영어로 공부하는
생물학+기초생리학
for AP Biology, A Level Biology

영어로 공부하는 생물학 + 기초생리학
for AP Biology, A Level Biology

초판 발행 2022년 8월 15일
초판 2쇄 2023년 12월 5일
지은이 배소윤
디자인 남경지

출판사 위키하우스 (WIKIHOUSE)
주　소 서울시 마포구 마포대로20길
전자우편 wikihousebooks@gmail.com

ISBN 979-11-979232-0-3 (13470)

© 위키하우스 (WIKIHOUSE), 2022
이 책의 저작권은 배소윤과 위키하우스에 있습니다.
이 책은 저작권법에 따라 보호받는 저작물이므로 무단전재와 무단복제를 금합니다.
이 책 내용의 전부 또는 일부를 사용하려면 반드시 저작권자와 출판사에 동의를 받아야 합니다.
이 책에 대한 의견이나 오탈자 및 잘못된 내용에 대한 수정 정보는 출판사 메일로 알려주십시오.
잘못 인쇄된 책은 서점에서 바꾸어 드립니다.

영어로 공부하는
생물학+기초생리학
for AP Biology, A Level Biology

저 자 | 배소윤

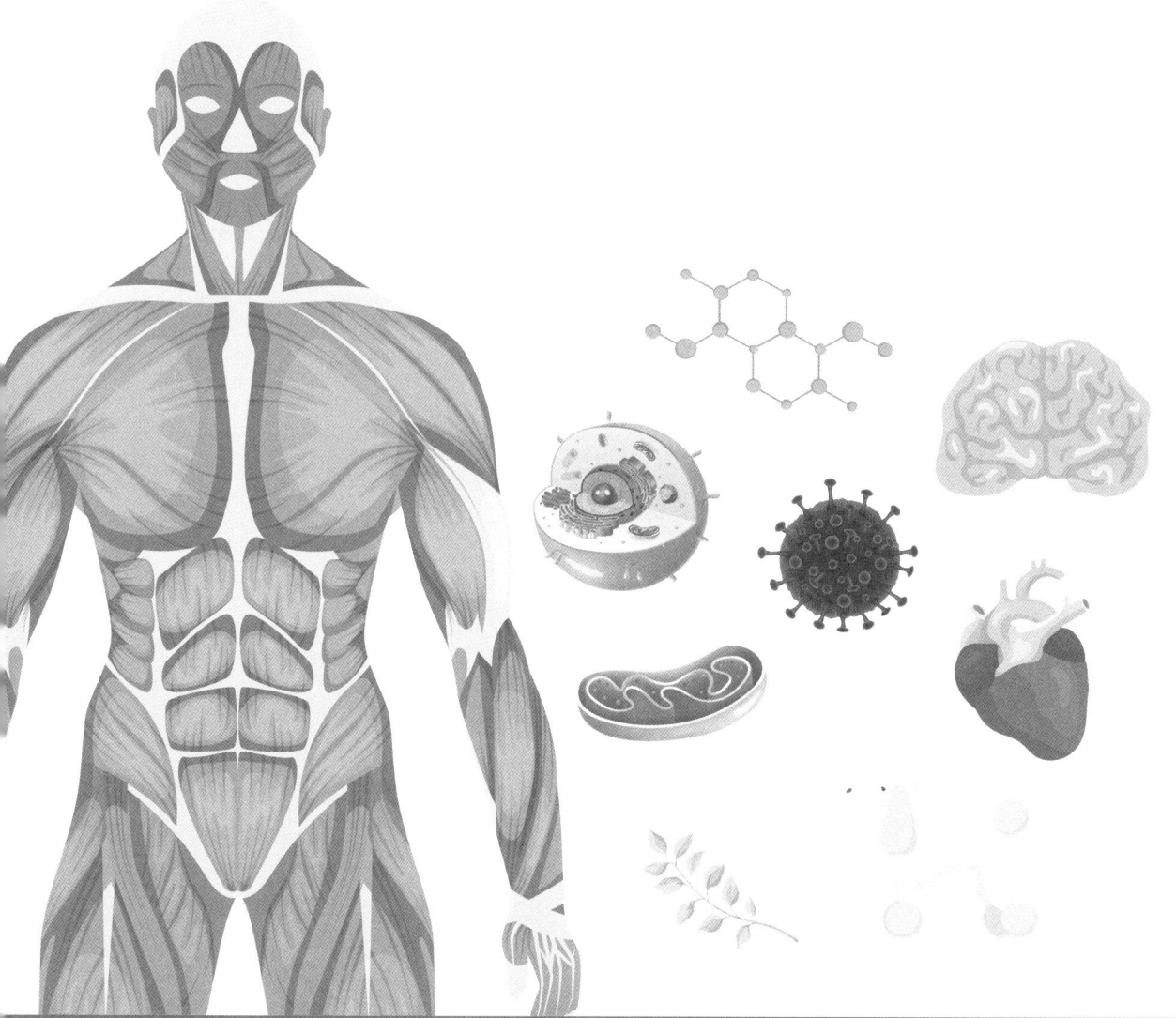

위키하우스

배소윤

정부기관 해외사업팀 소속 활동
세계 50개국 박람회, 컨퍼런스, 글로벌 프로젝트 진행
국제몬테소리협회 인증 기관 설립 프로젝트 진행
화학물 개발 글로벌 프로젝트 진행
기업 글로벌 비즈니스 컨설팅 진행
정부 장학생으로 수의학 공부

책 소개

이 책을 이런 분들께 추천합니다.

북미권 생물학, 의학 계열 유학 준비생
유럽권 생물학, 의학 계열 유학 준비생
국내외 생물학, 의학 계열 전공자
관련 계열 기술 이민 준비자
영어 전문 용어가 낯선 분
생물학, 생리학에 관심 있는 누구나!

1. **AP Biology, A Level Biology, 해외 의학 계열 대학 준비생 및 국내외 관련 종사자** 등 영어로 생물학, 기초 생리학을 공부하는 사람들을 위한 기본서

2. **AP Biology와 A Level Biology** 토픽 수록

3. 계통(System)별 **기초 생리학** 수록

4. '**표**'가 삽입되어, 핵심 주제 간결 명확한 비교

5. 2,500개 이상의 생물학 용어가 담긴 '**생물학 영어 단어장**'

6. Lipase는 [라이페이스], 영어식 발음을 위한 **단어와 발음기호**

7. 한 눈에 보는 **원소 기호표**

8. 세포 안까지 눈으로 보는 **컬러 이미지**

9. **비전공자, 생물학이 낯선 모두**를 위한 간결 핵심 포인트

이 책이 끝나면, 원핵생물보다 Prokaryote에 더 친숙해질 수 있다.
의외로 한글이 더 복잡한 용어가 많아, 영어가 더 쉽게 느껴질 수 있다. (희소돌기아교세포..?)
처음에는 영어 전문 용어가 익숙하지 않을 수 있지만,
이 책이 끝나면, 어느새 영어 전문 용어에 익숙함을 느끼고 있을 것이다.

목차

책 소개
Prologue
Periodic Table
Atomic Number
Biology English Vocabulary 2500

1. Cell biology ········· 88
Life signs
Cells
Methods of studying cells
Prokaryotes vs. Eukaryotes
Cell membrane
Non-membrane-bound organelles
Cell wall
DNA, RNA
Ribosome
Membrane-bound organelles
Nucleus
Endoplasmic reticulum
Golgi apparatus
Mitochondria
Vacuoles
Microbody
Lysosome
Peroxisome
Glyoxysome
Cell coat
Extracellular matrix
Cytoskeleton
Microtubules
Centriole, Centrosome
Cell membrane transport
Osmosis
Exocytosis, Endocytosis
Microorganisms
Bacteria
Virus
Fungi
Protist
Animal cell vs. Plant cell
Biomass
Organism sources

2. Acid, Base, pH ········· 117
Acid, Base
pH, pOH
Acid-Base theory
Acid-Base reactions
Strong and weak Acid, Base
Buffer system
Polar, Nonpolar

3. Organic compounds ········· 122
Isomers
Monomer, Polymer
Lipids
Carbohydrates
Proteins
Nucleic acids

4. DNA replication, Protein synthesis 136
DNA replication
Protein synthesis
Transcription
Post-transcription
Translation

5. Cell division ········· 143
Cell cycle
Interphase
Mitosis
Meiosis
Mitosis vs. Meiosis
Homologous pairs vs. Sister chromatids
Asexual reproduction
Nondisjunction

6. Inheritance ... 155
- Mendel's laws
- Homozygous, Heterozygous
- Exceptions to Mendel's laws
- Punnett square, Test cross
- Rules of probability
- Linked genes
- Sex chromosomes
- Chromosomal disease
- Operon
- Genetic equilibrium
- Microevolution
- Pedigree

7. Cellular respiration ... 169
- Glycolysis
- Acetyl CoA formation
- Citric acid cycle
- Electron transport chain
- Fermentation
- Photosynthesis
- Aerobic respiration vs. Photosynthesis
- Enzymes
- Inhibition

Biological system

8. Tissues ... 185
- Epithelial tissues
- Connective tissues
- Muscle tissues
- Nervous tissues

9. Skin and Skeletal system ... 196
- Skin
- Skeletal system
- Bone
- Bone metabolism
- Joints

10. Muscular system ... 203
- Sarcomere
- Muscle structure
- Muscle fibers
- Muscle contraction
- Junctions
- Muscle tissue types

11. Respiratory system ... 211
- Respiration
- Gas exchange
- Oxygen transport
- Carbon dioxide transport
- Partial pressure

12. Excretory system ... 219
- Urinary system
- Kidney
- Nephron
- Kidney-related hormones

13. Circulatory system ········· 226
- Blood
- RBC, WBC, Platelets
- Blood vessels
- Blood circulations
- Gas exchange
- Heart
- Cardiovascular disease
- Heart layers
- Heartbeat
- Cardiac cycle
- Blood pressure
- Blood clotting
- Lymphatic system

14. Immune system ········· 245
- Non-specific immune system
- Specific immune system
- Antibody-mediated immunity
- Cell-mediated immunity
- Lymphatic system
- Active, Passive immunity
- Immune disease

15. Digestive system ········· 257
- Animal classification
- Digestive tract
- Oral cavity
- Pharynx
- Esophagus
- Stomach
- Small intestine
- Pancreas
- Liver
- Large intestine
- Nutrients digestion
- Vitamins, Minerals

16. Reproduction ········· 273
- Male reproduction
- Spermatogenesis
- Female reproduction
- Oogenesis
- Ovarian follicles
- Menstrual cycle
- Menstruation hormones
- Fertilization

17. Endocrine system ········· 286
- Types of signaling
- Types of hormones
- Hypothalamus
- Anterior pituitary
- Posterior pituitary
- Thyroid glands
- Parathyroid glands
- Skins
- Adrenal glands
- Pancreas
- Kidney hormones
- Renin-Angiotensin-Aldosterone pathway
- Thymus
- Other hormones

18. Nervous system ········· 303
- Neurons
- Glial cells
- Electrical signals transmission
- Resting potential
- Action potential

19. Central nervous system and Peripheral nervous system ·········· 312
    Central nervous system
    Brain
    Spinal cord
    Peripheral nervous system
    Somatic nervous system
    Autonomic nervous system
    Synapse

20. Sensory system ·········· 324
    Sensory processing
    Sensory adaptation, Integration
    Types of receptors
    Photoreceptors
    Mechanoreceptors
    Auditory receptors
    Chemoreceptors
    Electroreceptors, Electromagnetic receptors
    Nociceptors
    Thermoreceptors

Credits

Prologue

"영어로 공부하는 생물학이 쉬워질 것이다."

Prokaryotes 그리고 Eukaryotes. 처음 원서로 된 생물학책을 펼쳤을 때, 이러한 낯선 단어들을 만났을 때의 그 당혹스러움을 잊을 수가 없다. 영어와는 또 다른 외계어의 느낌이었다.

해외 메디컬, 생명과학 계열 진출을 위한 필수 시험인 AP Biology, A Level Biology를 준비하기 위한 영어 생물학, 생리학 자료를 한국에서는 찾기가 쉽지 않았다. 하지만 여전히 많은 사람이 이러한 자료를 필요로 하기에, 해외 의사들과 글로벌 엔지니어 자문, 의사들의 감수를 바탕으로 AP Biology와 A Level Biology에서 요구하는 토픽들 그리고 의학 계열 전반에 필요한 기초 생리학을 정리하게 되었다. 긴 시간에 걸쳐 다듬어진 생물학 그리고 기초 생리학을, 국내외 의학 계열, 혹은 영어로 생물학 공부가 필요한 모두를 위하여 책으로 출간하였다.

저자가 공부할 때 겪었던 어려운 부분을 분석하여, 모국어가 아닌 언어로 어렵고 복잡한 내용에 최대한 쉽게 접근 할 수 있는 방법을 고민하여 책을 구성하였다. 그러므로 긴 영어 문장보다는 '표' 형태를 많이 볼 수 있으며, 이는 핵심 내용을 비교하는 데 도움이 될 수 있다.

이 책은, 오롯이 '영어로 생물학과 기초 생리학을 쉽게 공부할 수 있도록'에 그 본연의 초점을 두었다.
생물학을 영어로 공부한다는 것이 낯설게 느껴질 수도 있을 것이다. 당신의 그 '낯섦'에, 이 책이 조금이나마 도움이 되길 바란다.

생명을 사랑하는 길 위에 있는 모두를 응원하며.

배 소 윤

Thanks to

배덕환 엔지니어님, 천경윤 선생님, 남경지 작가님, Dr. Andrey, Dr. Chris, Dr. Jason, Jeremy S. Slavin, 사랑하는 부모님, 생명에 대한 경외감을 배우게 해준 모든 생명들과 보물 배몽구에게 감사의 마음을 표합니다.

Periodic Table

Group	1	2	3	4	5	6	7	8	9	10	11	12	13	14	15	16	17	18
Period 1	1 H																	2 He
2	3 Li	4 Be											5 B	6 C	7 N	8 O	9 F	10 Ne
3	11 Na	12 Mg											13 Al	14 Si	15 P	16 S	17 Cl	18 Ar
4	19 K	20 Ca	21 Sc	22 Ti	23 V	24 Cr	25 Mn	26 Fe	27 Co	28 Ni	29 Cu	30 Zn	31 Ga	32 Ge	33 As	34 Se	35 Br	36 Kr
5	37 Rb	38 Sr	39 Y	40 Zr	41 Nb	42 Mo	43 Tc	44 Ru	45 Rh	46 Pd	47 Ag	48 Cd	49 In	50 Sn	51 Sb	52 Te	53 I	54 Xe
6	55 Cs	56 Ba	71 Lu	72 Hf	73 Ta	74 W	75 Re	76 Os	77 Ir	78 Pt	79 Au	80 Hg	81 Tl	82 Pb	83 Bi	84 Po	85 At	86 Rn
7	87 Fr	88 Ra	103 Lr	104 Rf	105 Db	106 Sg	107 Bh	108 Hs	109 Mt	110 Ds	111 Rg	112 Cn	113 Nh	114 Fl	115 Mc	116 Lv	117 Ts	118 Og

57 La	58 Ce	59 Pr	60 Nd	61 Pm	62 Sm	63 Eu	64 Gd	65 Tb	66 Dy	67 Ho	68 Er	69 Tm	70 Yb		
89 Ac	90 Th	91 Pa	92 U	93 Np	94 Pu	95 Am	96 Cm	97 Bk	98 Cf	99 Es	100 Fm	101 Md	102 No		

Atomic Number

Atomic number	Symbol	Name	Signification	Atomic number	Symbol	Name	Signification
1	H	Hydrogen	수소	29	Cu	Copper	구리
2	He	Helium	헬륨	30	Zn	Zinc	아연
3	Li	Lithium	리튬	31	Ga	Gallium	갈륨
4	Be	Beryllium	베릴륨	32	Ge	Germanium	게르마늄
5	B	Boron	붕소	33	As	Arsenic	비소
6	C	Carbon	탄소	34	Se	Selenium	셀레늄
7	N	Nitrogen	질소	35	Br	Bromine	브롬
8	O	Oxygen	산소	36	Kr	Krypton	크립톤
9	F	Fluorine	플루오르	37	Rb	Rubidium	루비듐
10	Ne	Neon	네온	38	Sr	Strontium	스트론튬
11	Na	Sodium	소듐	39	Y	Yttrium	이트륨
12	Mg	Magnesium	마그네슘	40	Zr	Zirconium	지르코늄
13	Al	Aluminum	알류미늄	41	Nb	Niobium	니오븀
14	Si	Silicon	규소	42	Mo	Molybdenum	몰리브덴
15	P	Phosphorus	인	43	Tc	Technetium	테크네튬
16	S	Sulfur	황	44	Ru	Ruthenium	루테늄
17	Cl	Chlorine	염소	45	Rh	Rhodium	로듐
18	Ar	Argon	아르곤	46	Pd	Palladium	보장
19	K	Potassium	칼륨	47	Ag	Silver	은
20	Ca	Calcium	칼슘	48	Cd	Cadmium	카드뮴
21	Sc	Scandium	스칸듐	49	In	Indium	인듐
22	Ti	Titanium	티타늄	50	Sn	Tin	주석
23	V	Vanadium	바나듐	51	Sb	Antimony	안티몬
24	Cr	Chromium	크롬	52	Te	Tellurium	텔루르
25	Mn	Manganese	망간	53	I	Iodine	아이오딘
26	Fe	Iron	철	54	Xe	Xenon	크세논
27	Co	Cobalt	코발트	55	Cs	Caesium	세슘
28	Ni	Nickel	니켈	56	Ba	Barium	바륨

Atomic number	Symbol	Name	Signification	Atomic number	Symbol	Name	Signification
57	La	Lanthanum	란탄	88	Ra	Radium	라듐
58	Ce	Cerium	세륨	89	Ac	Actinium	악티늄
59	Pr	Praseodymium	프라세오디뮴	90	Th	Thorium	토륨
60	Nd	Neodymium	네오디뮴	91	Pa	Protactinium	프로탁티늄
61	Pm	Promethium	프로메튬	92	U	Uranium	우라늄
62	Sm	Samarium	사마륨	93	Np	Neptunium	넵투늄
63	Eu	Europium	유로퓸	94	Pu	Plutonium	플루토늄
64	Gd	Gadolinium	가돌리늄	95	Am	Americium	아메리슘
65	Tb	Terbium	테르븀	96	Cm	Curium	퀴륨
66	Dy	Dysprosium	디스프로슘	97	Bk	Berkelium	버클륨
67	Ho	Holmium	홀뮴	98	Cf	Californium	캘리포늄
68	Er	Erbium	에르븀	99	Es	Einsteinium	아인슈타늄
69	Tm	Thulium	툴륨	100	Fm	Fermium	페르뮴
70	Yb	Ytterbium	이테르븀	101	Md	Mendelevium	멘델레비움
71	Lu	Lutetium	루테튬	102	No	Nobelium	노벨륨
72	Hf	Hafnium	하프늄	103	Lr	Lawrencium	로렌시움
73	Ta	Tantalum	탄탈	104	Rf	Rutherfordium	러더포디움
74	W	Tungsten	텅스텐	105	Db	Dubnium	두브늄
75	Re	Rhenium	레늄	106	Sg	Seaborgium	시보르기움
76	Os	Osmium	오스뮴	107	Bh	Bohrium	보륨
77	Ir	Iridium	이리듐	108	Hs	Hassium	하슘
78	Pt	Platinum	백금	109	Mt	Meitnerium	마이트네리윰
79	Au	Gold	금	110	Ds	Darmstadtium	다름스타디움
80	Hg	Mercury	수은	111	Rg	Roentgenium	뢴트게늄
81	Tl	Thallium	탈륨	112	Cn	Copernicium	코페르니시움
82	Pb	Lead	선두	113	Nh	Nihonium	니호늄
83	Bi	Bismuth	창연	114	Fl	Flerovium	플레로비움
84	Po	Polonium	폴로늄	115	Mc	Moscovium	모스코비움
85	At	Astatine	아스타틴	116	Lv	Livermorium	리버모리움
86	Rn	Radon	라돈	117	Ts	Tennessine	테네신
87	Fr	Francium	프랑슘	118	Og	Oganesson	오가네손

Biology English Vocabulary 2500

Chapter 1

Vocabulary	Pronunciation	Signification
Ability	[əˈbɪləti]	능력
Absorb	[əbǀsɔːrb əbǀzɔːrb]	흡수하다, 빨아들이다
Acetyl	[əsíːtl,ǽsətl]	아세틸(기), 아세틸(기)을 함유한
Acid	[ˈæsɪd]	산, 산성의
Actin	[ǽktən]	액틴
Activity	[ækˈtɪvəti]	활동, 움직임
Adapt	[əˈdæpt]	맞추다, 적응하다
Adaptation	[ˌædæpˈteɪʃn]	적응
Adenosine	[ədénəsiːn,-sin]	아데노신
Adhesion	[ədˈhiːʒn]	접착, 부착
Aerobic	[eǀroʊbɪk]	호기성의
AIDS	Acquired Immune Deficiency Syndrome	후천성 면역 결핍 증후군
Alcohol	[ǀælkəhɔːl ǀælkəhɑːl]	알코올
Algae	[ˈældʒiː ˈælgiː]	조류
Amoeba	[əˈmiːbə]	아메바
Amoeboid	[əˈmiːbɔɪd]	아메바 모양의, 아메바 같은
Amphiphilic	[ˌam(p)-fə-ˈfi-lik]	양친매성
Anaerobic	[ǀæneǀroʊbɪk]	혐기성의, 무산소성의
Animal	[ˈænɪml]	동물
Apoptosis	[æ̀paptósis]	세포자멸사
Apparatus	[ǀæpəǀrætəs]	기관, 조직체
Archaea	[ˈɑrkiə]	고세균
Area	[ˈeriə]	영역, 부분
Artificial	[ǀɑːrtɪǀfɪʃl]	인공의, 인위적인
Asexual	[ˌeɪˈsekʃuəl]	무성의
Assembly	[əˈsembli]	조립
Associate	[əǀsoʊʃieɪt əǀsoʊʃiət]	어울리다
ATP	Adenosine Triphosphate	아데노신 삼인산
Attach	[əˈtætʃ]	들러붙다
Autolysis	[ɔːtálǝsis]	자가분해
Autotroph	[ǀɔːtətroʊf]	독립 영양 생물

Bacillus	[bæsíləs]	바실러스
Bacteria	[bæk|tɪrəriə]	박테리아, 세균 (복수)
Bacterium	[bækˈtɪəriəm]	박테리아 (단수)
Balance	[ˈbæləns]	균형, 균형을 이루다
Beam	[biːm]	빛줄기
Behavior	[bihéivjər]	행동
Beta	[ˈbiːtə]	베타
Bilayer	[báilèiər]	이중층
Bile	[baɪl]	담즙
Biochemistry	[|baɪoʊ|kemɪstri]	생화학, (생물의) 생리
Biological	[|baɪə|lɑːdʒɪkl]	생물학의, 생물체의
Biology	[baɪ|ɑːlədʒi]	생물학
Biomass	[|baɪoʊmæs]	생물량
Blood	[blʌd]	피, 혈액
Bond	[bɑːnd]	결합하다, 접착하다
Boundary	[ˈbaʊndri]	경계
Break	[breɪk]	부수다
Burst	[bɜːrst]	터지다
Calcium	[ˈkælsiəm]	칼슘
Camouflage	[ˈkæməflɑːʒ]	위장, 위장하다
Cancer	[ˈkænsə(r)]	암
Capsid	[kǽpsid]	캡시드
Capsule	[ˈkæpsjuːl]	협망, 낙망, 포
Carbohydrate	[|kɑːrboʊ|haɪdreɪt]	탄수화물
Carbon	[|kɑːrbən]	탄소
Carbon dioxide	[|kɑːrbən daɪ|ɑːksaɪd]	이산화탄소
Cell	[sel]	세포
Cellular	[ˈseljələ(r)]	세포의
Cellulose	[|seljuloʊs]	셀룰로오스
Centrifuge	[ˈsentrɪfjuːdʒ]	원심분리기
Centriole	[séntriòul]	중심립, 중심자, 중심 소체
Centrosome	[séntrəsòum]	중심체
Chain	[tʃeɪn]	일련, 띠, 사슬, 묶다
Change	[tʃeɪndʒ]	변하다, 변화
Characteristic	[ˌkærəktəˈrɪstɪk]	특성
Chemical	[ˈkemɪkl]	화학의, 화학적인
Chemiosmosis	[ˌkɛmɪɒzˈməʊsɪs]	화학삼투작용
Chemotroph	[kíːmətrɑ̀f]	화학합성 영양 생물
Chitin	[káitin]	키틴
Chloroplast	[ˈklɔːrəplæst]	엽록체

Cholesterol	[kəˈlestərɔːl]	콜레스테롤
Chromosome	[ˈkroʊməsoʊm]	염색체
Circle	[ˈsɜːrkl]	원형, 빙빙 돌다
Circular	[ˈsɜːrkjələ(r)]	원형의, 순환적인
Cisternae	[siˈstərnē]	시스터네(긴 액포)
Cisterna	[sistəˈnə]	수조, 조
Citric acid	[ˌsɪtrɪk ˈæsɪd]	구연산
Cling	[klɪŋ]	들러붙다
CoA	Coenzyme A	보조효소A
Coagulation	[koʊæˈgjuléiʃən]	응고 (작용)
Coat	[koʊt]	덮다, 털, 표면을 덮고 있는 것
Coccus	[kákəs]	구균
Collagen	[ˈkɑːlədʒən]	콜라겐
Combine	[ˈkɒmbaɪn ˈkɑːmbaɪn]	결합하다
Complex	[ˈkɒmpleks ˈkɑːmpleks]	덩어리, 집합체, 복잡한
Component	[kəmˈpoʊnənt]	요소
Composition	[ˈkɑːmpəˈzɪʃn]	구성 요소
Compound	[ˈkɒmpaʊnd ˈkɑːmpaʊnd]	화합물, 혼합물
Concentration	[ˈkɑːnsnˈtreɪʃn]	농도
Condition	[kənˈdɪʃn]	환경, 조건, 상태
Conjugate	[ˈkɑːndʒəgeɪt]	쌍을 이루고 있는
Consist	[kənˈsɪst]	이루어져 있다
Constituent	[kənˈstɪtʃuənt]	구성 성분
Contain	[kənˈteɪn]	포함하다, 들어 있다
Content	[kənˈtent]	내용물
Contribute	[kənˈtrɪbjuːt]	기여하다
Convert	[kənˈvɜːt kənˈvɜːrt]	전환하다
Copy	[ˈkɑːpi]	복사, 복제, 복제하다
Crista	[krístə]	크리스타
Curved	[kɜːrvd]	구부러진
Cycle	[ˈsaɪkl]	주기, 순환
Cytochrome	[sáitəkròum]	시토크롬
Cytoplasm	[ˈsaɪtoʊplæzəm]	세포질
Cytoskeleton	[sàitəskélitən]	세포 골격
Damage	[ˈdæmɪdʒ]	손상, 손상을 주다
Deactivate	[ˌdiːˈæktɪveɪt]	비활성화시키다
Decarboxylate	[diːkɑːrbáksəlèit]	카르복시기를 제거하다
Decrease	[dɪˈkris]	감소하다, 감소
Dense	[dens]	밀도가 높은, 빽빽한
Density	[ˈdensəti]	밀도, 농도

Deoxyribonucleic acid	[diːɑ̀ksirài̯bounjuːklíːik ˈæsɪd]	데옥시리보핵산, DNA
Derivative	[dɪˈrɪvətɪv]	파생물
Derive	[diráiv]	파생하다
Detoxify	[|diːˈ|tɑːksɪfaɪ]	해독하다
Develop	[dɪˈveləp]	성장하다, 발달하다
Differentiate	[ˌdɪfəˈrenʃieɪt]	구별하다
Diffusion	[difjúːʒən]	확산
Digestive	[daɪ|dʒestɪv dɪ|dʒestɪv]	소화의
Dimensional	[daɪ|menʃənl dɪ|menʃənl]	차원의
Dioxide	[daɪ|ɑːksaɪd]	이산화물
Direction	[dəˈrekʃn dɪˈrekʃn daɪˈrekʃn]	방향
Disease	[dɪˈziːz]	질병
Dispatch	[dɪˈspætʃ]	보내다
Distinguish	[dɪˈstɪŋgwɪʃ]	구별하다
Divide	[dɪˈvaɪd]	나누다
DNA	Deoxyribonucleic Acid	데옥시리보핵산
Ecosystem	[|iːkoʊsɪstəm]	생태계
Egg	[eg]	난자
Electron	[ɪ|lektrɑːn]	전자
Embed	[ɪmˈbed]	박다, 끼워 넣다
Endocytosis	[èndousaitóusis]	엔도시토시스, 세포내이입
Endoplasmic reticulum	[endōˌplazmik rəˈtikyələm]	소포체
Endosome	[ˈendəˌsōm]	엔도솜
Endotoxin	[èndoutáksin]	(균체) 내 독소
Energy	[|enərdʒi]	에너지
Enhance	[ɪn|hæns]	향상시키다
Envelop	[ɪnˈveləp]	감싸다
Envelope	[|envəloʊp |ɑːnvəloʊp]	엔벨로프
Environment	[ɪnˈvaɪrənmənt]	환경
Enzyme	[ˈenzaɪm]	효소
Eukaryote	[juːkǽriòut,-ət]	진핵생물
Evolution	[|iːvə|luːʃn |evə|luːʃn]	진화
Exchange	[ɪksˈtʃeɪndʒ]	교환하다
Exocytosis	[èksousaitóusis]	엑소시토시스
Exotoxin	[èksoutáksin]	외독소
External	[ɪkˈstɜːrnl]	외부의
Extra	[ˈekstrə]	추가의
Extracellular	[èkstrəséljulər]	세포 밖의
Facilitate	[fəˈsɪlɪteɪt]	가능하게 하다

Factor	[ˈfæktə(r)]	요인, 인자
Fall	[fɔːl]	떨어지다
Fat	[fæt]	지방
Fatty	[ˈfæti]	지방의, 지방이 많은, 지방으로 된
Female	[ˈfiːmeɪl]	여성, 암컷, 여성의, 암컷의
Fertilize	[ˈfɜːrtəlaɪz]	수정시키다
Fiber	[fáibər]	섬유질
Fibronectin	[fàibrounéktin]	피브로넥틴, 섬유결합소
Filament	[ˈfɪləmənt]	필라멘트
Filtration	[fɪlˈtreɪʃn]	여과
Flagella	[fləˈdʒelə]	편모 (복수)
Fluid	[ˈfluːɪd]	체액, 유체, 유동체
Fluidity	[fluːˈɪdəti]	유동성
Form	[fɔːrm]	형체, 형성하다
Fractionation	[frækʃənéiʃən]	분류(법)
Free	[friː]	자유로운
Fuel	[ˈfjuːəl]	연료
Fungus	[ˈfʌŋɡəs]	균류, 곰팡이류
Fuse	[fjuːz]	융합되다
Gene	[dʒiːn]	유전자
Generate	[ˈdʒenəreɪt]	생성하다
Genetic	[dʒəˈnetɪk]	유전의
Genome	[ˈdʒiːnoʊm]	게놈
Germinate	[ˈdʒɜːrmɪneɪt]	싹트다, 시작되다, 싹트게 하다
Glucagon	[glúːkəgɑ̀n]	글루카곤
Glucose	[ˈgluːkoʊs ǀ gluːkoʊz]	포도당
Glycocalyx	[glàikoukéiliks]	당질피질, 글리코칼릭스
Glycogen	[glái kədʒən,-dʒèn]	글리코겐
Glycolipid	[glàikəlípid]	당지질
Glycolysis	[glaikɑ́ləsis]	당 분해
Glycoprotein	[glàikəpróutiːn]	당단백질
Glycoside	[gláikəsàid]	글리코사이드
Golgi apparatus	[góːldʒ ǀæpəǀrætəs]	골지체
Gradient	[ˈgreɪdiənt]	변화도
Gravity	[ˈɡrævəti]	중력
Habitat	[ˈhæbɪtæt]	서식지
Hair	[her]	털
Hatch	[hætʃ]	부화하다
Helical	[ǀhelɪkl ǀ hiːlɪkl]	나선형의

Hemoglobin	[híːməglòubin, hémə glòubin, hìːməglóubin]	헤모글로빈
Heterotroph	[ˈhetərətrouf ˈhetərətrɑːf]	종속 영양 생물
High-resolution	[haɪ-ˌrezəˈluːʃn]	고해상도
Histone	[hístoun]	히스톤
Homeostasis	[ˌhoumiəˈsteɪsɪs]	항상성
Homogenization	[həˌmɒdʒənaɪˈzeɪʃən, hoʊ-]	균질화
Hormone	[ˈhɔːrmoun]	호르몬
Host	[houst]	숙주
Hydrogen	[ˈhaɪdrədʒən]	수소
Hydrolytic	[haɪdrəˈlɪtɪk]	가수 분해의
Hydrophilic	[hàidrəfílik]	친수성의
Hydrophobic	[haɪdrəˈfoʊbɪk]	소수성의
Hydrostatic	[hàidrəstǽtik(əl)]	정수학적인, 유체정력학의
Hydroxyapatite	[haɪˌdrɒksiˈæpəˌtaɪt]	수산화인회석
Hydroxyl	[haidrάksəl]	수산기, 수산기의, 수산기를 가진
Hypha	[háifə]	균사
Hypertonic	[hàipərtάnik]	고장성의, 삼투압이 높은
Hypotonic	[hàipətάnik]	저장성의, 삼투압이 낮은
Isotonic	[ˌaɪsoʊˈtɑːnɪk]	등장성의
Identical	[aɪˈdentɪkl]	동일한
Impermeable	[ɪmˈpɜːrmiəbl]	불침투성의
Inability	[ˌɪnəˈbɪləti]	불능
Inborn	[ˌɪnˈbɔːrn]	선천적인
Increase	[ɪnˈkris]	증가, 증가하다
Infect	[ɪnˈfekt]	감염시키다, 침투시키다
Infold	[infóuld]	감싸다
Inherit	[ɪnˈherɪt]	(유전적으로) 물려받다
Inorganic	[ˌɪnɔːrˈgænɪk]	무기물의
Instinct	[ˈɪnstɪŋkt]	본능
Instrument	[ˈɪnstrəmənt]	기구
Insulin	[ˈɪnsəlɪn]	인슐린
Integrin	[ˈɪntəgrɪn]	인테그린
Interior	[ɪnˈtɪriə(r)]	내부, 내부의
Intestine	[ɪnˈtestɪn]	장, 창자
Ion	[ˈaɪɑːn]	이온
Lamina	[lǽmənə]	층, 단층, 잎몸
Layer	[ˈleɪr]	막, 층
Lens	[lenz]	렌즈, 수정체
Linear	[lɪniə(r)]	선의, 선으로 된, 직선 모양의

Lipid	[lɪpɪd]	지질, 지방질
Liver	[ˈlɪvə(r)]	간
Living	[ˈlɪvɪŋ]	살아 있는
Lumen	[luːmen]	내강, 주머니 공간
Lysis	[láisis]	용해, 분해
Lysogenic	[làisədʒénik]	(바이러스, 세균이) 용원성의
Lysosome	[láisəsòum]	리소좀
Lytic	[lítik]	용해의
Macromolecule	[mæ̀krəmálikjuːl]	거대분자, 고분자
Magnify	[ˈmæɡnɪfaɪ]	확대하다
Mammal	[ˈmæml]	포유동물
Matrix	[ˈmeɪtrɪks]	행렬, 망
Mature	[məˈtʃʊr məˈtʊr]	성숙한, 다 자란, 성숙해지다, 발달하다
Measurement	[ˈmeʒərmənt]	측정, 치수
Mechanism	[ˈmekənɪzəm]	구조
Membrane	[ˈmembren]	막
Metabolism	[məˈtæbəlɪzəm]	신진대사
Micro-	[ˈmaɪkroʊ]	작은, 100만 분의 1의
Microbody	[ˈmaɪkroʊ ˈbɑːdi]	미소체
Microfilament	[màikrəfíləmənt]	미세 섬유
Microorganism	[ˈmaɪkroʊ-óːrɡənɪzəm]	미생물
Microscope	[ˈmaɪkrəskoʊp]	현미경
Microtubule	[màikroutjúːbjuːl]	미소관
Migrate	[ˈmaɪɡreɪt]	옮기다, 이동하다
Mimicry	[ˈmɪmɪkri]	흉내
Mineral	[ˈmɪnərəl]	무기물
Mitochondria	[ˈmitoxondria]	미토콘드리아 (복수)
Mitochondrion	[ˈmaɪtoʊˈkɑːndriən]	미토콘드리아 (단수)
Modify	[ˈmɑːdɪfaɪ]	수정하다, 바꾸다
Mold	[moʊld]	곰팡이
Molecule	[ˈmɑːlɪkjuːl]	분자
Mosaic	[moʊˈzeɪɪk]	모자이크
mRNA	messenger RNA	메신저 RNA
Multi-	[ˈmʌlti]	복수의, 다수의-
Multicellular	[mʌltiséljələr]	다세포의
Muscle	[ˈmʌsl]	근육
Mycelium	[maisíːliəm]	균사체
Myosin	[máiəsən]	미오신
Naked	[ˈneɪkɪd]	잎이 없는, 벗겨진
Nonliving	[ˌnänˈli-viŋ]	살아 있지 않은

Nonpolar	[nɑ̀npóulər]	무극성의
Nuclear	[|nuːkliə(r)]	핵의
Nucleic acid	[nuːˈkliːɪk ˈæsɪd]	핵산
Nucleoid	[ˈnüklēˌȯid]	핵양체
Nucleolus	[njuːklíːələs]	인, 핵소체
Nucleoplasm	[njúːkliəplæ̀zm]	핵질, 핵원형질
Nucleus	[|nuːkliəs]	세포핵, 원자핵
Nutrient	[|nuːtriənt]	영양소, 영양분
Nutrition	[nu|trɪʃn]	영양
Obligate	[άbləgèit]	(기생충·기생균 등이) 어떤 특정 환경에서만 생활할 수 있는, 절대의, 무조건적인
Offspring	[|ɔːfsprɪŋ | ɑːfsprɪŋ]	자식, (동식물의) 새끼
Oocyte	[óuəsàit]	난모 세포
Optic	[|ɑːptɪk]	광학의, 눈의
Organ	[ˈɔːrgən]	장기
Organelle	[ɔ̀ːrgənél,ɔ́ːrgənèl]	세포 기관
Organic	[ɔːr|gænɪk]	유기의, 장기 기관의
Organism	[|ɔːrgənɪzəm]	유기체
Organotrophic	[ɔ̀ːrgənoutróufik]	장기영양의, 종속영양의
Outer	[ˈaʊtə(r)]	바깥 표면의, 바깥의, 외부의
Oxidation	[ὰksədéiʃən]	산화
Oxygen	[|ɑːksɪdʒən]	산소
Pancreatic	[ˈpæŋkriǽtik]	췌장의
Parasite	[ˈpærəsaɪt]	기생물
Particle	[|pɑːrtɪkl]	입자
Penetrate	[ˈpenɪtreɪt]	뚫고 들어가다, 침투하다
Peptidoglycan	[pèptidagláikən]	펩티도글리칸
Peri-	[péri]	주위, 주변, 근처
Perinuclear	[pèrənjúːkliər]	핵 주위의
Period	[|pɪriəd]	기간
Peripheral	[pəˈrɪfərəl]	주변의, 말초의
Permeable	[|pɜːrmiəbl]	침투할 수 있는, 투과할 수 있는
Peroxide	[pə|rɑːksaɪd]	과산화물
Peroxisome	[pəráksəsòum]	페록시솜
pH	[ˌpiːˈeɪtʃ]	산도, 페하
Phagocyte	[ˈfǽgəsaɪt]	식세포
Phagosome	[fǽgəsòum]	식포
Phosphate	[|fɑːsfeɪt]	인산염
Phospholipid	[fὰsfoulípid]	인지질
Photosynthesis	[|foʊtoʊ|sɪnθəsɪs]	광합성

Phototroph	[fóutətrɑ̀f]	광영양 생물
Physical	[ˈfɪzɪkl]	물리적인, 육체의
Pili	[páili, píli]	선모
Pinosome	[pĭnˈəsōmˈ, pīˈnə-]	피노좀
Plant	[plænt]	식물
Plasma	[ˈplæzmə]	혈장, 플라스마
Plasmid	[plǽzmid]	플라스미드
Plastid	[plǽstid]	색소체
Polar	[ǀpoʊlə(r)]	극성의
Polymerase	[pɑ́limərèis]	폴리머레이스
Polysaccharide	[pɑ̀lisǽkəràid]	다당류
Pore	[pɔː(r)]	구멍
Porin	[ˈpɔːrɪn]	포린
Portion	[ˈpɔːrʃn]	부분
Pre-existing	[priːɪɡˈzɪstɪŋ]	이전부터 존재하던
Predator	[ˈpredətə(r)]	포식자, 포식 동물
Primary	[ǀpraɪmeri]	일차적인, 최초의, 주된
Prion	[ǀpriːɑːn]	프리온
Projection	[prəˈdʒekʃn]	투사, 투영, 투사도, 투영도
Prokaryote	[proukǽriòut,-riət]	원핵생물
Protein	[ǀproʊtiːn]	단백질
Protist	[próutist]	원생생물
Proton	[ˈproʊtɑːn]	양성자
Pyruvate	[páiruːveit]	피루브산
Reaction	[riˈækʃn]	반응
Receptor	[rɪˈseptə(r)]	수용체
Rectangular	[rektǽŋjulər]	직사각형의
Rectum	[ˈrektəm]	직장
Region	[ˈriːdʒən]	부위
Regulate	[ˈreɡjuleɪt]	조절하다
Release	[rɪˈliːs]	방출하다
Replicate	[ˈreplɪkeɪt]	복제하다
Representative	[ˌreprɪˈzentətɪv]	대표, 대표하는
Reproduce	[ǀriːprəǀduːs]	번식하다
rER	Rough Endoplasmic Reticulum	거친 소포체
Respiration	[ˌrespəˈreɪʃn]	호흡
Respond	[rɪˈspɑːnd]	반응을 보이다
Reticulum	[ritíkjuləm]	세망, 그물 모양의 것, 망상 조직
Retina	[ˈretənə]	망막
Retrovirus	[ǀretroʊvaɪrəs]	레트로바이러스

Ribonucleic acid	[ràibounjuːklíːikˈæsɪd]	리보핵산
Ribosome	[ráibəsòum]	리보솜
Rigid	[ˈrɪdʒɪd]	뻣뻣한, 단단한, 잘 휘지 않는
Ring	[rɪŋ]	고리
RNA	Ribonucleic acid	리보핵산
Rodlike	[rɑːdlaɪk]	막대 같은, 막대형의
Rough	[rʌf]	거친, 고르지 않은
rRNA	ribosomal RNA	리보솜 RNA
Sac	[sæk]	낭, 주머니
Salivary	[ˈsæləveri]	침의
Salt	[sɔːlt]	소금, 염(결정)
Secrete	[sɪˈkriːt]	분비하다
Seed	[siːd]	씨앗
Self-regulating	[ˌself-ˈregyəˌlātiŋ]	스스로 조절하는
Semi-	[ˈsemi]	반- (half)
Sensitive	[ˈsensətɪv]	예민한
Sexual	[ˈsekʃuəl]	생식의, 성적인
Sign	[saɪn]	징후, 신호
Signal	[ˈsɪgnəl]	신호, 신호를 보내다
Single	[ˈsɪŋgl]	단일의, 단 하나의
Site	[saɪt]	장소, 부위, 위치시키다
Smooth	[smuːð]	매끄러운
Span	[spæn]	걸치다, 가로지르다
Specialize	[ˈspeʃəlaɪz]	특수화하다
Species	[ˈspiːʃiːz]	종
Specimen	[ˈspesɪmən]	표본
Sperm	[spɜːrm]	정자, 정액
Spherical	[|sferɪkl]	구 모양의
Spindle	[ˈspɪndl]	축
Spiral	[ˈspaɪrəl]	나선, 나선형의
Spirillum	[spairíləm]	나선균
Spirochete	[spáiərəkìːt]	스피로헤타
Split	[splɪt]	분열, 분열되다, 나누다
Spore	[spɔː(r)]	포자
Spread	[spred]	확산
Sprout	[spraʊt]	싹이 나다, 생기다
Stabilize	[ˈsteɪbəlaɪz]	안정시키다
Stain	[steɪn]	얼룩, 얼룩지게 하다
Starch	[stɑːrtʃ]	녹말
Stereo-	[|sterioʊ]	굳은, 고체의, 입체의

Sticky	[ˈstɪki]	끈적거리는, 달라붙는
Stimulus	[ˈstɪmjələs]	자극
Store	[stɔː(r)]	저장하다
Strand	[strænd]	가닥
Strength	[strenθ]	힘, 내구성
Stripe	[straɪp]	줄무늬
Structure	[ˈstrʌktʃə(r)]	구조
Substance	[ˈsʌbstəns]	물질
Sugar	[ʃʊgə(r)]	설탕, 당
Surface	[ˈsɜːrfɪs]	표면
Surround	[səˈraʊnd]	가장자리, 둘러싸다
Surrounding	[səˈraʊndɪŋ]	주위의
Sustain	[səˈsteɪn]	지속시키다
Synthesize	[ˈsɪnθəsaɪz]	합성하다
System	[ˈsɪstəm]	계통, 기관계
Tail	[teɪl]	꼬리
Terminate	[ǀtɜːrmɪneɪt]	끝내다
Three-dimensional	[θriːdiménʃənl, dai-]	삼차원의
Tissue	[ˈtɪʃuː]	조직
Touch	[tʌtʃ]	만지다, 촉각
Toxic	[ǀtɑːksɪk]	유독성의
Toxin	[ǀtɑːksɪn]	독소
Transcription	[trænˈskrɪpʃn]	전사
Transfer	[ˈtrænsfɜː(r)]	옮기다, 이동하다
Transformation	[ǀtrænsfərǀmeɪʃn]	변환
Transport	[trænǀspɔːt ǀ trænǀspɔːrt]	수송하다
Triphosphate	[traɪˈfɒsfeɪt]	삼인산
tRNA	transfer RNA	전달 RNA
Tubulin	[tjúːbjulin]	튜불린
Turgor pressure	[tə́ːrgər ˈpreʃə(r)]	팽압
Uni-	[ˈjuːni]	하나의-
Unicellular	[ˌjuːnɪˈseljələ(r)]	단세포의
Unique	[juˈniːk]	고유의, 특유의
Unit	[ˈjuːnɪt]	구성단위
Vacuole	[ǀvækjuoʊl]	액포
Vertebrate	[ǀvɜːrtɪbrət]	척추동물
Vesicle	[ˈvesɪkl]	소낭
Vibrio	[váibriou]	비브리오
Virus	[ˈvaɪrəs]	바이러스
Visual	[ˈvɪʒuəl]	시각의

Wall	[wɔːl]	벽
Waste	[weɪst]	폐기물
Wrap	[ræp]	둘러싸다
Yeast	[jiːst]	효모균

Chapter 2

Vocabulary	Pronunciation	Signification
Acceptor	[ækséptər,ək-]	수용체
Acid	[ˈæsɪd]	산
Acidity	[əˈsɪdəti]	산성
Alkali	[ˈælkəlaɪ]	알칼리
Alkaline	[ˈælkəlaɪn]	알칼리성
Amine	[əmíːn,ǽmin]	아민
Amino	[əmíːnou,-nə,ǽmə-]	아민의
Apolar	[eipóulər]	무극성의
Appreciable	[əˈpriːʃəbl]	상당한
Aqueous	[eɪkwiəs]	수용액의
Base	[beɪs]	염기
Basic	[ˈbeɪsɪk]	염기성의
Bi-	[baɪ]	두 개-
Bicarbonate	[ǀbaɪǀkɑːrbənət]	중탄산염
Bitter	[ˈbɪtə(r)]	쓴
Buffer	[ˈbʌfə(r)]	완충액
Capacity	[kəˈpæsəti]	용량
Carbonate	[ˈkɑːrbənət]	탄산염
Carbonic	[kɑːrbɑ́nik]	탄소의
Catalysis	[kətǽləsis]	촉매 작용
Charge	[tʃɑːrdʒ]	전하
Digestion	[daɪǀdʒestʃən]	소화
Dihydrogen	[daɪˈhaɪdrədʒən]	이수소
Dipole	[ǀdaɪpoʊl]	쌍극자
Donor	[ǀdoʊnə(r)]	공여체
Electrical	[ɪˈlektrɪkl]	전기의
Equilibrium	[ǀiːkwɪǀlɪbriəm]	평형
Fatal	[ˈfeɪtl]	죽음을 초래하는
Gas	[gæs]	기체

Histidine	[hístədìːn,-din]	히스티딘
Hydroxide	[haɪˈdrɑːksaɪd]	수산화물
Indicator	[ˈɪndɪkeɪtə(r)]	지표
Interaction	[ˌɪntərˈækʃn]	상호 작용
Intermediate	[ˌɪntərˈmiːdiət]	중간의
Irreversible	[ˌɪrɪˈvɜːrsəbl]	되돌릴 수 없는
Level	[ˈlevl]	정도
Liberate	[ˈlɪbəreɪt]	자유롭게 하다
Litmus	[ˈlɪtməs]	리트머스
Measure	[meʒə(r)]	측정하다
Metal	[ˈmetl]	금속
Negative	[ˈneɡətɪv]	부정적인
Neuron	[ˈnʊrɑːn]	신경 세포, 뉴런
Neutral	[ˈnuːtrəl]	중립적인
Oil	[ɔɪl]	기름
Optimal	[ˈɑːptɪməl]	최적의
Oxide	[ˈɑːksaɪd]	산화물
Phosphoric	[fɑsfóːrik,-fár-]	인의
Physiological	[ˌfɪziəˈlɑːdʒɪkl]	생리학적
Polypeptide	[pɑ̀lipéptaid]	폴리펩티드
Poor	[pɔːr pʊr]	부족한
Positive	[ˈpɑːzətɪv]	긍정적인
Potential	[pəˈtenʃl]	잠재적인
Promote	[prəˈmoʊt]	촉진시키다
Pure	[pjʊr]	순수한
Range	[reɪndʒ]	범위
React	[riˈækt]	반응하다
Related	[rɪˈleɪtɪd]	관련된
Reversible	[rɪˈvɜːrsəbl]	되돌릴 수 있는
Rich	[rɪtʃ]	풍부한
Secondary	[sekənderi]	이차적인
Slight	[slaɪt]	약간의
Slippery	[ˈslɪpəri]	미끄러운
Soluble	[ˈsɑːljəbl]	용해성 있는
Solution	[səˈluːʃn]	용액
Sour	[saʊə(r)]	신
Tract	[trækt]	관
Trigger	[ˈtrɪɡə(r)]	촉발시키다
Variation	[ˌveriˈeɪʃn]	변이

Chapter 3

Vocabulary	Pronunciation	Signification
Abundant	[əˈbʌndənt]	풍부한
Aldehyde	[ǽldəhàid]	알데히드
Aldose	[ǽldous]	알도오스
Aldosterone	[ælˈdoustiróun, ældástəròun]	알도스테론
Aliphatic	[æ̀ləfǽtik]	지방족의
Alkaloid	[ǽlkəlɔid]	알칼로이드
Allotrope	[ǽlətroup]	동소체
Amylopectin	[æ̀məloupéktin]	아밀로펙틴
Amyloplast	[ˈa-mə-(ˌ)lō-ˌplast]	아밀로플라스트, 녹말체
Amylose	[ǽməlòus,-lòuz]	아밀로오스
Anabolic	[æ̀nəbɑ́lik]	합성대사작용의, 동화작용의
Androgen	[ǽndrədʒən]	안드로겐
Antifungal	[æ̀ntifʌ́ŋgəl,-tai-]	항진균성의
Arrangement	[əˈreɪndʒmənt]	배열
Atom	[ˈætəm]	원자
Backbone	[|bækboʊn]	중추
Bind	[baɪnd]	묶다
Biologically	[|baɪə|lɑːdʒɪkli]	생물학적으로
Body	[bɑːdi]	신체
Building block	[ˈbɪldɪŋ blɑːk]	구성 요소
Carboxyl	[kɑːrbɑ́ksil]	카르복시기
Carboxylic	[ˌkɑːbɒkˈsɪlɪk]	카르복시기의
Cardiac	[|kɑːrdiæk]	심장의
Cardiovascular	[|kɑːrdioʊ|væskjələ(r)]	심혈관의
Carotenoid	[kərɑ́tənɔ́id]	카로티노이드
Chemistry	[ˈkemɪstri]	화학
Cis-	[sis]	시스형의-
Class	[klæs]	강(綱)
Colorless	[|kʌlərləs]	무색의
Condensation	[|kɑːnden|seɪʃn]	응축
Configuration	[kən|fɪgjə|reɪʃn]	구성
Conformational	[kɑːnfɔːr|meɪʃnəl]	구조적인
Corticosteroid	[kɔ́ːrtikoustéroid,-stíər]	코르티코스테로이드
Cortisol	[kɔ́ːrtəsɔ́ːl,-sòul]	코르티솔
Covalent bond	[|koʊ|veɪlənt bɑːnd]	공유 결합
Covalently	[|koʊ|veɪləntli]	공유 결합으로

Cyclohexane	[sàikləhéksein]	시클로헥산
Cyclopentane	[ˌsaɪkləʊˈpɛnteɪn]	시클로펜탄
Deoxyribose	[diːɑksiráibous]	디옥시리보핵산
Di-	[daɪ]	둘의-
Diamond	[daɪəmənd]	다이아몬드
Digest	[daɪ|dʒest]	소화하다
Disaccharide	[daisǽkəràid]	이당류
Dissolve	[dɪˈzɑːlv]	녹이다
Electrolyte	[ɪˈlektrəlaɪt]	전해질
Element	[ˈelɪmənt]	요소
Enantiomer	[inǽntiəmər]	거울상 이성질체
Ergosterol	[əːrgɑ́sterɔ́ːl]	에르고스테롤
Ester	[ˈestə(r)]	에스터
Estrogen	[ˈiːstrədʒən]	에스트로겐
Excretion	[ikskríːʃən]	배설
Fat	[fæt]	지방
Fibrous	[ˈfaɪbrəs]	섬유질의, 섬유로 된
Flexible	[ˈfleksəbl]	신축성 있는
Flush	[flʌʃ]	씻어 없애다, 같은 높이의
Formula	[fɔːrmjələ]	공식
Fructose	[|frʌktoʊs	frʌktoʊz]	프록토오스
Fungal	[ˈfʌŋgl]	균류의
Galactose	[gəlǽktous]	갈락토오스
Geometric	[ˌdʒiːəˈmetrɪk]	기하학적인
Glucocorticoid	[glùːkoukɔ́ːrtəkɔ́id]	글루코코르티코이드
Glyceride	[glísəràid,-rid]	글리세리드
Glycerin	[glísərin]	글리세린
Glycerol	[glísərɔ́ːl,-rɑ̀l]	글리세롤
Glycoside	[gláikəsàid]	글리코사이드
Grain	[greɪn]	곡물
Granulosa	[græ̀njulóusə]	과립층
Graphite	[ˈgræfaɪt]	흑연
Grass	[græs]	잔디
HDL	High-Density Lipoprotein	고밀도 지질단백질
Humectant	[hjuː|mektənt]	습윤제, 보습제
Hydrocarbon	[|haɪdrə| kɑːrbən]	탄화수소
Hydrogenate	[háidrədʒənèit,haidrɑ́dʒ-]	수소화하다, 수소를 첨가하다
Hydrolysis	[haɪ|drɑːlɪsɪs]	가수 분해
Hydrolyze	[háidrəlàiz]	가수분해하다
Immune	[ɪˈmjuːn]	면역성 있는

Immunosuppression	[ɪmjunoʊsə│preʃn]	면역 억제	
Inflammatory	[ɪn│flæmətɔːri]	염증을 일으키는	
Inflexible	[ɪnˈfleksəbl]	구부러지지 않는	
Insoluble	[ɪn│sɑːljəbl]	용해되지 않는	
Integrity	[ɪnˈtegrəti]	완전한 상태, 온전함	
Intolerance	[ɪn│tɑːlərəns]	과민증	
Ionic bond	[aɪ│ɑːnɪk bɑːnd]	이온 결합	
Isomer	[ˈaɪsəmə(r)]	이성질체	
Isoprene	[ˈaɪsəpriːn]	이소프렌	
Isotope	[│aɪsətoʊp]	동위 원소	
Ketone	[kíːtoun]	케톤	
Ketose	[ˈkē-ˌtōs]	케토스	
Lactose	[│læktoʊs]	유당	
Lactose intolerance	[│læktoʊs │læktoʊz ɪn│tɑːlərəns]	유당 불내증	
LDL	Low-Density Lipoprotein	저밀도 지단백질	
Linkage	[ˈlɪŋkɪdʒ]	결합	
Lipoprotein	[│lɪpəproʊtiːn]	지단백질	
Liquid	[lɪkwɪd]	액체	
Lower	[│loʊə(r)]	낮추다	
Malt	[mɔːlt]	맥아	
Maltose	[│mɔːltoʊz │mɔːltoʊs]	말토오스	
Marker	[│mɑːrkə(r)]	표지	
Messenger	[mesɪndʒə(r)]	메신저	
Mimic	[ˈmɪmɪk]	모방하다	
Mineralocorticoid	[ˌmɪn(ə)rələ(ʊ)ˈkɔːtɪkɔɪd]	미네랄로코르티코이드	
Molecular	[məˈlekjələ(r)]	분자의	
Mono-	[mɑːnoʊ]	하나의-	
Monomer	[mánəmər]	단위체	
Monosaccharide	[mɑ̀nəsǽkəraid]	단당류	
Monounsaturated	[mɑ̀nəʌnsǽtʃəreitid]	단일불포화의	
Nitrogen	[ˈnaɪtrədʒən]	질소	
Nucleotide	[njúːkliətàid]	뉴클레오티드	
Odorless	[óudərlis]	냄새 없는	
Oily	[ˈɔɪli]	기름기가 함유된	
Pathogenic	[pæ̀θədʒénik]	병원성의	
Phytosterol	[faitɑ́stərɔ́ːl,-rɑ̀l]	피토스테롤	
Pigment	[ˈpɪgmənt]	색소	
Polarity	[pəˈlærəti]	극성	
Polymer	[│pɑːlɪmə(r)]	고분자	
Polyunsaturated	[pɑ̀liʌnsǽtʃəreitid]	고도불포화의	

Progesterone	[prə|dʒestəroʊn]	프로게스테론
Rearrange	[ˌriːəˈreɪndʒ]	재배열하다
Renal	[ˈriːnl]	신장의
Resource	[|riːsɔːrs rɪ|sɔːrs]	자원
Retinal	[rétənəl]	망막의
Ribose	[ráibous]	리보오스
Rotate	[ˈroʊteɪt]	회전하다
Saturate	[sætʃəreɪt]	포화시키다
Saturated	[ˈsætʃəreɪtɪd]	포화된
Sex	[seks]	성
Skin	[skɪn]	피부
Solid	[|sɑːlɪd]	고체
Solvent	[|sɑːlvənt]	용제, 용해하는
Split	[splɪt]	나누다
Steroid	[|stɪrɔɪd]	스테로이드
Stomach	[stʌmək]	위
Stroke	[stroʊk]	스트로크, 타격
Sucrose	[|suːkroʊs |suːkroʊz]	수크로오스
Sweetener	[ˈswiːtnə(r)]	감미료
Symmetrical	[sɪˈmetrɪkl]	대칭적인
Technically	[ˈteknɪkli]	기술적으로
Testosterone	[teˈstɑːstəroʊn]	테스토스테론
Tetracyclic	[ˌtɛtrəˈsɪklɪk]	네 개의 고리가 있는
Theca	[θíːkə]	포막
Trans-	[trænz- træns]	트랜스형의-
Transform	[træns|fɔːrm]	변형시키다
Tri-	[traɪ]	3개로 된-
Triglyceride	[traiglísəràid]	트리글리세리드, 중성지방
Triple	[ˈtrɪpl]	3배의
Unsaturated	[ʌnsætʃərèitid]	불포화의
Viscous	[ˈvɪskəs]	점성이 있는
Volume	[|vɑːljuːm |vɑːljəm]	용량

Chapter 4

Vocabulary	Pronunciation	Signification
Addition	[əˈdɪʃn]	부가물
Adenine	[ǽdənin,-nìːn,-nàin]	아데닌
Align	[əˈlaɪn]	정렬, 일직선으로 하다
Aminoacyl	[əmēˈnōăsˈəl]	아미노아실
Anticodon	[æ̀ntikóudɑn,-tai]	안티코돈
Antisense	[æ̀ntiséns,-tai-]	안티센스
Bidirectional	[bʌɪdɪˈrɛkʃ(ə)n(ə)l]	양방향의
Bubble	[ˈbʌbl]	기포, 거품
Cap	[kæp]	뚜껑, 캡
Code	[koʊd]	코드
Codon	[kóudɑn]	코돈
Complementary	[ˌkɑːmplɪˈmentri]	상호 보완적인
Conservative	[kənˈsɜːrvətɪv]	보수적인
Elongation	[ˌiːlɔːŋˈɡeɪʃn]	신장, 연장
Encode	[ɪnˈkoʊd]	부호화하다
Error	[ˈerə(r)]	오류
Exit	[eksɪt]	나가다
Exon	[éksɑn]	엑손
Exonuclease	[èksounjúːklieis]	엑소뉴클레에이스
Fixing	[fíksiŋ]	고정
Floating	[floʊtɪŋ]	떠 있는, 유동적인
Fork	[fɔːrk]	분기점
Fragment	[ˈfræɡmənt]	파편, 조각
Glue	[ɡluː]	붙이다, 접착제
Guanine	[ɡwάːniːn]	구아닌
Gyrase	[dʒáiəreis,-reiz]	자이레이스
Helicase	[ˈhiːlɪkeɪz]	헬리케이스
Helix	[ˈhiːlɪks]	나선
Initiation	[ɪˈnɪʃətɪv]	시작
Interact	[ˌɪntərˈækt]	상호 작용을 하다
Intron	[íntrɑn]	인트론
Lagging strand	[lǽɡiŋ strænd]	지연 가닥
Leading strand	[ˈliːdɪŋ strænd]	선도 가닥
Ligase	[láiɡeis]	라이게이스
Location	[loʊˈkeɪʃn]	위치
Match	[mætʃ]	짝을 맞추다

Maturation	[mætʃuˈreɪʃn]	성숙
Methionine	[meθáiənìːn]	메티오닌
Methyl	[méθəl]	메틸
Mutate	[mjuːteɪt]	돌연변이를 만들다
Nucleotide	[njúːkliətàid]	뉴클레오티드
Okazaki fragment	[okaˈzɑːki ˈfrægmənt]	오카자키 절편
Orientation	[ˌɔːriənˈteɪʃn]	방향
Origin	[|ɔːrɪdʒɪn	ɑːrɪdʒɪn]	기원
Peptide	[ˈpeptaɪd]	펩티드
Phosphorus	[|fɑːsfərəs]	인
Piece	[piːs]	조각
Point	[pɔɪnt]	지점, 시점, 가리키다
Poly-	[ˈpɑːli]	많은-
Polymerase	[pálimərèis]	폴리머레이스
Present	[prɪˈzent]	보여주다
Primer	[ˈpraɪmə(r)]	프라이머, 시발체
Promoter	[prə|moʊtə(r)]	촉진자, 프로모터
Read	[riːd]	읽다
Recycle	[ˌriːˈsaɪkl]	재활용
Repeat	[rɪˈpiːt]	반복하다
Replace	[rɪˈpleɪs]	교체하다
Replacement	[rɪˈpleɪsmənt]	교체, 대체
Repressor	[riprésər]	리프레서, 억제자
Sense	[sens]	감각
Sequence	[ˈsiːkwəns]	순서
Splice	[splaɪs]	붙이다
SSB	Single-Strand Binding (protein)	단일 가닥 결합 단백질
Stabilize	[ˈsteɪbəlaɪz]	안정시키다
Stress	[stres]	스트레스
Subunit	[sʌbjùːnit]	서브유닛
Supercoil	[|suːpə(r)kɔ́il]	슈퍼코일
Synthesis	[ˈsɪnθəsɪs]	합성
Synthase	[sínθeis]	신테이스
Template	[ˈtempleɪt]	템플릿, 형판
Termination	[|tɜːrmɪ|neɪʃn]	종료
Thymine	[θáimiːn]	티민
Topoisomerase	[ˌtɒpoʊˈʌɪsəmərɛɪz]	국소이성질화효소
Transcribe	[trænˈskraɪb]	전사하다
Translate	[træns|leɪt]	번역하다
Translation	[træns|leɪʃn]	번역

Triplet	[ˈtrɪplət]	세쌍둥이
Tube	[tuːb]	튜브
Unwind	[ʌnˈwaɪnd]	풀다
Uracil	[júərəsil]	우라실

Chapter 5

Vocabulary	Pronunciation	Signification
Allele	[əˈliːl]	대립 유전자
Anaphase	[ǽnəfèiz]	후기
Assortment	[əlsɔːrtmənt]	종류, 모음
Autosomal	[ɔ́ːtəsóuməl]	상염색체의
Binary	[ˈbaɪnəri]	2진수의, 두 부분으로 이뤄진
Centriole	[séntrìoùl]	중심소체
Centromere	[séntrəmìər]	중심립
Chance	[tʃæns]	가능성
Chiasma	[kaiǽzmə]	키아스마
Chromatid	[króumətid]	염색분체
Chromatin	[króumətin]	염색질
Clone	[kloʊn]	클론, 복제
Cohesin	[kōˈhēsən]	코헤신
Cohesion	[koʊlhiːʒn]	응집력
Condense	[kənˈdens]	응축하다, 농축하다, 응결하다
Cytokinesis	[sàitoukiníːsis]	세포질분열
Diploid	[ˈdɪplɔɪd]	이배체
Disjunction	[dɪsˈdʒʌŋkʃn]	분리
Diversity	[daɪlvɜːrsəti]	다양성
Duplication	[djùːplikéiʃən]	복제
Envelopment	[invéləpmənt]	포위
Equally	[ˈiːkwəli]	균등하게
Fission	[ˈfɪʃn]	핵분열
Fragile	[|frædʒl]	손상되기 쉬운
Gamete	[gæmiːt]	생식 세포
Gap	[gæp]	갭, 격차
Haploid	[ˈhæplɔɪd]	반수체
Hold	[hoʊld]	유지하다
Homologous	[hoʊ|mɑːləgəs he	mɑːləgəs]	상동의

Independent	[ˌɪndɪˈpendənt]	독립적인
Interphase	[íntərfèiz]	간기
Kinetochore	[kiníːtəkɔ́ːr]	방추사부착점
Klinefelter syndrome	[ˈklaɪn fɛl tər ǀ sɪndroʊm]	클라인펠터 증후군
Law	[lɔː]	법칙
Line	[laɪn]	라인
Meiosis	[maɪǀoʊsɪs]	감수 분열
Metaphase	[métəfèiz]	중기
Mitosis	[maɪǀtoʊsɪs]	유사 분열
Monosomy	[mənásəmi]	일염색체성
Nail	[neɪl]	손톱, 발톱
Nerve	[nɜːrv]	신경
Nondisjunction	[nɑndisdʒʌ́ŋkʃən]	비분리
Nonhistone	[ˌnänˈhiˌstōn]	비히스톤
Nucleoside	[njúːkliəsàid]	뉴클레오시드
Nucleosome	[njúːkliəsòum]	뉴클레오솜
Parental	[pəˈrentl]	부모의
Patau's syndrome	[ˈpataʊz ǀ sɪndroʊm]	파타우 증후군
Phase	[feɪz]	단계
Polyploid	[páliplɔ́id]	배수체
Preparatory	[prɪǀpærətɔːri]	준비를 위한
Prophase	[próufèiz]	전기
Randomly	[ˈrændəmli]	무작위로
Recombination	[rìːkɑmbənéiʃən]	재조합
Redistribute	[ǀriːdɪǀ strɪbjuːt ǀ riːǀ dɪstrɪbjuːt]	재분배하다
Reform	[rɪˈfɔːrm]	개편하다
Repair	[rɪǀper]	수리하다
Scaffold protein	[ǀskæfoʊld ǀproʊtiːn]	스캐폴드 단백질
Segregate	[ˈsegrɪgeɪt]	분리하다
Segregation	[segrɪˈgeɪʃn]	분리
Separation	[sepəˈreɪʃn]	분리
Sister chromatid	[ˈsɪstə(r) króumətid]	자매 염색분체
Somatic	[soumǽtik]	체강의
Synapse	[ǀsaɪnæps ǀ sɪnæps]	시냅스, 신경 접합부
Synapsis	[sinǽpsis]	시냅시스, 접합
Syndrome	[sɪndroʊm]	증후군
Tangle	[ˈtæŋgl]	엉킨
Telomer	[ˈteləmə(r)]	텔로머
Telophase	[téləfèiz]	말기
Tetrad	[tétræd]	사분염색체

Trait	[treɪt]	특성
Trisomy	[tráisoumi]	삼염색체
Visible	[vɪzəbl]	보이는
Zygote	[|zaɪgoʊt]	수정란

Chapter 6

Vocabulary	Pronunciation	Signification
Absence	[ˈæbsəns]	부재
Adapt	[əˈdæpt]	적응하다
Adaptive	[əˈdæptɪv]	적응하는
Additive	[ˈædətɪv]	첨가제
Affect	[əˈfekt]	영향을 미치다
Albino	[æl|baɪnoʊ]	알비노
Anemia	[əˈniːmiə]	빈혈
Aneuploid	[ǽnjuːplɔ́id]	이수체
Architectural	[|ɑːrkɪ|tektʃərəl]	건축의
Assortative	[əˈsɔ́rtətiv]	선택적인, 종을 선택하는
Autosomal	[ɔ́ːtəsóuməl]	상염색체의
Autosome	[ɔ́ːtəsòum]	상염색체
Barr body	[bɑːr ˈbɑːdi]	바소체
Bottleneck	[|bɑːtlnek]	병목
Breed	[briːd]	새끼를 낳다
Breeding	[briːdɪŋ]	번식
Carcinogen	[kɑːr|sɪnədʒən]	발암물질
Chromosomal	[ˌkroʊməˈsoʊməl]	염색체의
Circumstance	[|sɜːrkəmstæns]	환경
Cluster	[klʌstə(r)]	무리
Code	[koʊd]	부호, 암호
Codominant	[koudǽmənənt]	공동우성의
Coli	[kóulài]	대장균
Colony	[|kɑːləni]	군집
Colorblind	[ˈkʌlə(r)blàind]	색맹
Compensation	[|kɑːmpen|seɪʃn]	보상
Compose	[kəm|poʊz]	구성하다
Consistent	[kənˈsɪstənt]	일관된
Constant	[|kɑːnstənt]	끊임없는

Constitution	[kɑːnstəˈtuːʃn]	구조
Deletion	[dɪˈliːʃn]	삭제
Depression	[dɪˈpreʃn]	우울증
Determination	[dɪˌtɜːrmɪˈneɪʃn]	결정, 측정
Dihybrid	[daiháibrid]	양성잡종
Dilute	[daɪˈluːt]	희석시키다
Diploid	[dɪploɪd]	이배체
Directional	[dəˈrekʃənl]	지향성의, 방향의
Disruptive	[dɪsˈrʌptɪv]	붕괴시키는
Distance	[dɪstəns]	거리
Distinct	[dɪˈstɪŋkt]	특유의
Distribution	[dɪstrɪˈbjuːʃn]	분포
Disturb	[dɪˈstɜːrb]	방해하다
DNA	Deoxyribonucleic Acid	디옥시리보핵산
Dominance	[dɑːmɪnəns]	우성
Dominant	[dɑːmɪnənt]	우성의
Dosage	[ˈdoʊsɪdʒ]	복용량
Drift	[drɪft]	이동
Effect	[ɪˈfekt]	효과
Egg	[eg]	난자
Eliminate	[ɪˈlɪmɪneɪt]	제거하다
Embryo	[ˈembrioʊ]	배아
Environment	[ɪnˈvaɪrənmənt]	환경
Epistasis	[ipístəsis]	상위성
Equal	[ˈiːkwəl]	동일한
Equilibrium	[ˌiːkwɪˈlɪbriəm]	평형
Escherichia	[èʃəríkiə-]	대장균
Event	[ɪˈvent]	사건
Evolutionary	[ˌiːvəˈluːʃəneri]	진화의
Exception	[ɪkˈsepʃn]	예외
Exclusive	[ɪkˈskluːsɪv]	독점적인
Extreme	[ɪkˈstriːm]	극심한
Favored	[féivərd]	선호하는
Feather	[ˈfeðə(r)]	깃털
Fertile	[ˈfɜːrtl]	생식력 있는, 가임의
Fertilization	[ˌfɜːrtələˈzeɪʃn]	수정
Fingerprint	[fɪŋgərprɪnt]	지문
Fitness	[ˈfɪtnəs]	적응도
Flow	[floʊ]	흐름
Force	[fɔːrs]	힘

Founder	[ˈfaʊndə(r)]	설립자
Frame	[freɪm]	골격
Frameshift	[freɪmʃift]	프레임 시프트
Frequency	[friːkwənsi]	빈도
Functional	[ˈfʌŋkʃənl]	기능의
Gender	[dʒendə(r)]	성별
Gene pool	[dʒiːn puːl]	유전자풀
Generation	[dʒenəˈreɪʃn]	세대
Genomic	[dʒinóumik,-nά-]	게놈의
Genotype	[|dʒenətaɪp	dʒiːnətaɪp]	유전자형
Gender	[ˈdʒendə(r)]	성별
Height	[haɪt]	키
Hemizygous	[ˌhemiˈzīgəs]	반접합성
Hemophilia	[hìːməfíliə,hèm-]	혈우병
Heptaploid	[ˈhɛptəplɔ́id]	칠배체
Heterozygote	[hetərə|zaɪgoʊt]	이형접합체
Heterozygous	[hètərəzáigəs]	이형접합체의
Hexaploid	[héksəplɔ́id]	육배체
Homozygous	[ˌhɑːməˈzaɪgoəs]	동형접합의
Huntington disease	[hʌ́ntiŋtən dɪˈziːz]	헌팅턴병
Inactivate	[ɪnˈæktɪveɪt]	비활성화하다
Inactivation	[inæktəvéiʃən]	비활성의
Inactive	[ɪnˈæktɪv]	비활성
Inbred	[ˌɪnˈbred]	타고난
Incomplete	[ɪnkəmˈpliːt]	불완전한
Influence	[ɪnfluəns]	영향
Inheritance	[ɪnˈherɪtəns]	계승
Inhibit	[ɪnˈhɪbɪt]	억제하다
Insertion	[ɪnˈsɜːrʃn]	삽입
Intelligence	[ɪnˈtelɪdʒəns]	지능
Intensity	[ɪnˈtensəti]	강도
Interest	[|ɪntrəst]	관심
Intrinsic	[ɪn|trɪnsɪk ɪn| trɪnzɪk]	본질적인
Lighten	[ˈlaɪtn]	가볍게 하다
Locate	[loʊkeɪt]	위치하다
Locus	[|loʊkəs]	유전자자리
Male	[meɪl]	남성, 수컷, 남성의, 수컷의
Map	[mæp]	지도
Mate	[meɪt]	짝짓기 하다
Mating	[meɪtɪŋ]	교배

Melanin	[melənɪn]	멜라닌
Mendel	[méndl]	멘델
Microevolution	[ˌmaɪkrouèvəlúːʃən]	소진화
Migration	[maɪˈgreɪʃn]	이주, 이동
Miss	[mɪs]	놓치다
Missense	[míssèns]	미스센스
Monohybrid	[mɑ̀nəháibrid]	단성잡종
Muscular	[ˈmʌskjələ(r)]	근육의
Mutagen	[mjúːtədʒən]	돌연별이 유발 요인
Mutation	[mjuːˈteɪʃn]	돌연변이
Mutually	[ˈmjuːtʃuəli]	상호 간에
Nonsense	[nɑːnsens ǀ nɑːnsns]	무의미 돌연변이
Norm of reaction	[nɔːrm ʌv riˈækʃn]	반응 규격
Observable	[əbǀzɜːrvəbl]	식별할 수 있는
Observe	[əbˈzɜːrv]	관찰하다
Occurrence	[əǀkɜːrəns]	발생
Octaploid	[ɒktəˌplɔɪd]	팔배체
Operon	[ɑ́pərɑ̀n]	오페론
Order	[ɔːrdə(r)]	순서
Ovum	[ǀoʊvəm]	난자
Passing	[ǀpæsɪŋ]	지나가는
Pedigree	[pedɪgriː]	족보
Pentaploid	[péntəplɔ́id]	오배체
Phenotype	[fiːnətaɪp]	표현형
Phenotypic	[ˈfiːnətaɪpik]	표현의
Phenylketonuria	[fènlkiːtounjúəriə]	페닐케톤뇨증
Physically	[ˈfɪzɪkli]	육체적으로
Pleiotropy	[plaiɑ́trəpi]	다면발현
Polycistronic	[ˌpälēsiˈstränik]	다시스트론의
Polygenic	[ˌpɒlɪˈdʒɛnɪk]	다유전자의
Population	[ǀpɑːpjuǀleɪʃn]	개체군
Possibility	[ǀpɑːsəǀbɪləti]	가능성
Predictable	[prɪˈdɪktəbl]	예측 가능한
Principle	[ˈprɪnsəpl]	원칙
Probability	[ǀprɑːbəǀbɪləti]	확률
Punnett square	[ˈpənət skwer]	퍼넷스퀘어
Pureblood	[pjúərblʌ́d]	순혈
Radiation	[ˌreɪdiˈeɪʃn]	방사능
Random	[rændəm]	무작위의
Ratio	[ǀreɪʃoʊ]	비율

Real	[ˈriːəl]	진정한
Recessive	[rɪˈsesɪv]	열성의
Recognizable	[rekəgnaɪz]	확인할 수 있는
Regulatory	[ˈregjələtɔːri]	규제
Remain	[rɪˈmeɪn]	유지하다
Replicable	[réplikəbl]	복제 가능한
Rule	[ruːl]	규칙
Segment	[segmənt]	분절
Select	[sɪˈlekt]	선택하다
Selection	[sɪˈlekʃn]	선택
Self-fertilization	[sélffəːrtəlizéiʃən]	자가 수정
Separately	[ˈseprətli]	각기
Sickle cell anemia	[ˈsɪk(ə)l sèl əˈniːmiə]	겸상 적혈구 빈혈
Silent	[ˈsaɪlənt]	조용한
Similar	[sɪmələ(r)]	비슷한
Similarity	[ˌsɪməˈlærəti]	유사성
Stick	[stɪk]	붙다
Substitution	[ˌsʌbstɪˈtuːʃn]	치환
Supercoil	[ˈsuːpə(r)kɔíl]	초나선
Suppress	[səˈpres]	억제하다
Symptom	[sɪmptəm]	증상
Terminology	[tɜːrməˈnɑːlədʒi]	전문 용어
Tetraploid	[tétrəplɔ́id]	사배체
Theria	[ˈθɪərɪə]	수아강
Tool	[tuːl]	도구
Triploid	[tríplɔid]	삼배체
Turner syndrome	[təˈrnər ˈsɪndroʊm]	터너 증후군
Unrelated	[ʌnrɪˈleɪtɪd]	관련 없는
Variety	[vəˈraɪəti]	다양성
Vital	[vaɪtl]	필수적인

Chapter 7

Vocabulary	Pronunciation	Signification
Accept	[əkˈsept]	수용하다
Acceptor	[ækséptər]	수용체
Acetaldehyde	[æ̀sətǽldəhàid]	아세트알데히드
Acetyl	[əsíːtl, ǽsətl]	아세틸
Acid	[ǽsɪd]	산, 산성의
Act	[ækt]	행동하다
Activate	[ǽktɪveɪt]	활성화하다
Activation	[æ̀ktəvéiʃən]	활성화
Active	[ǽktɪv]	활동적인
Activity	[ækˈtɪvəti]	활동
ADP	Adenosine Diphosphate	아데노신 이인산
Aerobic	[eǀroʊbɪk]	호기성
Affect	[əˈfekt]	영향을 미치다
Air	[er]	공기
Alcohol	[ǀælkəhɔːl ǀælkəhɑːl]	알코올
Allosteric	[æləstérik]	알로스테릭한
Alpha	[ǽlfə]	알파
Alternative	[ɔːlǀtɜːrnətɪv]	대체 가능한
Amount	[əˈmaʊnt]	양
Anaerobic	[æneǀroʊbɪk]	혐기성
Animal	[ˈænɪml]	동물
Bacterium	[bæktíəriəm]	박테리아
Barrier	[bæriə(r)]	장벽
Bind	[baɪnd]	묶다
Bond	[bɑːnd]	접착하다
Brain	[breɪn]	뇌
cAMP	[kæmp]	고리형아데노신일인산
Carbon	[ǀkɑːrbən]	탄소
Carboxylic	[ˌkɑːbɒkˈsɪlɪk]	카르복실기의
Carrier	[kæriə(r)]	매개체, 보균자
Catalyst	[ˈkætəlɪst]	촉매
Catalyze	[kǽtəlàiz]	촉매 작용을 하다
Cell	[sel]	세포
Cellular	[seljələ(r)]	세포의
Chain	[tʃeɪn]	사슬, 띠, 묶따
Channel	[ˈtʃænl]	경로

Charge	[tʃɑːrdʒ]	전하
Chemical	[kemɪkl]	화학적인
Chemiosmotic	[kèmiɑzmɑ́tik]	화학 삼투
Chlorophyll	[|klɔːrəfɪl]	엽록소
Chloroplast	[ˈklɔːrəplæst]	엽록체
Circular	[sɜːrkjələ(r)]	순회하는, 원형의
Citrate	[sítreit]	구연산염
Citric acid cycle	[ˈsɪtrɪk ˈæsɪd ˈsʌɪk(ə)l]	시트르산회로
CoA	Coenzyme A	조효소 A
Coenzyme	[kouénzaim]	조효소
Combine	[|kɒmbaɪn]	결합하다
Competitive	[kəmˈpetətɪv]	경쟁을 하는
Complement	[kɒmplɪmənt]	보완물
Complex	[|kɒmpleks]	복잡한
Concentration	[|kɑːnsn|treɪʃn]	농도
Conformation	[kɑːnfɔːr|meɪʃn]	형태
Consume	[kən|suːm]	소비하다
Consuming	[kən|suːmɪŋ]	소비하는
Convert	[kən|vɜːrt kən|vɜːrt]	전환하다
Cycle	[saɪkl]	주기, 순환
Cytoplasm	[|saɪtoʊplæzəm]	세포질
Decarboxylation	[ˌdēkärˌbäksəˈlāshən]	탈카르복실화
Decrease	[ˈdiːkriːs]	줄이다, 감소하다
Denaturalize	[diːnætʃərəlàiz]	본래 성질을 바꾸다
Depend	[dipénd]	의존하다
Dependent	[dɪˈpendənt]	의존적인
Derive	[diráiv]	파생하다
Destroy	[dɪˈstrɔɪ]	파괴하다
Dioxide	[daɪ|ɑːksaɪd]	이산화물
Dipole	[daɪpoʊl]	쌍극자
DNA	Deoxyribonucleic Acid	DNA
Electron	[ɪ|lektrɑːn]	전자
Endergonic	[èndərgɑ́nik]	흡에너지성의
Energy	[|enərdʒi]	에너지
Enzyme	[enzaɪm]	효소
Ethyl	[eθɪl ˈiːθaɪl]	에틸
Eukaryote	[juːkǽriòut]	진핵생물
Exercise	[eksərsaɪz]	운동
Exergonic	[èksərgɑ́nik]	발에너지의
Factor	[fæktə(r)]	요인

FAD	Flavin Adenine Dinucleotide	플라빈 아데닌 디뉴클레오타이드
Fermentation	[fəːrmentéiʃən]	발효
Final component	[ˈfaɪnl kəmˈpoʊnənt]	마지막 요소
Fit	[fɪt]	맞다, 적합한
Fixed	[fɪkst]	고정된
Flow	[floʊ]	흐름
Fluid	[fluːɪd]	체액, 유체
Form	[fɔːrm]	형태, 형성하다
Formation	[fɔːrˈmeɪʃn]	형성
Fraction	[frækʃn]	부분
Fragment	[ˈfragm(ə)nt]	파편
Fuel	[ˈfjuːəl]	연료
Fumarate	[fjúːməreit]	푸마르산염
Function	[fʌŋkʃn]	기능
Functional	[fʌŋkʃənl]	기능의
Fungus	[fʌŋgəs]	진균류
Glucose	[gluːkoʊs ǀ gluːkoʊz]	포도당
Glycogen	[gláikədʒən]	글리코겐
Glycolysis	[glaikáləsis]	해당 과정
Gradient	[ˈgreɪdiənt]	변화도
Grana	[ˈgrɑːnə]	그라나 (복수)
Granum	[gréinəm]	그라나 (단수)
GTP	Guanosine Triphosphate	구아노신 삼인산
Hydrolysis	[haɪǀdrɑːlɪsɪs]	가수 분해
Inactivate	[ɪnˈæktɪveɪt]	비활성화하다
Inactive	[ɪnˈæktɪv]	비활성한
Increase	[ɪnˈkriːs]	증가하다
Independent	[ˌɪndɪˈpendənt]	독립적인
Induce	[ɪnǀduːs]	유도하다
Inhibit	[ɪnˈhɪbɪt]	저해하다
Inhibition	[ǀɪnhɪǀbɪʃn]	저해
Inhibitor	[ɪnˈhɪbɪtə(r)]	저해제
Initiate	[ɪˈnɪʃieɪt]	시작하다
Interaction	[ɪntərǀækʃn]	상호 작용
Irreversible	[ǀɪrɪǀvɜːrsəbl]	뒤집을 수 없는
Isocitrate	[àisousítreit]	이소시트레이트
Kelvin	[kelvɪn]	켈빈
Ketoglutarate	[ˌkētōglüˈtäˌrāt, -ˈglütəˌrāt]	케토글루타레이트
Kinase	[káineis]	키네이스
Krebs cycle	[krébz-ˈsaɪkl]	크렙스 사이클

Lactate	[læk'teɪt]	젖산
Lactic acid	[læktɪk 'æsɪd]	젖산
Level	[levl]	수준
Light	[laɪt]	빛
Limiting	[lɪmɪtɪŋ]	제한하는
Liver	['lɪvə(r)]	간
Location	[loʊ|keɪʃn]	위치
Lumen	[luːmen]	내강
Lysozyme	[láisəzàim]	리소자임
Malate	[Malate]	말린산염
Matrix	[meɪtrɪks]	행렬
Mechanism	[mekənɪzəm]	구조
Membrane	[membreɪn]	막
Mitochondrion	[maɪtoʊ| kɑːndriən]	미토콘드리아
Modify	[mɑːdɪfaɪ]	수정하다
Molecule	[mɑːlɪkjuːl]	분자
Multiple	[mʌltɪpl]	다수의
Muscle	['mʌsl]	근육
NAD	Nicotinamide Adenine Dinucleotide	니코틴아미드 아데닌 디뉴클레오티드
Net	[net]	그물
Optimal	[ɑːptɪməl]	최적의
Organelle	[ɔːrgənél,ɔːrgənèl]	소기관
Organism	[ɔːrgənɪzəm]	유기체
Osmosis	[ɑːz|moʊsɪs]	삼투
Oxaloacetate	[ˌäksəlō'asəˌtāt]	옥살로아세테이트
Oxidation	[ɑ́ksədéiʃən]	산화
Oxidative	[ɑ́ksədèitiv]	산화의
Oxidize	[ɑːksɪdaɪz]	산화시키다
Oxygen	[ɑːksɪdʒən]	산소
Pathway	[pæθweɪ]	경로
Pepsin	[pepsɪn]	펩신
pH	Potential of Hydrogen	산도, 페하
Phosphorylation	[fɑ̀sfɔːriléiʃən]	인산화
Photosynthesis	[foʊtoʊ| sɪnθəsɪs]	광합성
Pigment	[pɪgmənt]	색소
Plant	[plænt]	식물
Pore	[pɔː(r)]	구멍, 모공
Power	[paʊə(r)]	힘
Proportional	[prə|pɔːrʃənl]	비례하는
Protein	[proʊtiːn]	단백질

Proton	[proʊtɑːn]	양성자
Pump	[pʌmp]	펌프
Pyruvate	[páiruːveit]	피루브산
Rate	[reɪt]	비율
Reactant	[riˈæktənt]	반응물
Reaction	[riˈækʃn]	반응
Recycle	[ˌriːˈsaɪkl]	다시 이용하다
Reducing	[ridjúːsiŋ]	환원의
Reduction	[rɪˈdʌkʃn]	환원
Reflect	[rɪˈflekt]	반영하다
Regulator	[regjuleɪtə(r)]	조절기
Release	[rɪˈliːs]	풀어 주다
Resemble	[rɪˈzembl]	닮다
Respiration	[respəˈreɪʃn]	호흡
Reversible	[rɪǀvɜːrsəbl]	되돌릴 수 있는
Shape	[ʃeɪp]	모양
Site	[saɪt]	위치, 장소
Stack	[stæk]	무더기, 쌓다
Stoma	[ǀstoʊmə]	기공
Stroma	[stróumə]	스트로마
Substrate	[sʌbstreɪt]	기질
Succinate	[ˈsʌksɪneɪt]	숙신산염
Succinyl	[sʌ́ksinil]	숙시닐
Summary	[ˈsʌməri]	요약
Synthase	[sínθeis]	신테이스
Thylakoid	[ˈθʌɪləkɔɪd]	틸라코이드
Tricarboxylic	[traikɑːrbɑksílik]	3개의 카르복실기를 가진
Trypsin	[trípsin]	트립신
Vacuole	[vækjuoʊl]	액포
Yield	[jiːld]	생산하다
Yogurt	[ˈjoʊɡərt]	요거트

Chapter 8

Vocabulary	Pronunciation	Signification
Absorption	[əbˈsɔːrpʃn əbˈzɔːrpʃn]	흡수
Actin	[æktən]	액틴
Action	[ækʃn]	행동
Active	[æktɪv]	활동적인
Activity	[ækˈtɪvəti]	활동
Adipose	[ˈædɪpoʊs]	지방질의
Adrenal	[ədríːnl]	부신의
Air	[eə(r)]	공기
Alternative	[ɔːlˈtɜːrnətɪv]	대체 가능한
Animal	[ˈænɪml]	동물
Antagonistic	[ænˌtæɡəˈnɪstɪk]	대항하는, 길항하는
Anus	[ˈeɪnəs]	항문
Aorta	[eɪˈɔːrtə]	대동맥
Area	[eriə]	지역, 영역
Armpit	[ˈɑːrmpɪt]	겨드랑이
Artery	[ˈɑːrtəri]	동맥
Associate	[əˈsoʊʃieɪt]	연관 짓다
Astrocyte	[æstrəsàit]	별아교세포
Attach	[əˈtætʃ]	들러붙다
Awareness	[əˈwernəs]	의식
Axon hillock	[ˈæksɑːn ˈhɪlək]	축삭 언덕
Axon terminal	[ˈæksɑːn ˈtɜːrmɪnl]	축삭 말단
Bind	[baɪnd]	묶다
Bladder	[ˈblædə(r)]	방광
Blood	[blʌd]	피
Blunt	[blʌnt]	둔화시키다
Bone	[boʊn]	뼈
Brain	[breɪn]	뇌
Branch	[bræntʃ]	가지, 분과
Bronchus	[ˈbrɑːŋkəs]	기관지
Calcium	[kælsiəm]	칼슘
Canal	[kəˈnæl]	관
Carbohydrate	[kɑːrboʊˈhaɪdreɪt]	탄수화물
Carbon dioxide	[ˈkɑːrbən daɪˈɑːksaɪd]	이산화탄소
Cardiac	[ˈkɑːrdiæk]	심장의
Cardiac muscle	[ˈkɑːrdiæk ˈmʌsl]	심장 근육

Cardiovascular	[kɑːrdioʊˌvæskjələ(r)]	심혈관의
Carry	[ˈkæri]	운반하다
Cartilage	[ˌkɑːrtɪlɪdʒ]	연골
Cavity	[kævəti]	공동
Central	[ˈsentrəl]	중앙의
Characteristic	[kærəktəˈrɪstɪk]	특성
Chemistry	[ˈkemɪstri]	화학
Cilia	[síliə]	섬모
Circle	[ˈsɜːrkl]	원
Circulatory	[sɜːrkjələtɔːri]	순환기의
CNS	Central Nervous System	중추신경계
Cohesion	[koʊˌhiːʒn]	응집력
Collagen	[ˌkɑːlədʒən]	콜라겐
Columnar	[kəlʌ́mnər]	원주형의
Communicate	[kəˈmjuːnɪkeɪt]	의사소통하다
Compact	[ˌkɒmpækt]	소형의
Complex	[ˌkɒmpleks]	복잡한, 복합체
Component	[kəmˌpoʊnənt]	구성 요소
Compose	[kəmˌpoʊz]	구성하다
Concentric lamella	[kənˈsentrɪk ləmélə]	동심원층판
Connection	[kəˈnekʃn]	연결
Connective	[kəˈnektɪv]	결합하는
Consist	[kənˈsɪst]	이루어져 있다
Contain	[kənˈteɪn]	포함하다
Continuous	[kənˈtɪnjuəs]	이어지는, 반복하는
Contract	[ˌkɒntrækt]	수축하다
Contraction	[kənˈtrækʃn]	수축
Control	[kənˌtroʊl]	통제하다
Cross	[krɔːs]	가로지르다
Cuboid	[kjuːbɔɪd]	직육면체
Cushion	[ˈkʊʃn]	쿠션
Cylinder	[sɪlɪndə(r)]	원통
Cylindrical	[səˈlɪndrɪkl]	원통형의
Cytoplasmic	[saɪtoʊplǽzəmɪk]	세포질의
Damage	[dæmɪdʒ]	손상, 손상 입히다
Debris	[dəˌbriː]	조직 파편, 찌꺼기
Defend	[dɪˈfend]	방어하다
Defense	[dɪˈfens]	방어
Delicate	[ˈdelɪkət]	연약한, 섬세한
Dendrite	[dendraɪt]	수상돌기

Dense	[dens]	밀집한, 빽빽한
Dermis	[dɜːrmɪs]	진피
Destroy	[dɪˈstrɔɪ]	파괴하다
Diaphragm	[ˈdaɪəfræm]	횡격막
Diffusion	[difjúːʒən]	확산
Digestive	[daɪ|dʒestɪv dɪ|dʒestɪv]	소화의
Disease	[dɪˈziːz]	질병
Dispersed	[dispə́ːrst]	분산된
Division	[dɪˈvɪʒn]	분할
Dry	[draɪ]	마른
Duct	[dʌkt]	관
Ductless	[dʌ́ktlis]	관이 없는
Dust	[dʌst]	먼지
Elastic	[ɪˈlæstɪk]	탄력 있는
Elasticity	[iːlæ|stɪsəti	elæ|stɪsəti ɪ|læ|stɪsəti]	탄력
Elastin	[ɪˈlæstɪn]	탄력소
Electrical	[ɪˈlektrɪkl]	전기의
Eliminate	[ɪˈlɪmɪneɪt]	제거하다
Elongated	[ɪ|lɔːŋgeɪtɪd]	길쭉한
Embed	[ɪmˈbed]	포함된
Emotion	[ɪˈmoʊʃn]	감정
End	[end]	끝
Endocrine	[|endəkrɪn]	내분비
Enzyme	[enzaɪm]	효소
Ependyma	[ɛˈpɛndɪmə]	수강상피
Epidermis	[|epɪ|dɜːrmɪs]	표피
Epithelial	[èpiθíːliəl]	상피성의
Epithelium	[èpəθíːliəm]	상피
Esophagus	[i|sɑːfəgəs]	식도
Excess	[ɪkˈses]	초과한
Excrete	[ɪkˈskriːt]	배설하다
Excretion	[ikskríːʃən]	배설
Exocrine	[eksəkrɪn	eksəkriːn]	외분비
Expand	[ɪkˈspænd]	확장하다
Expose	[ɪkˈspoʊz]	노출하다
Extension	[ɪkˈstenʃn]	연장, 확대
Extensive	[ɪkˈstensɪv]	광범위한
External	[ɪkˈstɜːrnl]	외부의
Fat	[fæt]	지방
Fatigue	[fəˈtiːg]	피로

Fiber	[fáibər]	섬유
Fibroblast	[fáibrəblæ̀st]	섬유아세포
Flexible	[ˈfleksəbl]	유연한
Fluid	[fluːɪd]	체액
Force	[fɔːrs]	힘
Foreign	[ˈfɔːrən ˈfɑːrən]	다른
Form	[fɔːrm]	형태
Framework	[ǀfreɪmwɜːrk]	뼈대
Function	[ˈfʌŋkʃn]	기능
Gallbladder	[gɔ́ːlblæ̀dər]	담낭, 쓸개
Gap	[gæp]	갭
General	[dʒenrəl]	일반적인
Generate	[dʒenəreɪt]	생성하다
Germ	[dʒɜːrm]	세균
Gland	[glænd]	샘
Glial cell	[ˈgliːəl sel]	신경아교세포
Goblet cell	[ˈgɒblɪt sel]	배상 세포
Gonad	[goʊnæd]	생식선
Groin	[grɔɪn]	사타구니
Gut	[gʌt]	소화관
Haversian canal	[həvəːrʃən kəˈnæl]	하버스관
Heart	[hɑːrt]	심장
Heartbeat	[ǀhɑːrtbiːt]	심장박동
Hollow	[hɑːloʊ]	구멍
Hormone	[hɔːrmoʊn]	호르몬
Hypothalamus	[haɪpəˈθæləməs]	시상하부
Immune	[ɪˈmjuːn]	면역성이 있는
Immunity	[ɪˈmjuːnəti]	면역
Impulse	[ˈɪmpʌls]	자극
Information	[ǀɪnfərǀmeɪʃn]	정보
Injury	[ˈɪndʒəri]	부상
Innate	[ɪˈneɪt]	타고난
Insulation	[ǀɪnsəǀleɪʃn]	절연
Integumentary	[inˌtegyəˈment(ə)rē]	외피의
Intercellular	[ìntərséljulər]	세포간
Interlace	[ǀɪntərǀleɪs]	꼬이다
Intermediate	[ǀɪntərǀmiːdiət]	중간의
Interstitial	[ǀɪntərǀstɪʃl]	사이의
Intestine	[ɪnˈtestɪn]	장
Invade	[ɪnˈveɪd]	침략하다

Involuntary	[ɪnˈvɑːlənteri]		비자발적인
Joint	[dʒɔɪnt]		관절
Juice	[dʒuːs]		육즙
Junction	[ˈdʒʌŋkʃn]		접합
Kidney	[ˈkɪdni]		신장
Lacuna	[ləǀkuːnə]		골강
Lamellae	[ləmélə]		층판
Larynx	[ˈlærɪŋks]		후두
Layer	[ˈler]		층
Ligament	[lɪɡəmənt]		인대
Lining	[ˈlaɪnɪŋ]		내벽
Locomotion	[loʊkəˈmoʊʃn]		운동
Loose	[luːs]		헐렁한, 느슨한
Lubricate	[ˈluːbrɪkeɪt]		윤활하게 하다
Lung	[lʌŋ]		폐
Lymph node	[límfnoud]		림프절
Lymphatic	[lɪmˈfætɪk]		림프의
Macrophage	[ˈmækrəfeɪdʒ]		대식세포
Male	[meɪl]		남성, 수컷, 남성의, 수컷의
Mammary	[ˈmæməri]		유방의
Matrix	[meɪtrɪks]		행렬
Matter	[mætə(r)]		물질
Membrane	[membreɪn]		막
Memory	[meməri]		기억
Metabolic	[ǀmetəǀbɑːlɪk]		대사
Microglia	[maikróuglaiə]		미세아교세포
Mixed	[mɪkst]		혼합된
Modulate	[ǀmɑːdʒəleɪt]		조절하다
Motion	[moʊʃn]		움직임
Mouth	[maʊθ]		입
Mucosa	[mjuːkóuzə,-sə]		점막
Mucous	[ˈmjuːkəs]		점액
Mucus	[mjuːkəs]		점액
Multilayer	[mʌltiléiər,-tai]		다층
Muscle	[ˈmʌsl]		근육
Myofibril	[màiəfáibrəl]		근원섬유
Myriad	[mɪriəd]		무수함
Nasal cavity	[ˈneɪz(ə)l ˈkavɪti]		비강
Neck	[nek]		목
Neighboring	[néibəriŋ]		인접한

Nerve	[nɜːrv]	신경
Nervous	[nɜːrvəs]	신경의
Network	[netwɜːrk]	회로망
Neuromuscular	[njùəroumʌ́skjulər]	신경근
Neuron	[nʊrɑːn]	뉴런
Node of Ranvier	[nəʊd ʌv ˈrɑnvyeɪ]	랑비에결절
Nose	[noʊz]	코
Nourish	[ˈnɜːrɪʃ]	영양분을 공급하다
Nucleus	[nuːkliəs]	핵
Nutrient	[nuːtriənt]	영양소
Occupy	[ɑːkjupaɪ]	차지하다
Oligodendrocyte	[ɑ̀ligoudéndrousait]	희소돌기아교세포
Oral	[ɔːrəl]	구두의
Organ	[ˈɔːrgən]	장기
Original	[əˈrɪdʒənl]	본래의
Osteocyte	[ɑ́stiəsàit]	골세포
Ovary	[|oʊvəri]	난소
Oviduct	[oʊvɪdʌkt]	수란관
Oxygen	[|ɑːksɪdʒən]	산소
Pacemaker	[ˈpeɪsmeɪkə(r)]	맥박 조정 장치
Pancreas	[ˈpæŋkriəs]	췌장
Parathyroid	[pæ̀rəθáirɔid]	부갑상선
Passage	[pæsɪdʒ]	통로
Passageway	[pǽsidʒwèi]	통로
Pathogen	[pæθədʒən]	병원체
Penis	[piːnɪs]	음경
Peristaltic	[ˌperəˈstóltik]	연동의
Phagocytosis	[fæ̀gəsaitóusis]	식균 작용
Pharynx	[ˈfærɪŋks]	인두
Pineal	[paɪˈniːəl]	송과체
Pituitary	[pɪ|tuːəteri]	뇌하수체
Pleura	[ˈplʊrə]	늑막
PNS	Peripheral Nervous System	말초 신경계
Pointed	[ˈpɔɪntɪd]	뾰족한
Power	[paʊə(r)]	힘
Propel	[prəˈpel]	추진하다
Prostate	[prɑːsteɪt]	전립선
Pseudostratified	[ˈsuː.doʊˌstrætəfaɪd]	거짓 중층
Reasoning	[riːzənɪŋ]	추리
Reproductive	[riːprəˈdʌktɪv]	생식의

Reservation	[ˈrezərˈveɪʃn]	예약
Resistance	[rɪˈzɪstəns]	저항
Respiratory	[ˈrespərətɔːri]	호흡의, 호흡 기관의
Reticular	[ritíkjulər]	그물 모양의
Return	[rɪˈtɜːrn]	돌아오다, 돌아가다
Rhythm	[ˈrɪðəm]	리듬
Saliva	[səˈlaɪvə]	타액
Sarcomere	[ˈsɑːkə(ʊ)mɪə]	근절
Satellite	[sætəlaɪt]	위성
Scavenger cell	[skævɪndʒə(r) sel]	청소부 세포
Schwann cell	[ʃwάːn sel]	슈반 세포
Semifluid	[sèmiflúːid]	반유동체
Sensation	[senˈseɪʃn]	감각
Sheet	[ʃiːt]	한 장
Cilia	[síliə]	섬모
Skeletal muscle	[ˈskelətl ˈmʌsl]	골격근
Skeleton	[skelɪtn]	해골
Smooth muscle	[smuːð ˈmʌsl]	민무늬근
Spinal cord	[ˈspaɪnl kɔːd]	척수
Spleen	[spliːn]	비장
Squamous	[skwéiməs]	비늘 모양의
Stimulate	[stɪmjuleɪt]	자극하다
Stratify	[strætɪfaɪ]	층을 이루다
Stretch	[stretʃ]	늘이다
Striation	[straɪˈeɪʃn]	줄무늬
Subcutaneous	[ˌsʌbkjuˈteɪniəs]	피하의
Sweat	[swet]	땀
Tendon	[ˈtendən]	건
Tensile	[ˈtensl]	인장
Testis	[ˈtestɪs]	고환
Thickness	[ˈθɪknəs]	두께
Thoracic	[θɔːræsik]	흉부
Thymus	[θaɪməs]	흉선
Thyroid	[θaɪrɔɪd]	갑상선
Tip	[tɪp]	끝부분
Tonsil	[ˈtɑːnsl]	편도
Tough	[tʌf]	힘든
Trace	[treɪs]	추적하다
Transmission	[trænsˈmɪʃn]	전송, 전염
Transmit	[trænsˈmɪt]	전송하다

Ureter	[uəríːtər]	요관
Urethra	[jʊˈriːθrə]	요도
Urinary	[ˈjʊrəneri]	비뇨기의
Urine	[ʊrən]	오줌
Uterus	[ˈjuːtərəs]	자궁
Vagina	[vəˈdʒaɪnə]	질
Vas deferens	[væs ˈdefərenz]	정관
Vein	[veɪn]	정맥
Vessel	[ˈvesl]	혈관
Visceral	[vɪsərəl]	내장의
Voluntary muscle	[ˈvɒlənt(ə)ri ˈmʌs(ə)l]	자발적 근육
Wander	[wɑːndə(r)]	돌아다니다, 다른 데로 가다
Wavy	[weɪvi]	떨리는
WBC	White Blood Cell	백혈구
Wound	[wuːnd]	상처

Chapter 9

Vocabulary	Pronunciation	Signification
Appendicular skeleton	[æpəndíkjulər ˈskelɪtn]	충수 골격
Arch	[ɑːrtʃ]	아치형
Attachment	[əˈtætʃmənt]	부착
Axial bones	[ˈæksiəl boʊn]	축골
Axis	[ˈæksɪs]	중심축
Band	[bænd]	밴드
Blade	[bleɪd]	날, 날갯짓
Bony	[ˈboʊn]	뼈의
Cage	[keɪdʒ]	우리
Carnivorous	[kɑːr|nɪvərəs]	육식성의
Cattle	[ˈkætl]	소
Cervical	[ˈsɜːrvɪkl]	(자궁) 경부의, 목의, 경부의
Chest	[tʃest]	가슴
Clavicle	[ˈklævɪkl]	쇄골
Claw	[klɔː]	발톱
Climbing	[klaɪmɪŋ]	등반
Coccygeal	[kɑksídʒiəl]	미저골의
Coccyx	[|kɑːksɪks]	미골

Collapse	[kəˈlæps]	무너지다
Column	[ˈkɑːləm]	기둥
Complete	[kəmˈpliːt]	완벽한
Courtship	[kɔːrtʃɪp]	구애
Cover	[ˈkʌvə(r)]	씌우다
Covered	[|kʌvərd]	덮인
Cranial	[ˈkreɪniəl]	두개골
Crystal	[ˈkrɪstl]	결정
Curve	[kɜːrv]	곡선
Deposit	[dɪ|pɑːzɪt]	침전물
Diameter	[daɪˈæmɪtə(r)]	지름
Diaphysis	[daiǽfəsis]	골간
Digit	[dɪdʒɪt]	손가락
Dorsally	[ˈdɔːrsli]	등 쪽으로
Epiphysis	[ipífəsis]	솔방울샘
Facial	[ˈfeɪʃl]	얼굴의
Facilitation	[fəsilətéiʃən]	촉진
Feeding	[ˈfiːdɪŋ]	수유
Finger	[ˈfɪŋgə(r)]	손가락
Flexibility	[|fleksə|bɪləti]	유연성
Flexibly	[ˈfleksəbli]	유연하게
Follicle	[|fɑːlɪkl]	소낭
Foot	[fʊt]	발
Friction	[ˈfrɪkʃn]	마찰
Fur	[fɜː(r)]	털
Gel	[dʒel]	젤
Girdle	[gɜːrdl]	상지대
Groom	[gruːm]	(동물을) 손질하다, (털을) 다듬다
Guard	[gɑːrd]	보호하다
Hip	[hɪp]	둔부
Hoof	[huːf]	발굽
Horn	[hɔːrn]	뿔
Hyaline	[háiəliːn,-lin]	유리질, 하이알린
Immovable	[ɪˈmuːvəbl]	움직일 수 없는
Insulate	[|ɪnsəleɪt]	절연시키다
Keratin	[ˈkerətɪn]	케라틴
Lifetime	[ˈlaɪftaɪm]	생애
Limb	[lɪm]	팔, 날개
Lubricant	[ˈluːbrɪkənt]	윤활유
Lumbar	[ˈlʌmbə(r)]	요추

Marrow	[ˈmæroʊ]	골수
Metaphysis	[mitǽfisis]	뼈몸통 끝 골간단
Mixture	[ˈmɪkstʃə(r)]	혼합물
Movable	[ˈmuːvəbl]	움직일 수 있는
Osteoblast	[ɑ́stiəblæ̀st]	조골세포
Osteoclast	[ɑ́stiəklæ̀st]	파골세포
Osteocyte	[ɑ́stiəsàit]	골세포
Osteon	[ɑ́stiɑn]	골단위
Pad	[pæd]	패드
Pain	[peɪn]	통증
Pectoral	[ˈpektərəl]	흉부의
Pelvic	[ˈpelvɪk]	골반
Periosteum	[pèriɑ́stiəm]	골막
Plate	[pleɪt]	판
Platelet	[ˈpleɪtlət]	혈소판
Prey	[preɪ]	먹이
Ray	[reɪ]	광선
Reabsorb	[ˌriːəbˈzɔːb]	재흡수하다
Reform	[rɪˈfɔːrm]	재구성하다
Relative	[ˈrelətɪv]	상대적인
Remodel	[ˌriːˈmɑːdl]	개조하다
Rib	[rɪb]	늑골
Sacral	[séikrəl]	천골의
Sacrum	[ˈseɪkrəm ˈsækrəm]	천골
Scapula	[ˈskæpjʊlə]	견갑골
Sebum	[ˈsiːbəm]	피지
Self-defense	[sélfdiféns]	자기방어
Sensory	[ˈsensəri]	감각의
Shell	[ʃel]	껍데기
Shock	[ʃɑːk]	충격
Shoulder	[ˈʃoʊldə(r)]	어깨
Skull	[skʌl]	두개골
Spine	[spaɪn]	척추
Sponge	[spʌndʒ]	스펀지
Stability	[stəˈbɪləti]	안정성
Sternum	[ˈstɜːrnəm]	흉골
Stratum basale	[ˈstreɪtəm beisəli]	기저층
Stratum corneum	[ˌstrɑːtəm ˈkɔːnɪəm]	각질층
Synovial fluid	[sɪˈnoʊviəl ˈfluːɪd]	관절 낭액
Territory	[ˈterətɔːri]	영역

Vocabulary	Pronunciation	Signification
Toe	[toʊ]	발가락
Underfur	[ˈʌndərfəːr]	잔털
Upper	[ˈʌpə(r)]	위쪽의
UV (Ultra-Violet)	[ˈʌltrə ˈvaɪələt]	자외선
Vertebra	[ǀvɜːrtɪbrə]	척추골
Vertebral	[vəˈrtəːbrəl]	척추의
Vertical	[ǀvɜːrtɪkl]	수직의
Waterproof	[ǀwɔːtərpruːf ǀ wɑːtərpruːf]	방수의
Wax	[wæks]	밀랍

Chapter 10

Vocabulary	Pronunciation	Signification
Acetylcholine	[əsìːtlkóuliːn]	아세틸콜린
Adjacent	[əˈdʒeɪsnt]	인접한
Angle	[æŋgl]	각도
Antagonist	[ænˈtæɡənɪst]	길항
Antagonistically	[ænˌtæɡəˈnɪstɪkli]	길항적으로
Bridge	[brɪdʒ]	다리
Bundle	[ˈbʌndl]	묶음
Capillary	[kæpəleri]	모세관
Contact	[kɑːntækt]	접촉하다
Contract	[ǀkɒntrækt]	수축하다
Contractile	[kənˈtræktaɪl]	수축성의
Contraction	[kənˈtrækʃn]	수축
Deliver	[dɪˈlɪvə(r)]	전달하다
Depolarize	[diːpóuləràɪz]	탈분극화하다
Detach	[dɪˈtætʃ]	분리하다
Electrochemical	[ilèktroukémikəl]	전기 화학의
Endurance	[ɪnǀdʊrəns]	인내, 내구
Expel	[ɪkˈspel]	배출하다
Fascicle	[fǽsikl]	작은 다발
Filament	[ˈfɪləmənt]	필라멘트
Gate	[geɪt]	게이트
Innervate	[inəˈrveit, ínərvèit]	신경을 분포시키다, 신경을 자극하다
Intertwine	[ǀɪntərǀtwaɪn]	서로 얽히게 하다
Length	[leŋθ]	길이
Manipulation	[məǀnɪpjuǀleɪʃn]	조작

Mediate	[miːdieɪt]	중재하다
Motor	[moʊtə(r)]	모터
Multinucleated	[ˌməltēˈnükleˌātəd]	다핵의
Myocyte	[máiousait]	근세포
Myofilament	[màioufíləmənt]	근섬유
Myoglobin	[ˌmīəˈglōbən]	미오글로빈
Neurotransmitter	[ˈnʊroʊtrænzmɪtə(r)]	신경전달물질
Overlap	[əʊvəlæp]	겹치다
Pack	[pæk]	싸다
Perpendicular	[pɜːrpənˈdɪkjələ(r)]	수직의
Postsynaptic	[pòustsinǽptik]	시냅스 후부의
Posture	[ˈpɑːstʃə(r)]	자세
Presynaptic	[prìːsinǽptik]	시냅스 전부의
Relaxation	[ˌriːlækˈseɪʃn]	이완, 완화
Responsible	[rɪˈspɑːnsəbl]	원인이 되는
Running	[rʌnɪŋ]	연속의
Sarcolemma	[ˌsärkəˈlemə]	근초
Sarcomere	[ˈsärkəˌmir]	근절
Sarcoplasm	[ˈsärkəˌplazəm]	근형질
Slide	[slaɪd]	미끄러지다
Sprint	[sprɪnt]	스프린트
Striped	[straɪpt]	줄무늬의
Synaptic	[səˈnaptik]	시냅스의
Target	[ˈtɑːrgɪt]	표적
Terminal	[tɜːrmɪnl]	전극, 말기의
Transverse	[trænzvɜːrs]	횡축
Tropomyosin	[ˌträpəˈmīəsən]	트로포미오신
Troponin	[tróupənin, tráp]	트로포닌
Tubule	[tjúːbjuːl]	세관
Turn	[tɜːrn]	돌다
Zone	[zoʊn]	구역, 지역

Chapter 11

Vocabulary	Pronunciation	Signification
Acidic	[əˈsɪdɪk]	산성의
Affinity	[əˈfɪnəti]	친밀성
Alveolar	[ælˈviːələ(r)]	폐포의
Alveolus	[ælˈviːələs]	폐포
Arteriole	[ɑːrˈtɪrioʊl]	세동맥
Atmospheric	[ætməsˈferɪk]	대기의
Breath	[breθ]	호흡
Breathe	[briːð]	호흡하다
Bronchiole	[bráŋkiòʊl]	세기관지
Carbaminohemoglobin	[kɑːrbæ̀minəhìːmouglóubin]	카르바미노헤모글로빈
Ciliated	[sílièitid]	섬모가 있는
Correlate	[kɔːrəleɪt]	연관성이 있다
Cough	[kɔːf]	기침, 기침하다
Deoxidize	[diːɑ́ksədàiz]	산소를 제거하다
Diffused	[difjúːzd]	확산된
Dirt	[dɜːrt]	먼지
Dissociate	[dɪ|souʃieɪt]	해리하다
Dissociation	[disòusiéiʃən,-ʃi-]	해리
Epiglottis	[|epɪ|glɑːtɪs]	후두개
Exhalation	[èkshəléiʃən]	발산
Exhale	[eksˈheɪl]	숨을 내쉬다
Expiration	[ekspəˈreɪʃn]	날숨
Extent	[ɪkˈstent]	정도
Filter	[ˈfɪltə(r)]	여과하다
Inhalation	[ˌɪnhəˈleɪʃn]	들숨
Inhale	[ɪnˈheɪl]	숨을 들이마시다
Intercostal	[ˌɪntərˈkɑːstl]	늑간의
Intrapleural	[ìntrəplú(ː)rəl]	흉막 내의
Lobe	[loʊb]	엽
Maximal	[mæksɪml]	최대한의
Microbe	[|maɪkroʊb]	미생물
Moist	[mɔɪst]	촉촉한
Moisten	[mɔɪsn]	촉촉하게 하다
Monoxide	[mɑnɑ́ksaid]	일산화물
Nostril	[nɑːstrəl]	콧구멍
Oxyhemoglobin	[ɑ̀ksihíːməglòubin]	옥시헤모글로빈

Vocabulary	Pronunciation	Signification
Parietal	[pəráiətl]	정수리의
Partial	[ˈpɑːrʃl]	부분적인
Percent	[pərˈsent]	퍼센트
Pleura	[ˈplʊrə]	늑막
Pneumocyte	[ˈn(y)üməˌsīt]	허파꽈리세포, 폐포세포
Pulmonary	[ǀpʌlməneri]	폐의
Rapidly	[ˈræpɪdli]	급속히
RBC	[Red Blood Cell]	적혈구
Residual volume	[rɪǀzɪdʒuəl ǀvɑːljuːm ǀvɑːljəm]	잔기량
Respire	[rɪˈspaɪə(r)]	호흡하다
Resting	[réstiŋ]	휴식하고 있는, (세포 등이) 증식하지 않고 있는
Saturation	[sætʃəˈreɪʃn]	포화
Surfactant	[sɜːrǀfæktənt]	계면활성제
Tension	[tenʃn]	장력
Throat	[θroʊt]	목구멍
Tidal volume	[ˈtaɪdl ǀvɑːljuːm ǀvɑːljəm]	일 호흡량
Trachea	[treɪkiə]	기관, 기도
Ventilation	[ǀventɪǀleɪʃn]	환기
Venule	[vénjuːl]	세정맥
Way	[weɪ]	방법
Working	[wɜːrkɪŋ]	작동, 작동하고 있는

Chapter 12

Vocabulary	Pronunciation	Signification
ACE	Angiotensin-Converting Enzyme	안지오텐신 전환 효소
ADH	Antidiuretic Hormone	항이뇨호르몬
Adrenal cortex	[ədríːnl ǀkɔːrteks]	부신 피질
Adrenal medulla	[ədríːnl mədʌ́lə]	부신 수질
Afferent	[ǽfərənt]	수입관, 수입성의
Ammonia	[əǀmoʊniə]	암모니아
Angiotensin	[æ̀ndʒiouténsin]	안지오텐신
Angiotensinogen	[æ̀ndʒiouténsinoudʒen]	안지오텐시노겐
ANP	Atrial Natriuretic Peptide	심방 나트륨 이뇨 펩티드
Aquaporin	[ˌækwəˈpɔːrɪn]	아쿠아포린
Atrial	[āˈtrēəl]	심방의
Atrium	[ˈeɪtriəm]	심방

Calcitriol	[kælsítriɔ́ːl,-ɑ̀l]	칼시트리올
Circulation	[ˌsɜːrkjəˈleɪʃn]	순환
Collecting duct	[kəlektɪŋ dʌkt]	집합관
Concentrate	[kɑːnsntreɪt]	농축시키다
Cortex	[kɔːrteks]	피질
Dehydration	[diːhaɪˈdreɪʃn]	탈수
Deoxygenate	[diːɑ́ksidʒənèit]	탈산소화하다
Diabetes	[daɪəˈbiːtiːz]	당뇨병
Dilate	[daɪˈleɪt]	확장하다
Distal convoluted tubule	[ˈdɪstl kɑːnvəluːtɪd tjúːbjuːl]	먼 쪽 곱슬 세관
Drain	[dreɪn]	물을 빼내다
Duct	[dʌkt]	관
Efferent	[éfərənt]	수출관, 수출성의
Endometrial	[ˌendəˈmiːtri.əl]	자궁 내막의
Erythropoietin	[iriθroupɔ́iətn]	적혈구생성인자
Excretory	[ekskrətɔːri]	배설물
Funnel	[ˈfʌnl]	깔때기
Glomerulus	[gloumérjuləs,glə-]	사구체
Granular	[grǽnjələ(r)]	과립의
Hydration	[haidréiʃən]	수분 공급, 수화
Hyperosmotic	[hàipərɑsmóutik]	고삼투압의
Insipid	[ɪnˈsɪpɪd]	무미한 맛
Juxtaglomerular apparatus	[dʒʌ̀kstəgloumérjulər ˌæpəˈrætəs]	방사구체장치
Liter	[liːtə(r)]	리터
Loop of Henle	[luːp ʌv ˈhenlē]	헨레계제
Macula densa	[mǽkjulə ˈdensə]	밀집반
Magnesium	[mægˈniːziəm]	마그네슘
Nephron	[néfrɑn]	네프론
Nitrogenous	[naitrɑ́dʒənəs]	질소의
Obligatory	[əˈblɪɡətɔːri]	의무적인
Osmotic	[ɑːzˈmɑːtɪk]	삼투의
Output	[ˈaʊtpʊt]	산출량
Oxygenate	[ɑːksɪdʒəneɪt]	산소를 공급하다
Passive	[ˈpæsɪv]	수동적인
Pelvis	[ˈpelvɪs]	골반
Portal	[pɔːrtl]	포털
Posterior	[pɑːˈstɪriə(r)]	후부
Proximal convoluted tubule	[ˌprɑːksɪməl kɑːnvəluːtɪd tjúːbjuːl]	근위곡요세관

Pyramid	[pɪrəmɪd]	피라미드
Reabsorption	[ˌrēəbˈsȯrpshən]	재흡수
Receiving	[risíːviŋ]	수신의
Removal	[rɪˈmuːvl]	제거
Renin	[ríːnin]	레닌
Section	[sekʃn]	부분
Split	[splɪt]	분열되다
Thirst	[θɜːrst]	갈증
Thrombopoietin	[ˌθrɒmboʊˈpɔɪɪtn, -pɔɪˈɛtn]	혈소판자극인자
Transparent	[trænsˈpærənt]	투명한
Urea	[jʊˈriːə]	요소
Urination	[jùərənéiʃən]	배뇨
Vasopressin	[væ̀souprésn]	바소프레신

Chapter 13

Vocabulary	Pronunciation	Signification
Accumulate	[əˈkjuːmjəleɪt]	축적하다
Adhere	[ədˈhɪr]	부착하다
Agent	[ˈeɪdʒənt]	물질
Albumin	[ælbjúːmən]	알부민
Allergic	[əˈlɜːrdʒɪk]	알레르기성의
Antibody	[|æntibɑːdi]	항체
Aortic	[eˈor.tɪk]	대동맥의
Ascending	[əséndiŋ]	상승하는
Atherosclerosis	[æ̀θərouskləróusis]	죽상 동맥 경화증
Atrium	[ˈeɪtriəm]	심방
Autonomic	[ɔ́ːtənɑ́mik]	자율적인
AV node	Atrioventricular node	방실결절
Backflow	[ˈbak-ˌflō']	역류
Bacterial	[bæk|tɪriəl]	세균의, 세균성의
Baroreceptor	[bæ̀rouriséptər]	압력 수용체
Biconcave	[baikɑ́nkeiv,bàikɑ́nkeiv]	양면이 오목한
Bicuspid valve	[(ˌ)bī-ˈkə-spəd vælv]	이첨판
Bleeding	[ˈbliːdɪŋ]	출혈
Bruise	[bruːz]	멍
Capability	[keɪpəˈbɪləti]	용량

Circuit	[sɜːrkɪt]	회로
Circulate	[sɜːrkjəleɪt]	순환하다
Clear	[klɪr]	맑은
Closed circuit	[kloʊzd ˈsɜːrkɪt]	폐쇄 회로
Clot	[klɑːt]	응고
Colloidal	[kəlɔ́idl]	교질의
Conduction	[kənˈdʌkʃn]	전도
Confined	[kənˈfaɪnd]	막힌
Constrict	[kənˈstrɪkt]	수축하다
Constriction	[kən|strɪkʃn]	수축
Dehydrate	[diːˈhaɪdreɪt]	탈수시키다
Delay	[dɪˈleɪ]	지연시키다
Dendritic cell	[ˌdenˈdrɪtɪk sel]	수상돌기세포
Deoxygenate	[diːɑksidʒənèit]	산소를 제거하다
Depot	[ˈdiːpoʊ]	저장부
Destination	[destɪˈneɪʃn]	목적지
Diastole	[daɪˈæstəli]	이완기
Diastolic	[dàiəstálik]	이완기의
Dilation	[dailéiʃən]	팽창
Disc	[dɪsk]	판
Distribute	[dɪˈstrɪbjuːt]	분배하다
Divided	[dɪˈvaɪdɪd]	분할된
Edge	[edʒ]	가장자리
EKG	Electrocardiogram	심전도
Electrocardiogram	[ɪ|lektroʊ|kɑːrdioʊɡræm]	심전도
Endocardium	[èndoukáːrdiəm]	심장내막
Endothelium	[èndouθiːliəm]	내피
Eosinophil	[ìːəsínəfàil]	호산구
Epicardium	[èpikáːrdiəm]	이심막
Erythrocyte	[ɪˈrɪθrəsaɪt]	적혈구
Excessive	[ɪkˈsesɪv]	과도한
External	[ɪkˈstɜːrnl]	외부의
Fenestration	[fènəstréiʃən]	천공
Fibrin	[faɪbrɪn | fɪbrɪn]	섬유소
Fibrinogen	[faɪ|brɪnədʒən fɪ|brɪnədʒən]	섬유소원
Hematopoiesis	[hìːmətoupɔiíːsis]	조혈작용
Histamine	[hɪstəmiːn]	히스타민
Hypertension	[haɪpər|tenʃn]	고혈압
Illness	[ˈɪlnəs]	병
Immediately	[ɪˈmiːdiətli]	즉시

Immunoglobulin	[ìmjunouglábjulin]	면역글로불린
Inactivity	[ɪnˈæktɪv]	비활동, 휴지
Inappropriate	[ˌɪnəˈproʊpriət]	부적합한
Inelastic	[ìnilǽstik]	탄력이 없는
Inferior	[ɪnˈfɪriə(r)]	하위의
Infestation	[ɪnfeˈsteɪʃn]	침입
Inflammation	[ɪnfləˈmeɪʃn]	염증
Innermost	[ˈɪnərmoʊst]	가장 안쪽의
Intercalate	[intə́ːrkəlèit]	사이에 끼워 넣다
Interventricular	[ìntə(ː)rventríkjulə]	심실 간의
Intima	[íntəmə]	내막
Invader	[ɪnˈveɪdə(r)]	침입자
Leukemia	[luːkíːmiə]	백혈병
Leukocyte	[lúːkəsàit]	백혈구
Lymphocytes	[lɪmfəsaɪt]	림프구
Malfunction	[ˌmælˈfʌŋkʃn]	고장, 장애
Mellituria	[ˌmeləˈt(y)u̇rēə]	당뇨
Mitral valve	[máitrəl vælv]	이첨판
Molar	[moʊlə(r)]	어금니
Monocyte	[mɑːnəsaɪt]	단핵구
Myelogenous	[màiəládʒinəs]	골수성의
Myocardium	[màiəkáːrdiəm]	심근
Myocyte	[máiousait]	근세포
Neutrophil	[njúːtrəfil]	호중구
Nodule	[nɑːdʒuːl]	결절
Nourishment	[nɜːrɪʃmənt]	영양분
Obesity	[oʊˈbiːsəti]	비만
Outgoing	[aʊtgoʊɪŋ]	나가는
Oxygenation	[ɑːksɪdʒəneɪt]	산화
Parasitic	[pærəˈsɪtɪk]	기생하는
Parasympathetic	[pæ̀rəsìmpəθétik]	부교감 신경의
Patch	[pætʃ]	부분, 패치
Pathology	[pəˈθɑːlədʒi]	병리학
Pericardium	[pèrəkáːrdiəm]	심낭
Phagocytosis	[fæ̀gəsaitóusis]	식세포 작용
Pinocytosis	[pìnəsaitóusis]	음세포 작용
Plug	[plʌg]	막다
Polycythemia	[pàlisaiθíːmiə]	적혈구증가증
Polymerize	[pɑːlɪməraɪz]	중합하다
Producing	[prədjúːsiŋ]	생산하는

Protective	[prəˈtektɪv]	보호하는
Prothrombin	[prouθrámbin]	프로트롬빈
Reabsorb	[ˌrē-əb-ˈsȯrb]	재흡수하다
Recoil	[rɪˈkɔɪl]	다시 감다
SA node	Sinoauricular node	동방결절
Semilunar valve	[sèmilúːnər vælv]	반월판
Septum	[septəm]	격막
Sphincter	[sfɪŋktə(r)]	괄약근
Squeeze	[skwiːz]	짜내다
Stem	[stem]	줄기
Superior	[suːǀpɪriə(r)]	상위의
Sympathetic	[sɪmpəˈθetɪk]	교감 신경의
Systemic	[sɪˈstemɪk]	전신에 영향을 주는, 침투성의
Systole	[ˈsɪstəli]	심장 수축기
Systolic	[sɪstəlik]	심장 수축의
Thread	[θred]	가닥
Thrombocyte	[θrámbəsàit]	혈소판
Tricuspid valve	[traikʌspid vælv]	삼첨판
Tunica	[tjúːnikə]	막
Unidirectional	[jùːnidirékʃənl,-dai-]	단방향의
Valve	[vælv]	판막
Velocity	[vəǀlɑːsəti]	속도
Vena cava	[ˌviːnə ˈkeɪvə]	대정맥
Venous	[viːnəs]	정맥의
Ventricle	[ventrɪkl]	심실
Ventricular	[ventríkjulər]	심실의
Viral	[vaɪrəl]	바이러스성의
Viscosity	[viskɑ́səti]	점도
Web	[web]	망

Chapter 14

Vocabulary	Pronunciation	Signification
Acquired	[əkwáiərd]	획득한
Agranulocyte	[əgrǽnjulousàit]	무과립 백혈구
Allergen	[ˈælərdʒən]	알레르겐
Amplify	[ˈæmplɪfaɪ]	증폭시키다
Anaphylaxis	[ˌænəfɪˈlæksɪs]	아나필락시스
Anti-	[ˈænti]	~에 반대되는-
Antigen	[ˈæntɪdʒən]	항원
Antiviral	[ˌæntiˈvaɪrəl]	항바이러스성의
APC	Antigen Presenting Cell	항원제시세포
Army	[ˈɑːrmi]	집단
Attack	[əˈtæk]	공격하다
Autoimmune	[ˌɔːtoʊɪˈmjuːn]	자가면역의
Basophil	[béisəfil]	호염기성백혈구
Breastfeed	[ˈbrɛstˌfiːd]	모유를 먹이다
Chronic	[ˈkrɑːnɪk]	만성적인
Clearance	[ˈklɪrəns]	없애기, 간격, 정리
Cobra	[ˈkoʊbrə]	코브라
Contributor	[kənˈtrɪbjətə(r)]	기여자
Cooperation	[koʊˌɑːpəˈreɪʃn]	협동
Crucial	[ˈkruːʃl]	중대한, 결정적인
Cytokine	[sàitoukain]	사이토카인
Cytotoxic	[sàitoutáksik]	세포독성, 세포독성의
Defeat	[dɪˈfiːt]	패배, 패배시키다
Diapedesis	[dàiəpidíːsis]	혈구 누출
Disturbance	[dɪˈstɜːrbəns]	장애
Disulfide	[daisʌ́lfaid,-fid]	이황화물
Edema	[ɪˈdiːmə]	부종
Endogenous	[enˈdɑːdʒənəs]	내인성의
Engulf	[ɪnˈgʌlf]	완전히 에워싸다, 뒤덮다
Epinephrine	[èpənéfri(ː)n]	에피네프린
Exposure	[ɪkˈspoʊʒə(r)]	노출
Fever	[ˈfiːvə(r)]	열
Granule	[ˈgrænjuːl]	과립
Granulocyte	[grǽnjulousàit]	과립성 백혈구
Helper cell	[ˈhelpə(r) sel]	도움 세포
Heparin	[hépərin]	헤파린

Histocompatibility	[hìstoukəmpæ̀təbíləti]	조직적합성
HIV	Human Immunodeficiency Virus	후천성면역결핍증
Humoral	[hjúːmərəl]	체액의
Immunodeficiency	[ɪ|mjuːnoʊdɪ|fɪʃnsi]	면역결핍
Immunosuppressant	[ìmjunousəpré-sənt]	면역억제제, 면역억제제의
Incompatibility	[ìnkəmpæ̀təbíləti]	불화합성, 불친화성
Injection	[ɪnˈdʒekʃn]	주사
Interfere	[ˌɪntərˈfɪr]	간섭하다, 개입하다, 방해하다
Interferon	[ˌɪntərˈfɪrɑːn]	인터페론
Interleukin	[ìntərlúːkin]	인터루킨
Invasion	[ɪnˈveɪʒn]	침입
Latent	[ˈleɪtnt]	잠재하는, 잠복해 있는
Lead	[liːd]	이끌다, 이어지다
Leak	[liːk]	누출, 새다
Leaky	[ˈliːki]	새는
Life-threatening	[ˈlaɪf ˌθrɛtnɪŋ]	생명을 위협하는
Lymphocyte	[ˈlɪmfəsaɪt]	림프구
Maintenance	[ˈmeɪntənəns]	유지
Mediator	[ˈmiːdieɪtə(r)]	중재자
Medicine	[|medsn | medɪsn]	의학, 약
Megakaryocyte	[mègəkæriousait]	거핵세포
MHC	Major Histocompatibility Complex	주요 조직적합성 복합체
Mobilize	[|moʊbəlaɪz]	동원하다
Nausea	[ˈnɔːziə ˈnɔːsiə]	메스꺼움
Necrosis	[ne|kroʊsɪs]	괴사
Nonspecific	[nɑ̀nspəsífik]	비특이성의
Phagocyte	[ˈfægəsaɪt]	식세포
Precursor	[priː|kɜːrsə(r)]	전구체
Pregnancy	[ˈpregnənsi]	임신
Pregnant	[ˈpregnənt]	임신한
Proliferation	[prəˌlɪfəˈreɪʃn]	확산, 급증
Rash	[ræʃ]	발진
Recognize	[ˈrekəgnaɪz]	인식하다
Record	[ˈrekɔːd ˈrekərd]	기록하다
Reinfect	[rìːinfékt]	재감염시키다
Reinfection	[rìːinfékʃən]	재감염
Reject	[ˈriːdʒekt]	거부하다
Rejection	[rɪˈdʒekʃn]	거부
Rh	Rhesus	붉은 털(인자)
Severe	[sɪ|vɪr]	심각한

Vocabulary	Pronunciation	Signification
Slip	[slɪp]	미끄러지다, 악화되다, 조각
Spectrum	[ˈspektrəm]	범위
Suppressor	[səˈpresə(r)]	억제인자
Swelling	[ˈswelɪŋ]	부기
Trap	[træp]	덫, 가두다
Treat	[triːt]	치료하다
Unconsciousness	[ʌnˈkɑːnʃəsnəs]	무의식
Vaccine	[vækˈsiːn]	백신
Venom	[ˈvenəm]	독
Vomiting	[vάmitiŋ]	구토

Chapter 15

Vocabulary	Pronunciation	Signification
Absorbed	[əbˈsɔːrbd əbˈzɔːrbd]	흡수한
Acetate	[ˈæsɪteɪt]	아세테이트
Acquire	[əˈkwaɪə(r)]	습득하다
Aging	[ˈeɪdʒɪŋ]	노화, 노화하는
Alive	[əˈlaɪv]	살아있는
Amylase	[ˈæməleɪs]	아밀레이스
Antibacterial	[ˌæntibækˈtɪriəl]	항균성의
Antioxidant	[ˌæntiˈɑːksɪdənt]	항산화제
Anxiety	[æŋˈzaɪəti]	불안
Aspirin	[ˈæsprɪn ˈæspərɪn]	아스피린
Bolus	[ˈboʊləs]	(특히 삼킬 수 있도록 잘 씹은 음식) 덩어리, 약의 한 회 분
Border	[ˈbɔːrdə(r)]	가장자리
Brush	[brʌʃ]	솔, 붓
Buildup	[bíldʌp]	증강, 강화
Caffeine	[ˈkæfiːn]	카페인
Canine	[ˈkeɪnaɪn]	개, 개의
Capture	[ˈkæptʃə]	포획, 포획하다
Carboxypeptidase	[kɑːrbɑ̀ksipéptədèis,-dèiz]	카복시 펩티데이스
Carnivore	[ˌkɑːrnɪvɔː(r)]	육식 동물
Catalase	[kǽtəlèis,-lèiz]	카탈레이스
Chew	[tʃuː]	씹다
Chief Cell	[tʃiːf sɛl]	주세포

Cholecystokinin	[kòuləsistəkí:nin,kàl-]	콜레시스토키닌
Chylomicron	[kàiləmáikrɑn]	암죽미립
Chyme	[káim]	미즙
Chymotrypsin	[kàimoutrípsin]	키모트립신
CKK	Cholecystokinin	콜레시스토키닌
Classification	[ˌklæsɪfɪˈkeɪʃn]	분류
Coenzyme	[kouénzaim]	조효소
Consumer	[kənˈsuːmə(r)]	소비자
Converted	[kənvə́ːrtid]	전환된
Crush	[krʌʃ]	으스러뜨리다, 밀어 넣다
Deamination	[dɪˈamɪneɪʃ(ə)n]	탈아미노반응
Deficiency	[dɪˈfɪʃnsi]	결핍(증)
Degradation	[ˌdegrəˈdeɪʃn]	저하
Denature	[diːnéitʃər]	변성하다, 변성시키다
Dextrin	[dékstrin]	덱스트린
Diet	[ˈdaɪət]	식사
Dipeptidase	[daipéptədèis,-dèiz]	다이펩티데이스
Dipeptide	[dipéptaid,dai-]	디펩티드
Disaccharidase	[daisəkǽrideis]	이당분해효소
Discharge	[ˈdɪstʃɑːdʒ ǀ dɪstʃɑːrdʒ]	방출하다
Distinguishing	[dɪˈstɪŋgwɪʃ]	특징적인
Dizziness	[ˈdɪzɪnəs]	현기(증)
Droplet	[ˈdrɑːplət]	작은 방울
Duodenum	[ˈduːəǀdiːnəm]	십이지장
Earthworm	[ˈɜːrθwɜːrm]	지렁이
Eat	[iːt]	먹다
Egestion	[iˈjeschən]	배설
Elephant	[ˈelɪfənt]	코끼리
Elimination	[ɪǀlɪmɪǀneɪʃn]	제거
Emulsification	[imʌlsəfikéiʃən]	유화
Emulsify	[ɪˈmʌlsɪfaɪ]	유화시키다
Enterocyte	[ˈɛntərə(ʊ)sʌɪt]	장세포
Enterogastrone	[èntərougǽstroun]	엔테로가스트론
Enterokinase	[èntəroukáineis,-kíneis]	엔테로카이네이스
Esophageal	[isɑ̀fədʒíːəl]	식도의
Fang	[fæŋ]	송곳니
Feces	[fíːsiːz]	배설물
Flavonoid	[ˈfleɪvənɔɪd]	플라보노이드
Flesh	[fleʃ]	살, 피부, 고기
Fold	[foʊld]	주름, 접다

Front	[frʌnt]	앞쪽의
Gastric	[ˈgæstrɪk]	위의
Gastrin	[gæstrin]	가스트린
Gastrointestinal	[ǀgæstroʊɪnǀtestɪnl]	위장의, 소화관의
Glass	[glæs]	유리
Grasshopper	[ǀgræshɑːpər]	메뚜기
Herbivore	[hɜːrbɪvɔː(r)]	초식 동물
Hooved	[húːv]	발굽이 있는
Hydrochloric	[hàidrəklɔ́ːrik]	염화수소의
Ileum	[ˈɪliəm]	회장
Ingest	[ɪnˈdʒest]	섭취하다, 삼키다
Ingestion	[indʒéstʃən]	섭취
Ingredient	[ɪnˈgriːdiənt]	재료, 구성 요소
Insomnia	[ɪnǀsɑːmniə]	불면증
Insulin	[ǀɪnsəlɪn]	인슐린
Intestinal	[intéstənl]	장의
Islet	[ˈaɪlət]	작은 섬
Jejunum	[dʒɪˈdʒuːnəm]	공장
Lactase	[lǽkteis,-teiz]	락테이스
Lipase	[ˈlaɪpeɪz]	라이페이스
Maltase	[mɔ́ːlteis,-teiz]	말테이스
Mechanically	[məǀkænɪkli]	기계적으로
Microvillus	[ˌmʌɪkrəʊˈvɪləs]	미세 융모
Momentary	[ˈmoʊmənteri]	순간적인
Mood	[muːd]	기분
Motility	[moutíləti]	운동성
Mucosal	[mjuːˈkosəl]	점막의
Mucous cell	[ˈmjuːkəs sel]	점액 세포
Oligosaccharide	[àligousǽkəraid,òuli-]	올리고당
Omnivore	[ǀɑːmnɪvɔː(r)]	잡식 동물
Opening	[ǀoʊpnɪŋ]	구멍
Overdose	[ˈoʊvərdoʊs]	과다 복용(투여), 과다 복용하다
Pancreas	[ˈpæŋkriəs]	췌장
Paralyze	[pǽrəlàiz]	마비시키다
Parietal cell	[pəráiətl sel]	벽세포
Pepsinogen	[pepsínədʒən,-dʒèn]	펩시노겐
Peptidase	[péptədèis,-dèiz]	펩티데이스
Perfect	[ǀpɜːfɪkt ǀpɜːrfɪkt]	완벽한
Peristalsis	[ˌperɪˈstælsɪs]	연동운동
Peroxidase	[pəráksidèis,-dèiz]	페록시데이스

영어	발음	한국어
Phytochemical	[fʌɪtəʊˈkɛmɪk(ə)l]	피토케미칼
Poison	[ˈpɔɪzn]	독
Problem	[ǀprɑːbləm]	문제
Producer	[prəǀduːsə(r)]	생산자
Propulsive	[prəpʌlsiv]	추진하는
Proteolysis	[pròutiáləsis]	단백질 가수분해
Proteolytic	[pròutiəlítik]	단백질 가수분해의
Ptyalin	[táiəlin]	프티알린
Radical	[ˈrædɪkl]	기(基), 급진적인
Rickets	[ˈrɪkɪts]	구루병
Ruminant	[ˈruːmɪnənt]	반추 동물
Saccharide	[sǽkəràid,-rid]	당류
Secrete	[sɪˈkriːt]	분비하다
Secretin	[sikríːtin]	세크레틴
Sharp	[ʃɑːrp]	날카로운
Shred	[ʃred]	조각, 자르다
Somatostatin	[səmæ̀təstǽtn,sòumətə-]	소마토스타틴
Splitting	[ˈsplɪtɪŋ]	분리, 분할, 분할하는
Sucrase	[ˈs(j)uːkreɪz]	수크레이스
Surplus	[ǀsɜːrpləs]	과잉, 과잉의
Swallow	[ˈswɑːloʊ]	삼키다
Tentacle	[ˈtentəkl]	촉수
Tongue	[tʌŋ]	혀
Tooth	[tuːθ]	치아, 이빨
Transportation	[ǀtrænspɔːrǀteɪʃn]	수송
Triacylglycerol	[trīǎsˈəlglĭsˈərôlˈ, -rōlˈ]	트리아실글리세롤
Trypsinogen	[trɪpˈsɪnədʒ(ə)n]	트립시노겐
Unpaired	[ʌnpɛ́ərd]	짝이 없는
Villus	[ˈvɪləs]	융모
Wave	[weɪv]	파동, 급증
Windpipe	[ˈwɪndpaɪp]	(호흡) 기관
Zymogen	[záimədʒən,-dʒèn]	효소원

Chapter 16

Vocabulary	Pronunciation	Signification
Accessory gland	[ɪkˈsɛsəri ˈglænd]	부속샘
Acrosome	[ǽkrəsòum]	첨체
Age	[eɪdʒ]	나이, 수명, 시기, 나이가 들다, 노화시키다
Annelid	[ǽnəlid]	환형동물
Anterior	[æn|tɪriə(r)]	앞의, 앞쪽의
Approach	[əˈproʊtʃ]	접근하다
Aquatic	[əˈkwætɪk]	물속에서 자라는, 수생의
Birth	[bɜːrθ]	탄생, 출산
Breast	[brest]	(여자의) 유방, 젖, (남자의) 젖가슴
Bulbourethral gland	[bʌlbəjurí:θrəl glænd]	요도구샘
Cervix	[|sɜːrvɪks]	자궁 경부
Childbirth	[|tʃaɪldbɜːrθ]	출산
Clinical	[ˈklɪnɪkl]	임상의
Cnidarian	[naidέəriən]	자포동물
Corpus luteum	[ˈkɔːrpəs lúːtiəm]	황체
Cortical	[kɔ́ːrtikəl]	피질의, 외피의
Degenerate	[dɪˈdʒenərət]	퇴화하다
Depolarization	[diːpòulərizéiʃən]	탈분극화
Deteriorate	[dɪ|tɪriəreɪt]	악화되다
Drill	[drɪl]	송곳, 구멍을 뚫다
Ejaculatory duct	[ɪˈdʒækjələˌtori dʌkt]	사정관
Ejection	[idʒékʃən]	방출
Embryological	[embriəlɒdʒɪkəl]	발생학의
Endometrium	[èndoumíːtriəm]	자궁내막
Epididymis	[èpədídəmis]	부고환
Estrus	[éstrəs]	발정
Fallopian tube	[fəˈloʊpiən tuːb]	나팔관
Feedback	[ˈfiːdbæk]	피드백
Fetal	[ˈfiːt(ə)l]	태아의
Finish	[ˈfɪnɪʃ]	끝내다
Flagellum	[fləd3éləm]	편모
Flatworm	[|flætwɜːrm]	편형동물
Freeze	[friːz]	얼다
FSH	Follicle-Stimulating Hormone	난포 자극 호르몬
Genital	[ˈdʒenɪtl]	생식기의
Genitalia	[dʒènətéiliə]	성기, 생식기, 외음부

Glandular	[ˈɡlændʒələ(r)]	선상
GnRH	Gonadotropin-Releasing Hormone	성선자극호르몬 방출 호르몬
Gonadotropin	[gounæ̀dətróupin]	성선 자극 호르몬
Grayish	[ˈgreɪʃ]	회색의
Hermaphroditism	[həːrmæfrədaitizm]	자웅동체
Hole	[hoʊl]	구멍, 구멍을 내다
Immature	[ˌɪməˈtʃʊr ˌɪməˈtʊr]	미성숙한, 다 자라지 못한
Immediate	[ɪˈmiːdiət]	즉각적인
Implantation	[ìmplæntéiʃən]	착상, 이식, 피하 주입
Indirect	[ˌɪndəˈrekt ˌɪndaɪˈrekt]	간접적인
Invertebrate	[ɪnˈvɜːrtɪbrət]	무척추동물
Lactation	[lækˈteɪʃn]	수유
Leydig cell	[lāˈdĭKHʹ sel]	라이디히 세포
LH	Luteinizing Hormone	황체 형성 호르몬
Limited	[ˈlɪmɪtɪd]	제한된, 한정된
Lined	[laɪnd]	주름진, 줄이 쳐진
Luteal	[lúːtiəl]	황체의
Luteinize	[lúːtiənàiz]	황체를 형성하다
Menstrual cycle	[ˈmɛnstrʊəl ˈsaɪkl]	생리 주기
Menstruation	[ˌmenstruˈeɪʃn]	월경
Meiosis	[maɪˈoʊsɪs]	감수 분열
Myometrium	[ˌmʌɪə(ʊ)ˈmiːtrɪəm]	자궁 근층
Negative feedback	[ˈnɛɡətɪv ˈfiːdbak]	부적 피드백
Neutralize	[ˈnuːtrəlaɪz]	중화시키다
Oocyte	[óuəsàit]	난모세포
Oogenesis	[òuədʒénəsis]	난자 형성
Oogonium	[òuəgóuniəm]	난원세포
Ovarian	[oʊˈveriən]	난소
Ovulation	[ˌɑːvjuˈleɪʃn]	배란
Oxytocin	[àksitóusn]	옥시토신
Peak	[piːk]	정점
Pear-shaped	[ˈpeəʳ ʃeɪpt]	배 모양의
Positive feedback	[ˈpɑːzətɪv ˈfiːdbæk]	양성 피드백
Pre-	[priː]	전의-
Progesterone	[prəˈdʒestəroʊn]	프로게스테론
Prolactin	[proulǽktin]	프로락틴
Puberty	[ˈpjuːbərti]	사춘기
Rotifer	[róutəfər]	담륜층
Rupture	[ˈrʌptʃə(r)]	파열, (장기를) 파열시키다

Vocabulary	Pronunciation	Signification
Semen	[ˈsiːmen]	정액
Seminal	[ˈsemɪnl]	정액의
Seminiferous tubule	[sèmənífərəs tjúːbjuːl]	세정관
Sertoli cell	[səːtəʊli ˈsɛl]	세르톨리 세포
Slough off	[slʌf ɔːf ɑːf]	버리다, 벗다
Spermatid	[spə́ːrmətid]	정세포
Spermatocyte	[spəːrmǽtəsàit, spə́ːrmət-]	정모 세포
Spermatogenesis	[spə̀ːrmətoudʒénisis]	정자 형성
Spermatogonium	[spəːrmæ̀təgóuniəm, spə́ːrmət-]	정원세포
Transduction	[trænsdʌ́kʃən, trænz-]	(유전) 형질 도입, 변환
Uterine	[júːtərin, -ràin]	자궁의
Vaginal	[vǽdʒainəl]	질의
Woman	[ˈwʊmən]	여성
Zona Pellucida	[zóunə-pəlúːsidə, peljúː-]	투명대

Chapter 17

Vocabulary	Pronunciation	Signification
ACTH	Adrenocorticotropic Hormone	부신 피질 자극 호르몬
Adrenaline	[ədrénəlin, -lìːn]	아드레날린
Anxiousness	[ˈæŋkʃəsnəs]	불안함
Appetite	[ˈæpɪtaɪt]	식욕
Autocrine	[ˈɔːtə(ʊ)krʌɪn]	자가 분비
Basal	[ˈbeɪsl]	기저가 되는
Calcitonin	[kæ̀lsətóunin]	칼시토닌
Corresponding hormone	[ˌkɔːrə ˈspɑːndɪŋ ˌkɑːrə ˈspɑːndɪŋ ˈhoɚˌmoʊn]	상응하는 호르몬
Corticotropin	[kɔ́ːrtikoutróupin]	부신 피질 자극 호르몬
Cortisone	[ˌkɔːrtəsoʊn ˌkɔːrtəzoʊn]	코르티손
Cytosol	[sáitəsɔ́ːl, -sàl]	사이토솔
Degrade	[dɪˈɡreɪd]	저하시키다, 분해하다
Delta	[ˈdeltə]	델타
Dilute	[daɪˈluːt]	희석시키다
Diuretic	[ˌdaɪjuˈretɪk]	이뇨제
Dopamine	[doʊpəmiːn]	도파민
Eminence	[ˈemɪnəns]	저명
Enlargement	[ɪnˈlɑːrdʒmənt]	확대, 확장

Enthusiasm	[ɪn|θuːziæzəm]	열정
Exhibit	[ɪgˈzɪbɪt]	보이다
Forebrain	[|fɔːrbreɪn]	전뇌
Gamma	[ˈgæmə]	감마
Gonadotrophin	[gounædətróupin]	성선 자극 호르몬
Gonadotropic hormone	[gounædətrápik,-tróup- ˈhɔːrmoʊn]	생식선 자극 호르몬
Hormone	[ˈhɔːrmoʊn]	호르몬
Hyperthyroidism	[|haɪpə|θaɪrɔɪdɪzəm |haɪpər|θaɪrɔɪdɪzəm]	갑상선 기능 항진증
Hypophyseal portal system	[hàipɑfíziəl ˈpɔːrtl ˈsɪstəm]	하수체-문맥계
Hypophysis	[haipɑ́fəsis]	뇌하수체
Hypothalamic	[hàipəθəlǽmik]	시상하부의
Hypothyroidism	[|haɪpoʊ|θaɪrɔɪdɪzəm]	갑상선 기능 저하증
Inhibitory	[inhíbətɔ́ːri]	억제하는
Intermediate	[|ɪntər|miːdiət]	중간의
Iodine	[|aɪədaɪn]	아이오딘
Juxtaglomerular apparatus	[dʒʌ̀kstəgloumérjulər |æpə|rætəs]	사구체 옆 장치
Locally	[lóukəli]	국부적으로
Long-term	[ˈlɑːŋˈtəːm]	장기적인
Melanocyte	[məlǽnəsàit,mélənə-]	멜라닌 세포
MSH	Melanocyte-Stimulating Hormone	멜라닌 세포 자극 호르몬
Neurohypophysis	[njùərouhaipɑ́fəsis]	신경 하수체
Norepinephrine	[nɔ́ːrepənéfriːn]	노르에피네프린
Overstimulate	[|oʊvə(r)ˈstɪmjuleɪt]	과도하게 자극하다
Paracrine	[pǽrəkrain]	주변 분비의
Parafollicular	[ˈpærəfəlíkjulər]	소포 곁의
Postganglionic	[pòustgæŋgliɑ́nik]	신경절 이후의
Prostaglandin	[prɑ̀stəglǽndin]	프로스타글란딘
Proteolysis	[pròutiɑ́ləsis]	단백질 분해
Proximity	[prɑːk|sɪməti]	근접성
PTH	Parathyroid Hormone	부갑상샘 호르몬
Regulation	[ˌregjuˈleɪʃn]	규제
Reverse	[rɪˈvɜːrs]	반대의, 뒤바꾸다
Short-lived	[ʃɔːtˈlɪvd]	단명하는
Situation	[ˌsɪtʃuˈeɪʃn]	환경
Sodium	[|soʊdiəm]	소듐
Stressful	[ˈstresfl]	스트레스가 많은
Sudoriferous	[sùːdərífərəs]	땀을 내는, 발한하는
Sufficient	[səˈfɪʃnt]	충분한
Synthetic	[sɪnˈθetɪk]	합성한, 인조의, 합성 물질

Vocabulary	Pronunciation	Signification
Tetraiodothyronine	[tétrə-ʌɪˈəʊdəʊθīˈrənēnˈnīn]	테트라요오드티로닌
Thymosin	[θáiməsin]	티모신
Thyrotropin	[θàiərətróupin,θaiərátrə-]	갑상선 자극 호르몬
Thyroxine	[θaiəráksi:n,-sin]	티록신
Transcription	[trænˈskrɪpʃn]	전사
TRH	Thyrotropin-Releasing Hormone	갑상선 자극 호르몬 방출 호르몬
Triiodothyronine	[traɪ-ɪˈəʊdəʊθīˈrənēnˈnīn]	트리요오드티로닌
TSH	Thyroid-Stimulating Hormone	갑상선 자극 호르몬
Uretic	[juərétik]	이뇨의

Chapter 18

Vocabulary	Pronunciation	Signification
Absolute	[ˈæbsəluːt]	완전한
Acquisition	[ˌækwɪˈzɪʃn]	습득
Amplitude	[ˈæmplɪtuːd]	진폭
ATPase	[éitìːpíːeis,-eiz]	에이티피에이스
Cerebrospinal	[sərìːbrouspáinl,sèrə-]	뇌 척수의
Channel	[ˈtʃænl]	통로
Charged	[tʃɑːrdʒd]	전하를 띤
Consecutive	[kənˈsekjətɪv]	연속적인, 연이은
Default	[dɪˈfɔːlt | diːˈfɔːlt]	기본
Diffusible	[difjúːzəbl]	퍼지는, 확산성의
Effector	[ɪˈfektə(r)]	실행기, 반응기
Electric	[ɪˈlektrɪk]	전기의
Electronegative	[ilèktrounégətiv]	전기 음성의
Electroneutral	[ilèktrou|nuːtrəl]	전기 중성의
Electropositive	[ilèktroupázətiv]	전기 양성의
Exceed	[ɪkˈsiːd]	초과하다
Facilitate	[fəˈsɪlɪteɪt]	촉진시키다
Functionality	[ˌfʌŋkʃəˈnæləti]	기능
Generation	[ˌdʒenəˈreɪʃn]	세대
Helical	[|helɪkl | hiːlɪkl]	나선형의
Hyperpolarize	[hàipərpóuləraiz]	과분극화하다
Hypopolarize	[haɪpoupóuləraiz]	저분극화하다
Initial	[ɪˈnɪʃl]	처음의, 초기의
Internode	[íntərnòud]	마디와 마디 사이, 절간

Vocabulary	Pronunciation	Signification
Interpret	[ɪn|tɜːrprɪt]	해석하다
Myelin	[ˈmaɪəlɪn]	미엘린
Myelination	[màiəlinéiʃən]	미엘린화, 수초화
Neuroglia	[njuəráglіə]	신경교
Oscillation	[|ɑːsɪ|leɪʃn]	진동
Overshoot	[|oʊvər|ʃuːt]	(목표 지점보다) 더 가다
Permeability	[pə́ːrmiəbíləti]	투과성, 삼투성
Progression	[prəˈgreʃn]	진행
Propagation	[pràpəgéiʃən]	번식, 전파, 전달
Pushing	[púʃiŋ]	미는
Re-	[riː]	다시-
Refractory	[rɪˈfræktəri]	난치의
Repolarization	[riːpòulərizéiʃən]	재분극화
Saltatory	[sæltətɔ́ːri]	도약적인
Selectively	[sɪˈlɛktɪvli]	선별적으로
Sheath	[ʃiːθ]	초 (싸개)
Spike	[spaɪk]	급등하다
Stage	[steɪdʒ]	단계
Stimulation	[|stɪmju|leɪʃn]	자극
Threshold	[|θreʃhoʊld]	한계점
Transporter	[træn|spɔːrtə(r)]	수송자, 수송 단백질
Unmyelinated	[ʌnmáiələnèitid]	무수초의
Value	[ˈvæljuː]	값
Voltage	[|voʊltɪdʒ]	전압

Chapter 19

Vocabulary	Pronunciation	Signification
Alertness	[əˈlɜːrtnəs]	각성
Amygdala	[əˈmɪgdələ]	편도체
Analyze	[ˈænəlaɪz]	분석하다
Brainstem	[ˈbreɪnstem]	뇌간
Corpus callosum	[ˈkɔːrpəs kəlóusəm]	뇌량
Cerebellum	[ˌserəˈbeləm]	소뇌
Cerebral cortex	[səˈriːbrəl |kɔːrteks]	대뇌 피질
Cerebrum	[səˈriːbrəm ˈserəbrəm]	대뇌
Collection	[kəˈlekʃn]	무리, 더미

Complexity	[kəmˈpleksəti]	복잡성
Consciousness	[ˈkɑːnʃəsnəs]	자각, 의식
Conserve	[kənˈsɚv]	보존하다
Decision	[dɪˈsɪʒn]	판단
Dorsal	[ˈdɔːrsl]	후방의
Excitatory	[ɪkˈsʌɪtət(ə)ri]	흥분성의
Flexor	[ˈfleksə(r)]	굴근
Forward	[ˈfɔːrwərd]	앞으로
Ganglion	[ˈgæŋgliən]	신경절
Global	[ˈgloʊbl]	구체의
Glutamate	[glúːtəmèit]	글루타메이트
Gray	[gréi]	회색
Hearing	[ˈhɪrɪŋ]	청각
Hemisphere	[ˈhemɪsfɪr]	반구체
Hindbrain	[ˈhaɪndbreɪn]	후뇌
Hippocampus	[ˌhɪpəˈkæmpəs]	해마
Integration	[ˌɪntɪˈgreɪʃn]	통합
Interneuron	[ìntə(ː)rnjúːrɑn]	개재뉴런
Judgment	[dʒʌdʒmənt]	판단
Learning	[ˈlɜːrnɪŋ]	학습
Limbic system	[ˈlɪmbɪk sɪstəm]	변연계
Local	[ˈloʊkl]	지역의
Medulla oblongata	[mədʌ́lə àblɔːŋgáːtə,-laŋ-]	숨뇌
Mesencephalon	[mèsenséfəlàn]	중뇌
Mesozoan	[ˌmɛsəˈzəʊən]	중생 동물
Microscopic	[ˈmaɪkrəˈskɑːpɪk]	현미경을 이용한
Midbrain	[ˈmɪdbreɪn]	중뇌
Mind	[maɪnd]	마음
Mobile	[ˈmoʊbl]	이동하는
Monosynaptic	[ˌmɒnə(ʊ)sɪˈnaptɪk]	단시냅스의
Neural	[ˈnʊrəl]	신경의
Noradrenaline	[nɔ̀ːrədrénəlìːn]	노르아드레날린
Olfactory	[ɑːlˈfæktəri oʊlˈfæktəri]	후각의
Originate	[əˈrɪdʒɪneɪt]	시작하다
Participation	[pɑːrˈtɪsɪˈpeɪʃn]	참여
Perception	[pərˈsepʃn]	지각
Polysynaptic	[ˌpä-lē-sə-ˈnap-tik]	다시냅스의
Pons	[pánz]	뇌교
Postural	[ˈpɑːstʃərəl]	자세의
Preganglionic	[prìgæŋgliánik]	신경 절전의

Vocabulary	Pronunciation	Signification
Pupil	[ˈpjuːpl]	동공
Reflex arc	[ˈriːfleks ɑːrk]	반사궁
Regenerate	[rɪˈdʒenəreɪt]	재생되다, 재생시키다
Relay	[ˈriːleɪ]	전달하다
Retrieval	[rɪˈtriːvl]	회수
Root	[ruːt]	뿌리
Seeing	[síːiŋ]	시각, 시력, 보기
Self-control	[ˌsɛlfkənˈtroʊl]	자제력, 자기 조절
Slender	[ˈslendə(r)]	가느다란
Speech	[spiːtʃ]	연설, 언어 능력, 연설하다
Synapse	[ǀsaɪnæps ǀsɪnæps]	시냅스
Thalamus	[θǽləməs]	시상
Vagus	[véigəs]	미주 신경
Ventral	[ˈventrəl]	배 쪽의
Vision	[ˈvɪʒn]	시력, 시야
Wakefulness	[ˈweɪkfəlnəs]	각성

Chapter 20

Vocabulary	Pronunciation	Signification
Acceleration	[əkˌseləˈreɪʃn]	가속
Accelerometer	[əkǀseləǀrɑːmɪtər]	가속도계
Alligator	[ˈælɪgeɪtə(r)]	악어
Amphibian	[æmˈfɪbiən]	양서류
Amplification	[ǀæmplɪfɪǀkeɪʃn]	증폭
Arthropod	[ˈɑːrθəpɑːd]	절지동물
Auditory	[ǀɔːdətɔːri]	청각의
Auricle	[ˈɔːrɪkl]	외이
Avoid	[əˈvɔɪd]	피하다
Aware	[əˈwer]	알고 있는
Basilar membrane	[bǽsələr ˈmembreɪn]	기저막
Blindspot	[blaɪnd spɑːt]	사각지대
Blockage	[ǀblɑːkɪdʒ]	폐색
Blur	[blɜː(r)]	흐릿한
Bright	[braɪt]	밝은
Bud	[bʌd]	싹
Camphor	[ˈkæmfə(r)]	장뇌

Chemoreceptor	[ˌkiːmoʊrɪseptə(r)]	화학수용체
Choroid	[kɔ́ːrɔid]	맥락막
Ciliary	[sílièri]	섬모의, 속눈썹의
Cochlea	[ˈkoʊkliə ǀ kɑːkliə]	달팽이관
Cochlear	[ˈkoʊklijɚ]	달팽이관의
Colored	[ˌkʌlərd]	유색의
Combination	[ˌkɑːmbɪˈneɪʃn]	조합
Compression	[kəmˈpreʃn]	압축
Cone	[koʊn]	추상체
Convex	[ˌkɑːnveks]	볼록한
Cornea	[ˈkɔːrniə]	각막
Corpuscle	[ˌkɔːrpʌsl]	소체
Crayfish	[ˈkreɪfɪʃ]	가재
Cupula	[kjúːpjulə]	마루, 꼭대기, 정
Detect	[dɪˈtekt]	감지하다
Dome	[doʊm]	반구형 모양의 것
Duration	[duˈreɪʃn]	(지속되는) 기간
Eardrum	[ˈɪrdrʌm]	고막
Electro-	[iléktr]	전기의-
Electromagnetic	[ɪˌlektroʊmægˈnetɪk]	전자기의
Electroreceptor	[iˌlektrōriˈseptər]	전기 수용체
Elevation	[ˌelɪˈveɪʃn]	증가
Emit	[iˈmɪt]	방출하다
Endolymph	[éndoulìmf]	내림프
Endothermic	[ˌendoʊˈθɜːrmɪk]	흡열성의
Exteroceptor	[èkstərəséptər]	외수용기
Faint	[feɪnt]	희미한
Flavor	[fléivər]	맛
Focal	[ˈfoʊkl]	중심의, 초점의
Focus	[ˈfoʊkəs]	초점, 초점을 맞추다
Fovea	[fóuviə]	중심와
Fuzziness	[ˈfʌzinəs]	흐릿함
Gaseous	[ˈgæsiəs ˈgeɪsiəs]	기체의
Generator	[ˈdʒenəreɪtə(r)]	발생시키는 것
Grade	[greɪd]	등급
Gustation	[gʌstéiʃən]	미각
Gustatory	[gʌstətóːri]	미각의
Hit	[hɪt]	때리다
Homeostatic	[hòumiəstéitik]	항상성의
Hyperpolarize	[hàipərpóuləraiz]	과분극하다

Ignore	[ɪgˈnɔː(r)]	무시하다
Impinge	[ɪmˈpɪndʒ]	(특히 나쁜) 영향을 주다
Incus	[íŋkəs]	침골
Inform	[ɪnˈfɔːrm]	알리다
Insect	[ˈɪnsekt]	곤충
Integrate	[ˈɪntɪgreɪt]	통합시키다
Integrated	[ˈɪntɪgreɪtɪd]	통합된
Interoceptor	[ìntərouséptər]	내부 감각 수용기
Interpretation	[ɪn|tɜːrprɪ|teɪʃn]	해석
Iris	[ˈaɪrɪs]	홍채
Jellyfish	[ˈdʒelifɪʃ]	해파리
Kinocilium	[ˌkīnōˈsiléəm]	운동섬모
Lateral	[ˈlætərəl]	옆의, 측면의
Lever	[ˈlevər]	지렛대, 지렛대로 움직이다
Magnetic	[mægˈnetɪk]	자성의, 자성에 의한
Magnitude	[|mægnɪtuːd]	규모
Malleus	[mǽliəs]	추골
Mechanoreceptor	[mèkənouriséptər]	기계 수용기
Meissner corpuscles	[ˈmʌɪsnə ˈkoɚˌpʌsəl]	마이스너 소체
Merkel cell	[məˊːrkel sel]	메르켈 세포
Message	[ˈmesɪdʒ]	메시지
Migratory	[ˈmaɪgrətɔːri]	이주하는
Murky	[ˈmɜːrki]	어두컴컴한, 흐린
Musky	[ˈmʌski]	머스키 향
Navigation	[ˌnævɪˈgeɪʃn]	운항
Neuropeptide	[njùəroupéptaid]	신경 펩티드
Nociceptor	[nòusiséptər]	통각수용기
Obey	[əˈbeɪ]	따르다, 복종하다
Obstacle	[|ɑːbstəkl]	장애물
Odor	[óudər]	냄새
Olfaction	[ɑlfǽkʃən,oul-]	후각
Opsin	[ɑ́psin]	옵신
Organ of Corti	[ˈɔːrgən ʌv kɔ́ːrti]	코르티 기관
Ossicle	[ɑ́sikl]	청소골
Oval window	[ˈoʊvl ˈwɪndoʊ]	난원창
Pacinian corpuscles	[pəsínien| kɔːrpʌsl]	파치니안 소체
Papilla	[pəpílə]	유두, 돌기
Perilymph	[périlìmf]	외림프
Persist	[pər|sɪst]	지속하다
Persistent	[pər|sɪstənt]	지속되는

Photon	[ˈfoʊtɑːn]	광자
Photoreceptor	[|foʊtoʊrɪseptə(r)]	광수용기
Pinch	[pɪntʃ]	꼬집다
Pinna	[pínə]	귓바퀴
Pit	[pɪt]	패인 자국, 자국을 남기다
Predatory	[|predətɔːri]	포식성의
Predominately	[prɪ|dɑːmɪneɪti]	대개, 대부분
Prevailing	[prɪˈveɪlɪŋ]	우세한, 지배적인
Prolong	[prə|lɔːŋ prə|lɑːŋ]	연장하다
Proprioceptor	[pròupriəséptər]	자기수용기
Radial	[ˈreɪdiəl]	방사상의
Reception	[rɪˈsepʃn]	수용
Reptile	[|reptaɪl]	파충류
Rhodopsin	[roudápsin]	로돕신
Rod	[rɑːd]	간상체
Rotational	[roʊˈteɪʃənl]	회전의
Ruffini ending	[ruːˈfiːni ˈendɪŋ]	루피니 말단
Saccule	[sǽkjuːl]	구형낭
Salty	[ˈsɔːlti]	소금이 든
Scent	[sent]	향기
Sclera	[ˈsklɪrə]	공막
Semicircular	[|semi|sɜːrkjələ(r)]	반원형의
Sensillum	[sɛnˈsɪləm]	감각기
Sensitivity	[ˌsensəˈtɪvəti]	예민함
Shade	[ʃeɪd]	그늘, 가리다
Stapes	[stéipiːz]	등자뼈
State	[steɪt]	상태
Statolith	[stǽtəlìθ]	평형석
Stereocilium	[stɛriəˈsɪliəm]	부동섬모
Sucking	[sʌ́kiŋ]	빨아들이는
Tactile	[|tæktl]	촉각의
Taster	[ˈteɪstə(r)]	맛보기
Texture	[ˈtekstʃə(r)]	감촉, 질감
Thermal	[ˈθɜːrml]	열의
Thermoreceptor	[θəːrməriséptər]	온도 수용기
Tick	[tɪk]	진드기
Tight	[taɪt]	단단한, 꽉 조여 있는
Topography	[tə|pɑːgrəfi]	지형학
Transducer	[trænz|duːsər]	변환기
Transmembrane	[trænsmémbrein, trænz-]	막횡단, 막전이

Tuning	[tjúːnɪŋ]	조율
Tympanic	[timpǽnik]	고막의
Umami	[uːˈmɑːmi]	감칠맛
Utricle	[júːtrikl]	소낭
Vascular	[ˈvæskjələ(r)]	(혈관 등의) 관의
Vestibular apparatus	[vestíbjulər ˌæpəˈrætəs]	전정기관
Vibrate	[vaɪ|breɪt │vaɪbreɪt]	진동하다
Vibration	[vaɪˈbreɪʃn]	진동
Viper	[ˈvaɪpə(r)]	독사
Visibility	[ˌvɪzəˈbɪləti]	가시성
Vitreous humor	[|vitreous |humor]	유리액
Wavelength	[ˈweɪvleŋθ]	파장, 주파수

chapter 01
Cell biology

Life signs

A signal or collection of signals given off by a lifeform indicates that it is currently alive or functional.

Growth	Biological growth means organisms increase in size and the number of cells. Each part of the organism continues to function as it grows. - Continue to grow: Organisms grow throughout their whole life. Ex) Plants - Defined growth period: Organisms terminate in characteristic adult size. Ex) Animals
Development	Development takes place during an organism's life. Development is adapted to an organism's functions.

Metabolism	The sum of all the chemical activities of the organism.
	All organisms have chemical reactions, energy transformation, and energy conversion into useful forms.
	Metabolism occurs continuously in every organism.
	
	Regulates to maintain homeostasis and a balanced internal environment.
	- Turned off (decreased): Enough cell products are made.
	- Turned on (increased): A particular substance is required.
	
	• **Homeostasis mechanisms**
	Any process living things use to maintain fairly stable conditions necessary for survival actively.
	A self-regulating control system, sensitive and efficient.
	
	Ex) <u>Glucose concentration</u>
	- Glucose concentration in the blood rises above normal:
	  It is stored in cells, such as liver or muscle cells.
	
	- Concentration of glucose in the blood falls:
	  It converts stored nutritions to glucose + concentration in the blood brings it back to normal

01 Cell biology

Stimuli	All lives respond to stimuli, physical or chemical changes in internal and external environments.
	
	- Simple organisms: The entire individual may be sensitive to stimuli.
	  Ex) Amoeboid
	
	- Complex animals: Complex animals have specialized cells that respond to specific types of stimuli.
	  Ex) Retina of the vertebrate eyes
	
	- Plants: Plants respond to light, gravity, water, touch, and other stimuli.

Reproduction	The process by which living things produce offspring.
	
	- Asexual reproduction (simple organisms): Asexual reproduction generates genetically identical offspring to a single parent.
	  Ex) When an amoeba grows to a specific size, it reproduces by splitting in half and forms two new amoebas.
	
	- Sexual reproduction (most plants and animals): In sexual reproduction, two parents contribute genetic information to produce unique offspring by fusion of an egg and a sperm cell to form a fertilized egg.
	  Ex) New organism develops from a fertilized egg.

Adaptation	Enhances an organism's ability to survive in a particular environment. - Adaptation reasons: Behavior, Camouflage, Environment, Habitat, Inborn behavior (instinct), Mimicry, Predator Ex) Zebra stripes are an adaptation for visual protection from predators.
Evolution	All life tends to increase. More organisms are conceived, born, hatched, germinated from seed, sprouted from spores, or produced by cell division than can survive.

Cells

Cells are the basic unit structure in all organisms and the basic unit of reproduction. Keeping an appropriate internal environment is necessary to maintain a cell's homeostasis.
   Ex) Salt concentration, pH, Temperature

Cell size is limited due to the inability of large cells to provide nutrients and water, and efficiently remove waste. It is adapted to function.

All cells do secretion.
- Specific secretory cells: Specialized cells derived from elements belonging to other tissues. Ex) Hormone cells, Pancreatic cells, Salivary cells

- Cytochrome: Cell with colors
   Ex) Hemoglobin

• **Cell theory**
1) Living organisms are made up of cells.
2) Cells are the basic structural and organizational unit of all organisms.
3) All cells come from pre-existing cells.

Methods of studying cells

• **Cell microscopy**
Individual cells are too small to be seen with naked eyes, so scientists use microscopes to study them. A microscope is an instrument that magnifies an object.

1) Light microscopes
Produce an image of a specimen by using a beam of light.
Optical lens, 3-D

- Living cells: Possible to watch living cells carrying out their normal behaviors.
- Stereo light microscope: Artificial heart, Big cells
- Compound light microscope: Small cells, Microorganisms

2) Electron microscopes
Produce an image of a specimen by using a beam of electrons.
Detailed, high-resolution images: Strength, Direction, Cell interior structure, 3-D structure

- Non-living cells: Cannot watch cell normal behaviors.
- Transmission electron microscope: Ultrathin section less than 100 nm thick
- Scanning electron microscope: Secondary electrons, Back scattered electrons

• Cell fractionation
The process used to separate cellular components while preserving individual functions of each component.
Homogenization: Breaking open cell membrane + mixing
Differential centrifugation: Spinning at different speeds + separate the organelles by their different densities

- Low speed: Dense organelles. Ex) Nucleus, Membrane-bounded organelles
- High speed: Less dense organelles. Ex) Ribosome, Phospholipid layer

Prokaryotes vs. Eukaryotes

- Unicellular organisms: Consist of a single cell (single-celled organisms)
- Multicellular organisms: Consist of multiple cells (form tissues, organs, organ systems)

• Prokaryotic cells (Prokaryotes)

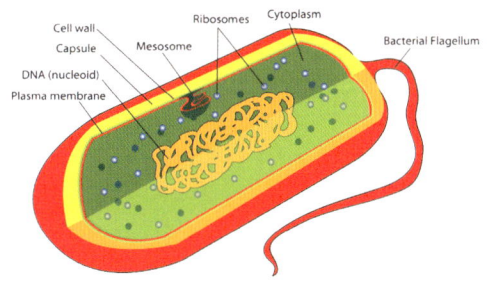

[1-1] Prokaryote

Unicellular organisms, basic single-celled organisms, no nucleus
Components: Cell membrane, Cell wall, DNA, RNA, Ribosome
Non-membrane-bound organelles: Bacteria, Archaea

Components
- Capsule: Sticky outermost layer
  Polysaccharides help cling to each other and prevent them from drying out.
- Cell wall: Encloses the entire organism.
- Cell membrane: Encloses the cell wall.
- Nucleoid: Contains genetic materials in DNA. Circular chromosomes
- DNA: Circular DNA, some have plasmids.
- Plasmid: Small rings of double-stranded DNA, sharing DNA through conjugation

- Pili: Adhesive hair-like projections for exchanging genetic materials during conjugation
- Ribosome: Protein synthesis
- Flagella: Allow prokaryotes to move.

• **Eukaryotic cells** (Eukaryotes)
Multicellular, highly-organized unicellular organisms, with a nucleus
Components: Cell membrane, Cell wall, DNA, RNA, Chromosome, Ribosome
Membrane-bound organelles: Animals, Plants, Fungi, Protist, Amoeba

Components
- Cell membrane: Semi-permeable membrane. Cell transport, Communication, Protection
- Cell wall: Plants (cellulose), Fungi (chitin)
- Nucleus: Nuclear double membrane, DNA, RNA, Genetic information
- Nucleolus: Center of the nucleus. Ribosomes synthesis
- DNA: Genetic information
- RNA: Protein synthesis
- Rough endoplasmic reticulum: Ribosomes, Protein synthesis
- Smooth endoplasmic reticulum: No ribosomes, Fatty acid synthesis, Detoxifying drugs
- Golgi apparatus: Packaging, sorting and modifying proteins. Secretory vesicles forming
- Secretory vesicle: Moving proteins outside (exocytosis)
- Ribosome: Protein synthesis
- Free ribosome: Ribosome in the cytoplasm. It synthesizes proteins in the cytoplasm.
- Cytoplasm: Thick solution that fills each cell enclosed by a cell membrane.
  Most chemical reactions occur. Ex) Protein and macromolecule synthesis, Cell division
- Lysosome: Contains hydrolytic enzymes. Breaks down unwanted materials.
- Peroxisome: Creates hydrogen peroxide.
  Breaks down fats and detoxifies dangerous substances.
- Centriole: Microtubule in animal cells. Spindle formation in cell division
- Mitochondria: Break down molecules. ATP synthesis. Have outer and inner membranes.

01 Cell biology

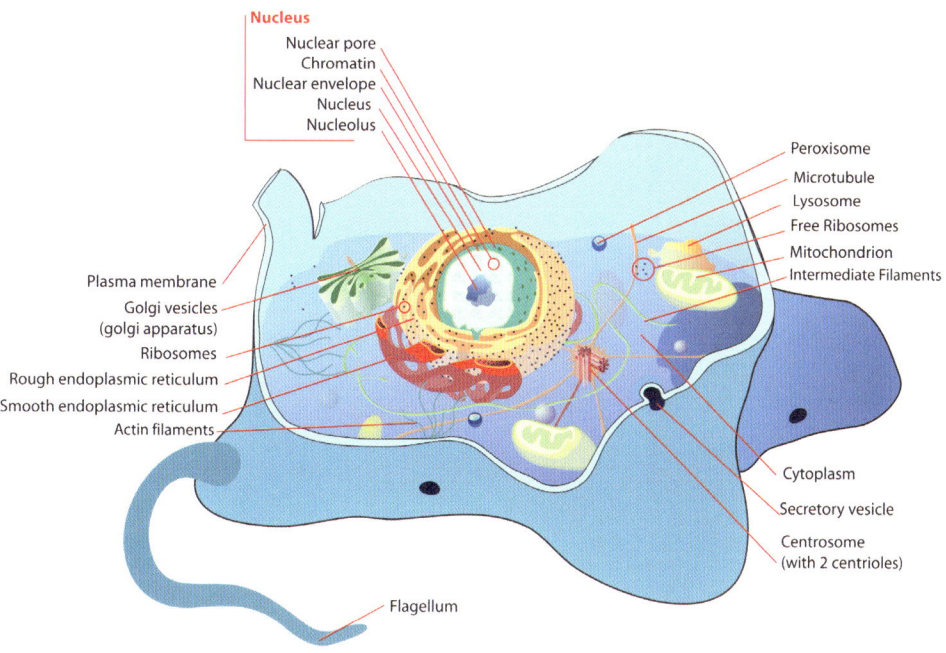

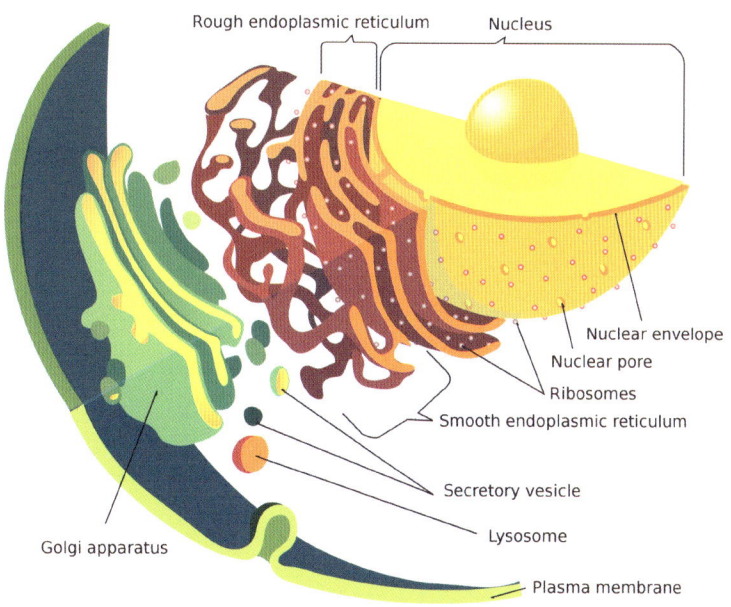

[1-2, 1-3] Eukaryote

Organelle	Prokaryotic cell	Eukaryotic cell
Cell type	Unicellular	Multicellular Highly organized unicellular
Cell wall	Bacteria: peptidoglycan	Plant cell: cellulose Fungi: chitin
Cell membrane	Yes	Yes
DNA, RNA	Circular Plasmid	Double helical Circular
Genetic material	Nucleoid	Chromosome
Ribosomes	Smaller	Larger
Membrane-bound organelles ↓	No	Yes
Nucleus	No	Double-layer
Mitochondria	No	Double-layer
Lysosomes	No	Single-layer
Endoplasmic reticulum	No	Single-layer
Golgi apparatus	No	Single-layer
Replication	Fast	Slow
Reproduction	Sexual, Asexual	Sexual, Asexual
Cell size	Smaller	Larger
Shape	Cocci (spherical) Bacilli (rod-shaped) Spirilli (spiral-shaped)	Various
Examples	Bacteria Archaea	Animal Plant Fungi Protist, Amoeba (unicellular)

Cell membrane

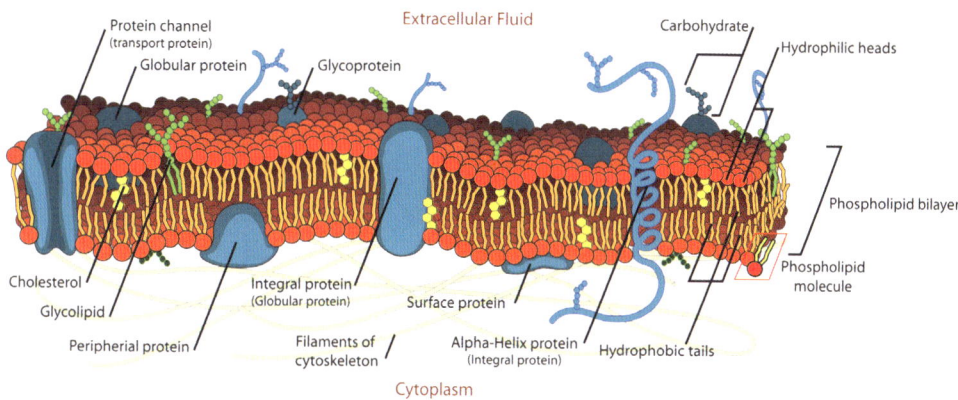

[1-4] Phospholipid bilayer cell membrane

A biological membrane that separates the interior of cells from the outside environment. It protects cells from the outer environment.
In both prokaryotes and eukaryotes.

• **Phospholipid bilayer**

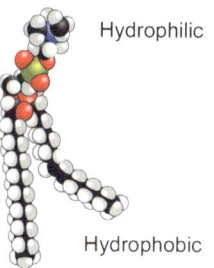

[1-5] Phospholipid

Head	Phosphate Hydrophilic Polar
Tail	2 Fatty acids Hydrophobic Nonpolar

- Amphiphilic: Polar, Nonpolar
- Inside: Nonpolar ↔ Water (separates from outside)
- Semi-permeable membrane: Controls movement of ions and molecules in and out.
- Fluid-mosaic model: Cell membrane is not fixed, moves around. (2-dimensional)
- Composition: Phospholipid, Cholesterol, Glycolipid, Glycoprotein

Cf. Cholesterol
- Phospholipid constituent which controls cell membrane fluidity.
- Nonpolar: Associates with fatty acids, spans inner membrane.
- Polar: Hydroxyl group (—OH) associates with phosphates, keeps phospholipids close together → rigid

• **Membrane proteins**

	Peripheral protein	Integral protein
Region	Hydrophilic	Hydrophilic + Hydrophobic Throughout the bilayer
Membrane	Cannot go through membrane	Can pass through membrane
Function	Adhesion, Cell signal Cell communication	Transport (in/out)

Non-membrane-bound organelles

In both prokaryotes and eukaryotes
Cell wall, DNA, RNA, Ribosome

Cell wall

Rigid and nonliving permeable wall surrounds the plasma membrane.
Encloses and supports the cells: Plants, Bacteria, Fungi, Algae

01 Cell biology

Prokaryotes	Eukaryotes
Bacteria: Peptiglycogen	Plant cell - Polysaccharide cellulose: Beta glycosidic bond - Surrounds the cell membrane. - Rigid, permeable, sustaining cell structure, cell protection - Turgor pressure: Makes a vacuole absorb water. Fungi: Chitin

DNA, RNA

DNA: Deoxyribonucleic acid, contains genetic materials.
RNA: Ribonucleic acid, participates in protein synthesis.

Prokaryotes	In the cytoplasm Type: Nucleic acid - DNA: Small, circular, single-strand, double-strands - Plasmid: Conjugates DNA and exchanges genetic information. - RNA: For protein synthesis, it does not contain genetic materials. - Prokaryotic chromosome: Nucleoid (single)
Eukaryotes	In the nucleus Type: Nucleic acid, wrapped with histones - DNA: Large, double-helical strands - RNA: Single strand - Mitochondria, Chloroplast: Own circular DNA, RNA - Eukaryotic chromosomes: Chromosomes (many)

Ribosome

A cellular particle made of RNA and proteins.
It gives the sites for protein synthesis in cells.

Prokaryotes	Eukaryotes
Protein synthesis In the cytoplasm	Protein synthesis Attached to the rough ER → Glogi apparatus → Lysosome - Free ribosome: Floats in the cytoplasm and synthesizes proteins. - Mitochondria: Have their own ribosomes and does own protein synthesis.
Small unit: 30S Large unit: 50S Total ribosomes: 70S	Small unit: 40S Large unit: 60S Total ribosomes: 80S

*S: Svedbergs, measurement of how fast molecules move in a centrifuge.

Membrane-bound organelles

Only in eukaryotes

- Single membrane: Vacuole, Lysosome, Golgi apparatus, Endoplasmic reticulum, Peroxisome, Glyoxysome
- Double membrane: Nucleus, Mitochondria

Nucleus

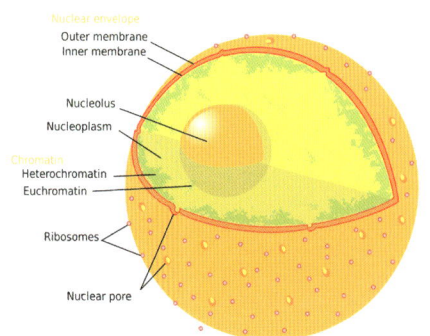

Double-membrane bound organelle

- DNA: Stores, protects, and expresses most of the genetic information
- Transcription: Regulates gene expression
- RNA synthesis: mRNA, rRNA, tRNA

[1-6] Nucleus

Nuclear membrane (Nuclear envelope)	Phospholipid bilayer - Perinuclear space: Between the inner and outer membrane - Outer membrane: Connects to the endoplasmic reticulum. - Inner membrane: Nucleoplasm fluid - Nucleus lamina: Inner membrane. Intermediate filament → Nucleus network Stabilizes the structure and involves gene expression.
Nucleolus	Center of the nucleus rRNA: Ribosome synthesis
Nuclear pore	Protein complex Helps transport materials: RNA, Ribosomal units, Polymerase → Cytoplasm Extends across the nuclear membrane.
Chromosome	Inside the nucleus Histone proteins + DNA Contains genetic information.

Endoplasmic reticulum

Single membrane-bound organelle, outside of the nucleus
ER lumen (Cisternal space): ER internal space, phospholipid bilayer membrane. Separates from the cytoplasm.

Rough ER	Contains ribosomes embedded: Synthesizes proteins. Connected to the nuclear envelope. (perinuclear region) Perinuclear region-ER lumen connection: Embedded into the cell membrane or leaves the cell. • **Protein synthesis process** rER → transported in vesicles → Gorgi apparatus → packaged into specialized secretory vesicle → released into the plasma membrane Ex) Insulin, Glucagon synthesis
Smooth ER	No ribosomes Synthesizes lipids: Fatty acids, Cholesterol, Phosphobilipids Detoxification, oxidation of drugs, toxins and alcohol → Liver Special enzymes: Glucose 6 phosphatases synthesize carbohydrates in muscle cells.

Golgi apparatus

Protein post office
Receiving proteins → packaging, sorting, modifying proteins → Secretory vesicles → dispatching into the cytoplasm

- Cisternae: Membrane sacs

Mitochondria

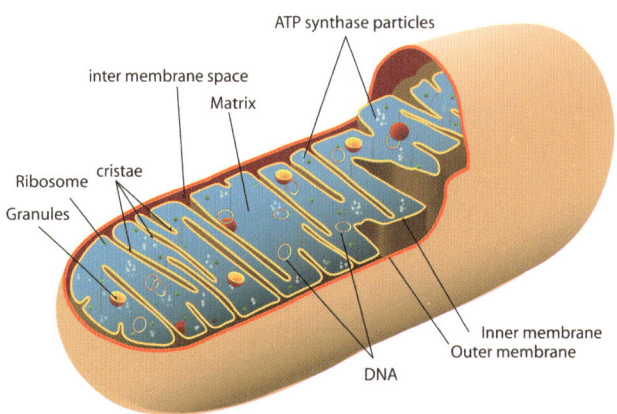

[1-7] Mitochondria

Double membrane organelle: Phospholipid bilayer membrane
Create cell energy: ATP (Adenosine triphosphate), Aerobic respiration
Cf. Anaerobic respiration: Cytoplasm

- ATP: Cell plasma → Mitochondria matrix → Inner membrane → out
- Glucose + Oxygen = ATP

Apoptosis: Program to cell death.
Calcium signaling: Different types of pathways with calcium
Cellular differentiation: Differentiates by cells.
Mitochondria's own DNA: Circular chromosomes
Mitochondrial ribosomes: Self-protein synthesis

- **Cellular respiration**: Cell plasma (glycolysis) → Mitochondria

Outer membrane
- Phospholipid bilayer
- Porin: Large integral protein. Facilitates diffusion
  → Exchanges ions, small molecules, NADH, and ATP

Mitochondrial matrix
- Mitochondrial circular DNA, Mitochondrial RNA
- Acetyl CoA formation (Pyruvate decarboxylation)
- Citric Acid cycle

Inner membrane: Cristae (infolds) → increases the surface areas to fit more proteins
- Higher proton concentration than the outer membrane
- Carries proteins in and out of the mitochondrial matrix.
- Electron transport chain: Electronic gradient between the intermembrane space and the mitochondrial matrix.

Intermembrane space: Ions, Molecules
- Many H^+, chemiosmosis (ion gradient) → makes ATP in the Electron transport chain
- Synthesizes ATP → many in muscles and liver

Vacuoles

Plants, Fungi, Some animals (highly reduced)
Many shapes, sizes, and functions

- Plants: Large, one. Store harmful materials, waste, and water.
  Maintain hydrostatic pressure. (Turgor pressure)
- Animals: Smaller, many. Helps endocytosis and exocytosis.

Microbody

Small, circle and single phospholipid bilayer
Vesicle + depends on what is inside determines → Lysosome, Peroxisome, Glyoxysome

- Lysosome: Lysis (digestive)
- Peroxisome: Produces and breaks down hydrogen peroxide.
- Glyoxysome: Plants

Lysosome

Contains digestive enzymes.
Low pH (by phosphate): Acid hydrolytic enzymes break down macromolecules and harmful waste.

- Primary lysosomes: Made in Golgi apparatus.
  Fuse with endosomes (phagosomes and pinosomes) → Secondary lysosomes
- Secondary lysosomes: Move throughout the cytoplasm.

- Autolysis: DNA damaged → Cell destroys itself
- Phagocytes have many lysosomes. (digestive hydrolytic enzymes)

Peroxisome

Synthesized in the smooth endoplasmic reticulum.
Reactive oxygen species detoxification: Toxins, drugs, alcohols → Liver
Oxidation reaction → produces hydrogen peroxide (H_2O_2)
Synthesizes lipids, cholesterols, and bile acids.
Lipid metabolism: Breaks down fatty acids and produces ATP.
Cell signaling

Glyoxysome

Peroxisomes of germinating plants
Fatty acids beta-oxidation → produce ATP until the chloroplasts mature to do photosynthesis

Cell coat

Protects the plasma membrane and participates in the filtration and diffusion process.
Glycocalyx, Polysaccharide chain

Extracellular matrix

Carbohydrate + Fiber proteins
Three-dimensional network consists of extracellular macromolecules and minerals.
Provides structural and biochemical supports to surrounding cells.
  Ex) Collagen, Enzymes, Glycoproteins, Hydroxyapatite

- Collagen: Main structural protein
- Fibronectin: Glycoprotein. Organizes matrix, and helps cells attach.
- Integrin: Receptor proteins in the cell membrane
  Adhesion between extracellular matrix and filaments inside the cell.
  Cell signal pathway controls signals and communication.

Cytoskeleton

Only in eukaryotes
A structure helps cells maintain their shape and internal organization.
Mechanical support enables cells to carry out essential functions: Cell division, Movement

	Microfilaments	Intermediate filaments	Microtubules
Size	6-7nm	10nm	23nm
Shape	Linear	Rope-like	Helical
Protein	Actin, Myosin	Many	Tubulin (α, β)
Function	Cell stability, shape, structure Tensile strength (resist pulling)	Cell stability, shape, structure Tensile strength Resist pulling Bond between cells Compose the nucleus Cytoplasm, Outside of cell	Compressive strength Resist pushing Cell transport Separate chromosomes
Example	Muscle contraction Phagocytosis	Nuclear lamina composition	Mitotic spindle Intracellular movement Cilia, Flagella Centrosomes Centrioles

Microtubules

• Cilia

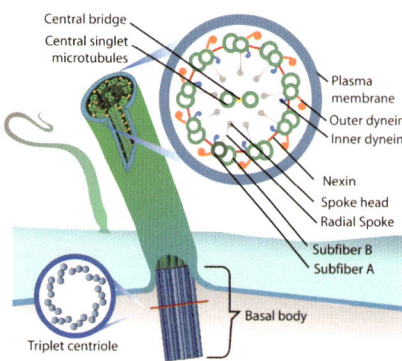

Long, hair-like, extend from the surface of the cell. Move through liquids and particles across the cell surface.

- Primary cilia: Single cilium, Cellular antenna
  The signaling pathway that regulates growth.

[1-8] Cilia

• Flagella

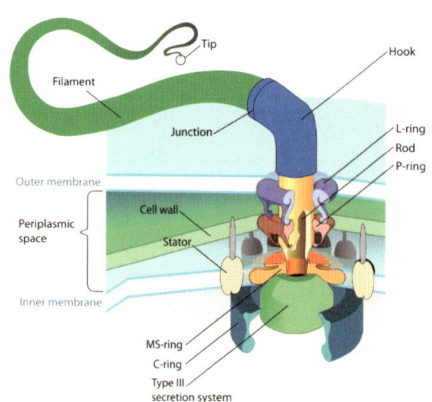

Long, they live on the cell's surface.
Longer than cilia

[1-9] Flagella

	Prokaryotes	Eukaryotes
Protein	Flagellin	Microtubules (protein filament) Dynein (motor protein) Radial spokes (polypeptide)
Energy	Proton pump (H^+ ions across the cell membrane)	ATP pump (Dynein → ATP → 9 doublet bending)
Motion	Rotation Counter clockwise	Bending

Centriole, Centrosome

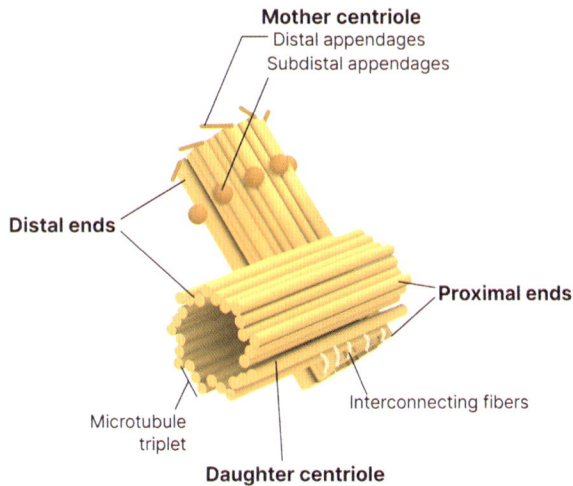

[1-10] Centrosome

Only in eukaryotes

• Centrosome
- 2 centrioles, 90 angles
- Embedded of proteins.
- Close to the nucleus.
- Mitotic spindle fibers: Separate chromosomes during cell division.
- Creating and extending microtubules of the cytoskeleton.
- MTOC: Microtubule organizing center

• Centrioles
- Basal body: 9+3 (nine-triplet) microtubules
- Mitotic spindle during cell division
- Determines positions of the nucleus and organelles.
- Flagella, Cilia: One mother centriole makes the basal body.

Cell membrane transport

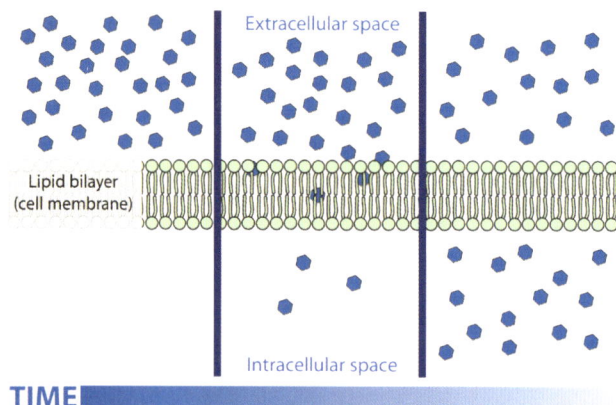

[1-11] Simple diffusion

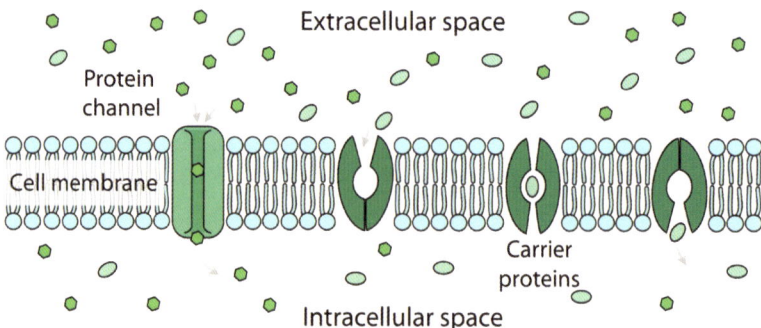

[1-12] Facilitated diffusion

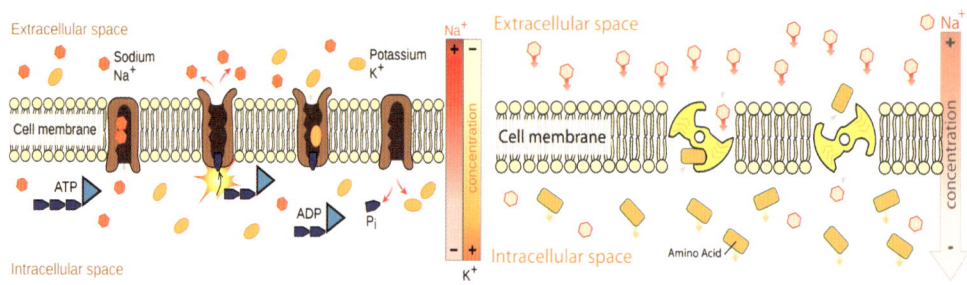

[1-13] Active transport 1, [1-14] Active transport 2

01 Cell biology

Substances movement passing in and out of cells.

Simple diffusion (Passive transport)	Facilitated diffusion (Passive transport)	Active transport
Small, Nonpolar solutes Move directly through the cell membrane	Special proteins help the solutes pass through the cell membrane	Movement of molecules across a cell membrane against the concentration gradient by using ATP
Concentration gradient: High → Low	Concentration gradient: High → Low	Concentration gradient: Low → High
Small particles Nonpolar solutes	- Channel protein (Porin): Hydrophilic pores (channels) - Carrier protein (Permease): Binds and changes shape to transfer the solutes → Proteins help solutes to pass membrane	- Sodium-potassium pump: Controls nerve cell signaling - Exocytosis: In → Out - Endocytosis: Out → In
No energy (ATP) No protein	No energy (ATP) Proteins: Channel protein, Carrier protein	Energy (ATP) Ion, Entropy
Nonpolar (hydrophobic)	Polar (hydrophilic)	Polarized
Small particles Nonpolar molecules Steroid hormones Osmosis	Polar ions Molecules Minerals Peptide hormones	Large molecules Bacteria Fungi Plants Humans Glucose transport Enzyme secretion Antibody releasing Neurotransmitters

Cf. Co-transportation: Secondary active transport. Transport of molecules across the cell membrane utilizing energy in other forms than ATP. This energy comes from the electrochemical gradient created by pumping ions out of the cell.

Ex) Movement of glucose in the proximal convoluted tubule, Glucose symporter SGLT1, Sodium-calcium antiporter

Osmosis

Passive diffusion of net movement of water through a semipermeable membrane to make equilibrium. Passive diffusion does not need ATP.

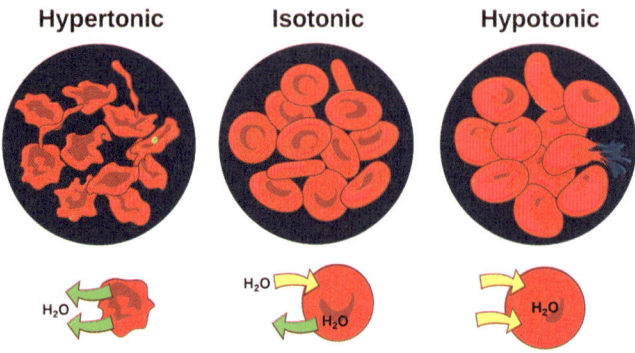

[1-15] Osmosis

Water concentration: High → Low
Solute concentration: Low → High

	Hypertonic	Hypotonic	Isotonic
Solute concentration	Inside < Outside	Inside > Outside	Equal
Water movement	Inside → Outside	Outside → Inside	Stay
	Cells shrink	Cells burst	Stay

Exocytosis, Endocytosis

Active transport: Movement of molecules across a cell membrane against the concentration gradient by using ATP.

- Concentration gradient: Low → High

• Exocytosis

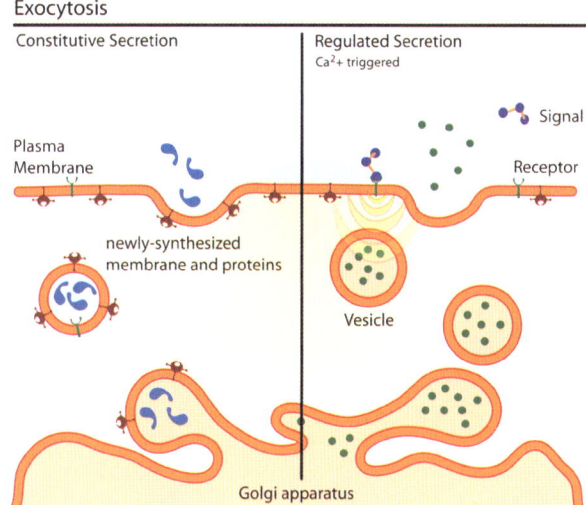

[1-16] Exocytosis

Push materials out of the cells.
Fusion of a vesicle with the cell membrane.
  Ex) Secrete hormones, enzymes, and antibodies.

• Endocytosis
Bring materials into the cells.

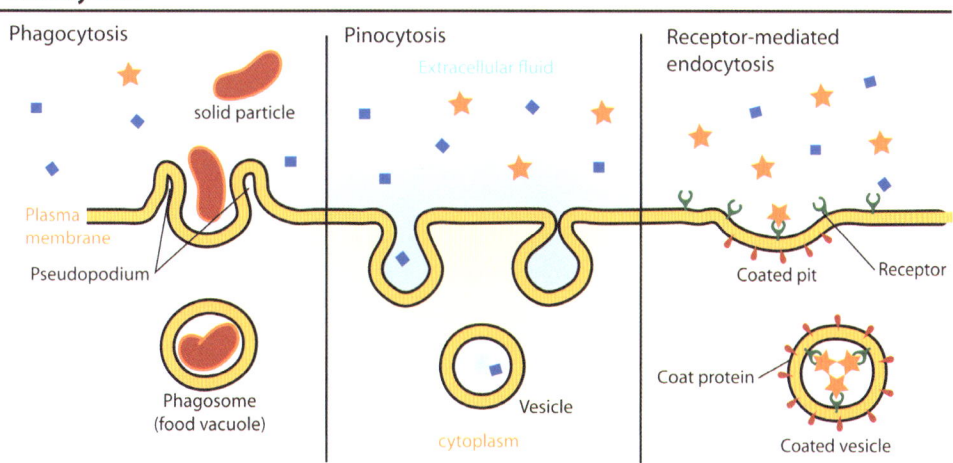

[1-17] Endocytosis

Pinocytosis (cell drinking)
Cell dissolves materials.
Almost every cell does.
Energy is used for the formation of vesicles.

- Process: Invaginating → Engulfing → Vesicle

   Ex) Small intestine absorbs nutrients from the lumen of the gastrointestinal tract.

Phagocytosis (cell eating)
Large materials: Molecules, Bacteria, Cells
Certain cells have the ability.
Energy is used for the formation of vesicles.

- Process: Binds to protein receptor → Protrudes outside → Engulfs → Vesicle (phagosome)
  → Lysosome → Digestion

   Ex) Macrophages, Antibodies, WBC

Receptor-mediated
Special active transport in eukaryotes

- Process: Binds to receptor → Clathrin (protein coat) binds to the cell membrane
  → Clathrin-coated vesicle

   Ex) Macromolecules: Sugar, Hormones
   Low-density-lipoprotein is removed from the blood by receptor-mediated endocytosis.

Microorganisms

Organisms of microscopic sizes may exist in their single-celled forms or as colonies of cells.
   Ex) Bacteria, Virus, Fungi, Protist

01 Cell biology

Bacteria

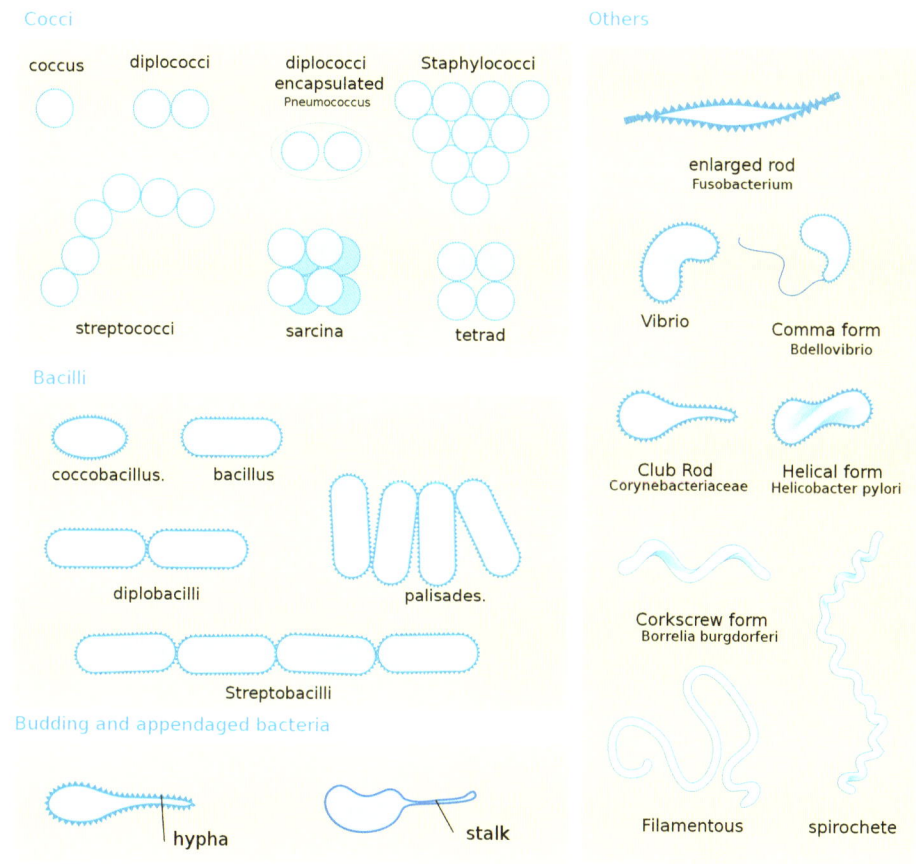

[1-18] Bacteria

Most representative prokaryotes are bacteria.
Prokaryotic cell: Unicellular organism
Shapes: Spherical (coccus), Rodlike (bacillus), Curved (vibrio, spirillum, spirochete)

Important bacteria in the rectum (large intestine) produce important molecules.
- Vitamin B12: DNA synthesis final component
- Vitamin K: Coagulation factor

• **YES:** Cell membrane, Ribosome, DNA, RNA, Cell wall
- DNA: Genetic materials in the nucleoid, single circular DNA

- Plasmid: Conjugates DNA with each other → transfers genetic materials
- RNA: Small, for protein synthesis. It does not contain genetic materials.
- Cell wall: peptidoglycan ↔ Plant cell wall: cellulose
  Bacterial protection against external environmental stimuli

- **NO:** Membrane-bound organelles
- Nucleus, Endoplasmic reticulum, Mitochondria, Lysosomes

- **Gram stain method**

Method of staining used to distinguish bacteria into 2 groups: Gram-positive, Gram-negative

	Gram-positive	Gram-negative
Concept	Positive result in the Gram stain test	Negative result in the Gram stain test
Stained	Purple	Red, Pink
Cell wall	Thick	Thin
Cell membrane	No	Yes
Production	Exotoxins (outward)	Endotoxins (in/outward)

Virus

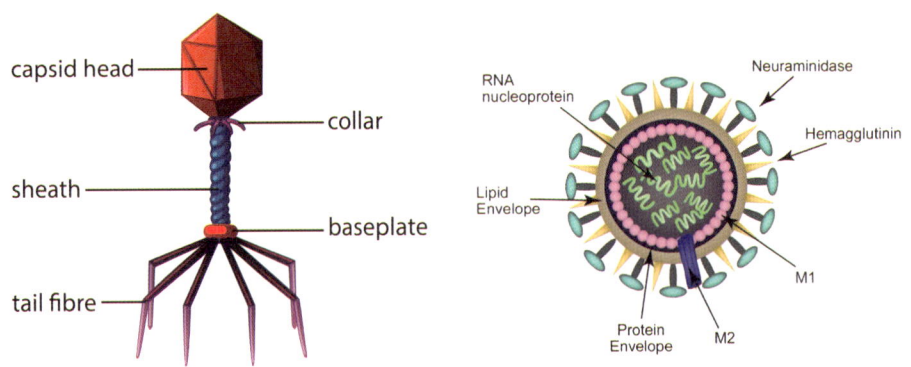

[1-19, 1-20] Virus

Not a cell (not a prokaryote nor a eukaryote) just a small particle.
Obligate cell parasite: Does metabolic activities only after penetrating the host cell.
Infects all kinds of organisms → can cause serious diseases
Shapes: Enveloped, Non-enveloped
Certain portion of DNA is from the deactivated virus.

- Retrovirus: A virus that uses RNA as its genetic material. When a retrovirus infects a cell, it makes a DNA copy of its genome inserted into the host cell's DNA.
  Ex) Cancer, AIDS

• Yes
- Nucleic acids (DNA, RNA): Double or single strand both contain genetic materials.
- Protein coat (capsid, envelope) + Genetic materials (DNA, RNA)
- Capsid: Protein, surrounds nucleic acids. (DNA, RNA)
- Cell envelope: Lipid and protein structure, surrounds capsid for some viruses.

• Life cycle
- Lytic cycle: Fast viral reproduction
  Penetrates the host cell → replicates genetic materials → assembles virus particles → cell bursts → virus spreads out → infects other host cells

- Lysogenic cycle: Slow viral reproduction
  Penetrates the host cell → combines with the host genetic information (DNA, RNA) → becomes a part of the host
  1) Host cell does not know → Cell division: Replicates the virus in infected cells
  2) Host cell knows → cuts out the virus → virus replicates (lytic cycle) → replicates genetic materials → assembles virus particles → cells bursts → virus spreads out → Infects other host cells

Fungi

Eukaryotic organism, heterotroph
Absorb nutrients from their surroundings.
Reproduction: Asexual, Sexual
Cell wall: Chitin
Types: Yeast, Mold

- Yeast: Unicellular
- Mold: Most fungi, multicellular, hyphae forms → Mycelium, reproduction with spores

	Fungi	**Plant**
Nutrients	Surroundings	Photosynthesis (autotrophs)
Cell wall	Chitin	Cellulose
Sunlight	Not necessary	Necessary
Reproduction	Spore	Sexual, Asexual

Protist

Unicellular organisms
The very first original eukaryotic cells

Animal cell vs. Plant cell

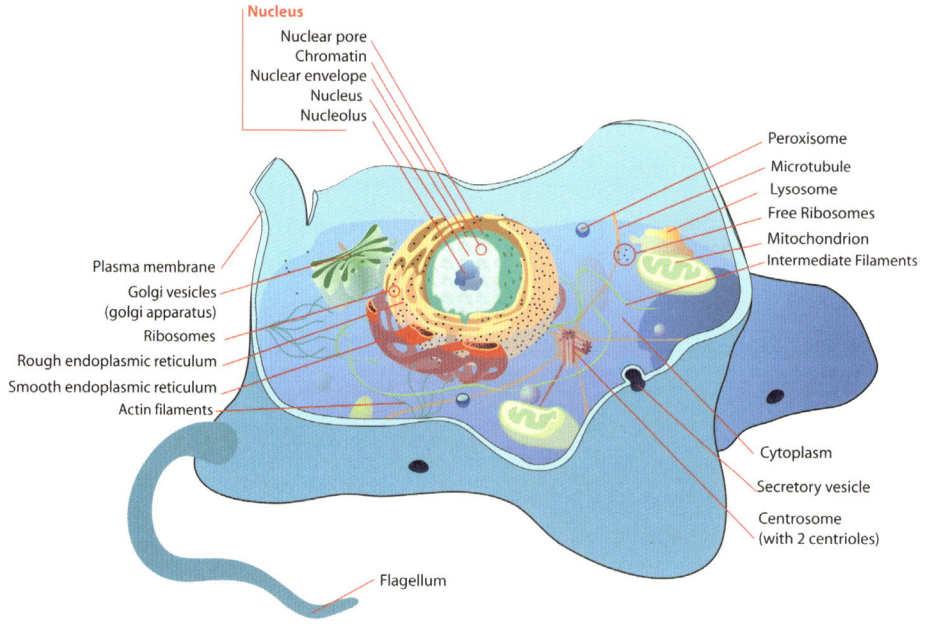

01 Cell biology

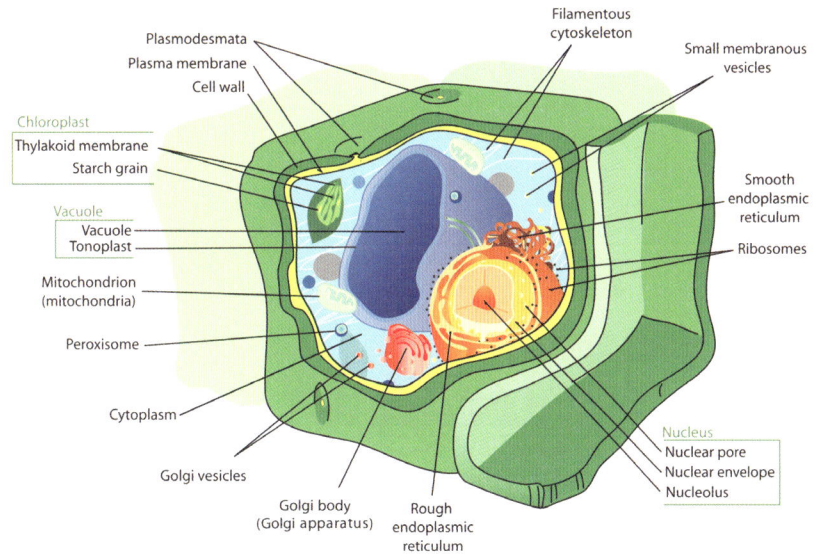

[1-21] Animal cell [1-22] Plant cell

	Prokaryotes	**Animal cell**	**Plant cell**
Type	Bacteria, Archaea	Mammal, Fungi, Protist	Eukaryote
Cell membrane	Yes	Yes	Internal to a cell wall
Cell wall	Peptidoglycan	Fungi (chitin)	Cellulose
Shape	Various	Various	Fixed, Rectangular
Vacuole	Small	Small	Large, Single
Chloroplast	No	Plants	Yes
Plastid	Yes	No	Double membrane
Mitochondria	No	Yes	Yes
Ribosomes	Yes	Yes	Yes
Lysosome	No	Yes	Yes
Peroxisome	No	Yes	Glyoxysome
Centrosome	No	Yes	No
Centriole	No	Yes	No
DNA	Single nucleoid Plasmid Circular DNA	Multiple chromosomes Double-helical Circular (Mitochondria)	Many chromosomes Chloroplast Circular DNA
Size	Smallest	Smaller	Small

Biomass

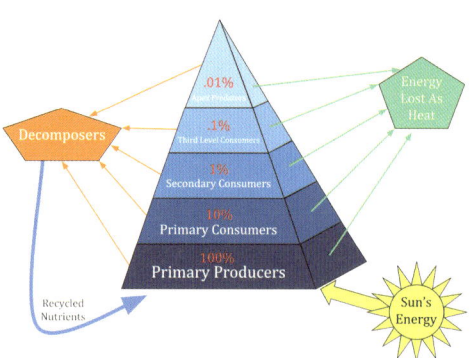

[1-23] Energy pyramid

The mass of living biological organisms in a given area or ecosystem at a given time.
Any fuel derived from organisms: Microorganisms, Animals, Plants

Organism sources

All living organisms need carbon, energy, and electrons.

Carbon source	**Autotrophs**	Inorganic	Organisms get energy sources from inorganic materials. Ex) Plants: Carbon dioxide, Water → Energy (Sugar, H_2O)
	Heterotrophs	Organic	Organisms get energy sources from other organisms. Ex) Human
Energy source	**Chemotrophs**	Oxidation	Get energy by breaking down macromolecules. Ex) Human: Sugar, Lipids, Proteins
	Phototrophs	Light	Get energy by using lights. Ex) Plant: Light → CO_2 + Water → Sugar, Oxygen
Electron source	**Organotroph**	Organic	Get electrons from organic molecules. Ex) Sugar
	Lithograph	Inorganic	Get electrons from inorganic sources.

Chapter 02: Acid, Base, pH

Acid, Base

• Acid
Any substance in water solution tastes sour, changes blue litmus paper to red, reacts with some metals to liberate hydrogen, reacts with bases to form salts, and promotes chemical reactions. (acid catalysis)

• Base
Any substance in water solution is slippery to the touch, tastes bitter, changes red litmus paper to blue, reacts with acids to form salts, and promotes specific chemical reactions. (base catalysis)

	Acid	Base
pH	Less than 7	Greater than 7
Taste	Sour	Bitter
Color of pH indicator	Red	Blue

Acid + Base → Salt + Water
(Salt: any chemical compound)

pH, pOH

• pH
Potential Hydrogen
A measure of the hydrogen ion (H^+) concentration of a solution
pH = -log [H^+]

• pOH
Potential Hydroxide
A measure of the hydroxide ion (OH^-) concentration of a solution
pOH = -log [OH^-]

Pure water: pH 7 (neutral)
pH + pOH = 14

- pH indicator: A substance that changes color at a certain pH.
  Ex) Acid: yellow, Base: blue

• **pH homeostasis**
To prevent changes in electrical charge in polypeptide chains.
  Ex) Proteins: Optimal pH, Enzymes, Muscles
Effective digestion throughout GI tract.
Ions can function properly in neuron signaling. (protein channels)

Acid-Base theory

• **Arrhenius theory** (narrow-range)
- Acid: Any species that increases the concentration of H^+ in an aqueous solution.
- Base: Any species that increases the concentration of OH^- in an aqueous solution.

• **Bronsted-Lowry theory** (intermediate-range)
- Acid: Proton donor
  + Conjugate base: An acid transfers a proton to a conjugate base.

- Base: Proton acceptor
  + Conjugate acid: A base receives a proton from a conjugate acid.

Only in a reversible reaction
Acid-base reaction: Proton transfer reaction
Conjugate acid-base pairs: A pair of molecules/ions, related to one another by gain or loss of a proton.

• **Lewis theory** (broad-range)
- Acid: Electron pair acceptor to form a chemical bond. (electron-poor)
- Base: Electron pair donor to form a chemical bond. (electron-rich)

Acid-Base reactions

Acid + Base → Salt + H_2O (neutral solution)
Acid + Metals → Salt + H_2

Acid + Metal oxide → Soluble salt + Water
Strong acid + Carbonate/Bicarbonate → CO_2 (g)
Strong acid + NH_3, Amine → Salt

(Salt: Any chemical compound)

Strong and weak Acid, Base

Strong acid	Strong base
H_3O^+	OH^-
HCl	LiOH
HBr	NaOH
HI	KOH
HNO_3	$Ba(OH)_2$
H_2SO_4	$Ca(OH)_2$
$HClO_4$	$Sr(OH)_2$

Weak acid	Weak base
H_2SO_3	
H_2PO_4	
HNO_2	NH_3
H_2CO_3	HCO_3
HF	
NH_4	

Buffer system

Aqueous solutions of acid and base which prevent large variations in pH levels.

• **Buffer conditions**
1) Must consist of a weak conjugate acid-base pair.
- A weak acid and its conjugate base
- A weak base and its conjugate acid

2) Buffers contain an equal amount of conjugate acid and conjugate base.
- Weak acid + Conjugate base solution → triggers slight change, not appreciable change
  Ex) $CH_3COOH + H_2O \rightleftharpoons CH_3COO^+ + H_3O^+$

- Strong acid, base → changes pH, irreversible reaction: difficult to go backward, not an equilibrium reaction

- Strong acid (H_3O^+) + Conjugate base solution
  Ex) $CH_3COO^- + H_3O^+ \rightarrow CH_3COOH + H_2O$

- Strong base (OH^-) + Conjugate acid solution
  Ex) $CH_3COOH + OH^- \rightarrow CH_3COO^- + H_2O$

- Buffer capacity: Maximum acid and the base amount by changing pH 1 of the solution.

• **Blood buffer**

Human blood pH: 7.4
Small changes can cause fatal disease and death.

Bicarbonate	Bicarbonate buffer system plays a significant role in maintaining the pH homeostasis of the blood. Bicarbonate buffer system converts a strong base to a weak base (bicarbonate ion) and a strong acid to a weak acid. (carbonic acid) $CO_2 + H_2O \rightleftharpoons H_2CO_3 \rightleftharpoons H^+ + HCO_3$
Phosphate	The phosphate buffer consists of phosphoric acid (H_3PO_4) in equilibrium with dihydrogen phosphate ion ($H_2PO_4^-$) and H^+. The pK for the phosphate buffer is 6.8, which allows this buffer to function within its optimal buffering range at physiological pH. It plays a very minute role in the blood. $H_3PO_4 \rightleftharpoons H_2PO_4^-$ $H_2PO_4^- \rightleftharpoons HPO_4^{2-}$ $HPO_4^{2-} \rightleftharpoons PO_4^{3-}$
Protein	Protein buffer helps maintain acidity in and around the cells. Proteins containing amino acid histidine are also good at buffering.

Polar, Nonpolar

Polar substances: Positive and negative charges on molecules.
Nonpolar substances: No (very small) charges on molecules.

	Polar	**Nonpolar** (apolar)
Charges	Positive, Negative	No charges
Movement	Dipole	No dipole
Interaction	With other polar substances	With other nonpolar substances
Water-friendly	Hydrophilic	Hydrophobic
Examples	Water, Alcohol	Carbon dioxide, Oil Most organic molecules

Chapter 03: Organic compounds

Any of a large class of chemical compounds in which one or more carbon atoms are covalently linked to atoms of other elements, most commonly hydrogen, oxygen, or nitrogen.
Compounds contain carbon-hydrogen bonds. (C-H)
Various in sizes and shapes: Lipids, Carbohydrates, Protein, Nucleic acids

- **Carbon** (C)

Join each other to form large molecules.
Carbon backbone: Binds large, complex molecules together. Strong, not easily broken.
Covalent bond: Sharing electrons and linked with another atom.

- Single bond: Rotate freely, flexible, and in many shapes.
- Double bond, Triple bond: Do not rotate and inflexible.

Isomers

Molecules with the same chemical formula but have different structures and properties.
Same formula and different bonds and structures.
Cf. Isotopes: Same # protons, different # nucleus. Same properties.

Structural isomer	Stereo isomer	Enantiomer
Same chemical formula	Same covalent bond (structure) Different 3-D	Mirror images of each other
Different covalent arrangement	Double bond (not flexible)	Center carbon is symmetrical
	Geometric Isomer - Cis-isomer - Trans-isomer	

Cf. Graphite-Diamond: Structural Isomers (allotropes)

03 Organic compounds

Monomer, Polymer

Monomer	Polymer
Basic unit of an organic compound Ex) Glucose, Amino acid, Fatty acid, Nucleotide	Many monomers
Condensation reaction: Covalently linked (water is removed during the reaction)	Hydrolysis reaction: Breaks down into monomers

Lipids

Organic compounds which are insoluble in water and soluble in nonpolar solvents.
A long carbon chain reduces the polarity of the carboxyl group.
Monomer: Fatty acid

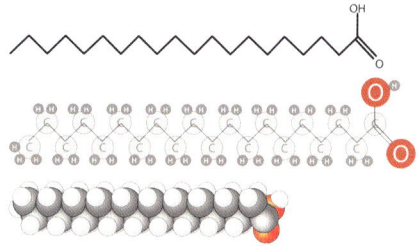

[3-1] Fatty acid

Functions
- Cell structure: Phospholipid bilayer (make up the building blocks of the structure)
- Store energy: Triglycerides (3 Fatty acids + Glycerol)
- Produce ATP: Beta oxidation → Acetyl CoA → ATP
- Steroid hormones
- Cell signaling, messengers
- Lipid-soluble vitamins: Vitamin D, A, E, K

• **Types of lipids**

Fatty acid	Single lipid Basic unit of triglyceride Carboxylic acids with a long aliphatic chain: $CH_3(CH_2)_nCOOH$ A long carbon chain reduces the polarity of the carboxyl group. - Saturated: No double covalent bond - Unsaturated: More than one double covalent bond
Triglyceride	Neutral fat Fat in our body Oily substance found in the body, under the skin, or around the organs. Triglyceride: Glycerol + 3 Fatty acids (Ester linkage: RCOOR') - Ester linkage: Alcohol + Acid → Ester linkage + Water Glyceride = Glycerol + Fatty acid (Ester linkage) - Glycerol + Fatty acid = Monoglyceride (1 Ester linkage) - Glycerol + 2 Fatty acids = Diglyceride (2 Ester linkages) - Glycerol + 3 Fatty acids = Triglyceride (3 Ester linkages)
Glycerol (Glycerin)	Colorless, odorless, viscous liquid that is sweet-tasting and non-toxic. Used as sweetener and humectant. Glycerol + 3 Fatty acids → Triglyceride
Steroid	Sex hormone, Corticosteroid, Anabolic steroid, Cholesterol

[3-2] Saturated fatty acid, [3-3] Unsaturated fatty acid, [3-4] Triglyceride

• Steroid

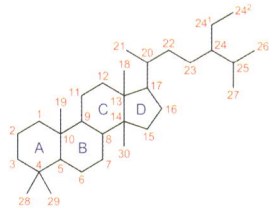

[3-5] Steroid

Biologically active organic compound with 17 carbons and four rings arranged in a specific molecular configuration.
17C + 4 rings (3 cyclohexane + 1 cyclopentane)

Fungal steroids	Maintaining the integrity of the fungal cell membrane. 　Ex) Ergosterol
Animal steroids	• **Sex hormone:** Progesterone, Testosterone, Estrogen, Androgen • **Corticosteroid:** Steroid drugs. Popularly referred to as a 'steroid.' - Glucocorticoids: Regulate metabolism, immune function, and inflammation. Powerful hormone drugs. Inhibit transformation of inflammatory molecules (modulate immune activity) and increase blood sugar levels. 　Ex) Cortisol: Immunosuppression - Mineralocorticoids: Control minerals. 　Maintain blood volume and renal electrolytes excretion. 　Ex) Aldosterone: Increases blood Na^+ concentration • **Anabolic steroids** Increase muscle and bone synthesis. • **Cholesterol** Animal cell membrane (phospholipids bilayer) structural component Controls the fluidity of cell membrane: Keeps cell membrane fluidity and warmth. More cholesterol → More rigid cell membrane Sex hormone resource: Cholesterol → Androgen, Estrogen ● Cholesterol → transformed into other steroids - LDL (Low-density lipoprotein): Bad cholesterol, makes up most of the body's cholesterol. Raises the risk of heart disease and stroke. - HDL (High-density lipoprotein): Good cholesterol, absorbs cholesterol and carries it back to the liver. The liver then flushes it from the body. High HDL levels can lower the risk for heart disease and stroke.
Plant steroids	Steroidal alkaloids, Cardiac glycosides, Phytosteroids, Brassinosteroids
Prokaryotes	Tetracyclic steroids, Pentacyclic steroids

- **Saturated, Unsaturated fatty acids**

	Saturated fatty acids	Unsaturated fatty acids	Trans fatty acids
	Maximum a possible number of H atoms (fully saturated) Full single bond C-H	1+ pairs C atoms: Double bond Not fully saturated with H atoms - Monounsaturated fatty acids - Polyunsaturated fatty acids	Artificially hydrogenated Double bonds → rearranged Trans configuration Resemble saturated fatty acids properties
Bonds	Single bond	Extra double bond	Trans double bond
Room temperature	Solid	Liquid	Solid
Examples	Animal fat	Plant fat	High risk of cardiovascular disease

- **Isoprene**

Unsaturated 5-hydrocarbon monomers (C_5H_8)

Ex) Carotenoids
- Plants: Pigments produce orange, yellow and red colors. Essential in oxygenic photosynthesis.
- Provitamin A carotenoids: Plant pigments that the body converts into vitamin A in the intestine.

Carbohydrates

Sugar molecules and organic compounds that occur in living tissues or food and that can be broken down into energy.
Monomer: Monosaccharide

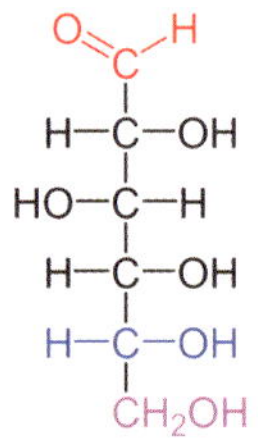

[3-6] Carbohydrate

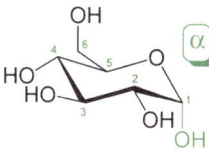 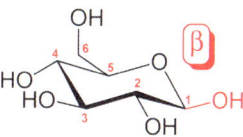

[3-7] α Anomer, [3-8] β Anomer

Functions
- Energy source: Glucose (animals, plants)
- Cell walls: Cellulose (plant), Chitin (fungi), Peptidoglycan (bacteria)
- Cell marker: Glycoprotein (blood types)
- Polar, Hydrophilic: —OH (hydroxyl) group, easily dissolved in the water.

Monosaccharides	One sugar unit • **Glucose** Most abundant energy source Gluconeogenesis: Synthesis from amino acids, fatty acids Maintain metabolism concentration. Ring structure • **Fructose** • **Galactose** Structural isomers: Fructose-Galactose (configurational, conformational) • **Ribose, Deoxyribose** RNA, DNA: 5C sugar
Disaccharides	Two sugar units • **Maltose** (malt sugar) Glucose + Glucose Alpha linkage: Digestible • **Sucrose** (table sugar) Glucose + Fructose Alpha linkage: Digestible • **Lactose** (milk sugar) Glucose + Galactose Beta linkage: Indigestible 　Ex) Lactose intolerance: Difficult to fully digest the lactose in milk because of a lack of enzymes.

Polysaccharides	Many sugar units • **Starch** Stored energy form in plant cells Amylose (a straight-chain) Amylopectin (a branched-chain) • **Amyloplast** Plant, store starch Hydrolyze starch → Energy • **Glycogen** Stored energy form in animal cells: Liver, Muscle cells Water-soluble: Alpha-glycosidic bond • **Cellulose** Plant cell wall component The most abundant organic compound on Earth Water-insoluble: Beta glycosidic bond. It cannot be split by enzymes. Cf. Grass-eating animals have cellulose digestive bacteria in the stomach.

• **Types of carbohydrates**
1) Monosaccharide: #C=1
Glucose, Galactose, Fructose: Structural isomers (configurational, conformational)
- Aldose: Monosaccharide + Aldehyde
- Ketose: Monosaccharide + Ketone
  Ex) Silver-mirror test: Positive: aldehyde ↔ Negative: ketone

2) Disaccharide: #C=2
Sucrose: D-glucose + D-fructose (α-glycosidic bond)
Lactose: D-glucose + D-galactose (β-glycosidic bond)
Maltose: D-glucose + D-glucose (α-glycosidic bond)

- Glycosidic bond: Covalent bond

3) Oligosaccharide: #C=3~6

4) Polysaccharide: #C=7+
Amylose, Amlypectin, Starch, Amyloplast, Glycogen, Cellulose
- Glycogen: D-glucopyranose, α-glycosidic bond
- Cellulose: Linear, D-glucopyranose, β-glycosidic bond

03 Organic compounds

• **Stereoisomer**
Same formula and bond atom sequence, different 3-D orientation
- D-monosaccharide: D-glyceraldehyde
- L-monosaccharide: L-glyceraldehyde

• **Reducing sugars**
- Reducing sugar: Sugar can act as a reducing agent, reduce others.
  Aldehydes, Ketones: oxidation ↔ Carboxylic acid: reduction
  Monosaccharides: Galactose, Glucose, Fructose
  Ribose, Xylose, Arabinose, Glyceraldehyde

- Non-reducing sugar: Sugar cannot act as a reducing agent and cannot reduce others.
  Polysaccharides, Sucrose, Raffinose, Gentianose

Cf. Benedict test: The reducing sugars that show positive results with Benedict solution.

• **The major dietary carbohydrates**

Sugars	Monosaccharides	Glucose, Galactose, Fructose, Xylose
	Disaccharides	Sucrose, Lactose, Maltose, Isomaltulose, Trehalose
	Polyols	Sorbitol, Mannitol
Oligosaccharides	Malto-oligosaccharides	Maltodextrins
	Other oligosaccharides	Raffinose, Stachyose, Fructo-oligosaccharides
Polysaccharides	Starch	Amylose, Amylopectin, Modified starches
	Non-starch	Glycogen, Cellulose, Hemicellulose, Pectins, Hydrocolloids

Proteins

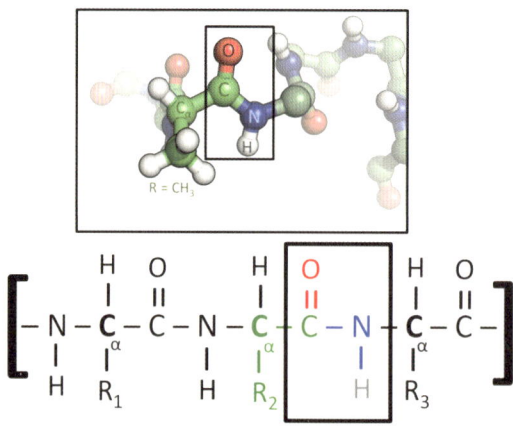

[3-9] Protein

Amino acids based organic compounds
Alpha C + Amino group + Carboxylic acid group + R group (side chain)
Monomer: Amino acid

- Denaturalization of proteins: With changes of heat, pH, chemicals, protein structures are disordered chains are unfolded, make random structures, and break bonds. They lose normal functions.

Functions
- Cell transporters
- Immune function: Antibody, Cytokine, Complement protein
- Cell structure: Cells growth, Cell repair, Cell maintenance (cytoskeleton, collagen)
- Enzymes: Accelerate different chemical reactions in organisms.
- Peptide hormones: Insulin, Glucagon
- Muscle contraction: Actin, Myosin

03　　Organic compounds

Amino acid	Monomer of proteins Consist of carbon, hydrogen, oxygen, and nitrogen - α Carbon: Carbon (+ Amino group + Carboxyl group) - Amino group: Polar, with nitrogen - R group: Side chain (bond to α carbon). It determines the characteristics. - All amino acids have the same amine and COOH, but different R groups. 　→ This classifies the type of amino acid - Peptide bond: Covalent bond between amino acids - Nonpolar: R group - Polar: 　Amino group: N, basic, accepts H^+ ions 　Carboxyl group: —COOH, acidic
Essential amino acid	Animals cannot synthesize essential amino acids → should obtain from the diet Plants and prokaryotes can synthesize.
Peptide bond	Covalent bond between amino acids via condense-dehydration reaction
Polypeptide bond	Proteins consist of 2+ peptide bonds. - One side: Amino group + Carboxyl group - Backbone: Linear, repeating sequence 　(Except R group: R group is not involved in the peptide bond.) - Amino acid sequence: Determines a protein's structure.

[3-10] Amino acid

4 Types of protein structure

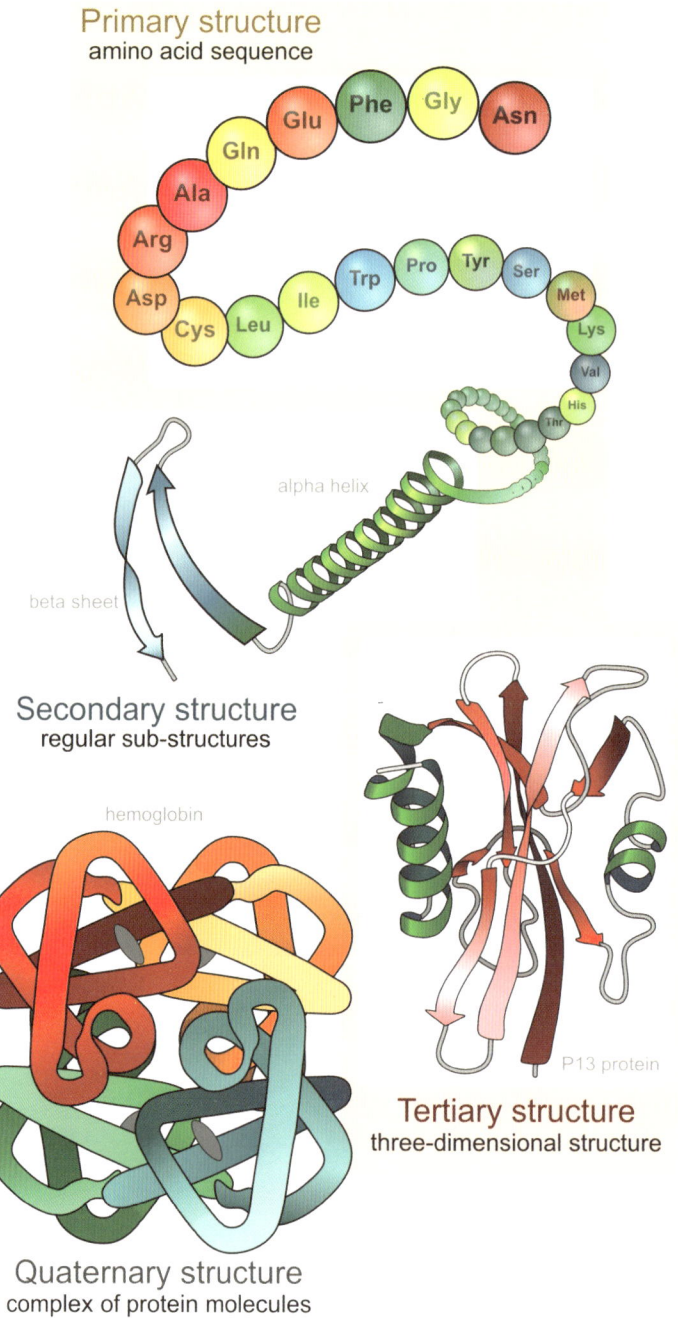

[3-11] 4 Types of protein structure

03 Organic compounds

Primary	Secondary	Tertiary	Quaternary
Simple, Linear	Highly regular	Interactions among side chains (R group)	Multiple polypeptide chains together (2'+3' structures)
Amino acid sequence gene instructor	• **α-helix** Helical coil Hydrogen bond Fibrous proteins Elasticity, bookable, reform Ex) Wool, Skin, Hair, Nail • **β-pleated sheet** Zigzag structure Different polypeptide chains Foldable, strong, flexible Not elastic Pleats distance fixed Ex) Silk	3-D structure Hydrophobic Hydrophilic Interactions Hydrophobic interaction Hydrophilic interaction Ionic bond H-bond Dipole-dipole London dispersion force Disulfide covalent bonds: Strong, stabilize Molecules in the external environment	Ionic bond H-bond Dipole-dipole London dispersion force Disulfide covalent bond
Insulin, Glucagon	Keratin Skin, Hair, Nail	Enzymes Globular protein Myoglobin Transport protein	Hemoglobin Collagen Antibody (Immunoglobulin)

Nucleic acids

Macromolecules composed of nucleotides, which are the monomers made of three components: Alpha 5-carbon sugar, a phosphate group, and a nitrogenous base.
Monomer: Nucleotide

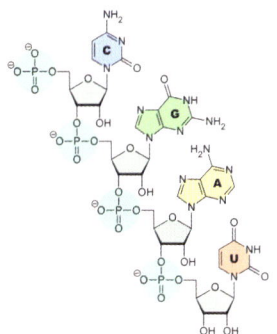

Functions
 - DNA: Transmits genetic information
 - RNA: Protein synthesis
 - ATP (Adenosine triphosphate): Adenine + Ribose + 3 phosphates
    Transfers chemical energy to other molecules
 - cAMP(cyclic Adenosine monophosphate): Cell secondary messenger transmits information

[3-12] Nucleic acid

- Structure: CHO + N + P
  CHO: 5C sugar (Deoxyribose, Ribose)
  P: Phosphate
  N: Nitrogenous base

- Backbone (CHOP): 5-Carbon sugar + Phosphate group (phosphodiester bond)
- Ring: Nitrogenous base

• DNA, RNA

	DNA (Deoxyribonucleic acid)	**RNA** (Ribonucleic acid)
Function	Store genetic information for protein synthesis	Transfer genetic information for protein synthesis from DNA
	In the nucleus and mitochondria	In the nucleus and mitochondria
Structure	Double-strands, helix	Single-strand, helix
	Backbone: 5-Carbon sugar + Phosphate group (phosphodiester bond)	
5C sugar	Deoxyribose	Ribose
	+ Phosphate group	
	Nitrogenous base	
	Hydrogen bond (complementary bond)	
Pyrimidines	Cytosine Thymine	Cytosine Uracil
Purines	Guanine Adenine	Guanine Adenine
Pairs	Cytosine-Guanine (3 H-bonds) Thymine-Adenine (2 H-bonds)	Cytosine-Guanine (3 H-bonds) Uracil-Adenine (2 H-bonds)

03 Organic compounds

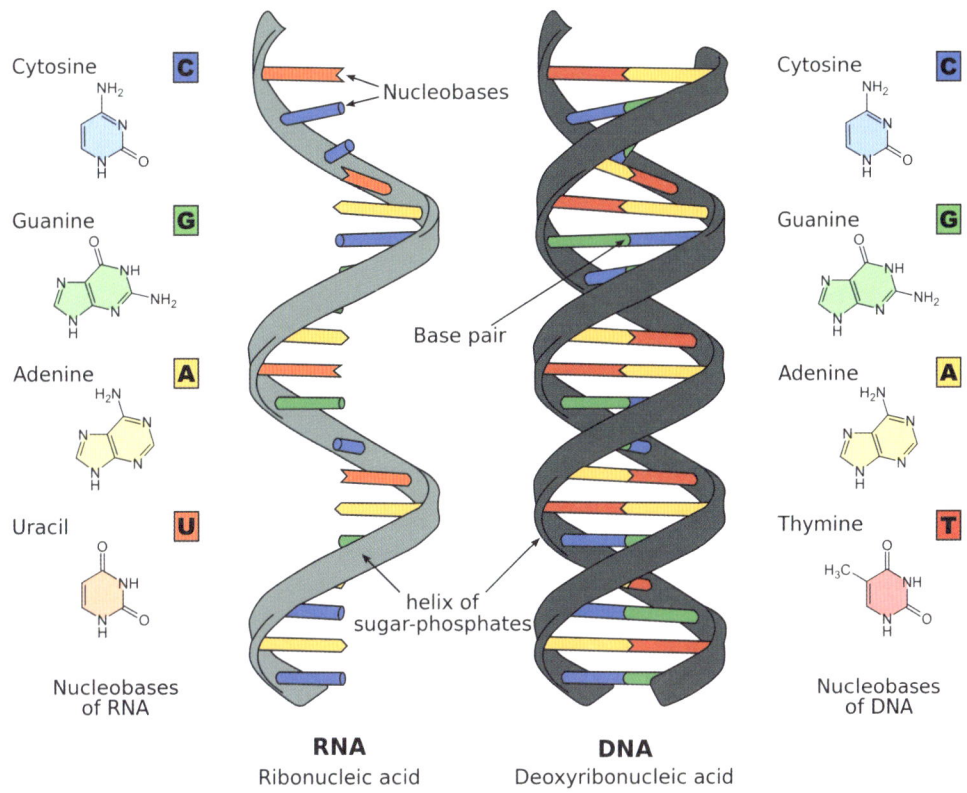

[3-13] DNA, RNA

chapter 04 DNA replication, Protein synthesis

DNA replication

The process by which a double-stranded DNA molecule is copied to produce two identical DNA molecules.
Semi-conservative process: Half strand is from the original strand, and the other half strand is newly replicated.
Bidirectional process: Both strands are synthesized in opposite directions.

• Process: Unwind → Replication → Termination

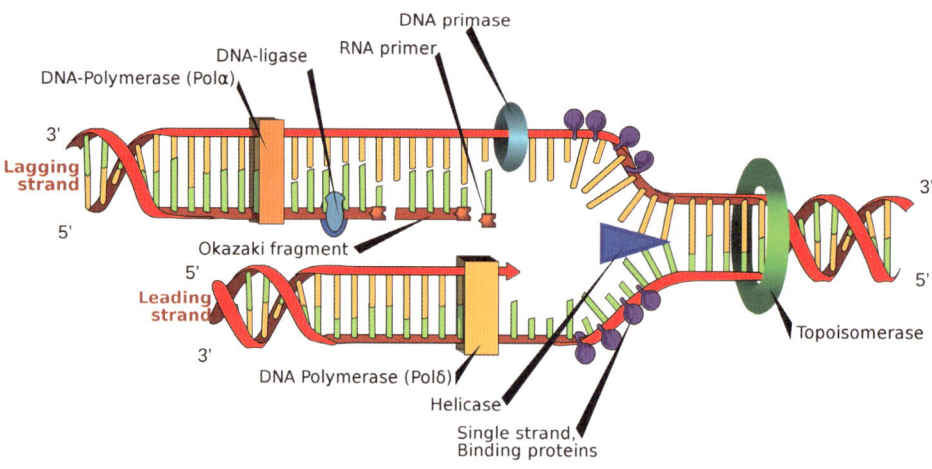

[4-1] DNA replication

04   DNA replication, Protein synthesis

Unwind

1. Helicase: Unwinds the double-helix.
→ Forms 'Replication fork (origin of replication)'
Unwinding double-helix: Positive supercoils, stress ↑

- Eukaryotes: Have multiple origins.
- Prokaryotes: Have a single origin.

2. SSB protein (Single-strand binding protein): Attaches to the single strand. Stabilizes the single-helix.

3. Gyrase (Topoisomerase): Helps helicase to reduce stress and distinguish bacteria and DNA.

4. Primase: Synthesizes RNA primer.

Replication (Leading strand)

1. RNA primer: Adds the 1st nucleotide. (checks starting point)

2. DNA polymerase
Reads: 3' → 5' parent strand
Makes: 5' → 3' daughter strand (Leading strand)

Adds nucleotides in the sequence.
Synthesis direction: 5' → 3' (same in both RNA and DNA synthesis)

Replication (Lagging strand)

1. RNA primer: Goes as far as possible and adds the 1st nucleotide. (checks starting point)

2. DNA polymerase
Reads: 5' → 3' parent strand
Makes: 5' → 3' daughter strand (Lagging strand)

Adds nucleotides piece by piece.
Because the parent strand reading direction is the same as the daughter strand, it makes fragments on the lagging strand, which is called as 'Okazaki fragment.'

- RNA primer goes as far as possible → DNA polymerase synthesizes
  5' → 3' + makes Okazaki fragment → RNA primer goes as far as possible
  → DNA polymerase synthesizes 5' → 3' + makes Okazaki fragment

The lagging strand synthesis is slower than the leading strand synthesis.

3. Ligase: Glues the Okazaki fragments.

Termination

1. Error fixing
2. RNA primer: Removed and replaced with DNA.

Protein synthesis

The process in which cells make proteins, participating with DNA and three RNAs.
• Process: Transcription → Post-transcription → Translation

• **RNA**
Nucleic acid, single strand with DNA's gene information
RNAs are synthesized in the transcription process: mRNA, tRNA, rRNA

Why use RNA in protein synthesis?
- DNA is more stable than RNA: Useful for keeping genetic information safely.
- Less damaging or mutating DNA

• **RNA types**

mRNA (messenger RNA)	A single strand, which is shorter than DNA strands and has codons. Nucleotide replacement: Thymine (DNA) is replaced → Uracil
	
	Codon
	A three nucleotides sequence (triplet) present on mRNA for translation.
	Genetic codes
	Gives coding instructions.
	Complementary to anticodons
	
	- Start codons: AUG
	- Stop codons: UAA, UGA, UAG
	
	- Eukaryotes: mRNA encodes a single polypeptide chain.
	- Prokaryotes: mRNA encodes multiple polypeptide chains.
	
	- Process: Synthesized in the nucleus → goes out into the plasma
	   → + Ribosome → Translation (tRNA, anticodons, amino acids)
	   → forms polypeptides chains → synthesizes proteins

tRNA (transfer RNA)	Anticodon + Amino acid Amino acids: Become polypeptide chains to proteins. The first amino acid is Methionine. Anticodon A three nucleotides sequence (triplet) present on tRNA, which binds to the complementary sequence present on mRNA. - Process: 1 Amino acid + Anticodon (3 nucleotides) → attach to mRNA → Translation (encoding) → Multiple amino acids → Polypeptide chain
rRNA (ribosomal RNA)	rRNA + Proteins → form a Ribosome Provides a site for polypeptide synthesis. It aligns the amino acids up in the correct orientation to synthesize proteins.

Transcription

The process of translating the sequence of a messenger RNA (mRNA) molecule to a sequence of amino acids during protein synthesis.

- Location: Nucleus
- Gene expression: Copy DNA's gene sequence and make RNA. (mRNA, tRNA, rRNA)
- DNA (nucleotides) + RNA (nucleotides): Easy to transcribe, no need to translate or codons.
- Prokaryotes translate mRNA as soon as it is transcribed by RNA polymerase.

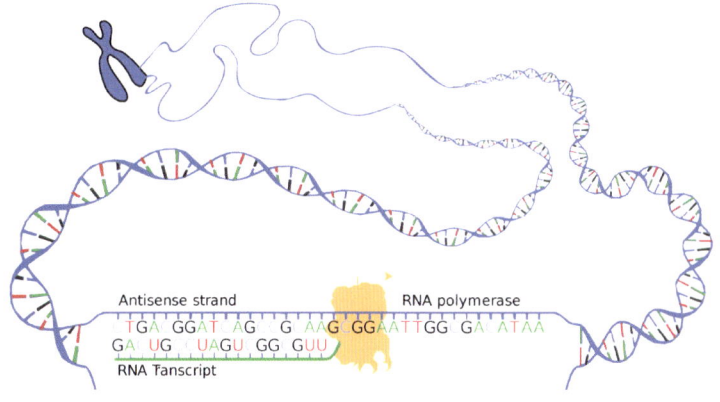

[4-2] Transcription

Initiation	1. Initiation factor: Checks Initiation point, makes the 'Promoter region.' - Promoter region: Synthesizes region, Nucleotides sequence 2. RNA polymerase: Binds to the promoter region and unwinds DNA double-helix.
Elongation	1. RNA polymerase makes bubbles. 2. Reads: 3' → 5' DNA coding strand (sense strand) Makes: 5' → 3' mRNA template strand (antisense strand) → synthesize mRNA
Termination	1. RNA polymerase terminates transcription. 2. After transcription, DNA reassociates and forms its original structure.

Post-transcription

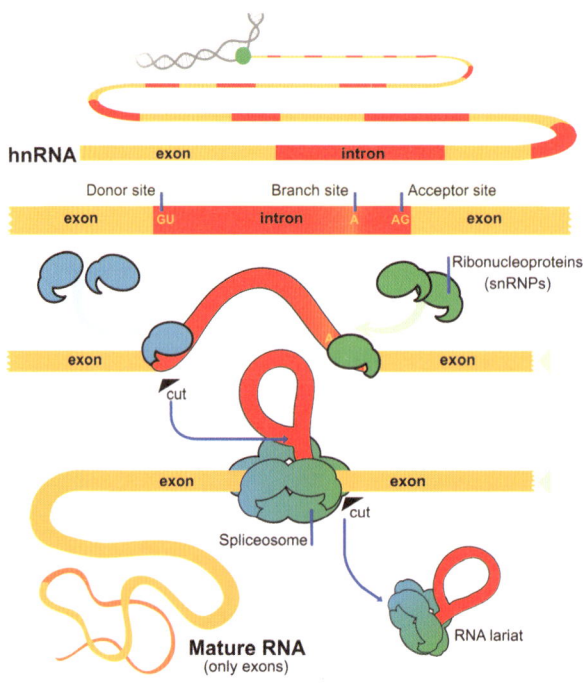

[4-3] Splicing exons

5' Methyl cap	7-methylguanosine cap added to the 5' end of mRNA. Regulation of nuclear export Prevention of degradation by exonucleases Promotion of translation Stabilizing
3' Poly A tail	Adenosine added to the 3' end of mRNA. Stabilizing Prevention of degradation
Splicing exons	Cut the introns and splice them together with the exons. - Exons: Protein coding region (encode genetic information) - Intron: Non-coding region (encode nothing)

→ mRNA, rRNA, tRNA go out of the nucleus → to the plasma
→ ready for the protein synthesis

Translation

The process by which a cell makes proteins with mRNA, rRNA, tRNA.
- DNA (nucleotides) + RNA (nucleotides): Easy to transcribe, no need to translate and encode.
- RNA (nucleotides) + Protein (amino acids): Needs encoding (codon + anticodon)

• **Ribosome**
rRNA + Protein
Organelle which is involved in the process of making proteins.
Small subunit + Large subunit
Can be found floating freely in the cytoplasm or attached to the rough endoplasmic reticulum.

- Svedberg units: How fast a particle of given size and shape settles to the bottom of a solution.

	Small subunit	Large subunit	Combination
Eukaryotes	40S	60S	80S
Prokaryotes	30S	50S	70S

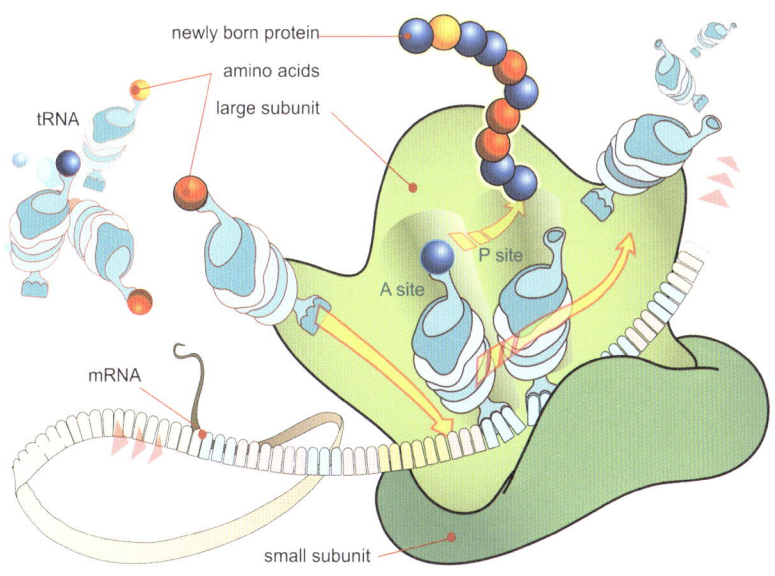

[4-4] Translation

Initiation	Location: Cytoplasm 1. Initiation factor: Helps ribosomal small unit + large unit bind to mRNA Interacts with repressors to slow down or to prevent translation. 2. Ribosomal small unit + large unit binding 3. Ribosome: Binds to mRNA (5'-3') start codon. - Start codon: 5'-AUG-3' 4. tRNA: Binds to the start codon (complementary to anticodon: 5'-UAC-3') + Methionine (the first amino acid) - tRNA synthetase: Helps tRNA can bind to proper amino acids.

Elongation	Addition of amino acids → formation of peptide chains
	
	1. Ribosome: Provides binding sites for amino acids.
	
	2. Encoding: Anticodon (tRNA) + Codon (mRNA) → Amino acid
	→ Polypeptide chains → Proteins
	
	- Binding sites
	  P-site (Peptidyl): Put Methionine (1st amino acid)
	  A-site (Aminoacyl): Amino acids binding → forms polypeptide chains
	  E-site (Exit): RNA goes out

Termination	1. Ribosome: Binds to mRNA stop codon. - Stop codons: UAA, UGA, UAG 2. Release factor: Comes instead of tRNA, binds on E-site. No encoding, No amino acid Ribosome releases the polypeptide chain → Proteins 3. Maturation: At the rough endoplasmic reticulum

chapter 05
Cell division

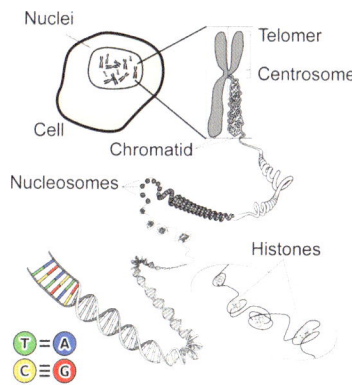

Organisms do cell division for growth and development through mitosis.
For reproduction, cell division transfers the genetic materials of organisms to their offspring through meiosis.

[5-1] Chromosome

Nucleotide ⇩⇩⇩	Basic unit (monomer) of nucleic acids Hydrolysis: Phosphate group + Nucleosides Composition: Phosphate + 5C sugar + Base
Nucleic acid	Polymer of nucleotide
Histone protein	Histone + packaging DNA → Nucleosome
Nucleosome ⇩⇩⇩	147 base pairs of DNA sequence + wrapping around 8 histone proteins It prevents DNA from tangling.
Chromatin ⇩⇩⇩	Basic unit of chromosomes DNA + Histone proteins

Chromatid Chromosome	Chromatins condensation (DNA + Histone protein) → Chromatid/Chromosome
	Contains gene information
	In the nucleus
	
	- Chromatid: DNA condensation
	- Chromosome: Chromatid → stable structure
	  Only in eukaryotes nucleus (prokaryotes: nucleoid)
	  Mitochondria: Circular DNA (not a chromosome form)
	
	- Haploid cell: n, 1 chromosome (meiosis, gametes)
	- Diploid cell: 2n, 2 chromosomes in a pair (mitosis, zygotes)

- Scaffold protein: Nonhistone protein
- Telomer: End of a chromosome. Telomeres are made of repetitive sequences of non-coding DNA that protect the chromosome from damage. Each time a cell divides, the telomeres become shorter. Eventually, the telomeres become so short that the cell can no longer divide.

Cell cycle

Cf. Prokaryotes: Binary fission
   (Prokaryotes produce new individuals genetically identical to the parent organism.)

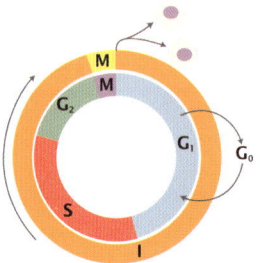

[5-2] Cell cycle

• Interphase
Most of the cell cycle
Preparatory phase, DNA duplication, Histone protein synthesis, Organelles duplication
Phase: G1 phase → S phase → G2 phase → M phase

• M phase
Cell division phase
Phase: Mitosis (cell growth, cell repair), Meiosis (reproduction)

- Parent cell: 2n (both mitosis, meiosis)
   # Chromosomes: 46
   # Chromatids: 92

	Mitosis	Prophase	Metaphase	Anaphase	Telophase	Cytokinesis
Interphase	2n					2n / 2n
	Meiosis 1	PMAT	Cytokinesis	Meiosis 2	PMAT	Cytokinesis
	2n		n / n			n / n / n / n

Interphase

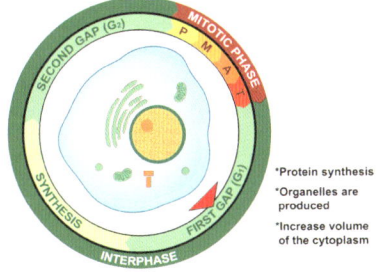

- **G1 phase** (Gap)
Cell growth, Organelles replication, Microtubules replication

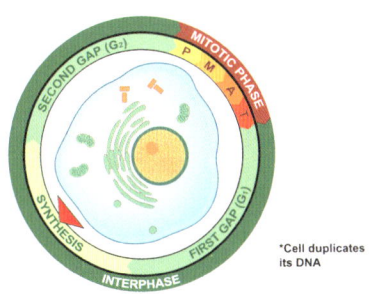

- **S phase** (Synthesis)
Replication: DNA (nucleus, homologous pairs), Chromosomes, Centrioles, Sister chromatids, Histone proteins

  - Chromosome (chromatids) replication
    → 2 sister chromatids

  46 original chromatids + 46 replicated chromatids → 92 sister chromatids (46 chromosomes)

  - Cohesin: Holds 2 sister chromatids

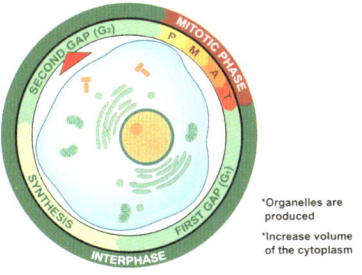

- **G2 phase**
Cell grows more
More proteins, organelles
Microtubules synthesis, grow

  - MPF (Maturation promoting factor): Regulates the passage of a cell from G2 phase to M phase

[5-3] G1 phase, [5-4] S phase, [5-5] G2 phase

Mitosis

Cell division for cell growth and repair.
Makes 2 identical diploid cells.
Skin cells, stomach cells: constantly dividing ↔ Nerve cells: no cell division

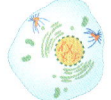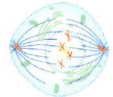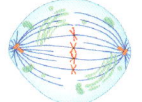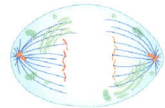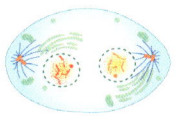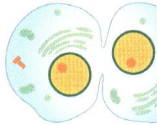

[5-6] Mitosis

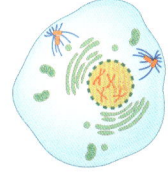

2n
#C: 46
#T: 92

- **Interphase**
DNA replication
46 original chromatids + 46 replicated chromatids = 92 sister chromatids

---

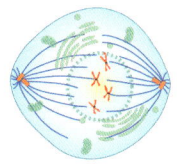

2n
#C: 46
#T: 92

- **Prophase**
Centrioles → go to opposite sites
→ form spindle bodies (spindle apparatus)

Nucleus, Nuclear membrane → gone
Chromosomes condense → become visible

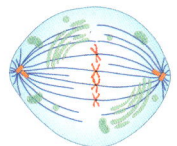

2n
#C: 46
#T: 92

- **Metaphase**
Chromosomes → go to the middle
Spindle fibers bind to centromeres (kinetochores)

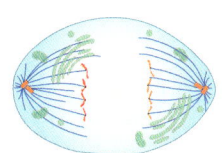

2n x 2
#C: 92
#T: 92

- **Anaphase**
Disjunction: Spindle fibers pull the sister chromatids → separated
→ go to the opposite ends

Sister chromatids separation
Form daughter chromosomes

05 Cell division

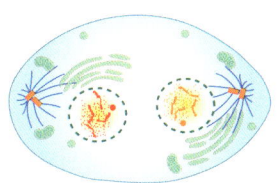

2n × 2
#C: 92
#T: 92

• **Telophase**
Each cell contains identical chromosomes
Nucleus, Nuclear membrane → reform around the chromosomes

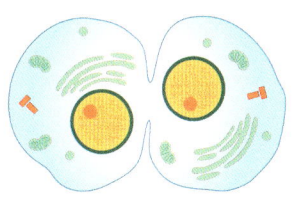

2n × 2
#C: 46
#T: 46

• **Cytokinesis**
Nuclear envelopment forms
Redistribute organelles

Final products
2 × 2n (diploid cells)
Genetically identical daughter chromosomes

[5-7] Interphase, [5-8] Prophase, [5-9 Metaphase], [5-10] Anaphase, [5-11] Telophase, [5-12] Cytokinesis

#C: Number of chromosomes
#T: Number of chromatids

Meiosis

Cell division for sexual reproduction process, forming gametes. (egg, sperm)
Makes 4 genetically different haploid cells. (2n → 4 × n)

- Gamete: Haploid (n), has a single set of unpaired chromosomes.
   Ex) Egg cell, Sperm cell
- Zygote: Diploid (2n), contains two complete sets of chromosomes, one from each parent.
   Ex) Fertilized egg

Meiosis 1: Genetic recombination, makes 2 genetically different haploid cells. (2n → n × 2)
Meiosis 2: Sister chromatids separation, makes 4 genetically different haploid daughter cells. (n × 2 → n × 4)
→ Meiosis (1+2): 1 zygote → 4 genetically unique haploid cells (2n → n × 4)

• **Meiosis 1**
Genetic recombination, makes 2 genetically different haploid cells. (2n → n × 2)

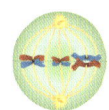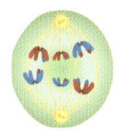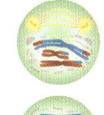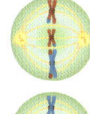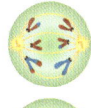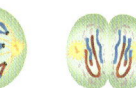

[5-13] Meiosis

2n
#C: 46
#T: 92

- **Interphase**
DNA replication
46 original chromatids + 46 replicated chromatids
= 92 sister chromatids

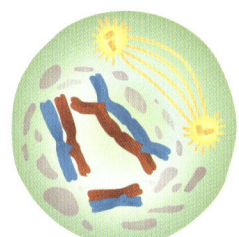

2n
#C: 46
#T: 92

- **Prophase 1**
Centrioles → go to opposite sites
→ form spindle bodies (spindle apparatus)

Nucleus, Nuclear membrane → gone
Chromosomes condense → become visible

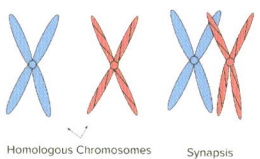

1) **Synapsis**
Pairing of homologous chromosomes
(homologous pair)

2) **Crossing over**
Genetic recombination
Recombination of non-sister chromatids
Exchange genetic materials for genetic diversity.
Each sister chromatid is genetically unique, not identical.
  - Tetrad: 4 sister chromatids are visible
  - Chiasma: Gene exchange region

3) **New homologous chromosomes**
  - The law of segregation: The parental genes must separate randomly and equally, so there is an equal chance of the offspring inheriting
    → genetic diversity to offspring

  - The law of independent assortment: The alleles from parents are passed on independently to the offspring

05 Cell division

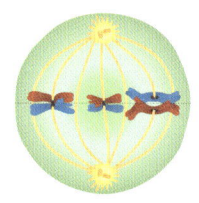

2n
#C: 46
#T: 92

- **Metaphase 1**
Spindle fibers bind to centromeres (kinetochores) of the tetrads: Human 23 tetrads

Tetrads go to the center
Homologous chromosomes line up

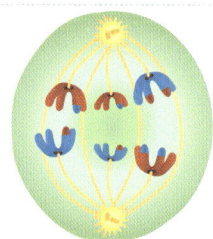

2n
#C: 46
#T: 92

- **Anaphase 1**
Disjunction: Chromosome tetrads are separated → go to opposite sites, bind to centrioles

Tetrad separation: Still sister chromatids are together

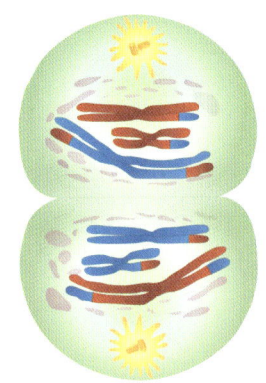

n x 2
#C: 23
#T: 46

- **Telophase 1**
Nucleus, Nuclear membrane → reform around the chromosomes

- **Cytokinesis 1**
Nuclear envelopment forms
Redistribute organelles
Create haploid cells (n)

Final products
Genetic recombination
2 genetically different haploid daughter chromosomes: 2n → n x 2 (sister chromatids)

[5-14.1] Prophase 1, [5-14.2] Synapsis, [5-15] Metaphase 1
[5-16] Anaphase 1, [5-17] Telophase 1, Cytokinesis 1

#C: Number of chromosomes
#T: Number of chromatids

- **Meiosis 2**

Sister chromatids separate. Make 4 genetically different haploid daughter cells.
No Interphase.

n x 2
#C: 23
#T: 46

- **Prophase 2**
Centrioles → go to opposite sites
→ form spindle bodies (spindle apparatus)

Nucleus, Nuclear membrane → gone
Chromosomes condense → become visible

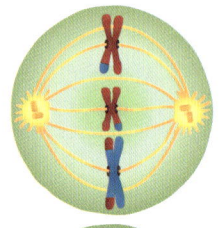
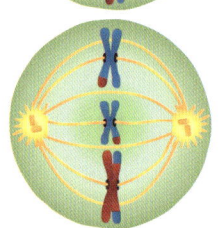

n x 2
#C: 23
#T: 46

- **Metaphase 2**
Chromosomes → go to the middle
Spindle fibers bind to centromeres (kinetochores)

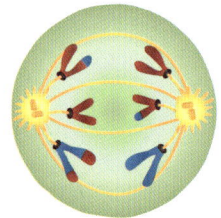
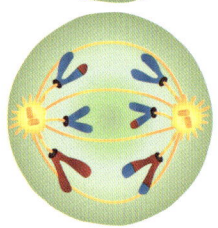

2n x 2
#C: 46
#T: 46

- **Anaphase 2**
Disjunction: Spindle fibers pull chromosomes (not homologous) → separated → go to the opposite ends, bind to centrioles

Sister chromatids separation

05 Cell division

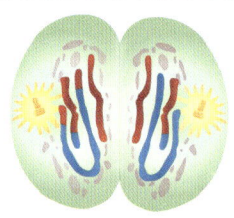

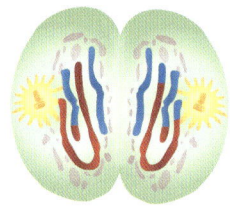

n x 4
#C: 23
#T: 23

• **Telophase 2**
Nucleus, Nuclear membrane → reform around the chromosomes

• **Cytokinesis 2**
Nuclear envelopment forms
Redistribute organelles

Final products
Genetically different 4 daughter chromosomes
4 x n (haploid cells)
Genetic diversity

[5-18] Prophase 2, [5-19] Metaphase 2, [5-20] Anaphase 2, [5-21] Telophase 2, Cytokinesis 2

#C: Number of chromosomes
#T: Number of chromatids

Mitosis vs. Meiosis

Mitosis	Meiosis
Make 2 identical diploids	Make 4 genetically different haploids
Interphase: 46 chromatid replication → 46 chromosomes (2 sister chromatids each)	Interphase: 46 chromatid replication → 46 chromosomes (2 sister chromatids each) Meiosis 2: No interphase
2n → 2n	2n → n x 2 → n x 4
1 nuclear division	2 nuclears division
Somatic cells: Nail cells, Stomach cells, Skin cells	Gametes, Sexual reproduction

Homologous pairs vs. Sister chromatids

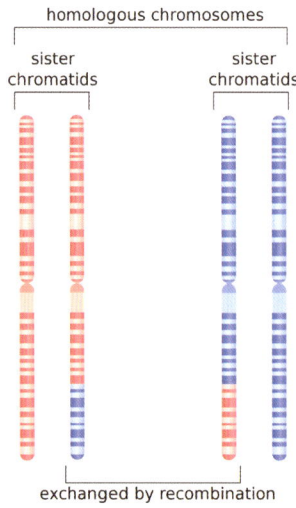

[5-22] Homologous chromosomes and sister chromatids

Homologous pairs	Sister chromatids
Somatic cells 22 homologous autonomal chromosome pairs + 2 sex chromosomes (X,Y)	
Prophase 1 (Meiosis)	**Interphase - S Phase** (Mitosis, Meiosis)
Chromosomes → Synapse → Homologous pair (tetrad)	Chromosomes are copied → Sister chromatids 1 chromatid → 1 chromosome (2 sister chromatids)
Not identical (1 from mom, 1 from dad) Same type information	2 identical chromatids
Not held together by centromere	Held together by centromere (cohesion)
Different alleles	Same alleles

Asexual reproduction

Single parent splits.
Genes and inherited traits are like the parent.
   Ex) Hydra, Paramecium, Starfish, Planaria, Mint plants

Nondisjunction

A pair of homologous chromosomes has failed to separate or segregate at anaphase so that both chromosomes of the pair pass to the same daughter cell.

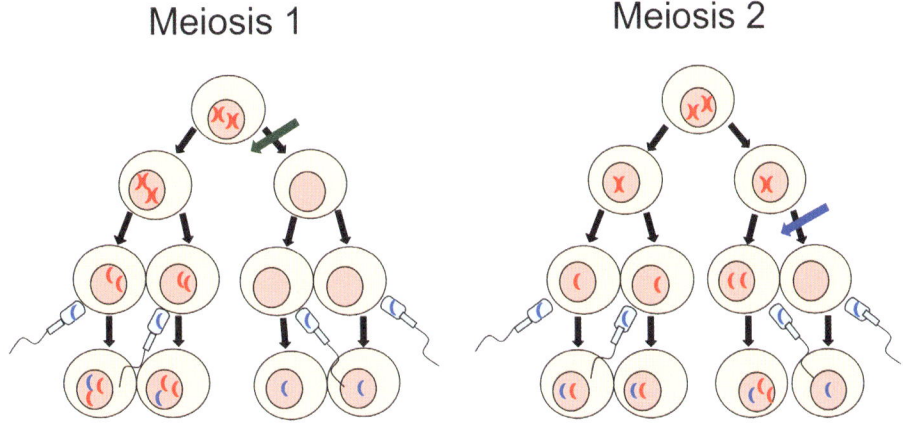

[5-23] Chromosomes nondisjunction

- Meiosis 1: Homologous pair nondisjunction
- Chromosomes: n+1, n+1, n-1, n-1

- Meiosis 2: Sister chromatids nondisjunction
- Chromosomes: n+1, n-1, n, n (2 normal)

- **Nondisjunction disease**

Disease	Factor
Colorblindness	X-linked recessive disease
Hemophilia A, B	X-linked recessive disease
Duchenne muscular dystrophy	X-linked recessive disease
Turner syndrome	One X chromosome is missing
Klinefelter syndrome	A boy with an extra X chromosome
Sickle-cell anemia	Autosomal recessive disease
Phenylketonuria	Autosomal recessive disease
Huntington's disease	Autosomal dominant disease
Patau's syndrome	Chromosome 13 trisomy
Edwards syndrome	Chromosome 18 trisomy
Down syndrome	Chromosome 21 trisomy

chapter 06
Inheritance

A process that involves the passing of genetic property from one generation to another.

True breeding (pureblood)	The offspring will show consistent, replicable, and predictable characteristics of their parents.
Phenotype	What an organism actually looks like. (a set of observable and physical traits)
Genotype	Genetic constitution (a set of genes) Genotype can help determine phenotypes.
Gene	DNA segment codes for a protein used to express that trait.
Locus (Loci)	Specific location on a chromosome that contains a gene for some trait.
Allele	A pair of genes that codes for similar polypeptides. (genetic information) Expresses the same trait. Between homologous chromosomes A specific location in chromosomes An allele's property is related to another allele. For any trait, there are 2 homologous alleles for expressing the trait.
Somatic cell	Body cell Diploid (2n), 46 chromosomes 44 autosomal chromosomes + 2 sex chromosomes (XX or XY)
Gamete	Sex cell Haploid (n), 23 chromosomes 22 autosomal chromosomes + 1 sex chromosome (X or Y)
Zygote	Gamete (from mom) + Gamete (from dad) → Fertilization → Zygote (embryo) Ex) Human: Male gamete (sperm) 23 chromosomes (haploid) + Female gamete (egg) 23 chromosomes (haploid) = 46 chromosomes (Fertilized egg, diploid)

[6-1] Allele

• **Human chromosomes**

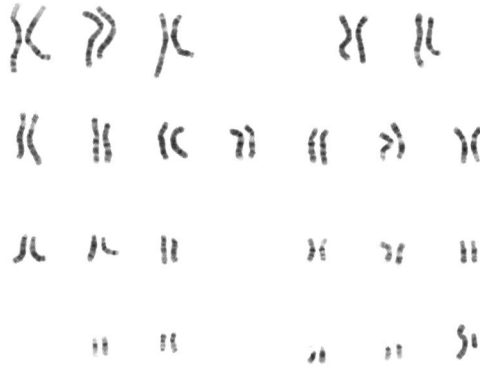

[6-2] Human chromosome

46 chromosomes (23 homologous pairs per 1 somatic cell)

= 44 autosomal homologous chromosomes
  + 2 sex chromosomes (XX or XY)

Mendel's laws

Laws about how genes are inherited by offspring.

• **Law of dominance**
There are 2 genotypes: Dominant, Recessive
The presence of a dominant allele will always mask the presence of a recessive allele.

• **Law of segregation**
During meiosis, each gamete has one gene separately.

• **Law of independent assortment**
Each gene is independently, randomly received, and does not affect each other.

06　Inheritance

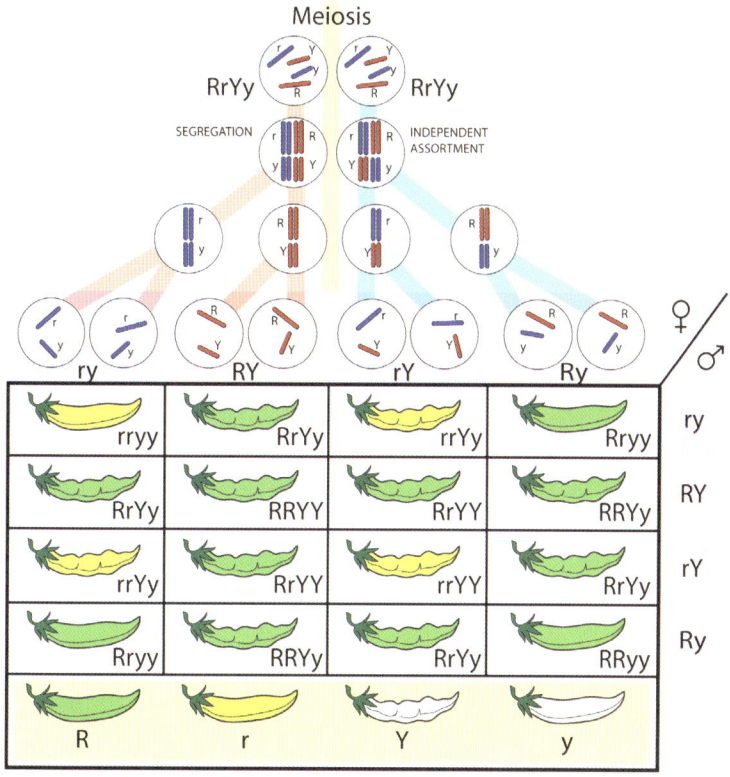

[6-3] Mendel's law

Homozygous, Heterozygous

For any trait, 2 homologous alleles code for proteins that express the trait.

Homozygous	Heterozygous
TT, tt	Tt
2 alleles are identical for this locus	2 different alleles for this locus
TT: Both dominant tt: Both recessive	One dominant, another recessive
	1 allele is dominant → Phenotype is dominant

Exceptions to Mendel's laws

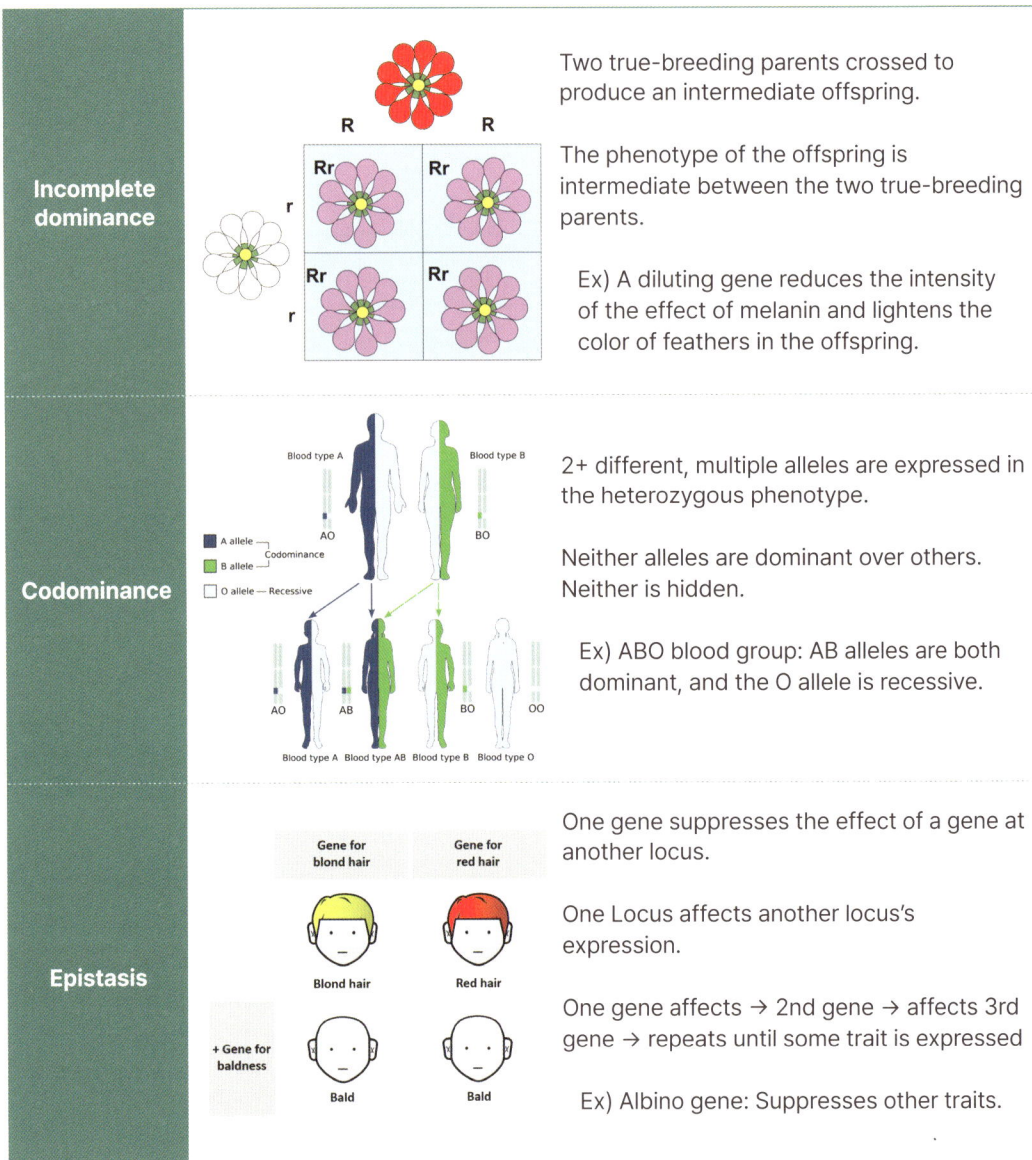

Incomplete dominance

Two true-breeding parents crossed to produce an intermediate offspring.

The phenotype of the offspring is intermediate between the two true-breeding parents.

Ex) A diluting gene reduces the intensity of the effect of melanin and lightens the color of feathers in the offspring.

Codominance

2+ different, multiple alleles are expressed in the heterozygous phenotype.

Neither alleles are dominant over others. Neither is hidden.

Ex) ABO blood group: AB alleles are both dominant, and the O allele is recessive.

Epistasis

One gene suppresses the effect of a gene at another locus.

One Locus affects another locus's expression.

One gene affects → 2nd gene → affects 3rd gene → repeats until some trait is expressed

Ex) Albino gene: Suppresses other traits.

06 Inheritance

Pleiotropy

Genotype

Phenotype

A single gene influences two or more unrelated phenotypic traits.

Ex) Phenylketonuria: Causes amino acids to increase in the amount in the body.

Polygenic inheritance

Many genes (alleles) have an additive effect on a single phenotypic trait.
Additive effect: 2+ alleles are combined, showing their individual effects.

Ex) Skin. Eye color, Height, Intelligence, Depression

Norm of reaction

Range of phenotype expression of a genotype in various environments.

Ex) Siamese cats: Different colors according to different temperatures

[6-4] Incomplete dominance, [6-5] Codominance, [6-6] Epistasis
[6-7] Pleiotropy, [6-8] Norm of reaction

Punnett square, Test cross

A tool to determine genotype. See potential genotypes of offspring in a given cross.

• Monohybrid cross
A cross between two organisms with different variations at one genetic locus of interest.

[6-9] Punnett square

• Dihybrid cross
A cross between two individuals with two observed traits controlled by two distinct genes.

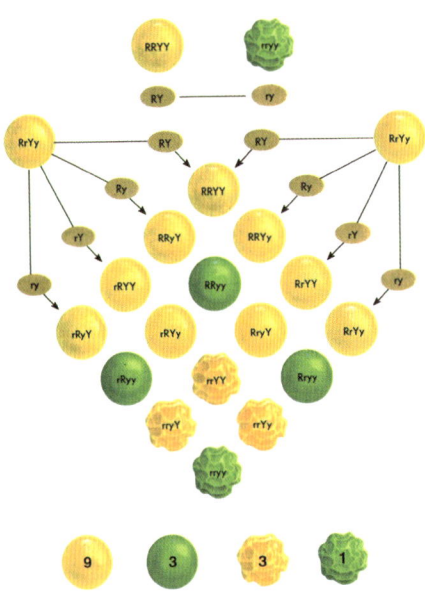

[6-10] Dihybrid cross

Rules of probability

• **Product rule**
Product rule: Possibility A x Possibility B
Probability of 2+ independent events occurring is equal to the products of their individual probabilities.

- 2 events are independent if the occurrence of one does not affect the occurrence of the other. 2 events are independent, one and the other.
  Ex) Gender of the 1st child does not affect the gender of the 2nd child.

• **Sum rule**
Sum rule: Possibility A + Possibility B
Probability of 2+ mutually exclusive events occurring equals the sum of their individual probabilities.

- 2 events are mutually exclusive if the occurrence of one event prevents the occurrence of the other.
  Ex) Having a boy is mutually exclusive to having a girl.

Linked genes

Genes that are likely to be inherited together because they are physically close to one another on the same chromosome during meiosis prophase 1.
Gametes are different after meiosis because of crossing over.

- Crossing over: Genetic materials exchange during meiosis 1. (prophase 1)
- Synapsis: In prophase 1, sister chromatids exchange genetic information.
- Genetic recombination: Genetic variety, does not make identical chromosomes.
  Ex) Offspring's fingerprints ≠ Parents' fingerprints

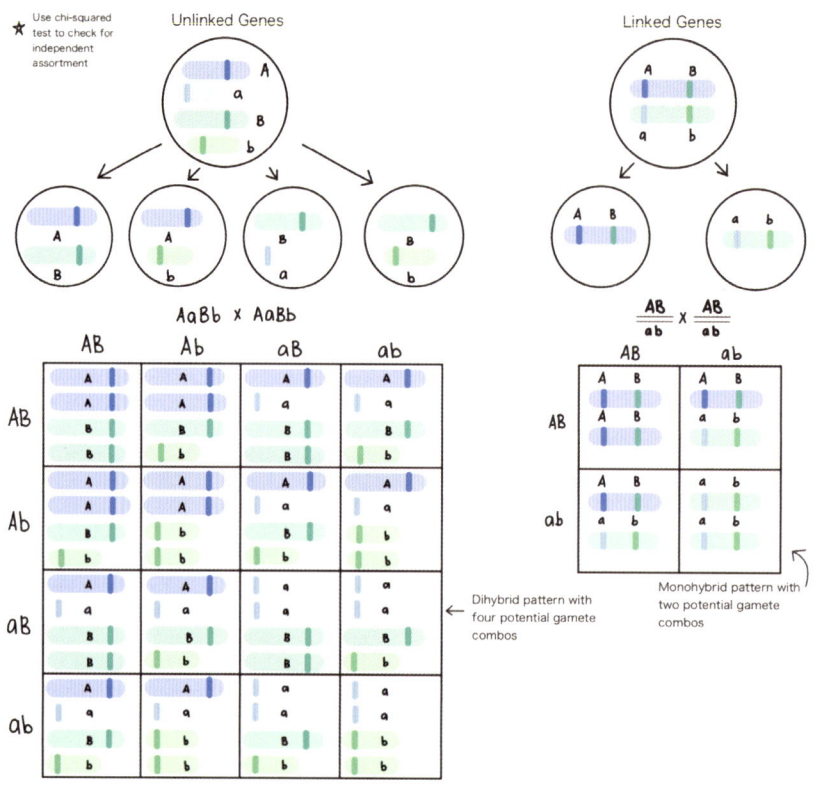

[6-11] Linked genes

Unlinked gene	Linked gene
Loci far apart	Loci close together
Inherited independently because loci are located far apart on the same chromosome, or on different chromosomes altogether.	Inherited together due to their loci being close. Inhibits independent assortment.

Sex chromosomes

A type of chromosome that participates in sex determination.
Sex chromosomes determine the gender.
Types: Chromosome X, Chromosome Y

- Female mammals: 2X chromosomes
- Male mammals: X chromosome + Y chromosome

06 Inheritance

- Ova (egg cell): One X chromosome
- Sperm: One X chromosome, or one Y chromosome

Cf. Autosomal chromosomes (Autosomes): Chromosomes except for sex chromosomes.
   Human: Autosomal chromosomes (22 pairs) + Sex chromosomes (XX or XY)
   = 23 pairs (46 chromosomes)

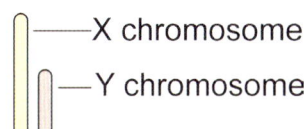

[6-12] Sex chromosomes

X chromosome	Y chromosome
Female mammals	Male mammals
Size identical	Y chromosome is shorter Y determines the gender
X-linked genes Make genes necessary for both genders	A few genes for males
Homozygous dominant Homozygous recessive	Hemizygous Y is shorter than X
Female individual Egg cell: X (100%)	Male individual Sperm cell: X or Y
Egg cell x Sperm cell (X) = XX zygote Egg cell x Sperm cell (Y) = XY zygote	

• **Dosage compensation** (X Inactivation)
X chromosome has vital proteins to make genes. A Female has 2X chromosomes, whereas a male has 1X chromosome. So, one of the copies of the X chromosome is inactivated in female mammals for equilibrium with the Y chromosome.
X chromosomes inactivation occurs randomly in female cells during development.

- Barr body: Inactive X chromosome. Female has one Barr body per cell.
  Ex) Colorblindness (X recessive diseases):
  Mom has the symptom (Xx) → Son has the symptom (xY)

Chromosomal disease

X-linked disease	Colorblindness: X-linked recessive disease Hemophilia A, B: X-linked recessive disease Duchenne muscular dystrophy: X-linked recessive disease Turner syndrome: One X chromosome is missing Klinefelter syndrome: A boy with an extra X chromosome
Autosomal disease	Sickle-cell anemia: Autosomal recessive disease Phenylketonuria: Autosomal recessive disease Huntington's disease: Autosomal dominant disease Patau's syndrome: Chromosome 13 trisomy Edwards syndrome: Chromosome 18 trisomy Down syndrome: Chromosome 21 trisomy

Operon

Genetic regulatory system found in bacteria and their viruses in which genes are coding for functionally related proteins are clustered along with the DNA.

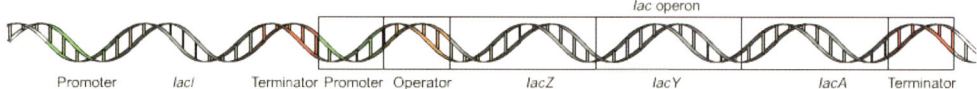

[6-13] Lac operon

- Prokaryotic operons: Generation of polycistronic mRNA
- Eukaryotic operons: Generation of monocistronic mRNA

- E.coli DNA: The Escherichia coli chromosome or nucleoid is composed of the genomic DNA, RNA, and protein. The nucleoid forms by condensation and functional arrangement of a single chromosomal DNA with the help of chromosomal architectural proteins, RNA molecules, and DNA supercoiling.

Genetic equilibrium (Hardy-Weinberg)

A principle that genetic variation in a population will remain constant from one generation to the next without disturbing factors.
A population's allele and genotype frequencies are constant between generations, without evolutionary forces.

• **Population** (Gene pool)
Total genetic diversity (alleles) in a species population
The same species can breed each other and have fertile offspring.

• **Genetic equilibrium conditions**
1) No natural selection
2) No mutation
3) No migration: No allele exchange
4) Large population
5) Random mating: Each individual has an equal chance of mating.

→ Disruptive forces of the conditions could exist commonly in nature.
→ No genetic equilibrium → occurs 'Microevolution'

Genetic equilibrium	Microevolution
No natural selection	Natural selection
No migration	Gene flow
No mutation	Mutation
Large population	Gene drift: Population bottleneck, Founder effect
Random mating	Non-random mating: Inbreeding, Assortative mating

Microevolution

Changes of allele, genotype frequency in a population as generations change.
↔ Genetic equilibrium (Hardy-Weinberg equilibrium)

Non-random mating	**• Inbreeding** Mating genetically similar are closely related. Increases homozygous genotypes. Ex) Self-fertilization: Plants Changes genotype frequency. - Inbreeding depression: Inbred individuals have lower fitness than not inbred. **• Assortative mating** Individuals select similar phenotypes mates. (positive assortative mating) Increases homologous result. Does not change the overall allele frequency.
Mutation	Changes DNA nucleotide sequences. **• Basic-pair substitution mutation** - Silent mutation: Not change amino acid sequence. - Missense mutation: Replaces amino acids. - Nonsense mutation: Changes an amino acid to a stop codon. **• Frameshift mutation** - Insertion: Inserts nucleotides into the frame. - Deletion: Deletes nucleotides from the frame. **• Chromosome mutation** Chromosomal structure change - Polyploid: Change in whole sets of chromosomes (rarely occurs in human) - Aneuploid: +1, -1 in a chromosome Cf. Triploid (3n): Three sets of chromosomes Tetraploid (4n): Four sets of chromosomes Pentaploid (5n): Five sets of chromosomes Hexaploid (6n): Six sets of chromosomes Heptaploid (Septaploid, 7n): Seven sets of chromosomes Octaploid (Octoploid, 8n): Eght sets of chromosomes **• Mutagen** Chemical or physical agent capable of inducing changes in DNA 　Ex) Carcinogens

06 Inheritance

Genetic drift	Change in allele frequency due to change. Change allele frequency from one generation to another. • **Population bottleneck** Random genetic properties are only shown. The rest are stuck in the bottleneck. • **Founder effect** A small number of individuals from a large population → found a new colony Offspring allele frequency ≠ Parents allele frequency
Gene flow (Migration)	Breeding migration between populations → alleles movement Genetic difference ↓ Genetic variety ↓ Genetic similarity ↑

Natural selection	More successfully adapted to the environment have greater fitness.
	(adaptive evolutionary change)
	
	Affects phenotype → genotype expression
	
	• **Stabilizing selection**
	Most common natural selection: Well-adapted to the environment.
	Favored: Average, intermediate phenotype
	Eliminate the extreme phenotypes.
	Genetic variation ↓
	
	• **Directional selection**
	Favored: 1 extreme phenotype
	Environment changes over time in new circumstances.
	
	  Ex) Moth in a forest: After the factory → only the black moths survive
	
	• **Disruptive selection**
	Favored: More than 1 phenotype (2 phenotypes normally)
	In a new circumstance, we could know how the phenotypes are developed.
	
	  Ex) Moth in a forest: After the factory → 2 types of moths survive
	  (in different areas)

- Fitness: average # of surviving offspring

Pedigree

Family tree
Gene map between generations
Important factor: Female mitochondria

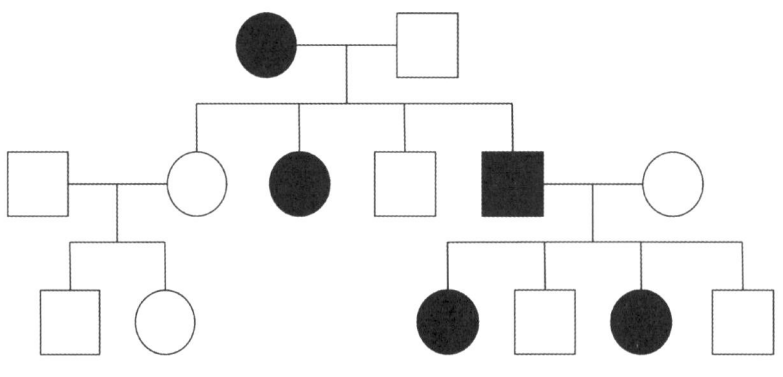

[6-14] Pedigree

chapter 07
Cellular respiration

Organisms use oxygen to break down glucose to get chemical energy for cell functions.
Exergonic process (energy-releasing)
Eukaryotes, Prokaryotes, Animals, Plants

- Substrate-level phosphorylation:
  Making ATP by physically adding a phosphate group to ADP.

- Oxidative phosphorylation:
  Using energy released by the oxidation of nutrients to produce ATP.

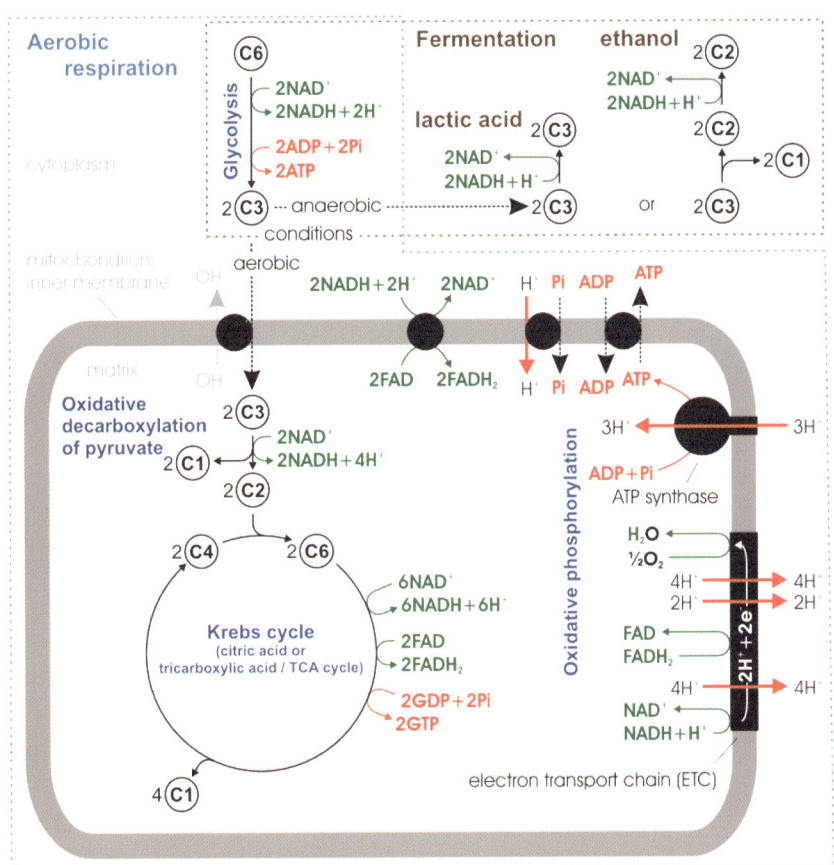

[7-1] Cellular respiration

- **Overview**

Reaction	Location	Aerobic	Phosphorylation	Net yield
1. Glycolysis Glucose → 2Pyruvate + 2NADH + 2H$_2$O + 2ATP	Cytoplasm	Aerobic Anaerobic	Substrate-level phosphorylation	2 Pyruvate 2 NADH 2 H$_2$O 2 ATP
2. Acetyl CoA (Pyruvate decarboxylation) 2Pyruvate + 2CoA → 2Acetyl CoA + 2NADH + 2CO$_2$	Mitochondria Matrix	Aerobic		2 Acetyl CoA 2 NADH 2 CO$_2$
3. Citric Acid Cycle (Krebs cycle, Tricarboxylic acid cycle) 2Acetyl CoA → 6NADH + 2FADH$_2$ + 2ATP	Mitochondria Matrix	Aerobic	Substrate-level phosphorylation	6 NADH 2 FADH$_2$ 4 CO$_2$ 2 GTP(ATP)
4. Electron Transport Chain 10NADH + 2FADH$_2$ → H$_2$O + CO$_2$ + 32ATP	Inner membrane	Aerobic	Oxidative phosphorylation	H$_2$O CO$_2$ 32 ATP
			Total ATP	**36**

Glucose (C$_6$H$_{12}$O$_6$) + 6O$_2$ → 6H$_2$O + 6CO$_2$ + 36ATP

- Some high energy required organs produce 38ATP (Brain, Liver)

- **ATP**

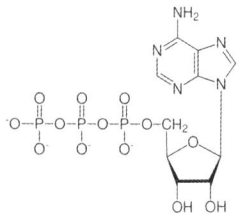

ATP hydrolysis, many (-) charges separated → yield energies
Energy is always produced (ATP, NADH, FADH) but most ATP is synthesized in the Electron transfer chain.

[7-2] ATP (Adenosine triphosphate)

07   Cellular respiration

Glycolysis

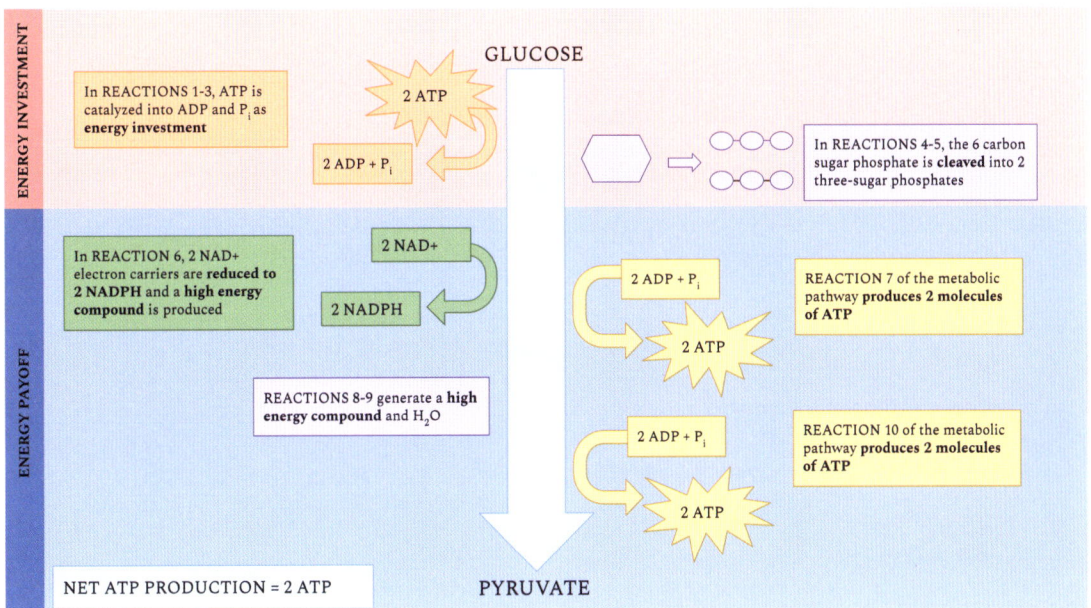

[7-3] Glycolysis

- **Location:** Cytoplasm
- **Air:** Aerobic, Anaerobic (fermentation)
- **Phosphorylation:** Substrate-level phosphorylation
- **Reaction:** 1Glucose → 2Pyruvate, 2NADH, 2ATP

- **Process**

Start: Glucose (6C)

1. 2ATP is used: 2ADP + 2P

2. P + Glucose (6C) + P

3. Separation: P+3C, P+3C
- G3P: P+3C

4. NAD⁺ → NADH
- Reduction

5. ADP+P → ATP
- Substrate-level phosphorylation

6. 3C → Pyruvate

- **Final products:** 2Pyruvate, 2NADH, 2ATP

Acetyl CoA formation
(Pyruvate decarboxylation, Oxidative decarboxylation)

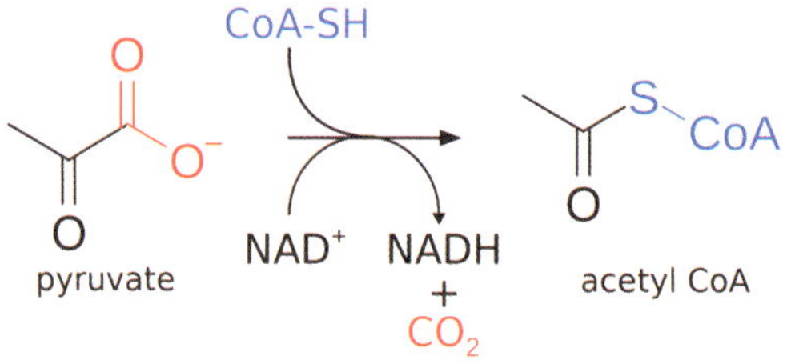

[7-4] Acetyl CoA formation

- **Location:** Mitochondria matrix
- **Air:** Aerobic
- **Reaction:** 2Pyruvate → 2Acetyl CoA, 2NADH, 2CO_2

- **Process**

Start: Pyruvate (3C)

1. Pyruvate 1C → 1CO_2 (-1C)
- Pyruvate decarboxylation

2. Pyruvate 2C oxidation
- Oxidized 2C fragment
- Pyruvate oxidation

3. NAD^+ → NADH
- Reduction

4. Oxidized 2C fragment + Coenzyme A → Acetyl Coenzyme A (Acetyl CoA)

- **Final products:** 2Pyruvate → 2Acetyl CoA, 2NADH, 2CO_2

07 Cellular respiration

Citric acid cycle
(Krebs cycle, Tricarboxylic acid cycle)

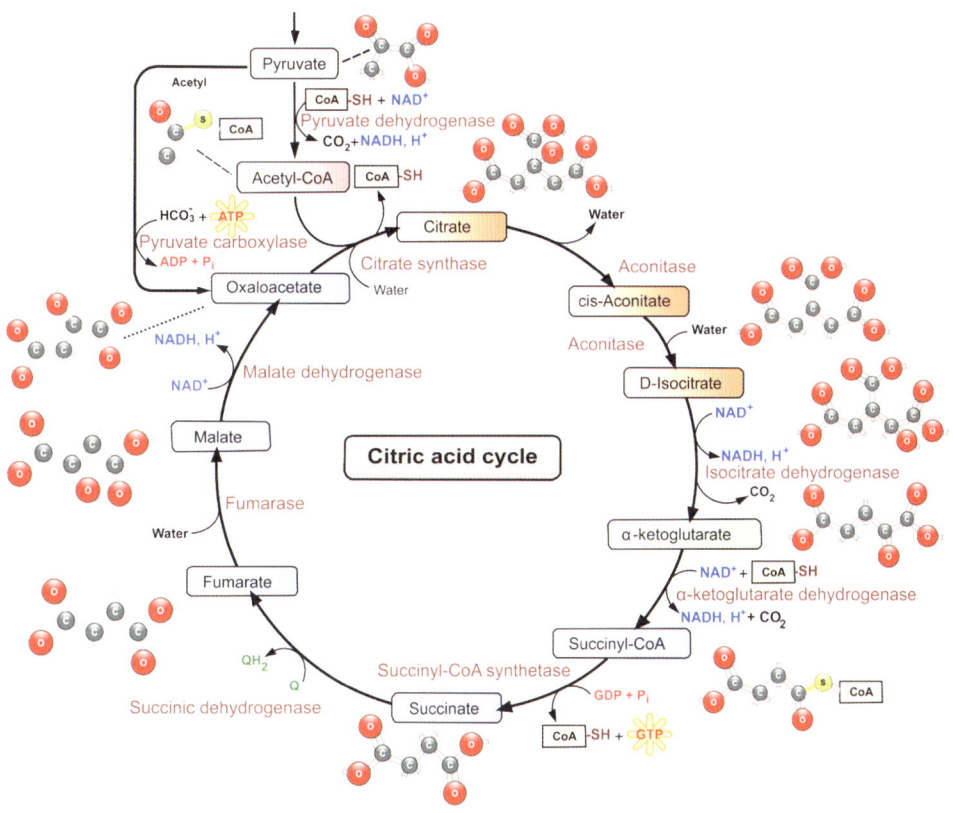

[7-5] Citric acid cycle

- **Location:** Mitochondria matrix
- **Air:** Aerobic
- **Phosphorylation:** Substrate-level phosphorylation
- **Reaction:** 2Acetyl CoA → 6NADH, 2FADH$_2$, 2ATP, 4CO$_2$, 6H$_2$O

- **Process**
Start: 2Acetyl CoA (2C)

1. Acetyl CoA(2C) + Oxaloacetate(4C) → Citrate(6C)

2. Citrate(6C): $2H_2O$

3. Isocitrate(6C): NAD^+ → NADH (reduction) + CO_2 (- 1C)

4. Alpha-Ketoglutarate(5C): NAD^+ → NADH (reduction) + CO_2 (- 1C)

5. Succinyl CoA synthetase: GTP → ATP

6. Succinate(4C): FAD → $FADH_2$ (reduction)

7. Fumarate(4C): H_2O

8. Malate(4C): NAD^+ → NADH (reduction)

9. Oxaloacetate(4C) + New Acetyl CoA
- New Citric acid cycle starts
- Oxaloacetate repeats the Citric acid cycle

- **Final products:** 2Acetyl CoA → 6NADH, $2FADH_2$, 2ATP, $4CO_2$, $6H_2O$

Electron transport chain
(Chemiosmosis, Oxidative phosphorylation)

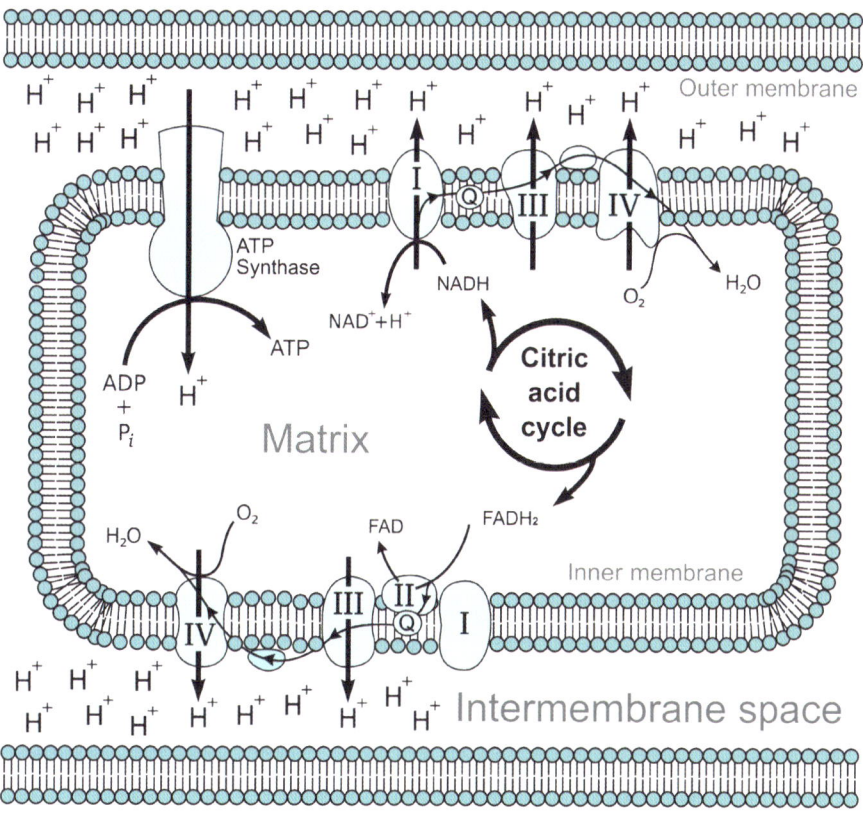

[7-6] Electron transport chain

- Electron transport chains: Proteins, each has a different mechanism for accepting and passing electrons. (e-)
- Protein complexes 1~4: Carrier proteins, transport protons. (H^+)
- Inner membrane space: NADH → NAD^+ + H^+
- Chemiosmosis: Proton osmosis between inner membrane space and matrix. The flow of protons through ATP synthase

- **Location**: Mitochondria inner membrane
- **Air**: Aerobic

- **Phosphorylation**: Oxidative phosphorylation
- NADH, $FADH_2$: Oxidation → ATP
- Most ATP is made through the oxidative phosphorylation.

- **Reaction**: 10NADH, $2FADH_2$ → 32ATP
- 2NADH (Glycolysis) + 2NADH (Acetyl CoA) + 6NADH, $2FADH_2$ (Citric acid cycle) → 32ATP

- **Process**
Start: 10NADH, $2FADH_2$

1. NADH, $FADH_2$ oxidation
- Give e- to the Electron transport chains
- Give H^+ to the protein complexes (1~4)

2. Protein complexes pump H^+ : Matrix → Inner membrane space: high H^+ concentration
- Chemiosmosis pressure: H^+ concentration gradient between inner membrane space and the matrix
- H^+ wants to come inside the inner membrane (gradient: high → low)

3. ATP Synthase: Proton (H^+) → flows through ATP synthase → ATP
- Proton gradient energy: ADP + P → ATP
- Use energy derived from a gradient of protons
- Oxidative phosphorylation

4. Electron (e-) passes through the Electron transport channels
→ The last electron + O_2 → H_2O

- O_2: Final electron acceptor

- **Final products:** 10NADH, $2FADH_2$ → 32ATP

Fermentation

Recycling of NAD^+ for sustaining glycolysis

- **Location:** Cytoplasm
- **Air:** Anaerobic
- **Phosphorylation:** Substrate-level phosphorylation
- Alcohol fermentation: Glucose → 2Ethyl alcohol, $2CO_2$, 2ATP
- Lactic acid fermentation: Glucose → 2Lactate, 2ATP

07 Cellular respiration

Alcohol fermentation	Lactic acid fermentation
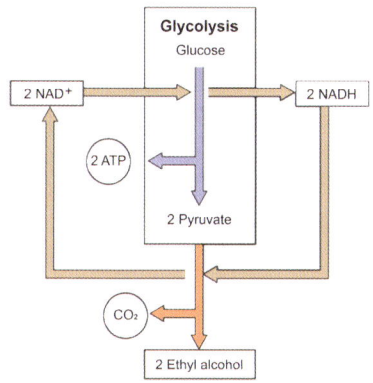	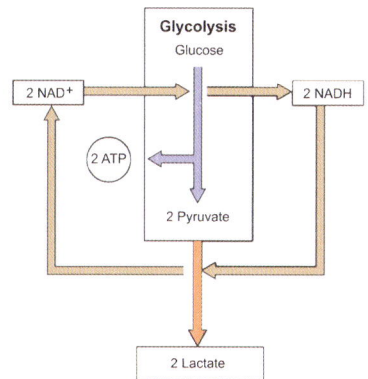
Start: Glucose → 2Pyruvate + 2ATP + 2NADH 1. Pyruvate(3C) decarboxylation - Acetaldehyde(2C) + CO_2 2. NADH → NAD^+ + H - Oxidation: lose H^+ 3. Acetaldehyde(2C) + H^+ (reduction) → Ethyl Alcohol(2C) - NADH → NAD^++H → NADH (recycling)	Start: Glucose → 2Pyruvate + 2ATP + 2NADH 1. NADH → NAD^+ + H^+ - Oxidation: lose H^+ 2. Pyruvate + H^+ (reduction) → Lactate(3C) - NADH → NAD^+ + H → NADH (recycling)
• **Reaction** Glucose → 2Ethyl alcohol, $2CO_2$, 2ATP	• **Reaction** Glucose → 2Lactic acids, 2ATP
Bacteria, Yeast, Beer, Wine	Animals, Fungi, Muscle cells (exercising), Yogurt

[7-7] Alcohol fermentation, [7-8] Lactic acid fermentation

- 2NADH → $2NAD^+$ + H → 2NADH → $2NAD^+$ + H : Recycling
- Lactic acid: When a muscle lacks O_2 → produces lactic acids

Photosynthesis

The process used by plants and other organisms to convert light energy into chemical energy through cellular respiration can later be released to fuel the organism's activities.

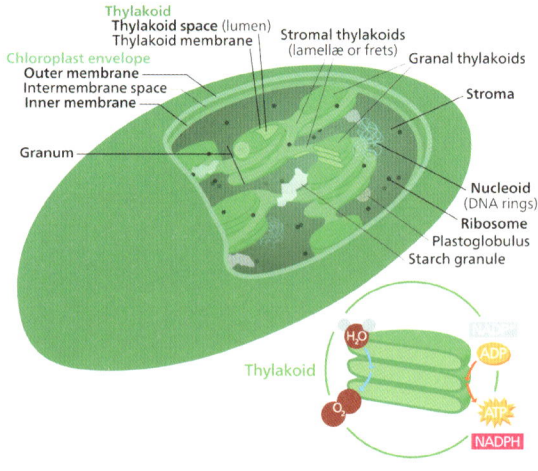

[7-9] Chloroplast

- **Chloroplast**

Photosynthesis location
Has own circular DNA.

- Chlorophyll: Absorbs lights (red, blue), reflects green color to human eyes.
- Plastid: Double-membrane, stores energy.
- Thylakoid lumen: Inside of the thylakoid

- **Light-dependent organelles**
- Thylakoid: Pigment apartment, ATP synthesis
- Granum: A stack of the thylakoid
- Grana: Multiple stacks of the thylakoids

- **Light-independent organelles**
- Stroma: Fluid outside of the thylakoid
- Stomata (Stoma): Pores on the bottom of the leaves (ATP + NADPH + CO_2 enter)

● **Photosynthesis**
- **Location:** Chloroplast
- **Air:** Aerobic
- **phosphorylation:** Photophosphorylation
- **Reaction:** $6CO_2 + 6H_2O + (Light) \rightarrow C_6H_{12}O_6$ (Glucose) $+ 6O_2$

07 Cellular respiration

Process	Yield
• **Light-dependent reaction** - Location: In the thylakoid - Reaction: $12H_2O + 12NADP + 18ADP + (Light) \rightarrow 6O_2 + 12NADPH + 18ATP$	ATP NADPH O_2

• **Light-independent reaction** (Kalvin cycle, dark reaction)
 	
- Location: In the stroma
- Reaction: $6CO_2 + 18ATP + 12NADPH \rightarrow C_6H_{12}O_6 + 12NADP + 18ADP + 18P + 6H_2O$
- Process: ATP + NADPH + CO_2 → Stomata (pores, stoma) opens
  → Stroma absorbs CO_2 → +Enzyme → fixed → CO_2 usable form
  → ATP + NADPH + CO_2 → Glucose
	Glucose

$6CO_2 + 6H_2O + (Light) \rightarrow C_6H_{12}O_6 + 6O_2$	

Aerobic respiration vs. Photosynthesis

	Aerobic respiration	Photosynthesis
Who	Animals	Plants
Summary	Glucose + Oxygen → Carbon dioxide + Water + ATP	Carbon dioxide + Water (Light) → Glucose + Oxygen
Reaction	$C_6H_{12}O_6 + 6O_2 \rightarrow 6CO_2 + 6H_2O + ATP$	$6CO_2 + 6H_2O + (Light)$ $\rightarrow C_6H_{12}O_6 + 6O_2$
Organelles	Mitochondria (circular DNA)	Chloroplast (circular DNA)
Glucose	Use glucose	Make glucose
Storage place	Liver, Muscle	Vescuole
Energy	Pyruvates Acetyl CoA NADH $FADH_2$ ATP	ATP NADPH
Process	Glycolysis Acetyl CoA formation Citric acid cycle Electron transport chain	Light-dependent Light-independent
Energy	Released	Stored

Enzymes

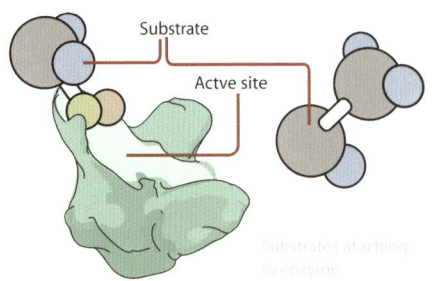
Substrates attaching to enzyme

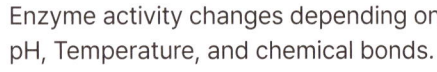
enzyne chnages form to fit substrates and start its catalytic function

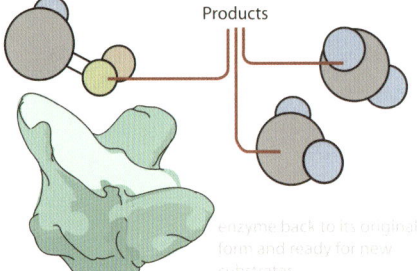
enzyme back to its original form and ready for new substrates

Special proteins which regulate the rates of chemical reactions of cells by providing an alternative pathway of lowering the activation energy.

It affects the reaction rate by providing an alternative pathway for lowering the activation energy necessary to initiate a chemical reaction.

Enzyme activity changes depending on pH, Temperature, and chemical bonds.

- Optimal pH: Body pH (pH 6-8)
  Cf. Pepsin: pH 2 (stomach)

- Optimal temperature: Body temperature (35-40°C)

- Enzyme denaturalization:
  High temperature, not reversible

Cf. Enzymes nomenclature:
  ~ase, ~zyme, ~sin

[7-10] Enzyme

07 Cellular respiration

• Activation energy

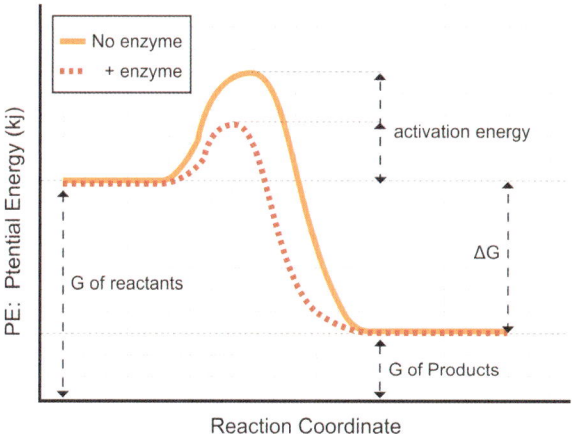

[7-11] Activation energy graph

Amount of energy input necessary for all chemical reactions to occur.
The energy is required to break the existing bonds and to begin the reaction.
Activation barrier ↓ Needs energy ↓ Reactant molecule fraction ↑ Reaction process ↑

Cf. Catalyst: Substance that increases the reaction rate without itself being consumed.

• Substrate
A molecule upon which an enzyme reacts.
Enzymes catalyze chemical reactions involving the substrates.

Enzymes form an unstable complex with substrates.
- Unstable complex: Low activation energy → reaction → Products (stable)
- Induced fit: Enzyme + Substrate
  → changed a little bit, not completely complement each other

• Enzyme-substrate complex (ES complex)
Substrate bonds with the enzyme active site, and an enzyme-substrate complex is formed.

- Enzyme + Substrate → ES complex (unstable)
- ES complex → reaction → Enzyme + Products (stable)

Inhibition

Inhibitor: A molecule that binds to an enzyme and decreases its activity.

[7-12] Inhibitions

Reversible inhibition	Inhibitor forms weak chemical bonds with the enzyme. Most inhibitions Ex) H-bond, Nonpolar, Dipole-dipole interaction	
	Competitive inhibition	An inhibitor that resembles the normal substrate binds to the enzyme, usually at the active site, and competes with the substrate for binding.
	Non-competitive inhibition	An inhibitor molecule binds to the enzyme at a location other than the active site. (allosteric site) → changes the enzyme's shape → prevents the substrates from binding - Allosteric enzyme: Enzymes that change their conformation by binding inhibitors. - Allosteric site (receptor site): A site that allows molecules to either activate or inhibit enzyme's activity ↔ Active site: modifies enzyme's activity - Allosteric regulators: Allosteric inhibitors that keep the enzyme in its inactive shape. Ex) cAMP, Kinase
Irreversible inhibition	Inhibitor forms strong chemical bonds with the enzyme. An inhibitor permanently inactivates or destroys an enzyme when the inhibitor combines with one of the enzyme's functional groups at the active site or anywhere.	

Biological system

Integumentary system	Protects the body, helps regulate body temperature, receives stimuli. - Skin, Nails, Hair, Sweat glands
Skeletal system	Supports and protects the body, important movement and stores calcium. - Bones, Cartilage, Ligaments, Joints
Muscular system	Contractibility and movement. They are composed of specialized cells called muscle fibers. - Skeletal muscles - Cardiac muscles of the heart - Smooth muscles of internal organs
Respiratory system	Supplies oxygen to the blood and excretes carbon dioxide. - Lungs, Air passageways, Nasal cavity, Pharynx, Oral cavity, Larynx, Bronchus, Diaphragm
Excretory system	Kidney removes metabolic waste and excess materials from the blood. Produces urine and helps regulate blood chemistry. - Kidney, Ureter, Urinary bladders, Urethra
Circulatory system	Transports nutrients, oxygen, hormones, and other substances throughout the body. - Heart, Blood vessels, Arteries, Veins, Blood
Immune system	Network of cells and proteins defends the body against infection. - White blood cells, Skins, Fluid, Lymphatic system
Digestive system	Secretes digestive juices. Processes food and eliminates waste. - Oral cavity, Pharynx, Salivary glands, Esophagus, Liver, Stomach, Gallbladder, Pancreas, Small intestine, Large intestine, Rectum, Anus
Reproductive system	The tissues, glands, and organs which function in reproduction. Sexual reproduction maintains sexual characteristics. - Female: Oviduct, Ovary, Uterus, Vagina - Male: Prostate gland, Vas deferens, Penis, Testis

Endocrine system	Works with nervous systems regulating metabolic activities and other functions. Ductless glands that release hormones. - Hypothalamus, Pineal, Pituitary, Thyroid, Parathyroids, Thymus, Adrenals, Pancreas, Ovaries, Testis
Nervous system	Major controlling, Regulatory and communicating system in the body. - Brain, Spinal cord, Sense organs, Nerves
Sensory system	A part of the nervous system responsible for processing sensory information. - Photoreceptors, Mechanoreceptors, Auditory receptors, Chemoreceptors, Electroreceptors, Nociceptors, Thermoceptors

chapter 08

Tissues

● Definition: Consist of a group of closely associated, similar cells that carry out specific functions.

● Functions: Protection, Absorption, Secretion, Sensation, Connection, Muscle contraction, Transmit signals

Tissues	Location	Functions	Examples
Epithelial	All around the body	Protection, Absorption, Secretion, Sensation Excretion, Filtration, Diffusion	Squamous: simple, stratified Cuboidal: simple, stratified Columnar: simple, stratified Pseudostratified
Connective	Between organs	Bind structures together. Form a framework. Support organs and body. Store fats. Transport substances. Protect against disease. Help repair tissue damage.	Connective: dense, elastic, loose, reticular, adipose Supportive: cartilage, bone Fluid: blood, lymph
Muscle	All	Contraction Movement Respond to stimuli Generating pulling force	Skeletal Cardiac Smooth
Nervous	Brain Spinal cord Nerves	Receive, transmit signals	Neurons Glial cells

Epithelial tissues

A type of body tissue that forms the covering on all internal and external surfaces of the body, lines body cavities and hollow organs and is the major tissues in glands.

Locations	Skin, organs, tracts, throughout the whole body.
Types	Squamous: simple, stratified Cuboidal: simple, stratified Columnar: simple, stratified Pseudostratified
Functions	Protection, Absorption, Secretion, Sensation, Excretion, Filtration, Diffusion - Innate immunity: The first line of defense against invading pathogen. Everything that enters the body must cross at least one layer of the epithelium. - Digestive organs: Absorb nutrients and secrete HCl to protect the body from germs. - Secretion: Enzymes, Hormones - Repair injury: Routinely exposed to various inflammatory stimuli.
Information	Outermost layer Lining of organs and organs, tissues and tissues Cells fitted tightly together to form a continuous layer or sheet of cells.

- Epidermis: An epithelial layer of the skin
- Glands: More than one epithelial cells
  Produce and secrete hormones, enzymes, sweat, milk, mucus, wax, and saliva.

- Exocrine glands: Secrete products → free epithelial surfaces (goblet cells, sweat glands)
- Endocrine glands: Hormones → tissue fluid (interstitial fluid), blood

- Goblet cells: Specialized mucus-secreting cells.
  Mucus lubricates the tissue and protects it from drying.

- Epithelial membrane: A sheet of epithelial tissue, a layer underlying connective tissue.
- Mucous membrane (mucosa): Lines. It opens to the outside. (digestive, respiratory tract)
- Serous membrane: Simple squamous epithelium over a thin layer of loose connective tissue. Not open to the outside. Secretes fluid into the cavity lines.
  Ex) Pleural membrane

• Epithelial tissue types

Name	Info	Photo
Simple squamous	**Locations** Lungs, Blood vessels **Functions** Material passage, Diffusion **Info** Thin layer	
Stratified squamous	**Locations** Skin, Mouth, Vagina **Functions** Protection, Diffusion **Info** Several layers Basal layer is metabolically active Division: Older cells are pushed upward	
Simple cuboidal	**Locations** Kidney, Gland ducts **Functions** Secretion, Absorption **Info** Medium-thickness Single layer, Short cylinder	
Stratified cuboidal	**Locations** Sweat glands, Salivary glands, Mammary glands **Functions** Secretion, Absorption	

Simple columnar	**Locations** Stomach, Intestine, Digestive organs, Mucus, Goblet cells **Functions** Secretion, Absorption, Protection, Move the layer of mucus **Info** Cilia: Increase absorption area	
Stratified columnar	**Locations** Male urethra, Gland ducts **Functions** Secretion, Absorption	
Pseudostratified	**Locations** Respiratory passages, Glands ducts, Male reproductive trace, Bladder **Functions** Secretion, Protection, Moves layer of mucus **Info** Cilia, Mucus-secreting	

[8-1] Simple squamous epithelial tissue, [8-2] Stratified squamous epithelial tissue, [8-3] Simple cuboidal epithelial tissue, [8-4] Stratified cuboidal epithelial tissue, [8-5] Simple columnar epithelial tissue [8-6] Stratified cuboidal epithelial tissue, [8-7] Pseudostratified epithelial tissue

Connective tissues

A group of tissues in the body that maintains the form of the body and its organs. It provides cohesion and internal support.

Locations	Between organs, tissues, systems
Types	Connective: Dense, Elastic, Regular, Loose, Reticular, Adipose Supportive: Cartilage, Bone Fluid: Blood, Lymph
Functions	Bind structures together Form organ framework Support and cushion for organs and the body Store fats Transport substances Protect against disease Help repair tissue damage
Information	Consist of fibers throughout a matrix (polysaccharides, cell secretion) Embedded in extensive intercellular substances (fibers, polysaccharides) Fewer cells than epithelial tissues

- Collagen fibers: Made of collagens. A group of fibrous proteins in all animals
  25% to 35% of total protein. Tough, tensile, strength, wavy, and flexible.

- Elastic fibers: Branches to form networks. Elastin protein
  Stretched by force, return to its original size and shape without force.

- Reticular fibers: Thin and branched fibers. Collagen + Glycoprotein
  Delicate networks between connective tissues and neighboring tissues.

- Fibroblasts: Connective tissue cells produce ECM's structural proteins (collagen, elastin)
  Release proteins → characteristic fibers
  Developing tissues, Healing wounds
  Tissue matured → fibroblasts ↓
  Clean up cell dust and phagocytose foreign matters.

- Macrophages: Body's scavenger cells, Wandering through connective tissues,
  Cleaning up debris, Phagocytose foreign matters

• Connective tissue types

	Connective function	
Dense	**Locations** Tendons, Ligaments, Dermis **Functions** Support, transmits mechanical forces **Info** Collagen fibers More fibers than loose tissues Fewest cells per volume	
Elastic	**Locations** Lungs tissue, Large arteries, Aorta **Functions** Elasticity, Structures expand Return to the original size **Info** Elastic fibers + Fibroblasts	
Loose	**Locations** Blood vessels, Organs **Functions** Support, Fluid and salts reservation **Info** Fibers embedded in semifluid matrix + mixed with other cells	
Reticular	**Locations** Liver, Lymph nodes, Spleen **Function** Support **Info** Consists of interlacing reticular fibers	

08 Tissues

Adipose
Locations
Subcutaneous layer, Internal organs

Functions
Food storage, Insulation, Support organs

Supportive

Cartilage
Locations
Supporting skeletons, Ends of bones,
Respiratory tubes walls,
A tip of the nose, External ears

Function
Flexible support

Info
Cells separated from one another
Cells occupy lacunae

Bone
Locations
Forms skeletal structure

Functions
Supports and protects internal organs
Calcium, phosphorus reservation
Skeletal muscles attach to bones

Info
Osteocytes in lacunae in compact bone
Lacunae embedded in lamellae
Concentric circles of matrix
+ surrounding Haversian canals

Fluid

Blood
Locations
Within the heart and blood vessels of circulatory system

Functions
Transports oxygen, nutrients, waste, proteins, and glucose
Immune function (WBC)

Info
Consists of cells dispersed in fluid intercellular substance (plasma)

Lymph	**Locations** Throughout the body Neck, Armpits, Groin, Gut, Lungs **Functions** Remove toxins, waste Remove unwanted materials Transports lymph fluid, containing infection-fighting white blood cells

[8-8] Dense connective tissue, [8-9] Elastic connective tissue, [8-10] Loose connective tissue, [8-11] Reticular connective tissue, [8-12] Adipose connective tissue, [8-13] Cartilage, [8-14] Bone, [8-15] Blood, [8-16] Lymph

Muscle tissues

Location	All
Types	Skeletal muscle tissue, Cardiac muscle tissue, Smooth muscle tissue
Functions	Contraction Movement (antagonistical) Support skeleton and the body Respond to stimuli Contractile: Generating pulling force
Information	Muscle (muscle fibers): Long, cylindrical, spindle shaped cells Myofibrils + Myofibrils …. + Myofibrils → Muscle Proteins: Myosin, Actin Peristaltic movement of digestive tract

• Muscle tissue types

	Skeletal	**Cardiac**	**Smooth**
Location	Attach to bones	Heart walls	Hollow visceral organ walls except the heart
Types	Voluntary	Involuntary	Involuntary
Functions	- Forces, Motion Locomotion - Powers physiological actions - Homeostasis	- Pumping blood throughout the boy - Relaxing in alternative rhythm - Propelling blood contraction	- Simple stretching - Regulating blood pressure - Control fluid by hormones
Electrical signal	Neuromuscular junction	Gap junction	Gap junction
Fiber shapes	Elongated Cylindrical Blunt ends	Elongated Cylindrical Branch and fuse	Elongated Spindle shaped Pointed ends
Striation (sarcomere)	Yes (sarcomere)	Yes (sarcomere)	No (no sarcomere)
# Nuclei	Many	1-2	1
Nuclei location	Peripheral	Central	Central
Contraction speed	Rapid	Intermediate	Slow
Fatigue resistance	Small (easily tired)	Intermediate	Great (not easily tired)
Nervous system	Directly controlled	Indirectly controlled	Directly controlled

[8-17] Skeletal muscle tissue, [8-18] Cardiac muscle tissue, [8-19] Smooth muscle tissue

Nervous tissues

The main tissue component of the nervous system.
The nervous system regulates and controls bodily functions and activity.

Location	Nervous system: CNS (brain, spinal cord), PNS, Nerves
Types	Neurons, Glial cells
Functions	Receives and transmits signals. Stimulates muscle contraction. Awareness, Emotions, Memory, Reasoning

• Nervous tissue types

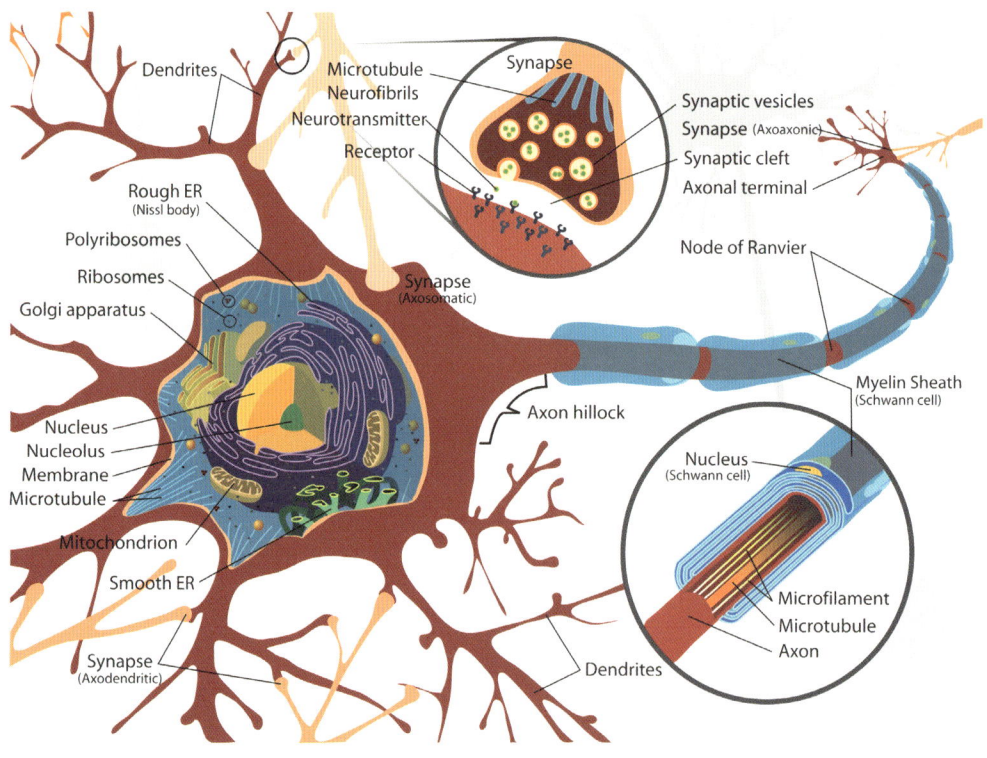

[8-20] Neuron

Neurons	Generate electrical signals. (action potential) - Cell body: Nucleus location, General functions Two cytoplasmic extensions (dendrites, axon) - Dendrites: Cytoplasmic extensions for receiving, transmitting signals → cell body - Axon (nerve impulses): Transmits signals far from the cell body. - Axon hillock: Generates an action potential.
Glial cells	Support, nourish, and protect neurons. (no signal generation) Destroy pathogens, modulate the transmission of impulses. (not transmit impulses) - CNS: Astrocytes, Microglia, Oligodendrocytes, Ependymal cells - PNS: Satellite cells, Schwann cells

Skin and Skeletal system

Skin

● Definition: The largest organ that covers the entire body.

● Functions
- It protects from heat, light, injury, infection, and toxic substances.
- Regulates the body temperature and performs immune function by secreting sebum and sweat.

• **Relative organs for mammals**

Fur	Thick growth of hair that covers the skin. Oily guard hair (top) + Thick underfur (bottom) Protection, Sensation, Waterproof, Camouflage
Claw	Narrow and an arched structure that curves downward from the end of a digit in animals. Catch and hold prey in carnivorous mammals. Digging, Climbing, Self-defense, Grooming
Horn	One of the hard bony growths on the head of many hoofed animals. (cattle, goats, or sheep) Defense from predators, tools in fighting other species members for territory or mating, feeding, courtship displays, and cooling.
Hoof	Foot to a horse, a goat, or a giraffe Protects the animal and helps it to walk and run.

09 Skin and Skeletal system

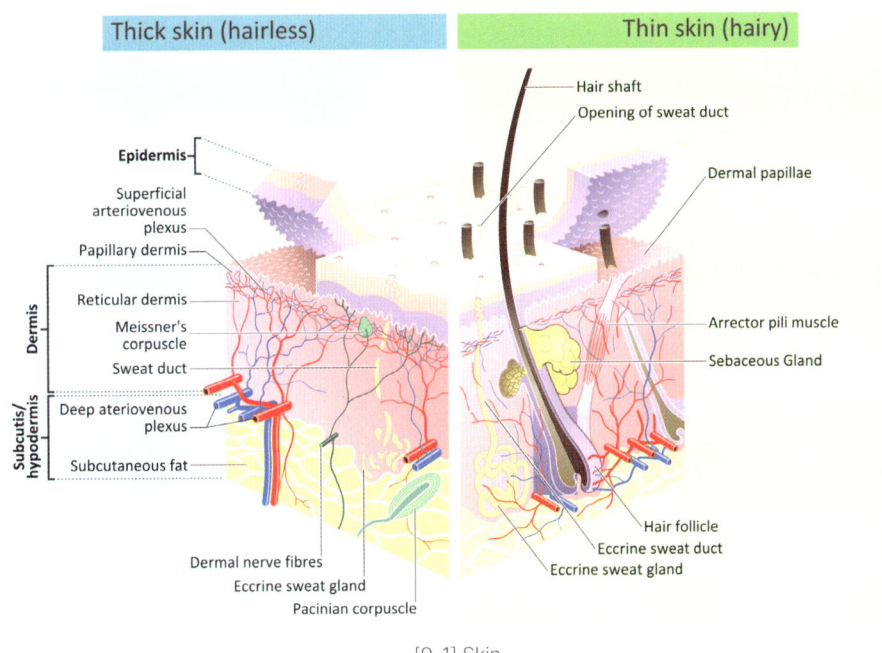

[9-1] Skin

Epidermis	Outermost layer of the skin. 2 sublayers of epithelial tissue. • **Stratum corneum** With dead cells - Oil ducts: Secrete sebum. - Sebum: Mixtures of fats and waxes inhibit harmful bacteria growth. • **Stratum basale** Keratin: Protein, which gives skin strength and flexibility in living cells. Cells divide towards the skin surface → dead: form Stratum corneum - Melanin: Pigment cells protect the skin against the sun. Absorb harmful UV rays.
Dermis	Dense connective tissue, fibrous connective tissue, with collagen fibers Collagen: Strength, flexibility to the skin Blood vessels: Nourish skins. Ex) Arteries, Veins Sensory receptors: Sense touch, pain, and temperature. Sweat glands: Epithelial tissues Hair follicles: Hair below the skin surface. Surround epithelial tissues. Nerve endings, Oil glands
Subcutaneous tissue	Adipose tissue that insulates the body from the outside temperature.

Skeletal system

- Definition: Internal framework of the body

- Functions
- Bodily support
- Facilitation of movement
- Protection of internal organs
- Storage of minerals (Ca, P) and fat
- Blood cell formation

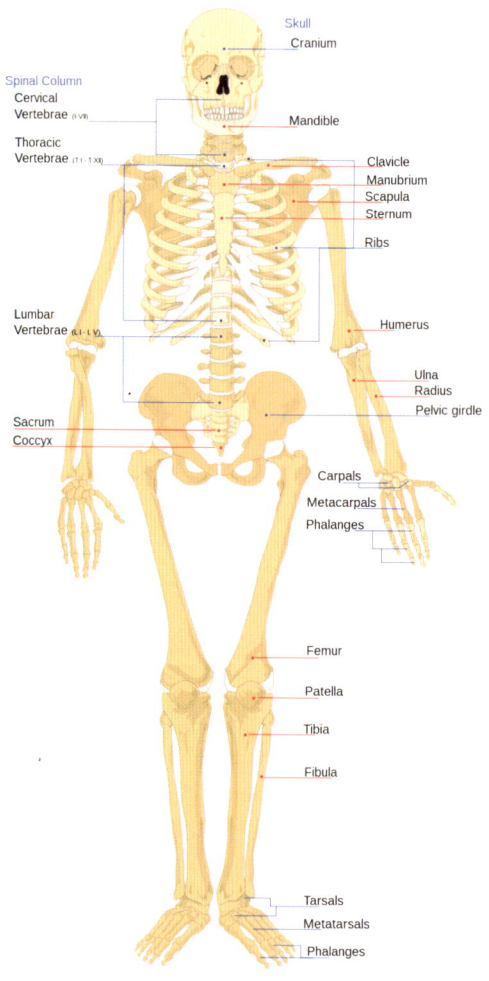

[9-2] Skeletal system

Axial skeleton	Along the central axis of the body. • **Skull** Bony framework of the head - Cranial bones: 8, enclose the brain - Facial bones: 14 • **Vertebral column** (spine) 24 vertebrae + 2 bones (sacrum + coccyx) - Cervical (neck): 7 vertebrae - Thoracic (chest): 12 vertebrae - Lumbar (back): 5 vertebrae - Sacral (pelvic): 5 fused vertebrae - Coccyx: 3-5 fused vertebrae • **Rib cage** 12 pairs, bony basket formed by the sternum and thoracic vertebrae. Protects the internal organs of the chest: The heart and lungs. Supports chest wall, preventing from collapsing diaphragm. Each pair is attached dorsally to a separate vertebra. - Sternum: 7 pairs - Cartilage: 3 pairs - No attachment: 2 pairs (floating)
Appendicular skeleton	• **Pectoral girdle** (shoulder) Flexibly attached by muscles. - Clavicles - Scapulas: 2 shoulder blades • **Pelvic girdle** (hip) Attached to the vertebral column. A pair of large bones: Each has 3 fused hip bones. • **Upper limbs** (arms): 30 bones + 5 digits (fingers) • **Lower limbs** (legs): 30 bones + 5 digits (toes)

Bone

The substance that forms the skeleton of the body.
Covered by a connective tissue membrane.
Formed by replacement of hyaline cartilage with bony tissue.

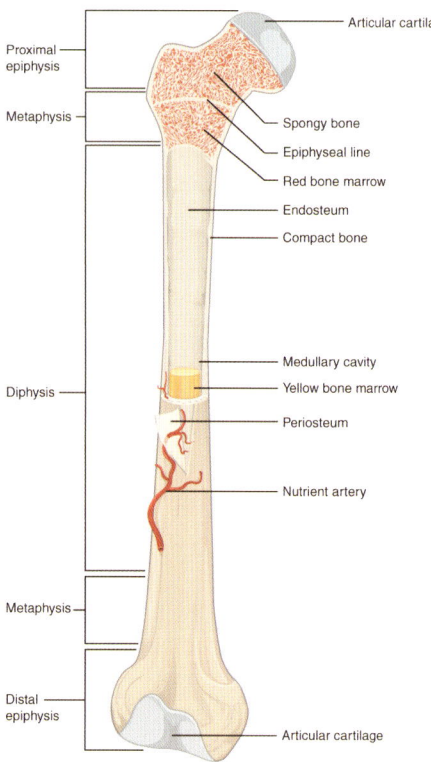

- **Periosteum**
Produces a new layer of bone.
Increases bone diameter.

- **Epiphysis**
Each end of diaphysis

- **Metaphysis**
Between epiphysis and diaphysis

  - Growth plate (Epiphyseal plate): Matured → disappeared → forms Epiphyseal lines

- **Diaphysis**
Compact bone, thin outer shell
Dense, hard, gives strength.
Near the surface of a bone
   Ex) Lacunae, Osteon, Osteocyte, Haversian canal

  - Sponge bone
    Inside of compact bone
    Mechanical strength
    Thin strands of bone
    Filled with bone marrow.

  - Bone marrow
    Inside the sponge bone

  - Red marrow
    Produce all blood: Red, White, Platelet
    Carry oxygen to the lungs and organs.

  - Yellow marrow
    Store fat, nourish, support, and protect red marrow.

[9-3] Bone

Bone metabolism

Bone is living connective tissue.
Cells in bone are continually breaking down and reforming the extracellular matrix in an active process.
Bone remodeling continues throughout the lifetime of the bone.
30% - 50% Bones are reformed in a year.
It helps reform bone when the bone is broken: Osteoclast + Osteoblast

[9-4] Osteoclast [9-5] Osteoblast

Bone matrix	A part of the bone tissue and forms most of the mass of the bone.
Osteoclast	Breaks down bones. Cells that reabsorb bones. Breaks down the matrix into constituents, Ca, P → releases into the blood
Osteoblast	Makes bones. Cells that produce collagen → secrete into the surroundings → form the organic compound of the matrix Receive Ca, P from the blood → deposit into the matrix → form the bone crystals (Inorganic component of the matrix)

Joints

Junctions between bones
Facilitate flexibility and movement.

- Immovable joints: Thin layer + Dense fibrous connective tissue. Ex) Skull
- Slightly movable joints: Between vertebrae, made of cartilage, absorbs shocks.
- Freely movable joints: Most joints. Ex) Fingers

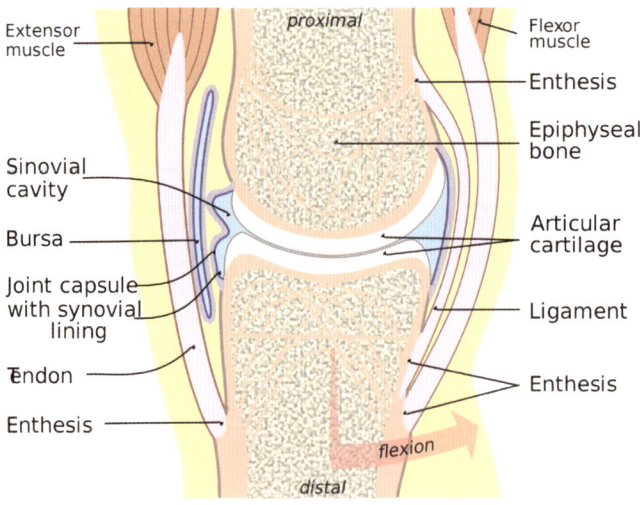

[9-6] Joint

Cartilage	Soft, gel-like pad, supportive tissue between bones The outer surface of each bone Protects joints and facilitates movement. Terminates a person's vertical growth. Completes conversion of the growth plate from cartilage to bone.
Ligament	The outermost part, dense connective tissues The elastic band of connective tissue It connects between bones and provides stability to the joint.
Tendon	Dense connective tissue Connects between bones and muscles.
Joint capsule	Sac-like envelope surrounds the joint and cavity and protects the joint. Joint cavity + Synovial fluid
Joint cavity	The space between bones is filled with synovial fluid. Provides nutrition and lubricates cartilage.
Synovial fluid	Lubricant fluid that reduces friction during movement. Absorbs shock.

chapter 10
Muscular system

- Definition: Tissue of the body, attached by tendons to bones.

- Functions
- Power source
- Generates the forces and motion for locomotion.
- Manipulation of objects
- Powers physiological actions to maintain homeostasis through contractile movement.

• **Antagonist**

Antagonistical movement: Muscles act antagonistically (reversible) to one another.
Muscle contracts to produce an opposite movement.
Several antagonists take part in any action.

Sarcomere

A functional unit of skeletal muscles and cardiac muscles

- Proteins: Actin, Myosin
- Voluntary movement: The expression of thought through action. Ex) Skeletal muscles
- Involuntary movement: Uncontrolled movement. Ex) Cardiac muscles

• **Sarcomere filaments**

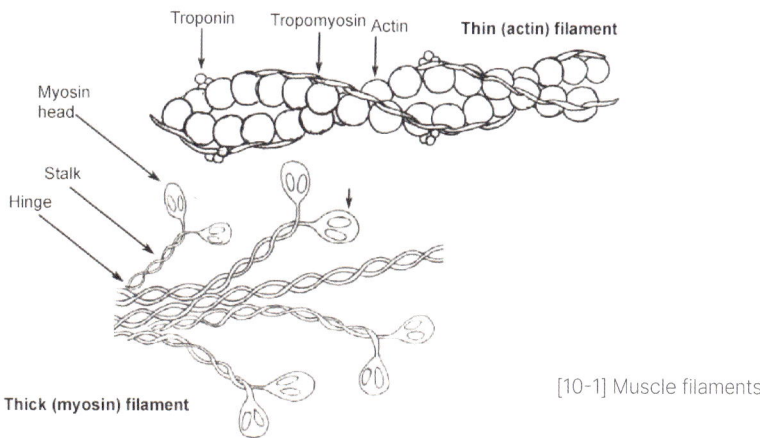

[10-1] Muscle filaments

- Thin filament: Actin + Troponin + Tropomyosin
  Intertwined in a helical form.

- Thick filament: Myosin + Myosin head

• **Muscle contraction**
The fibers overlapping only. Muscle fiber's length does not change.

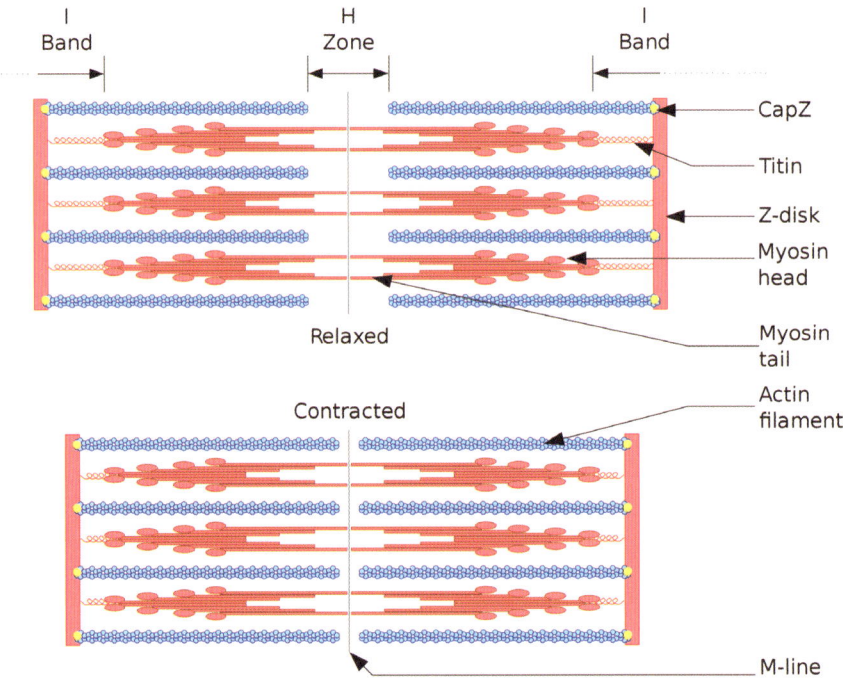

[10-2] Sarcomere and muscle contraction

	Relaxation	Contraction
A band	Thick filaments + Thin filaments (Myosin + Actin overlapping)	Does not change
H zone	Thick filaments only	Decrease Overlapping thin + thick filaments
I band	Thin filaments + over 2 sarcomeres	Decrease
Z line	Boundaries of a sarcomere Responsible for a striped look	Decrease

Muscle structure

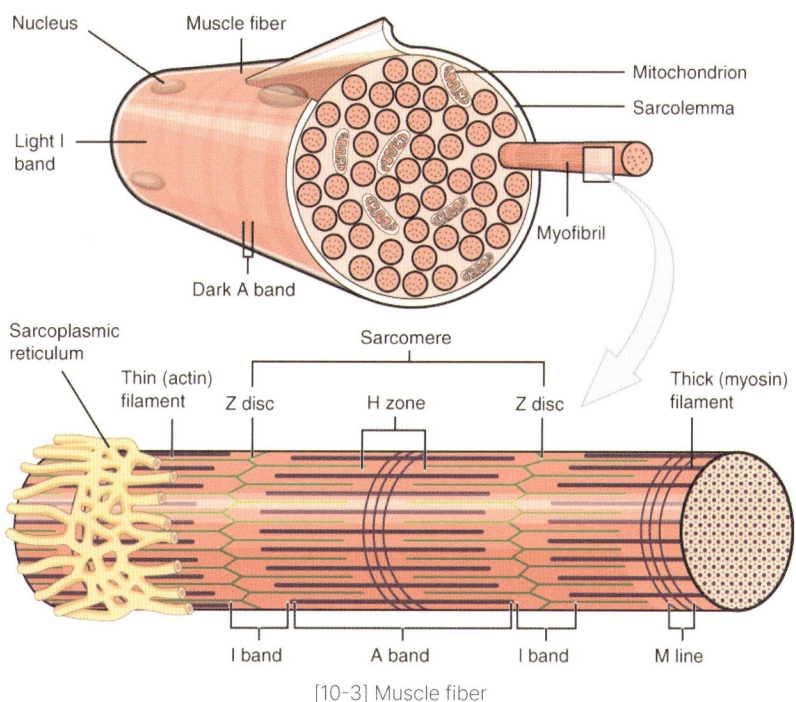

[10-3] Muscle fiber

Sarcomeres → Myofibrils → Muscle fibers → Fascicle → Muscle

Fascicles	Muscle fibers packed into cylindrical bundles. Fascicles + Fascicles → Muscles Muscles are long, multinucleated.
Muscle fiber	Consists of a single muscle cell. (myocyte)
Myofibril	A basic organelle of a muscle cell Sarcomeres are connected → form long fibers
Sarcoplasm	Muscle cell's cytoplasm Myofibril packed into the muscle cell.
Sarcoplasmic reticulum	Each myofibril is surrounded by the sarcoplasmic reticulum. Contains high calcium. Releases calcium during muscle contraction.

Sarcolemma	Muscle cell's membrane, surrounds muscle cells. • Sarcolemma + T tubules (transverse tubules) - Deep in the cells - Perpendicular (90°) to myofibril → delivers action potential quickly • Sarcolemma + Axon terminals - Innervated with muscle fibers + Somatic nervous system • Sarcolemma + Capillaries - Linked to blood
Sarcomere	Basic functional unit of skeletal muscles and cardiac muscles

• **Motor unit**

Motor unit: 1 Motor neuron + many muscle fibers
Force ↑ motor units ↑ ↔ Force ↓ motor units ↓
Large muscle: motor units ↑ ↔ Small muscle: motor units ↓

Muscle fibers

	Slow-oxidative fibers	Fast-glycolytic fibers	Fast-oxidative fibers
Contraction speed	Slow	Fast	Fast
Fatigue	Slow	Fast	Intermediate
ATP synthesis	Aerobic	Glycolysis	Aerobic
Mitochondria	Many	Few	Many
Contraction intensity	Low	High	Intermediate
Myoglobin	High	Low	High
Fiber color	Red	White	Red
When	Endurance activities	Great power Rapid movement	Primary movement
Examples	Swimming, Posture Long-distance running	Sprinting Weight lifting	Walking

Muscle contraction (Cross bridge cycle)

Sliding filaments theory that myosin and actin myofilaments slide over each other.

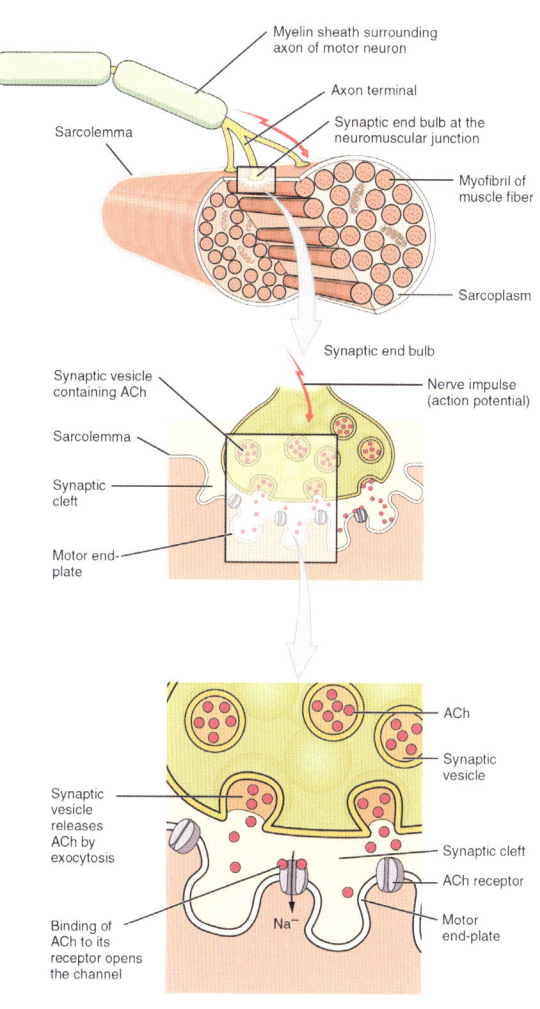

- **Deliver nerve signals**

1. Brain → Electrical signal (action potential) → Motor neuron → Axon terminal

- Action potential: Electrical signals from neurons

2. Synapse at the motor-end plate: Motor neuron + Muscle fiber

- Neuromuscular junction: Junction between nerve cells and muscle cells through neurotransmitters

3. Release acetylcholine (neurotransmitter) → binds to sarcolemma → depolarizes sarcolemma → permeable to Ca^{2+} at the sarcoplasmic reticulum

4. Sarcoplasmic reticulum: releases Ca^{2+}

5. Ca^{2+} ions go down its electrochemical gradient to sarcoplasm + interact with troponin (actin filament)

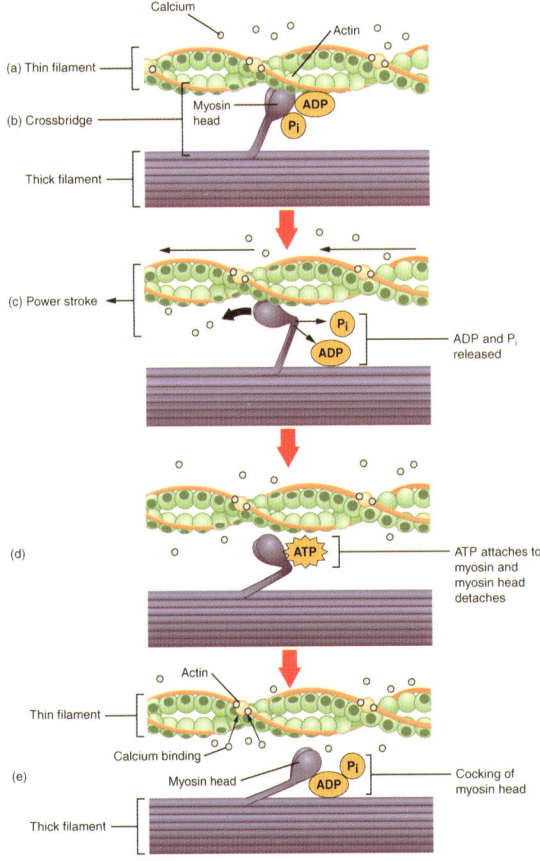

- **Actin filaments side**

6. Ca²⁺ ions bind to troponins on the actin filaments.

7. Actin filaments turn and move tropomyosin → expose myosin-binding site

- **Myosin filaments side**
Myosin heads + ATP is ready from the ex-cross bridge cycle when the myosin heads detach ADP + P

8. ATP hydrolyzed → ADP + P

9. Myosin heads change angles, open heads (45° → 90°)

10. <u>Cross bridge</u>: Myosin head (+ADP) binds to the myosin-binding site.

11. Myosin head expels ADP.

12. <u>Power stroke</u>: Myosin filament pulls the actin filament. When the actin filament is pulled, it moves approximately 10nm toward the M line.

13. New ATP binds to the myosin head.

14. Ca²⁺ is detached and goes back to the sarcoplasmic reticulum.

15. ATP hydrolysis: ATP → ADP + P
- Blocking the binding sites
- Muscle relaxation

16. Ready for the next cross bridge cycle.

- Myosin head attaching factor: Ca²⁺
- Myosin head detaching factor: ATP

[10-4] Muscle contraction 1, [10-5] Muscle contraction 2

Junctions

Gap junction	Channels that physically connect adjacent cells. Mediates the rapid exchange of small molecules between neurons and muscles. It directly passes through a regulated gate between cells. - Location: CNS, Cardiac muscles, Smooth muscles - Targets: Small molecules, Ions, Inorganic salts, Sugars, Amino acids, Nucleotides, Vitamins
Synapse	Neurons pass the electrical signals (action potential, receptor potential) to other neurons or skeletal muscles through neurotransmitters. - Location: PNS, Skeletal muscles - Target: Electrical signals (action potential, receptor potential) • **Neuromuscular junction** Synapse between a motor neuron and a muscle cell through neurotransmitters In skeletal muscles • **Neurotransmitter** Transmit electrical signals (action potential, receptor potential) between neurons or from neurons to skeletal muscles. Made in the neuron's cell body and transported down the axon to the axon terminal. Vesicle form is released at the presynaptic membrane. - Hydrophilic: Neurotransmitters cannot pass the membrane by themselves, so they bind to receptor proteins on the postsynaptic cells. - Active transport: When a nerve impulse is produced, neurotransmitters leave the vesicles and open channels of the adjacent cell at the point of the synaptic contact. - Presynaptic neuron: Transmits the signal toward a synapse with neurotransmitters. - Postsynaptic neuron: Transmits the signal away from the synapse with neurotransmitters.

Muscle tissue types

	Skeletal	Cardiac	Smooth
Location	Attach to bones	Heart walls	Hollow visceral organ walls except the heart
Types	Voluntary	Involuntary	Involuntary
Functions	- Forces, Motion Locomotion - Powers physiological actions - Homeostasis	- Pumping blood throughout the boy - Relaxing in alternative rhythm - Propelling blood contraction	- Simple stretching - Regulating blood pressure - Control fluid by hormones
Electrical signal	Neuromuscular junction	Gap junction	Gap junction
Fiber shapes	Elongated Cylindrical Blunt ends	Elongated Cylindrical Branch and fuse	Elongated Spindle shaped Pointed ends
Striation (sarcomere)	Yes (sarcomere)	Yes (sarcomere)	No (no sarcomere)
# Nuclei	Many	1-2	1
Nuclei location	Peripheral	Central	Central
Contraction speed	Rapid	Intermediate	Slow
Fatigue resistance	Small (easily tired)	Intermediate	Great (not easily tired)
Nervous system	Directly controlled	Indirectly controlled	Directly controlled

[10-6] Skeletal muscle tissue, [10-7] Cardiac muscle tissue, [10-8] Smooth muscle tissue

Chapter 11: Respiratory system

● Definition: Organs and structures used for gas exchange involve breathing.

● Functions
- Gas exchange: O_2, CO_2
- Breathing: Air movement
- Temperature regulation
- Sound production
- Acid-base balance
- Pulmonary defense and metabolism
- Protection from dust and microbes entering the body through mucus, cilia, coughing

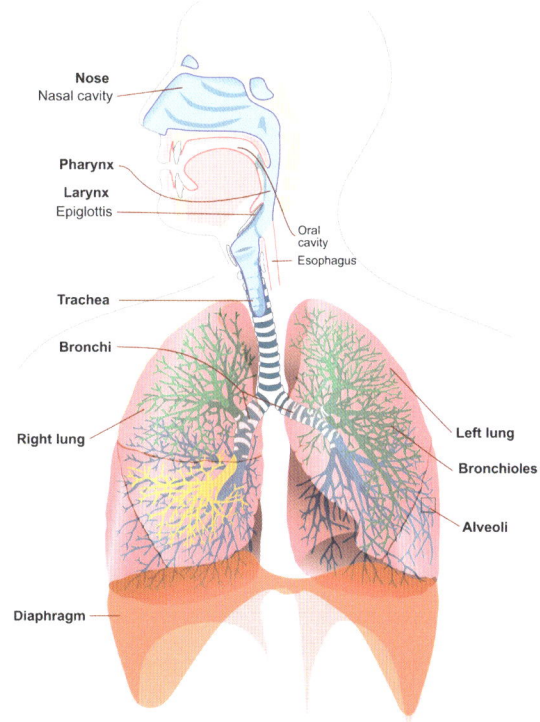

[11-1] Respiratory system

● **Respiration pathway:** Nostril (nose) → Nasal cavity → Pharynx → Larynx → Trachea → Lungs (bronchi → bronchioles → alveoli)

Nostril	Provides air for respiration, Serves the sense of smell, Cleans foreign debris Conditions the air by filtering, warming, and moistening
Nasal cavity	Moist, ciliated epithelium, rich in blood vessels. Sends inhaling dirt, bacteria, other particles → Mucus → Throat (cilia) → Lungs, digestive system
Epiglottis	Open: breathing (Air → Larynx) Close: digestion (Food, liquid → Esophagus) ↔ Failed: cough
Larynx	→ Trachea
Trachea	Windpump, prevents collapsing by cartilage rings. → Lungs (Bronchi → Bronchioles → Alveoli)
Lungs	Large, a pair of spongy organs, air-filled, located on either side of the chest. Gas exchange (Alveoli) - Respiration pathway: 2 Bronchi (bronchus) → Bronchioles → Alveoli - Left lung: Smaller than right lung (heart space), 2 lobes (upper, lower) - Right lung: 3 lobes (upper, middle, lower) - Pleural membranes: Cover lungs - Pleural cavity: Space between the pleural membranes When foreign materials come in: Mucous membrane + Cilia → move upward → Pharynx → Foreign materials go out of the lungs

Respiration

Gas exchange: $O_2 \leftrightarrow CO_2$
Moving air from the environment → into the lungs, expel air from the lungs → outside

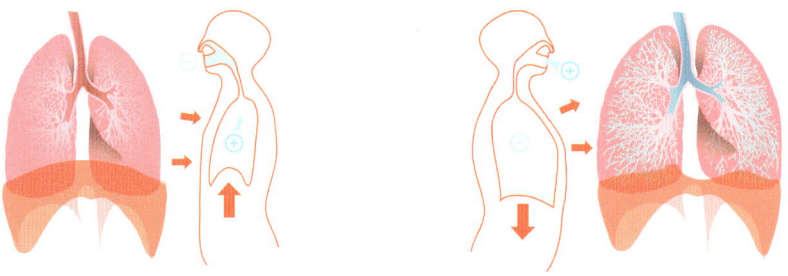

[11-2] Inhalation [11-3] Exhalation

11   Respiratory system

Inhalation	Exhalation
Absorb O_2	Release CO_2
Diaphragm-contraction, move ↓	Diaphragm-relax, move ↑
External intercostal muscle contraction move ↑	External intercostal muscle relaxation move ↓
Thoracic cavity ↑ (Lungs space ↑)	Thoracic cavity ↓ (Lungs space ↓)
Air pressure ↓ (inside the lungs)	Air pressure ↑ (inside the lungs)
Pressure in the lungs < Atmospheric pressure	Pressure in the lungs > Atmospheric pressure

- **Pleura:** Serous membrane covers the lungs.
- Parietal pleura: Outer membrane
- Visceral pleura: Inner membrane (linked with the parietal pleura by fluid-filled space)
- Intrapleural space: With fluid, decreases friction during breathing.
- Diaphragm: Skeletal muscle (voluntary movement), separates from digestive organs.

- **Respired air capacity**

Tidal volume	Amount of air moved in and out of the lungs in a normal resting breath. Approximately 500ml per inspiration
Residual volume	Volume of air in the lungs at the end of the maximal expiration.
Vital capacity	Maximum amount of air a person can exhale after filling the lungs to the maximum extent. Normal range: 3L - 5L

Gas exchange

Exchange $O_2 \leftrightarrow CO_2$ gas diffusion at alveolar sac space, by gas (O_2, CO_2) partial pressure gradient difference between alveolar walls and capillary walls.

- **Alveoli**

Pathway: Bronchi (bronchus) → Bronchioles → Alveoli
Sac-like structure, 2 thin layers (alveolar wall, capillary wall): Gas exchange (diffusion)
Exchange gas: $O_2 \leftrightarrow CO_2$

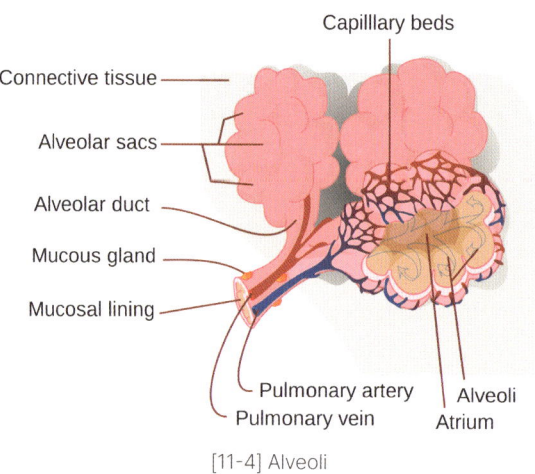

[11-4] Alveoli

With gas (O_2, CO_2) partial pressure gradient between alveolar walls and capillary walls at alveolar sac space.

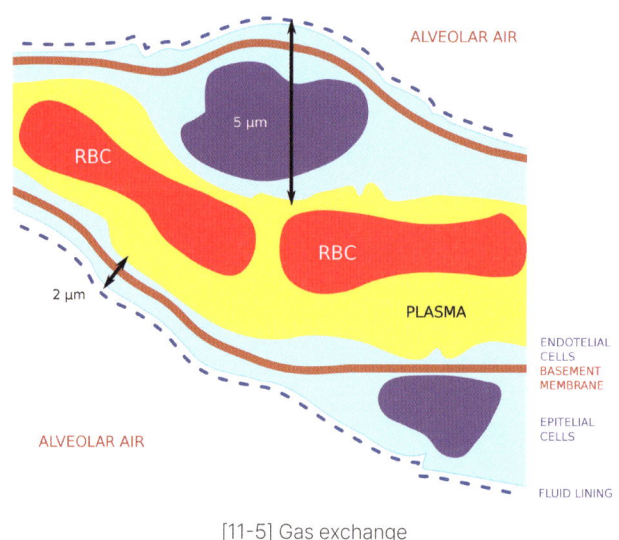

[11-5] Gas exchange

Gas molecules move from a region of high concentration to a region of low concentration. (Air flow is not-reversible, one way.)

O_2: Inhale → Lungs → Alveoli → Capillary → RBC → binds to Hemoglobin → Organs
CO_2: Organs → Capillaries → Alveoli → Lungs → Exhale

Pulmonary arteriole (artery): Heart → deoxidized blood → Lungs
Pulmonary venule (vein): Lungs → oxidized blood → Heart
Capillary: Exchange gases (O_2 ↔ CO_2)

11 Respiratory system

Lumen gas pressure: O_2 = CO_2
Pneumocyte (pulmonary surfactant): Decreases the surface tension and prevents collapsing during breathing.

Oxygen transport

Gas exchange → binds to Hemoglobin (Hemoglobin has strong oxygen affinity)
→ transported by the red blood cell
Respiratory pigments (Hemoglobin) bring O_2: Increase blood transport capacity.

- **Oxygen transportation**

Hemoglobin (99%)	O_2 binds to hemoglobin
Plasma (1%)	O_2 dissolved in the red blood cell plasma

- **Oxyhemoglobin**

Hemoglobin with O_2: Strong O_2 affinity, but stronger CO affinity
If oxygen and CO present at the same time, the hemoglobin brings more CO than O_2
Hemoglobin after delivering oxygen to the tissue cells → combines with CO_2, H^+

- The amount of O_2
  Blood leaving an exercising muscle < Blood entering the exercising muscle

- **Oxygen-hemoglobin dissociation curve**

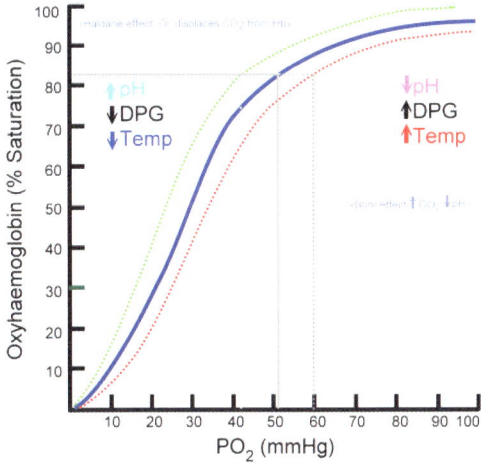

[11-6] Oxygen transport graph

Hemoglobin saturation with oxygen is related to the partial pressure of oxygen in the blood.

- Oxygen content. Amount of O_2 bound to hemoglobin
- Oxygen-carrying capacity: Maximum amount of O_2 that hemoglobin can transport
- Percent O_2 saturation: O_2 content per oxygen carrying capacity

• Hemoglobin-oxygen dissociation factors

1) The partial pressure of CO_2
   Increasing CO_2: Oxygen affinity ↓ (shifts the curve to the right)
   Hyperventilation, Hypocapnia: Oxygen affinity ↑ (shifts the curve to the left)

2) pH, independent of CO_2
   Decreasing pH: Oxygen affinity ↓ (shifts the curve to the right)
   Alkalosis: Oxygen affinity ↑ (shifts the curve to the left)

3) Temperature
   Hyperthermia shifts the curve to the right
   Hypothermia shifts the curve to the left

4) The concentration of 2,3-DPG inside the erythrocytes
   Increased 2,3-DPG: Oxygen affinity ↓ (shifts the curve to the right)
   Decreased 2,3-DPG: Oxygen affinity ↑ (shifts the curve to the left)

5) The presence of unusual haemoglobin species
   Sulfhaemoglobin: Oxygen affinity ↓ (shifts the curve to the right)
   Methemoglobin, Carboxyhemoglobin, Foetal hemoglobin: Oxygen affinity ↑ (shifts the curve to the left)

• Bohr effect
Movement of Oxygen-hemoglobin dissociation curve by the change in pH and the acidity. Acidity and the concentration of carbon dioxide are inversely related to the hemoglobin's oxygen binding affinity.

- pCO_2 ↑ pH ↓ (Acidity ↑) → Hemoglobin's O_2 affinity ↓ (Hemoglobin releases more O_2)

Carbon dioxide transport

Gas exchange → binds to red blood cells (bicarbonate ions, hemoglobin, plasma) → transported by the blood

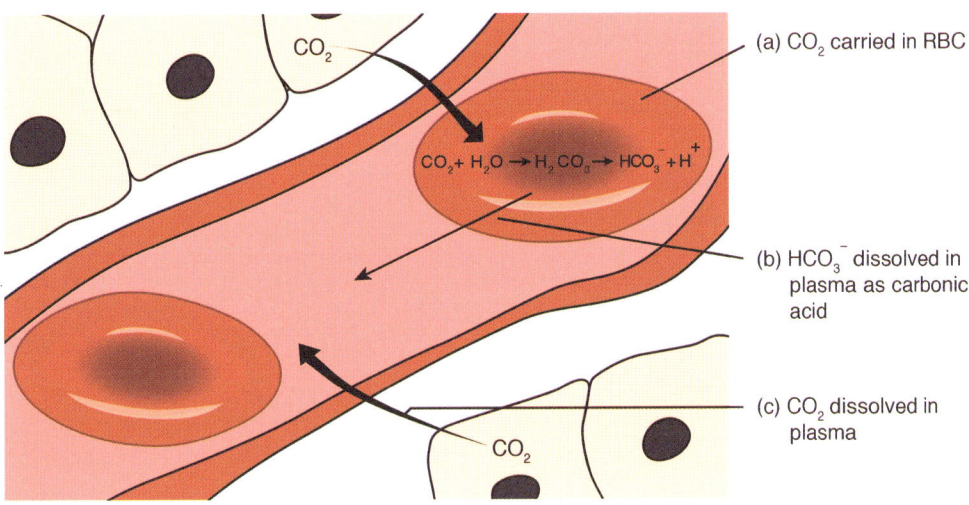

(a) CO_2 carried in RBC

(b) HCO_3^- dissolved in plasma as carbonic acid

(c) CO_2 dissolved in plasma

[11-7] Carbon dioxide transport

• Carbon dioxide transportation

Bicarbonate ions (70%)	Diffused through the capillaries → go into the RBC → + Water → Bicarbonate ions $CO_2 + H_2O \rightarrow H_2CO_3 + H^+$ (weak acid) Blood buffer: Maintains pH balance in the body. - Bicarbonate (HCO_3^-): Alkaline - Bicarbonate + Hydrogen ions ($HCO_3^- + H^+$): Acid
Carbaminohemoglobin (20%)	Diffused into RBC + binds to the hemoglobin
Plasma (10%)	Dissolved in the red blood cell plasma

Partial pressure

It alone occupies the original mixture's entire volume at the same temperature.
- Partial pressure oxygen: pO_2
- Partial pressure carbon dioxide: pCO_2

When Volume ↓, Pressure ↑, Partial pressure ↑
- pO_2 ↑ : O_2 amount ↑ O_2 volume ↓
  CO_2 volume ↑, Hemoglobin binds to O_2 more readily.

- pCO_2 ↑ : CO_2 amount ↑ CO_2 volume ↓
  O_2 volume ↑, Hemoglobin binds to CO_2 more readily.

Tissue: pO_2 < pCO_2
Tissues (organs) continuously use O_2 and release CO_2 to capillaries.

Blood: pO_2 > pCO_2
Blood vessels receive O_2 from the lungs and the heart, and deliver it to organs.

Excretory system

● Definition: Systems remove waste from the body. The main organ is the kidney.

● Functions
- Blood filtration, Nutrients reabsorption, Removal of waste and toxins
- Control balance: Acid-base, Electrolytes, Blood pressure, Water
- Release hormones: Calcitriol, Erythropoietin, Thrombopoietin

Urinary system

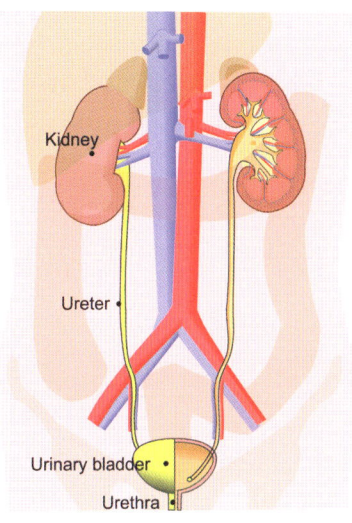

[12-1] Excretory system

● Urination pathway: Kidney → Ureters → Urinary bladder → Urethra

Kidney

Two bean-shaped organs, located below the rib cage, one on each side of the spine.
Covered by connective tissues.
Basic functional unit: Nephron

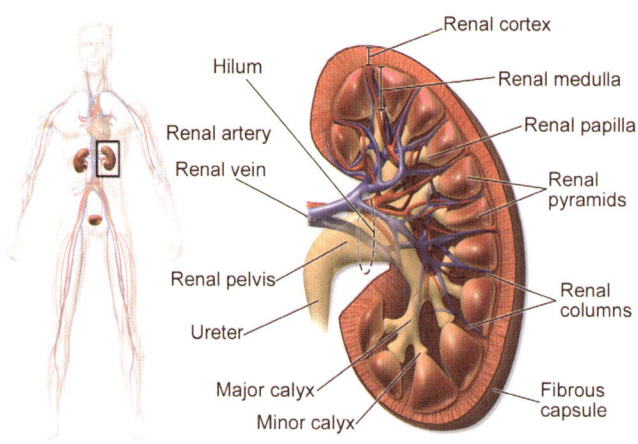

[12-2] Kidney

● Functions
- Blood filtration, Nutrients reabsorption, Removal of waste and toxins
- Control balance: Acid-base, Electrolytes, Blood pressure, Water
- Release hormones: Calcitriol, Erythropoietin, Thrombopoietin
- The daily volume of the kidney filtration: 180 liters

- Reabsorption: Nephron removes water and solutes from the tubular fluid
  and returns them to the circulating blood.
  Ex) Glucose, NaCl, K^+, HCO_3^-, Amino acids, Water

- Excretion: Removal of waste from the body.
  Ex) Waste, Toxic substances, Urea, Ammonia, Creatine, Excess fluid

Renal capsule	Thin and outermost part Transparent fibrous membranes and nephrons Surrounds and encloses the kidney. It helps the kidney maintain its structure and protects the kidney.
Renal cortex	The outer layer of the kidney Contains the nephron, bowman's capsule, glomerulus, proximal convoluted tubule, and distal convoluted tubule.
Renal medulla	Inner portion (Medulla + Renal pyramid) Part of the nephron: Loop of Henle, Collecting duct, Vasa recta
Renal pelvis	Funnel-shaped, collects and drains the urine to the ureters.
Renal artery	Delivers oxygenated blood to the kidney.
Renal vein	Receives deoxygenated blood from the kidney.
Ureters	Move the urine from the kidney to the urinary bladder.
Urinary bladder	Smooth muscle, flexible, holds up to 800mL of urine.

Nephron

Basic functional unit of the kidney

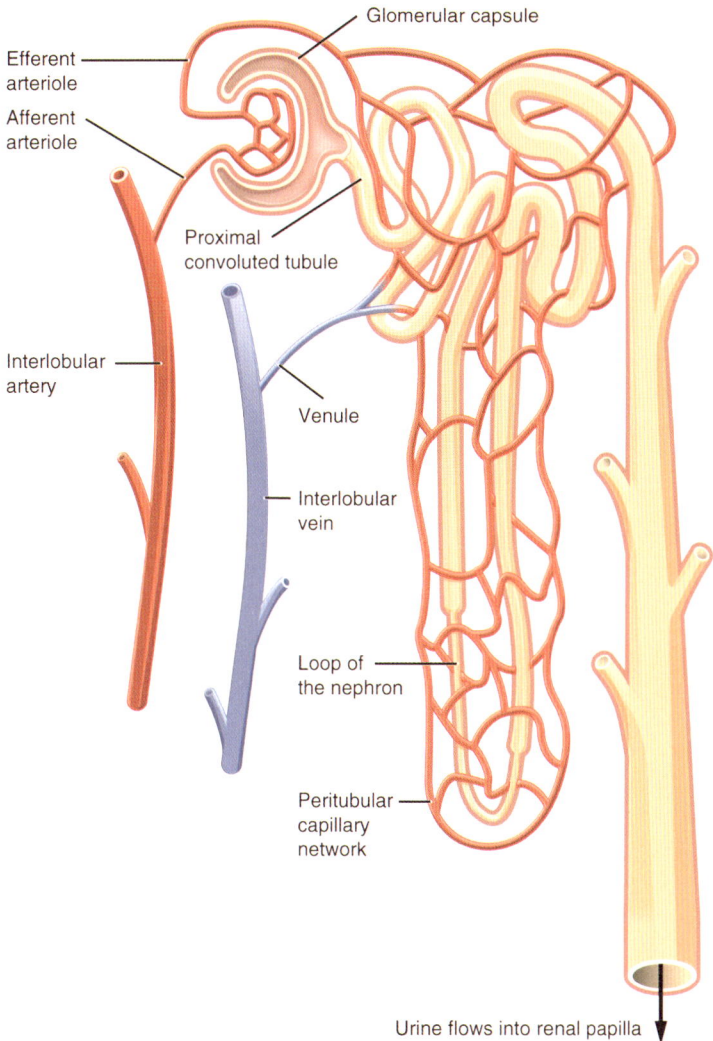

[12-3] Nephron

● **Nephron filtration pathway:** Afferent arterioles → Glomerulus → Bowman's capsule → Proximal convoluted tubule → Loop of Henle → Distal convoluted tubule → Collecting duct → Ureters → Urinary bladder → Urethra

	Renal cortex	
Afferent arteriole	Oxygenated, nutrient blood, waste → Nephron	
Glomerulus	First network of capillaries After the afferent arteriole, filtration starts here. - Large molecules cannot pass through: Cells (RBC, WBC), large proteins - After filtration components are same as the blood plasma.	<u>Filtration</u> Large molecules, Cells <u>After filtration</u> Glucose, Amino acids, Water, Sodium chloride, Potassium, Creatinine, Bicarbonate ions, Urea
Bowman's capsule	Encloses the glomerulus.	<u>Filtration</u> Blood from glomerulus
Proximal convoluted tubule	Obligatory reabsorption - Active transport: Glucose, Amino acid - Passive transport: Water, small nonpolar particles pH control - Filtration: 80% HCO_3^- - Reabsorption: New HCO_3^- Receiving hormones - Aldosterone: Increase Na^+ reabsorption	<u>Reabsorption</u> 100%: Amino acid, Glucose 80%: HCO_3^- 65%: NaCl, Water, K^+ <u>Excretion</u> Nitrogenous waste
	Renal medulla	
Loop of Henle	Concentrates the urine with the least energy. Hyperosmotic concentration: Reabsorbs water very efficiently.	<u>Reabsorption</u> 25%: NaCl Water
Distal convoluted tubule	Receiving hormones - ADH: Increases the water reabsorption - Aldosterone: Increases Na^+ reabsorption	<u>Reabsorption</u> 5%: NaCl Water <u>Excretion</u> H^+, K^+
Collecting duct	Receiving hormones - ADH: Increases water reabsorption - Aldosterone: Increases Na^+ reabsorption Concentrating urine: Final segment of the nephron	<u>Reabsorption</u> 5%: NaCl Water

→ Ureters → Urinary bladder → Urethra

- Kidney portal system network: Glomerulus, Vasa recta

● **Nephron filtration pathway**
Afferent arterioles → Glomerulus → Bowman's capsule → Proximal convoluted tubule → Loop of Henle → Distal convoluted tubule → Collecting duct → Ureters → Urinary bladder → Urethra

● **Blood circulation** (Two sets of capillaries in the kidney)
Afferent arteriole → Glomerulus capillaries (no gas exchange) → Efferent arteriole → Peritubular capillaries (gas exchange) → Small veins → Renal veins

● **Juxtaglomerular apparatus**
3 types of cells regulate the function of nephron.
- Granular cells: Secrete 'Renin'.
- Macula densa: Sense Na^+ concentration, control the filtration rate.
- Agranular cells (Lacis cells)

Kidney-related hormones

Regulate the body's fluid volume. (hydration)
Regulate electrolyte concentration.
Regulate blood pH and blood pressure.

- When blood pressure is low: ADH, Renin-Angiotensin-Aldosterone pathway
- When blood pressure is high: ANP

Antidiuretic Hormone (ADH, vasopressin)	Production: Hypothalamus Function: Increase water reabsorption in the kidney. ● **Pathway** Body dehydration → salt concentration ↑ (osmotic pressure) → Hypothalamus: 'Thirst center' is sensitive to the osmotic pressure → signals to the posterior pituitary: releases ADH → Kidney water reabsorption → hydration → Blood volume ↑ Blood pressure ↑ ● **ADH (Antidiuretic Hormone)** Increase water reabsorption. Increase blood pressure. Makes collecting ducts more permeable to water → Water reabsorption: less urea Acts on aquaporins: Membrane proteins. Make a water channel in the collecting ducts. Cf. Diabetes insipidus: Not enough ADH is released → lots of urine releasing

Renin-Angiotensin-Aldosterone pathway	Production: Kidney, Liver, Adrenal cortex Function: Increase Na⁺ reabsorption and blood pressure in the kidney. ● **Pathway** When blood pressure is low, Juxtaglomerular apparatus: secretes 'Renin'. → **Renin**: activates Angiotensinogen (Liver) → Renin + Angiotensinogen: **Angiotensin I** → ACE: converts Angiotensin I to **Angiotensin II** → Adrenal cortex secretes **Aldosterone**: Na⁺ reabsorption ↑ Blood pressure ↑ ● **Angiotensin II** Peptide hormone Stimulates aldosterone secretion. Blood pressure ↑ (by contracting blood vessels) Stimulates releasing ADH ↑ Stimulates thirst. Extracellular fluid volume ↑ ● **Aldosterone** Steroid hormone: Mineralocorticoid Production and releasing: In the adrenal cortex Increases Na⁺ reabsorption, blood pressure ↑ - Renin: Enzyme, produced and released in the kidney. - Angiotensin I, II: Peptide hormones, produced in the liver. - Aldosterone: Steroid hormone, produced and released in the adrenal cortex. - ACE (Angiotensin-converting enzyme): Produced by the endothelial cells in the walls of pulmonary capillaries.
Atrial Natriuretic Peptide (ANP)	Production: Heart atrium Functions: Promote urine output and Na⁺ excretion, Blood pressure ↓ ● **Pathway** When Na⁺ concentration ↑ Blood volume, pressure ↑ → Heart atria: releases ANP → Inhibits Na⁺ reabsorption, inhibits Aldosterone secretion → Large urine volume comes out: Blood volume ↓ Blood pressure ↓ ● **ANP** Dilates afferent arterioles. Inhibits Na⁺ reabsorption. (collecting ducts) Inhibits Renin secretion → inhibits Aldosterone secretion Large urine volume comes out ↑ Na⁺ excretion ↑ Decreases the blood volume and the blood pressure.

Erythropoietin	Red blood cell production
Thrombopoietin	Promotes platelet production
Calcitriol	Activates vitamin D

Chapter 13: Circulatory system

● Definition: Made up of blood vessels that carry blood away from and towards the heart.

● Functions
- Transport nutrients: Digestive system, storage depots → cells
- Transport O_2: Respiratory structures → cells
- Transport waste: Cells → excretion organs
- Transport hormones: Endocrine glands → target tissues
- Maintain fluid balance.
- Distribute metabolic heat within the body: Maintain a body temperature.
- Maintain appropriate pH.
- Defends the body against invading microorganisms: WBC
- Faster than diffusion and immediately provide resources.

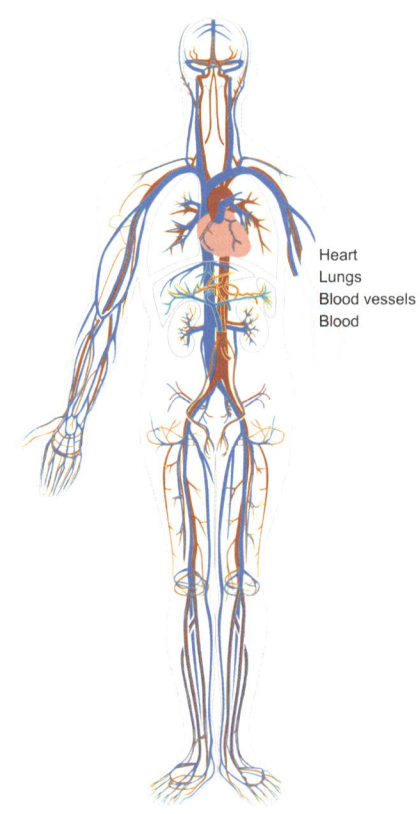

Heart
Lungs
Blood vessels
Blood

13 Circulatory system

[13-1] Circulatory system

• Circulatory system organs

The system permits blood to circulate and transport nutrients, O_2, CO_2, hormones, and blood → cells
It provides nourishment to the body.
It helps fight diseases, stabilizes temperature and pH, and maintains homeostasis.

Blood	Transport the nutrients, O_2 → cells Exert the CO_2 and waste. Transport hormones to the target organs. Maintain homeostasis, pH: Bicarbonate, Phosphate, Protein Immune system: WBC ● **Blood:** Plasma, Nutrients, O_2, CO_2
Blood vessels	Circulate the blood between organs, tissues, and the heart. ● **Arteries:** Heart → carry oxygenated blood (Aorta → Arteries → Arterioles → Capillaries) ● **Veins**: Carry deoxygenated blood → Heart (Vena cava → Veins → Venules → Capillaries) ● **Capillaries:** Tiniest blood vessels, exchange O_2, CO_2, nutrients, ions, and waste. - Extensive capillary organs: Skeletal muscle, Liver, Kidney
Lymphatic system	Produce antibodies, protect the body from illness-causing invaders. Maintain body fluid levels. Reabsorb digestive tract nutrients, return them into the veins. Remove cellular waste. Capillaries cannot absorb excessive fluid → rest of the nutrients accumulated in the interstitial fluid → Lymph nodes + Lymphatic vessels - Nutrients reabsorption → Vena cava → Heart - Waste: Clear, excretion → Excretory system
Heart	Cardiac muscle with more than 2 pumps (right/left ventricle pumps) Not attached to bones → Web-like net: contraction Create the hydrostatic pressure, move the blood throughout the body.

- Closed-circuit: Blood remains within the circuit the entire time.

Blood

Fluid transports oxygen and nutrients to the cells and carries away carbon dioxide and other waste products.
Proper pH: pH 7.35 - pH 7.45
Immune system: WBC
Transport nutrients, O_2 → cells
Exert the CO_2 and waste.
Transport hormones to the target organs.
Maintain homeostasis and pH: Bicarbonate, Phosphate, Protein
Adult has 5L blood in the body on average.

Blood plasma (up)	55% of the total blood volume Fluid-like matrix **95%** Water **5%** - Proteins: Albumin, Fibrinogen, Immunoglobulins - Nutrients: Glucose, Fatty acids, Amino acids - Electrolytes: Na^+, Ca^{2+}, Mg^{2+}, H_3O^+ - Waste: Lactic acid, CO_2, Urea - Hormones: ADH, Aldosterone - Maintain homeostasis, pH (bicarbonate, phosphate, protein), body temperature Functions: - Transport essential nutrients, minerals, waste, and hormones. - Regulate the composition of the matrix of cells.	
Cells (bottom)	45% of the total blood volume From the hematopoietic stem cells	
	Red blood cells (Erythrocytes)	Transport O_2: Lungs → carry O_2 → destination Transport CO_2: Tissues → carry CO_2 → Lungs Hemoglobin: Holds O_2, CO_2 (RBC cytoplasm) No nucleus (no DNA), no organelles → maximizes the space → stores more Biconcave shape: Maximizes surface → efficiently exchanges O_2 + squeezes through capillaries

White blood cells (Leukocytes)	Immune cells: Infection, WBC ↑ Fight off bacteria and viral agents Neutrophils, Eosinophils, Basophils, Lymphocytes, Monocytes 1% of the blood cells Have nuclei Ex) Blood, Lymphatic system	
Platelets (Thrombocytes)	Blood clotting: Move through the blood → stick to torn endothelium regions → bind → release chemicals → blood clotting No nucleus Not actual cells but merely circulating fragment of cells	

RBC, WBC, Platelets

	Normal range	Function	Pathology
Red blood cells	M: 4.2-5.4m /μL F: 3.6-5.0m /μL	Transport: O_2, CO_2 Involve in homeostasis	Anemia Polycythemia
Platelets	150k-400k /μL	Blood clotting	Clotting malfunctions
White blood cells: 5k-10k /μL			
Neutrophils	60% WBC	Phagocytosis	Bacterial infection Inflammation Myelogenous leukemia
Eosinophils	1-3% WBC	Make proteins: Toxic to parasites Immune response	Allergic reaction Parasitic infestation
Basophils	1% WBC	Prevent inappropriate clotting Make histamine: Allergic response, Inflammatory response	

Lymphocytes	25~35% WBC	Make antibodies: Destroy foreign cells B, T lymphocytes: Adaptive immunity Maintaining body fluid levels Absorbing digestive tract fats Removing cellular waste	Virus infection Lymphocytic leukemia
Monocytes	6% WBC	Make macrophages, dendritic cells Cannot pass the wall of capillaries	Monocytic leukemia Fungal infection

Blood vessels

Circulate the blood between organs, tissues, and the heart.

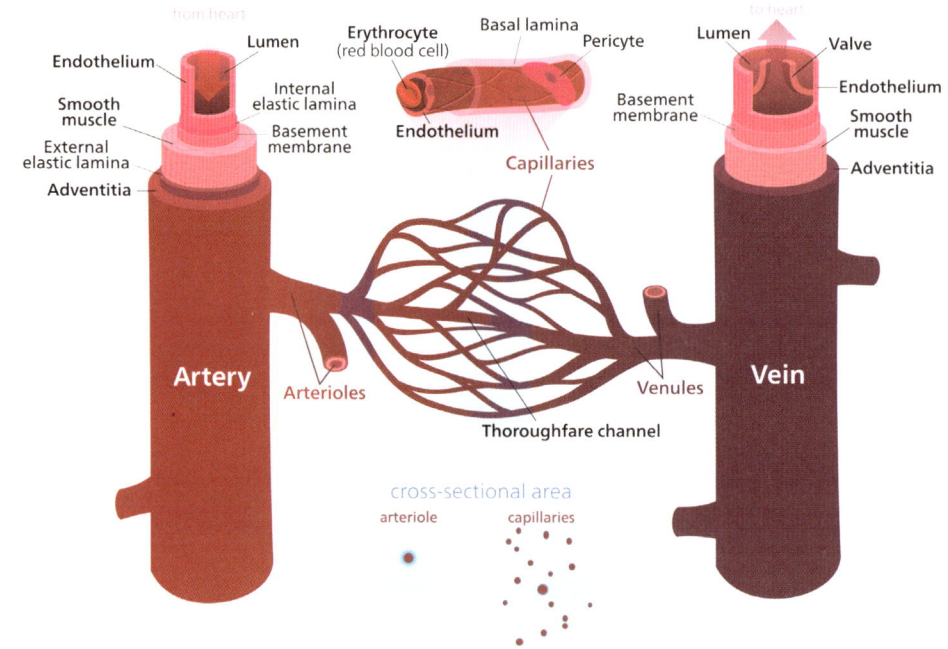

[13-2] Blood vessels

Arteries

Heart → Arteries → carry oxygenated blood → Organs

Oxygenated blood (mostly)
+ Deoxygenated blood (lungs)

Aorta → Arteries → Arterioles → Capillaries

● Functions
- Thick, smooth muscle layer: Elastic dense epithelial tissue
- Elasticity: High resistance to blood flow
- Smooth muscle + Innervated nervous system
- Dilate + Constrict vessels → control blood flow and pressure
- High recoil capabilities: Blood moving efficiently
- No valves: The pressure is so intense that it does not need the valves.
- Sphincter muscles: Control vessel walls.

● Types
- Aorta: Heart → organs, tissues
- Arteries: Heart → organs, tissues
- Arterioles: The smallest branch of the artery

● 3 layers
- Tunica intima: Innermost layer (endothelial cell + elastin fiber)
- Tunica media: Middle (thick smooth muscle + elastin fiber)
- Tunica externa: Outermost layer (collagen fiber)

Veins

Organs → Veins → carry deoxygenated blood → Heart
Deoxygenated blood (mostly)
+ Oxygenated blood (lungs)

Vena cava → Veins → Venules → Capillaries

● Functions
- Inelastic, do not recoil.
- Expand to carry more blood: 60% of total volume
- Energy by muscle contraction: Sends the fluid → Heart
- One-way valves: Ensure blood flows in one-way direction.
- Fewer muscles

● Types
- Vena cava: Organs, tissues → Heart
- Veins: Organs, tissues → Heart
- Venules

● 3 layers (smaller than arteries)
- Tunica intima: Innermost layer (endothelial cell + elastin fiber)
- Tunica media: Middle (thick smooth muscle + elastin fiber)
- Tunica externa: Outermost layer (collagen fiber)

Capillaries	Arterioles: O_2 → Capillaries: gas diffusion with CO_2 → Venules ● Functions - Tiniest blood vessels, 1 layer - Gas diffusion: O_2, CO_2 - Exchange materials between the blood and interstitial fluid. - Materials: O_2, CO_2, Nutrients, Electrolytes, Waste - Run close to the cells for blood travel. ● Hydrostatic pressure: Exchanges nutrients for waste. - Through cell membrane of endothelium - Through fenestrations - Through space between cells - Through pinocytosis

● **Blood vessels comparision**

	Arteries	Veins	Capillaries
Direction	Heart → Blood → Organs	Organs → Blood → Heart	Materials exchange with tissues
Blood pressure	High ↑	Low ↓	Low ↓
Wall	Thick layer smooth muscle tissue	Thin layer smooth muscle tissue	Extremely thin (single-cell layer)
Wall layer	3	3	1
Muscle fibers	Many	A few	No
Valves	No	Yes	No
Blood velocity	Fast	Intermediate	Slow

Blood circulations

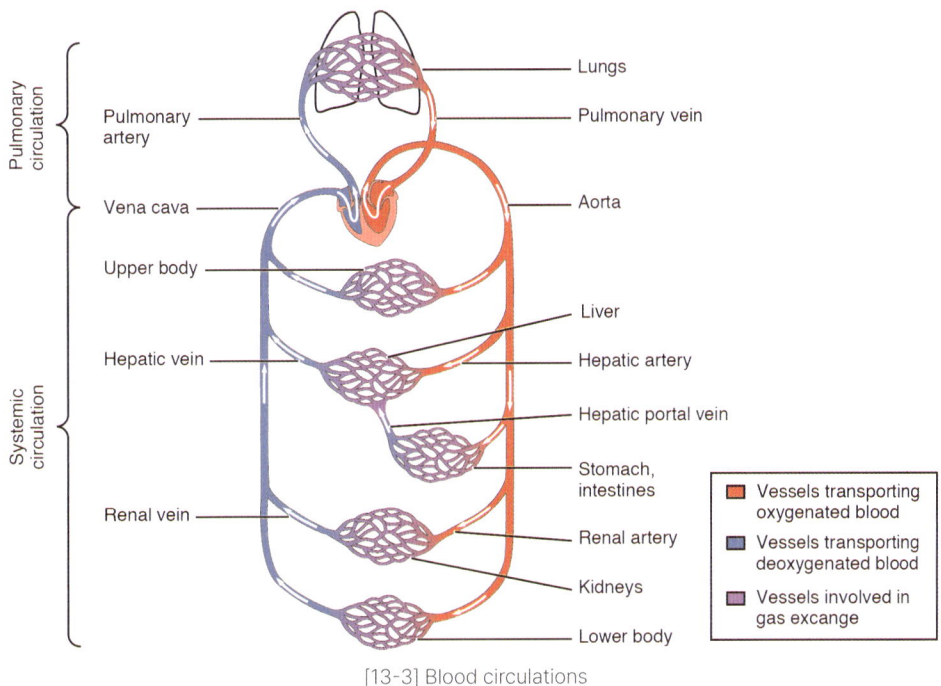

[13-3] Blood circulations

Blood circulation: Pulmonary circulation + Systemic circulation

Deoxygenated blood: Vena cava → Right atrium → Tricuspid valve → Right ventricle → Pulmonary artery valve → Pulmonary artery → Lungs (gas exchange)
→ **Oxygenated blood:** Pulmonary vein → Left atrium → Bicuspid valve → Left ventricle → Aortic valve → Aorta

● **Pulmonary circulation**
Deoxygenated blood → Right atrium → Right ventricle → Pulmonary artery → Capillaries in the lungs: Gas exchange → Oxygenated blood → Pulmonary vein → Left atrium → Left ventricle → Aorta

- Aorta: Outgoing oxygen-rich blood
- Vena cava: Receiving oxygen-poor blood

● **Systemic circulation**
Oxygenated blood → Aorta → Ascending, Descending Aorta → Upper, Lower organs → Superior, Inferior Vena cava → Right atrium

- Aorta: Receiving oxygen-rich blood
- Vena cava: Outgoing oxygen-poor blood

Gas exchange

Exchange $O_2 \leftrightarrow CO_2$ gas diffusion at alveolar sac space, by gas (O_2, CO_2) partial pressure gradient difference between alveolar walls and capillary walls.

- **Alveoli**

Pathway: Bronchi (bronchus) → Bronchioles → Alveoli
Sac-like structure, 2 thin layers (alveolar wall, capillary wall): Gas exchange (diffusion)
Exchange gas: $O_2 \leftrightarrow CO_2$

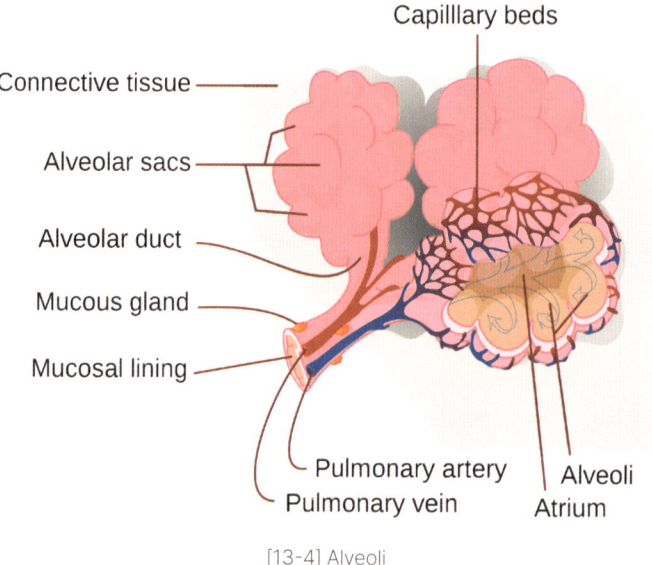

[13-4] Alveoli

With gas (O_2, CO_2) partial pressure gradient between alveolar walls and capillary walls at alveolar sac space.

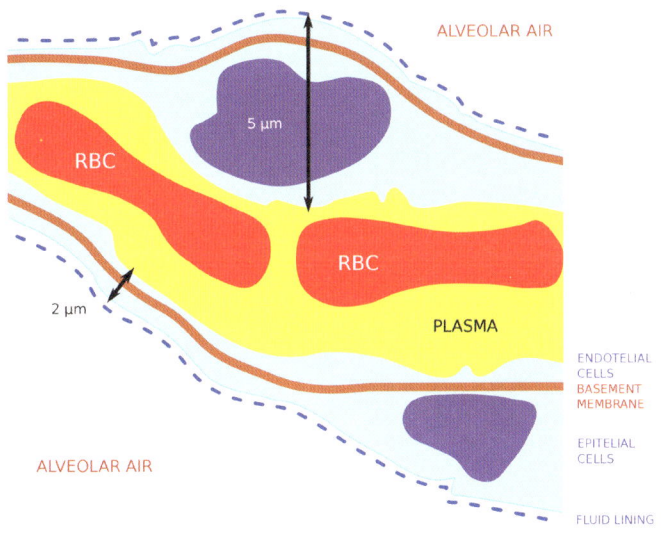

[13-5] Gas exchange

Gas molecules move from a region of high concentration to a region of low concentration. (Air flow is not-reversible, one way.)

O_2: Inhale → Lungs → Alveoli → Capillary → RBC → binds to Hemoglobin → Organs
CO_2: Organs → Capillaries → Alveoli → Lungs → Exhale

Heart

Heart: Cardiac muscles + 2 pumps + 4 chambers + 4 valves
Creates the hydrostatic pressure and moves the blood throughout the body.
Not attached to bones → contraction with a web-like net

Pumps	Right ventricle pump: Oxygen-poor blood to the lungs through the pulmonary valve Left ventricle pump: Oxygen-rich blood through the aortic valve to the rest of the body
Chambers	Right atrium, Right ventricle Left atrium, Left ventricle
Valves	Tricuspid valve Pulmonary artery valve Bicuspid valve Aortic valve Semilunar valve: Pulmonary artery valve + Aortic valve

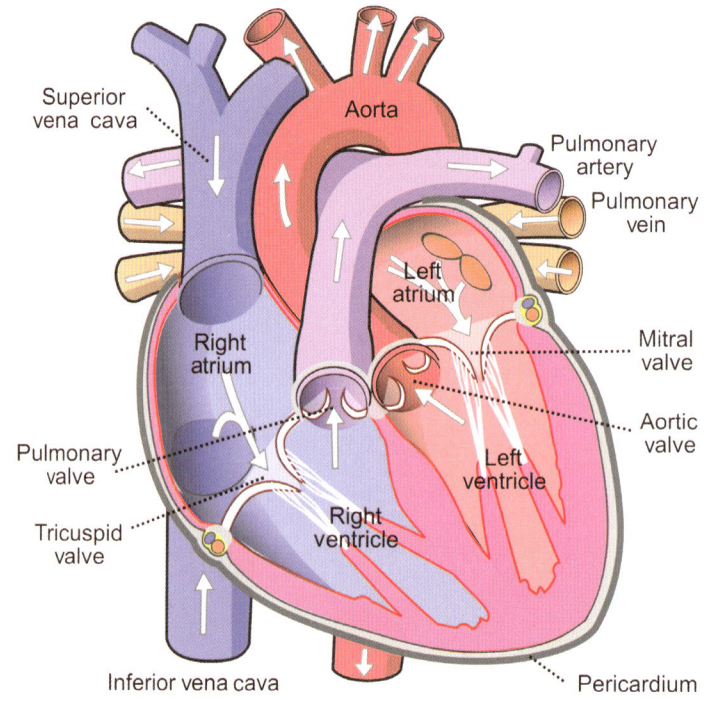

[13-6] Heart

13 Circulatory system

• Blood circulation pathway in the heart

Vena cava ⇩	Deoxygenated blood	
Right atrium ⇩	Deoxygenated blood Systemic circulation → receives deoxygenated blood	
Tricuspid valve ⇩	Deoxygenated blood Right atrium → Right ventricle Contraction: Prevents blood moving back to right ventricle → Right atrium	
Right ventricle ⇩	Deoxygenated blood Right ventricle → Pulmonary artery valve	
Pulmonary artery valve ⇩	Deoxygenated blood Right ventricle → Pulmonary artery	
Pulmonary artery ⇩	Deoxygenated blood Pulmonary artery → Lungs capillary	
Lungs: Oxygenation (gas exchange) (Bronchi → Bronchioles → Alveoli)		**Pulmonary circulation**
Pulmonary vein ⇩	Oxygenated blood Pulmonary vein → Left atrium	
Left atrium ⇩	Oxygenated blood Pulmonary circulation → receives oxygenated blood	
Bicuspid valve ⇩ (Mitral valve)	Oxygenated blood Left atrium → Left ventricle	
Left ventricle ⇩	Oxygenated blood Left atrium → Aortic valve	
Aortic valve ⇩	Oxygenated blood Left ventricle → Left atrium Aortic valve opens → prevents the blood backflow into the ventricle	
Aorta ⇩	Oxygenated blood Heart → Organs (upper/lower)	
Organs, Tissues ⇩	Deoxygenation: use O_2	**Systemic circulation**
Vena cava ⇩	Deoxygenated blood Organs, tissues → Right atrium (heart)	

Cardiovascular disease

Coronary artery disease	Damage or disease in the heart's major blood vessels.
High blood pressure	A condition in which the force of the blood against the artery walls is too high.
Cardiac arrest	Sudden, unexpected loss of heart function, breathing, and consciousness.
Congestive heart failure	A chronic condition in which the heart does not pump blood as well as it should.
Arrhythmia	Improper beating of the heart, whether irregular, too fast, or too slow.
Peripheral artery disease	A circulatory condition in which narrowed blood vessels reduce blood flow to the limbs.
Stroke	Damage to the brain from interruption of its blood supply.
Congenital heart disease	An abnormality in the heart that develops before birth.

Heart layers

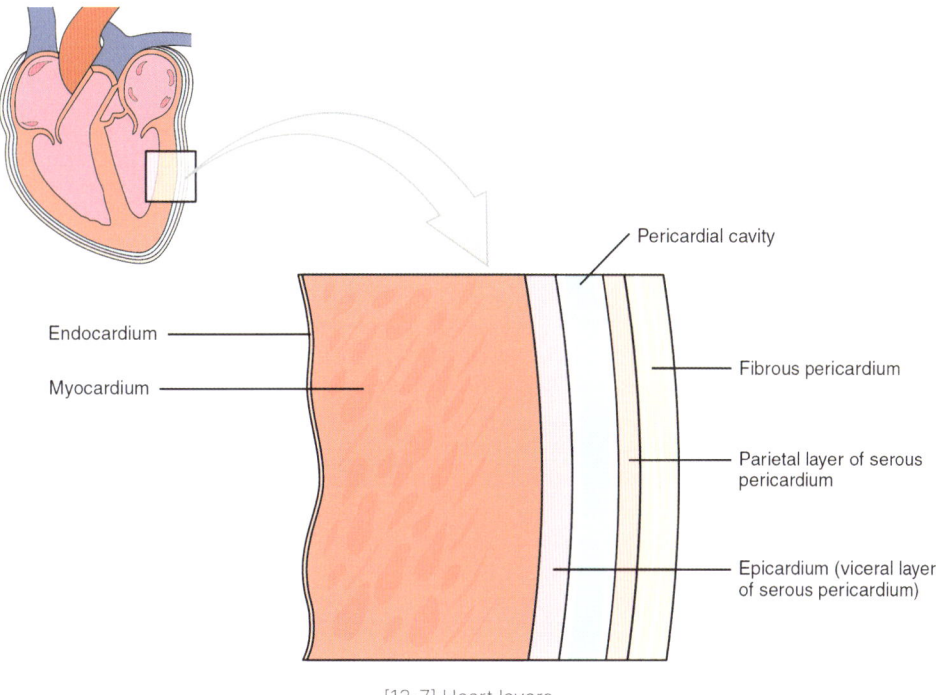

[13-7] Heart layers

	Pericardium: Protective sac that covers the heart.
Outer layer	Tough Fibrous proteins: Attach the heart to the body, and protect the heart.
Inner serous layer	Parietal layers + Visceral layers Separated by fluid (pericardial fluid): Lubricate the heart.
	Heart layers
Epicardium	Lubricate the heart. Decrease damage during contraction. Epicardium + Visceral layer (Inner pericardium)
Myocardium	Cardiac muscle contraction
Endocardium	Simple squamous endothelial cells contact with blood in chambers.

Heartbeat (Pacemaker)

A heartbeat is triggered by electrical impulses that travel down a special pathway through the heart.
Pacemaker control components: SA node, AV node, Bundle of His, Purkinje fiber

- Pacemaker: Special cardiac muscle fibers regulate the heartbeat in effective rhythm in the SA node.
- SA node: Sets basic heart rate in the right atrium.
- Vagus nerve: Parasympathetic nervous system
- EKG (Electrocardiogram): Electrical conduction of the heart monitoring
- Gap junction: 2 cells connect through pores. Very little resistance to pass an action potential.
- Autonomic nervous system: Regulate the heart rate.
- Sympathetic nervous system: Speed up the heart rate.
- Parasympathetic nervous system: Slow down the heart rate via the vagus nerves.

SA node (Sinoatrial node)	Generate action potential (electrical signal) Trigger electrical events → contract the heart + pump the blood Regulate the heart rate (heart contraction): 60-100 beats/min Special cardiac muscle cells Natural pacemaker Right atrium upper part Set the basic heart rate
AV node (Atrioventricular node)	● **Pacemaker impulse pathway** SA node → spread → atriums, atrial muscle fibers contraction → (AV node) → SA node action potential → AV node → receives action potential → delays slightly: Makes atrium contracts effectively, all the blood enters the ventricles → depolarizes and sends the electrical signal → Bundles of His (special cardiac fiber) → His splits into Left + Right branches → interventricular septum → bundles divided + form 'Purkinje fibers' Bundle of His + Purkinje fibers: Distribute electrical signals → both ventricles makes contraction at the same time Special cardiac myocytes At the base of the right atrium

● **Cardiac fibers impulsion**
SA node → Atrial muscle fibers (atria contract) → AV node → AV bundle → Right and left bundle branches → Purkinje fibers → Impulses to muscle fibers of both ventricles
→ Ventricles contract

13 Circulatory system

Cardiac cycle (Blood flow)

Cardiac cycle: One complete heartbeat (0.8 seconds)
- Systole: Contraction period
- Diastole: Relaxation period

- Cardiac output (CO): Volume of blood pumped by the left ventricle into the aorta in 1 minute.
- Stroke volume: Volume of the blood one ventricle pumps in one beat.
- Depends on venous return: The amount of blood the veins deliver to the heart.

● Starling's law of the heart
If the veins deliver more blood to the heart, the heart pumps more blood into the arteries.
Venous return ↑ Stretch cardiac muscle fiber ↑ Contraction force ↑ Stroke volume ↑

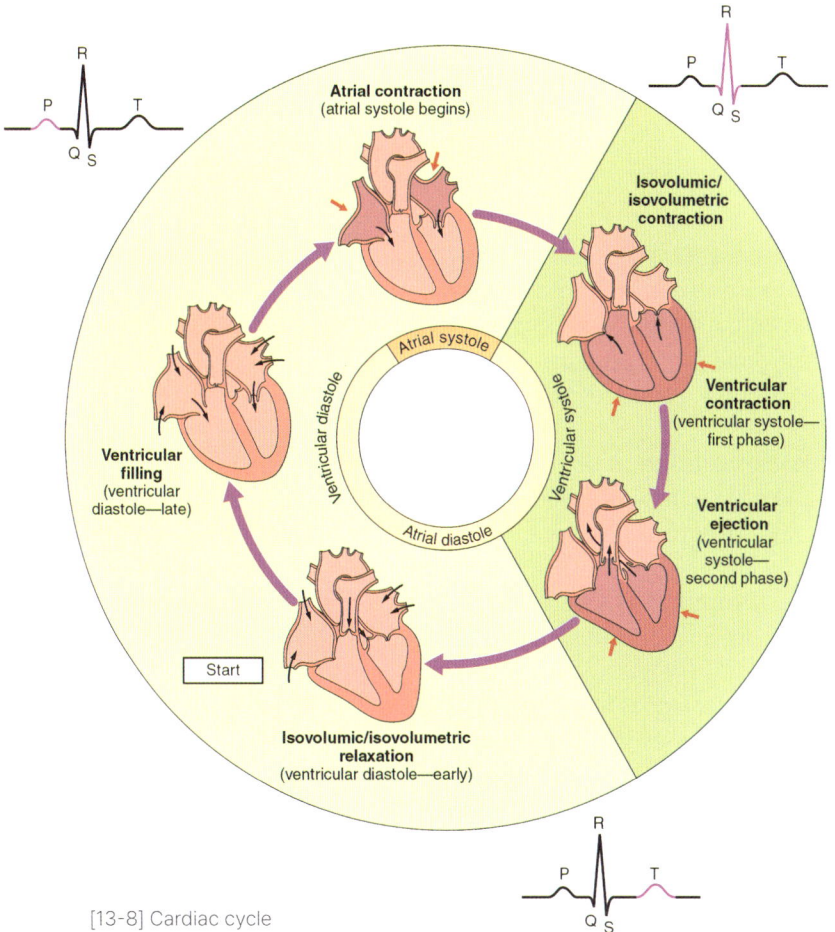

[13-8] Cardiac cycle

Right pump: Right atrium, Right ventricle
Left pump: Left atrium, Left ventricle

Atrial systole (contraction)	Atria contract → blood → open tricuspid and mitral valves → ventricles. Semilunar valves are closed.
Ventricular systole (contraction)	Ventricles contract → pressure ↑ → close tricuspid, mitral valves → heart sound
Rising pressure	Semilunar valves open → blood into aorta + pulmonary artery
Ventricular diastole (relaxation)	Ventricles pressure ↓ in arteries → semilunar valves closed → 2nd heart sound
Falling pressure	Vein → blood → relaxed atria

→ Repeats unidirectionally, continuously.

Blood pressure

• Blood pressure
The blood exerts on the walls of the blood vessels.
When blood moves, molecules, ions, and cells push against the walls: Force
- Systolic: Normal blood pressure < 120-139
- Diastolic: Normal blood pressure < 80-89

• Peripheral resistance
Resistance to blood flow by blood viscosity and by friction between the blood and the blood vessel walls: Resistance ↑ Blood pressure ↑ Blood velocity (flow) ↓

Length and diameter of a blood vessel determine the amount of the surface area. Length does not change, but diameter in arterioles changes.

Blood pressure decreases in the direction of the blood flow. (pulmonary, systemic)
- Blood vessel constriction: Blood pressure ↑
- Blood vessel dilation: Blood pressure ↓

- Baroreceptors: Special receptors in artery walls. (aortic arch, carotid sinus)
  Sense changes in blood pressure.

Ex) Blood pressure ↑ Baroreceptor stretch → Negative feedback → Heart rate decreases → Blood pressure ↓

- **Blood pressure related hormones**

Renin-Angiotensin-Aldosterone pathway	Kidney: activates 'Renin-angiotensin-aldosterone pathway' → Angiotensin 2 → Aldosterone: Blood mineral ↑ Blood pressure ↑
ADH (Antidiuretic hormone)	Body dehydrated → Osmotic concentration in the blood ↑ → release ADH: Hydration, Blood volume ↑ Blood pressure ↑ Restore homeostasis
ANP (Atrial natriuretic peptide)	Blood volume ↑ → Atria release ANP → Na^+ excretion ↑ → dilute urine → Blood pressure ↓

- **Body pressures**
- Osmotic pressure: Pressure produced by or associated with osmosis and dependent on molar concentration.
- Hydrostatic pressure: Pressure that any fluid in a confined space exerts.
- Colloidal pressure: In a blood vessel's plasma, the proteins, notably albumin, induce osmotic pressure.

Blood clotting

When the body gets hurt, the mass of blood forms when platelets, proteins, and cells in the blood stick together.

● Platelets: Fragment of cytoplasm + membrane
- Blood clotting
- Stimulate immune system

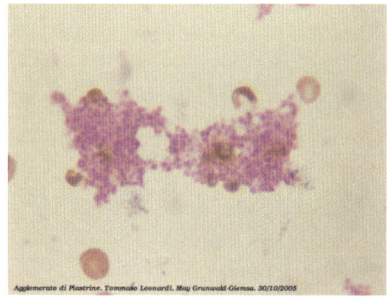

[13-9] Platelet

1. The blood vessel is cut → Platelets patch by sticking to the cut edges
2. Release substances → attract other platelets
3. Become sticky + adhere to collagen fibers
4. Form a 'Platelet plug' (temporary clot) in a short time. (5 mins)
5. Chemical substances interaction (in 30 mins)
6. Platelets release Ca^{2+}, K^+
   → Prothrombin (plasma protein from the liver) → transformed into Thrombin
7. Thrombin: Synthesized in the liver, catalyzes Fibrinogen
   (plasma protein, made by the liver) → converted into Fibrin
8. Fibrin: Made in the liver, found in blood plasma, polymerizes, produces long thread
   → sticks to damaged blood vessels → webbing of the clot

Cf. Hemophilia: Genetic disease, lack of 1 clotting factor.

Lymphatic system

Part of the circulatory system and the immune system
Consist of: Lymph nodes + Lymph nodules
Connective tissue, has many lymphocytes.
Location: Armpit, Neck, Thoracic duct

- Adaptive immune system: Produces antibodies and lymphocytes. (B-cell, T-cell)
  It defends the body against disease.
- Innate immune system: WBC, Natural killer cell

● Functions
- Producing antibodies
- Protecting the body from illness-causing invaders
- Maintaining body fluid levels
- Reabsorbing digestive tract nutrients and returning them into the veins
- Removing cellular waste
- Balance of interstitial fluid: Reabsorption, Clearing waste

● **Lymphatic system pathway**
Capillaries cannot absorb excessive fluid → Rest of the nutrients accumulated in the interstitial fluid → Lymph nodes + Lymphatic vessels

- Nutrients reabsorption → Vena cava → Heart
- Waste: Clear, excretion → Excretory systems
- Interstitial fluid: White blood cells
- Small molecules: Glucose, Amino acid, Nutrients, Oxygen, Salts

Chapter 14: Immune system

● Definition
- Network of cells and proteins that defends the body against infection.
- The immune system is spread through the entire body.

● Functions: Immune system blocks entry of pathogen and keeps a record of every germ it has ever defeated so it can recognize and destroy the microbe quickly if it enters the body again.

● **Pathogen**
Agent, living or non-living, causes harm to the cells of the body.
It travels through the air, food, and wounds.
   Ex) Microorganisms: Viruses, Bacteria, Protists, Fungi, Parasites

● **Antigen**
Macromolecules (substances) initiate an immune response.
Recognize and distinguish between its own cells and foreign cells.

● Immune system overview

Non-specific (Innate) immune system	Specific (Adaptive) immune system
Response immediately. Broad-spectrum	Response in several days. Specialized immunity for particular pathogens
● Physical barrier Skin: Prevents pathogens. Mucous membrane: Traps pathogens.	**● Antibody-mediated immunity** (Humoral immunity) Activation of B-cells and secretion of antibodies when in contact with a pathogen.

● Fluid secretions
 	
Stomach: Secretes HCl kills pathogens.
Skin, mouth, eyes: Secrete enzymes kill bacteria.
Oil glands: Sebum kills bacteria.
	- B-lymphocytes (B-cells)
	  Made and matured in the bone marrow.
	  Synthesize and store antibodies.
	
	Plasma B-cells: Produce and store antibodies.
	Memory B-cells: Protect from reinfection.

● White blood cells
 	
Blood, Lymphatic system
Phagocytes: Special cells engulf and destroy pathogens (Neutrophils, Monocytes)
Eosinophils: Parasitic reaction
Basophils: Allergic reaction
Megakaryocytes: Make platelets
	- Antibodies
	  Special defense molecules
	  Circulate in the blood.
	  Bind to specific antigens.
	  Initiate a defense response.

● Interleukin, Cytokine Interleukin: Regulate immune responses. Cytokine: Regulate cell activation, apoptosis, and cell proliferation.	**● Cell-mediated immunity** The immune response that does not involve antibodies. Activation of phagocytes, T-lymphocytes, and interleukins in response to antigens.

● Inflammation, Fever
 	
Special chemicals lead to inflammation.
Fever kills pathogens.
	- T-lymphocytes (T-cells)
	  Made in the bone marrow,
	  matured in the thymus.

● Complement system Enhance (complement) the ability of antibodies and phagocytic cells. Promote inflammation and attack the pathogen's cell membrane.	Helper T-cells Killer T-cells Suppressor T-cells Memory T-cells
● Lymphatic system Natural killer cells	**● Lymphatic system** B, T lymphocytes

Non-specific immune system

Innate immune system
Primary line of defense against pathogens
Broad-spectrum and reacts immediately after infection.

Physical barriers	● **Skin** The first line of defense system against invading pathogens. Glands: Secrete sebum → Bacteria cannot grow in the environment ● **Mucous, Cilia** Mucous sticky layer → traps pathogens Ex) Goblet cells Cilia: Move the pathogens to the outside or to the stomach.
Fluid secretion	● **Stomach acidity** Release HCl: Strong acid → destroys bacteria, viruses ● **Tears, Saliva** Lysozymes: Break down bacterial cell walls.

White blood cells	Leukocytes which defend the body from pathogens.
	Made in the hematopoietic stem cells in the bone marrow.
	
	- Leukocytes migration: WBC moves in and out of the cell walls.
	- Diapedesis: WBC moves independently and slips through the wall of capillaries → enters tissues
	
	● **Granulocytes**
	With granules, bi-lobed nuclei
	Phagocytic cells engulf bacterial cells.
	
	- Neutrophils: Phagocytosis (nonspecific), destroy pathogens.
	- Eosinophils: Parasitic infection reactions
	
	- Basophils
	  Histamine: Allergic response + Inflammation response
	  Heparin: Anti-clotting
	  Edema: Infected area becomes leaky.
	
	- Mast cells
	  Release histamines and cytokines → promoting inflammation
	  Help control other types of immune responses.
	
	● **Agranulocytes**
	Without granules
	Spherical, kidney-shaped nuclei

	- Monocytes 　Precursors of macrophages 　Engulf pathogens through phagocytosis. - Lymphocytes 　Circulatory system 　Innate immune system 　Adaptive immune system ● **Megakaryocytes**: Create platelets.
Inflammation	After physical barriers are broken → inflammation starts Blood flow increases to the infected area: Bringing white blood cells Symptom: Fever (38-39°C), germs cannot activate.
Signaling proteins	● **Interleukin**: Regulates immune responses. ● **Cytokine**: Regulates cell activation, apoptosis, and cell proliferation. ● **Interferon**: A group of signaling proteins (cytokines) released by host cells in response to the viruses. A cell is infected → releases Interferons → travels to neighboring healthy cells → binds to special receptors on the cells → initiates preparation for viral infection - Produce antiviral proteins: Block viral replication. 　Neighbor cells prepare for a defense. - Call natural killer cells: Seek and destroy infected cells and cancer cells. - Call macrophages: Engulf and break down infected cells. - Macrophages release their own interferons and amplify the immune response. - Stimulate the infected host cell's death.
Complement system	Enhance (complement) the ability of antibodies and phagocytic cells to clear microbes and damaged cells from an organism, promote inflammation, and attack the pathogen's cell membrane. A crucial mediator of the innate immune response, contributing to cell homeostasis, tissue development, repair, reproduction, and cross-talk with other endogenous systems. ● **Classical pathway** A major contributor to the defense against infections Clearance of pathogens Removal of apoptotic/necrotic cells Maintenance of homeostasis ● **Alternative pathway** Activated by viruses, fungi, bacteria, parasites, cobra venom, immunoglobulin A, and polysaccharides. Independent of the immune response
Lymphatic system	Contain white blood cells and natural killer cells. Seek and destroy infected cells and cancer cells. Apoptotic reaction

Specific immune system

Adaptive immune system
Specialized immunity for particular pathogens
Response in several days

- Antibody-mediated immunity (Humoral immunity)
- Cell-mediated immunity
- Lymphatic system

Antibody-mediated immunity (Humoral immunity)

Activation of B-cells and secretion of antibodies when in contact with a pathogen.
B-lymphocytes (B-cells) + B-cell receptors
Antigen-presenting cell (APC)
Synthesizing, storing antibodies
Cooperation with CD4 T-cells

- Pathogenic antigens: Float freely in tissues and attached to the membranes of macrophages or dendritic cells.

● Antibody-mediated immunity process

- Primary: Pathogens invasion → Antigens bind to B-cells → Interleukins, Helper T-cells stimulate B-cells → Plasma B-cells make antibodies + produce memory B-cells

- Secondary: Pathogens invasion → Memory B-cells recognize + bind to the pathogenic antigen → Memory B-cells produce plasma B-cells → produce and store antibodies

• B-lymphocytes (B-cells)

Made and matured in the bone marrow.
Synthesize and store antibodies.

- Plasma B-cells: Produce and store antibodies.
- Memory B-cells: Protect from reinfection.

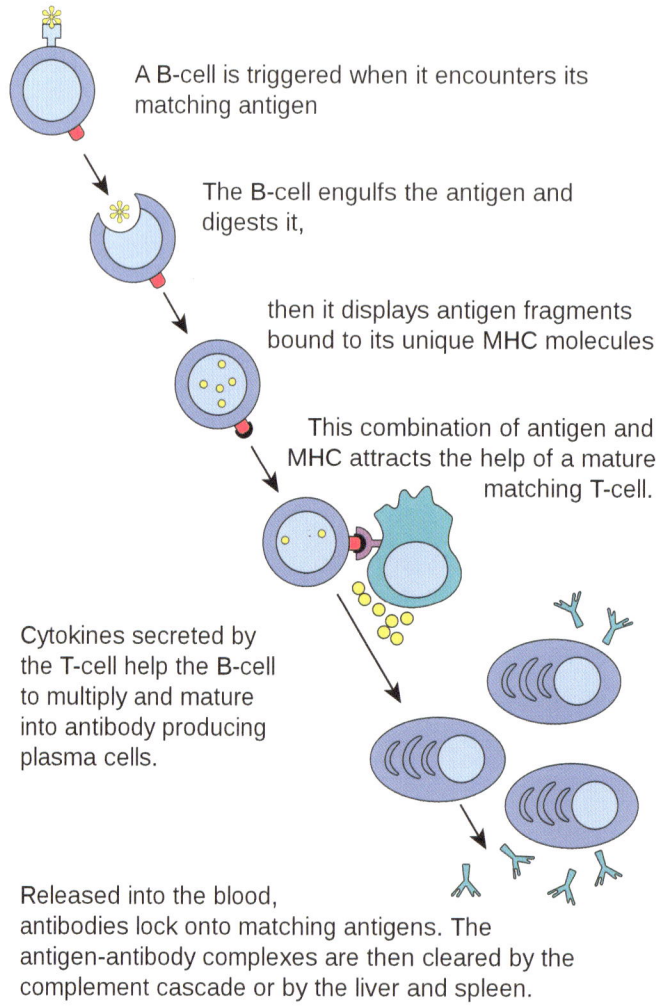

[14-1] B-cell

14 Immune system

• Antibodies (Immunoglobulins)

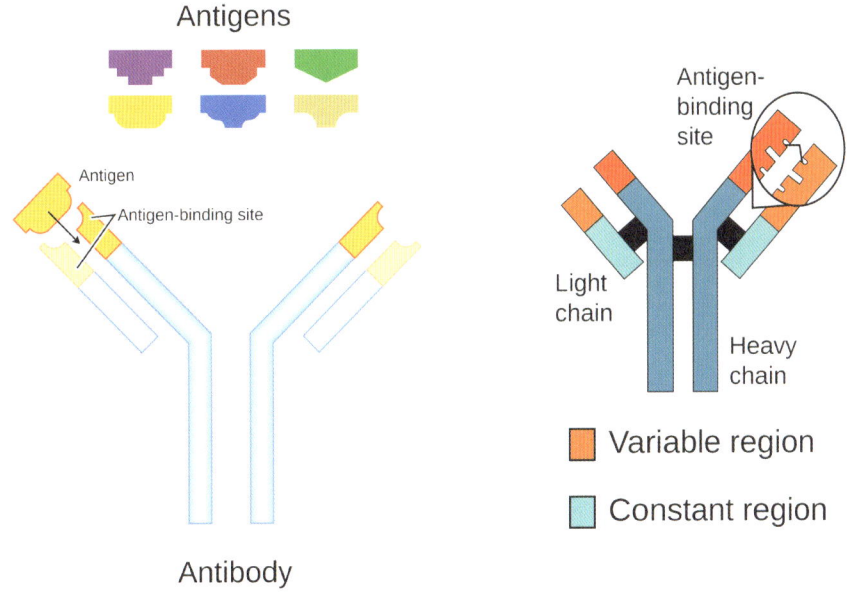

[14-2] Antibody [14-3] Antibody chains

Special defense proteins of the immune system
Components: Polypeptide subunits + Disulfide bridges + Y shape
Made by the plasma B-cells to fight infections like viruses.
Help to ward off future occurrences of the same infections.
Circulate in the blood.
Bind to specific antigens.
Initiate a defense response.

• Immunoglobulin types

IgM	Primary Immune response: Effective in virus
IgG	Secondary immune response: Majority antibodies
IgE	Binds to mast cells and basophils. Releases histamine: Allergic reaction
IgD	In B-lymphocytes: Antigen receptor, Antibody production
IgA	In the air passageways and digestive tracts

● Primary, Secondary immune response

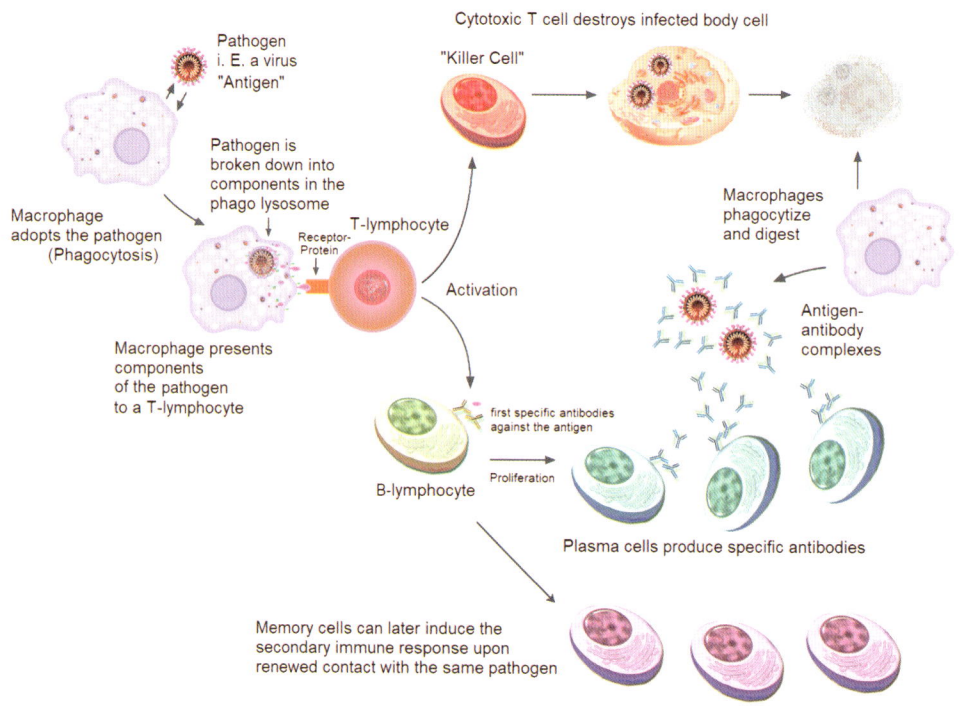

[14-4] Primary immune system

Primary immune response	The first exposure to some pathogenic antigens. During the adaptive immune system is being mobilized, lymphocytes are cloned. The latent period is long. - Major antibody: IgM
Secondary immune response	The same type of pathogen reinfects the body. More rapid immune response. The latent period is shorter than the primary immune response. - Major antibody: IgG

Cell-mediated immunity

Immune response that does not involve antibodies.
Activation of phagocytes, T-lymphocytes, and Interleukins in response to antigens.

- T-cells (T-lymphocytes) + T-cell receptors
- White blood cells
- MHC + Pathogenic antigen → T-cells recognize + bind to it

● **Cell-mediated immunity process**
Infected cells and APC (Antigen-presenting cells) display foreign antigens bind to T-cells
→ Interleukins activate T-cells (with MHC 1 or 2)

- MHC 1 + Cytotoxic T-cells + CD8 receptors
- MHC 2 + Helper T-cells + CD4 receptors: Release Interleukins
  → Stimulate B-cells to produce antibodies

● **T-lymphocytes** (T-cells)

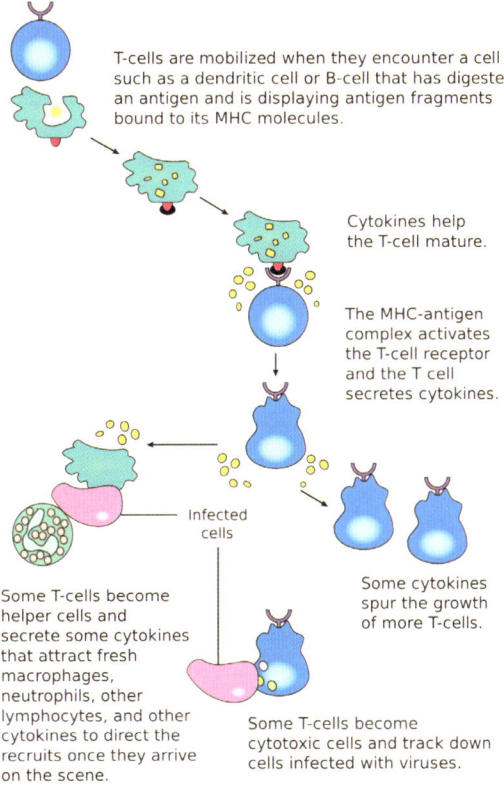

[14-5] T-cell

Made in the bone marrow and matured in the thymus.
It cannot bind to pathogenic antigens directly.

- Killer T-cells (cytotoxic T-cells): Seek foreign antigens and destroy pathogens.
- Helper T-cells: Release chemicals and assist communication with other immune cells.
- Memory T-cells: Protect from reinfection.
- Suppressor T-cells: Regulate and suppress T-cells.

● **MHC 1, 2** (Major Histocompatibility Complex)

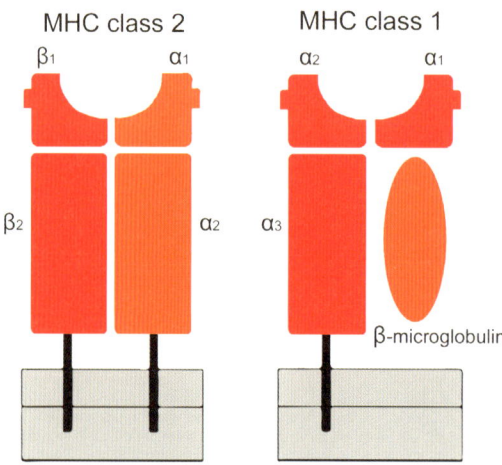

[14-6] Major histocompatibility complex

An immune system that recognizes and distinguishes its own cell and foreign cells, depending on a group of the protein complex on the cell membranes.

● **Antigen-presenting cells** (APC)

An immune cell detects, engulfs and informs the adaptive immune response about an infection.
When a pathogen is detected, these APCs will phagocytose the pathogen and digest it to form many different antigen fragments.
APCs naturally have a role in fighting tumors via stimulation of B and cytotoxic T-cells. Produce antibodies against the tumor-related antigens and kill malignant cells.

- T-lymphocytes cannot bind to pathogenic antigens directly.
  APC + Antigens → T-lymphocytes can bind

- Antigen-presenting cells: Macrophages, Dendritic cells, B-lymphocytes

Lymphatic system

Produce lymphocytes (B-cell, T-cell) and antibodies to defend the body against disease.

● **B-lymphocytes**
Plasma B-cells: Produce and store antibodies.
Memory B-cells: Protect from reinfection.

● **T-lymphocytes**
Killer T-cells: Seek foreign antigens and destroy pathogens.
Helper T-cells: Release chemicals, assist maturation of other cells, and communicate between immune cells.
Memory T-cells: Protect from reinfection.
Suppressor T-cells: Regulate and suppress T-cells.

Active, Passive immunity

When the body is exposed to pathogenic antigens, it produces antibodies for the antigen. Ever infected with the same antigen, the body already has the antibodies to deal with it.

Active immunity	Has immunity reaction. Body develops immunity to the pathogen by directly being exposed to the antigen. Memory cells are produced. - Natural: Naturally through exposure to the pathogen. Ex) Infection - Artificial: Give pathogens to make antibodies. Ex) Vaccine
Passive immunity	No immunity reaction Immunity acquired from someone or something else. Temporary immunity Memory cells are not produced. - Natural: Pregnant (IgG), Breastfeeding (IgA) - Artificial: Give antibodies directly. Ex) Immune medicine, Injection

Immune disease

Organ transplants immunosuppression	After an organ transplant, it will need to take immunosuppressant (anti-rejection) drugs. These drugs help prevent the immune system from attacking (rejecting) the donor organ.
Rh blood disease	Having an Rh-negative blood type is not an illness and usually does not affect health. However, it can affect pregnancy. Pregnancy needs special care if the mom is Rh-negative and the baby is Rh-positive (Rh incompatibility). A baby can inherit the Rh factor from either parents. (Type 2 hypersensitivity reaction)
Autoimmune disease	Condition in which the immune system mistakenly attacks the body. The immune system normally guards against germs like bacteria and viruses. When it senses these foreign invaders, it sends out an army of fighter cells to attack them.
HIV	Human Immunodeficiency Virus (HIV) is a virus that attacks the body's immune system. If HIV is not treated, it can lead to AIDS. (acquired immunodeficiency syndrome)
AIDS	Acquired immunodeficiency syndrome (AIDS) is a chronic, potentially life-threatening condition caused by the human immunodeficiency virus (HIV). By damaging the immune system, HIV interferes with the body's ability to fight infection and disease.
Allergic reactions	- Allergens: Substances that can cause an allergic reaction. - Anaphylaxis: A severe, potentially life-threatening allergic reaction. The reaction can occur within seconds or minutes of exposure to an allergen. Symptoms include a skin rash, nausea, vomiting, difficulty breathing, and shock. If not treated right away, usually with epinephrine, it can result in unconsciousness or death. - Histamine: Histamine is released by the body during an allergic reaction, response to an antibody called immunoglobulin E (IgE), causing the blood vessels to expand, which in turn causes a dangerous drop in blood pressure. Fluid can leak into the lungs, causing swelling (pulmonary edema). Anaphylaxis can also cause heart rhythm disturbances.

Chapter 15: Digestive system

● Definition
Breaks down food into the energy for the body.
Gastrointestinal tract + Organs for digestion

● Functions
Food digestion
Nutrient absorption
Move food by digestive tract motility.
Secrete hormones, enzymes to digest.

Nutrients	Substances in food, used as energy sources to power the system of the body ingredients needed for metabolic process.
Feeding	Process of selecting, acquiring, and ingesting food. Animals have a digestive system to eat.
Ingestion	Process of taking food into the digestive cavity.
Digestion	Process of breaking down food.
Absorption	Nutrients pass through the digestive tract into the blood.
Egestion (elimination)	Food is not digested or absorbed → discharged from the body

Animal classification

Herbivores	Primary consumers Eat producers (plants) Most of what they eat is not efficiently digested. Plant protein is difficult to digest, so it needs more time. Eat lots of food to get nourishment. Spend most of the time eating. 　Ex) Grasshopper, Elephant, Cattle
Ruminants	Hooved animals with stomachs divided into four chambers. Slow digestion: Long digestive tracts Bacteria and protists are living in 1, 2 chambers. Microbial digestion for cellulose of plant walls Digest cellulose, splitting molecules → sugars Produce fatty acids → energy source 　Ex) Cattle, Sheep, Deer, Giraffe, Cow
Carnivores	Secondary consumer Eat meat and flesh of animals. Predators capture and kill prey. Swallow alive, paralyze, crush, and shred. Adaptation: Tentacle, Claws, Fangs, Poison glass, Teeth Meat protein is easy to digest. Similar to the digestive system of human. Rapid digestion: Short digestive tracts Less and sharp teeth: K9 (Canine, 9th teeth of carnivores) Cannot digest plants: Need bacteria to digest.
Omnivores	Eat both plants and animals. Developed distinguishing many kinds of food from smells and tastes. 　Ex) Human, Earthworm, Whale, Pig, Dog

15 Digestive system

Digestive tract (Gastrointestinal tract)

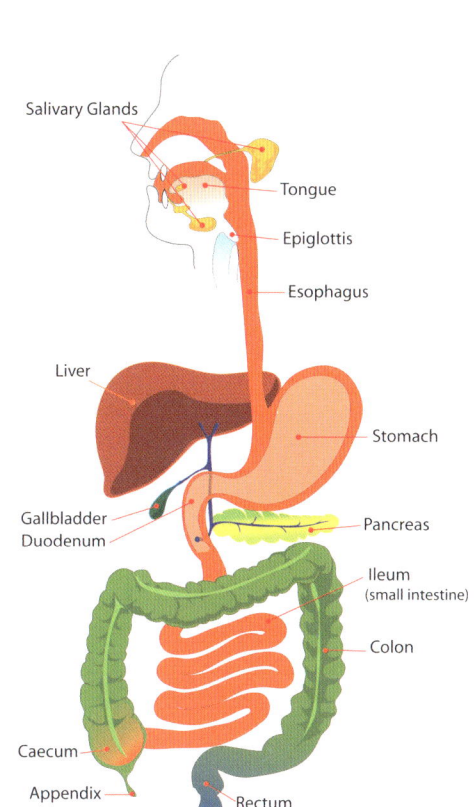

[15-1] Gastrointestinal tract

● **Pathway**: Oral cavity (mouth) → Pharynx → Esophagus → Stomach → Small intestine → Large intestine → Anus

Two-opening digestive tract: Tube-within-a-tube body
- Outer tube: Body wall
- Inner tube: Digestive tract + Two openings (mouth + anus)

Motility propulsive movements of the digestive tract
- Peristalsis: Propulsive activity characteristic

● **Types of digestion**
- Mechanical digestion: Physical movement to make foods smaller.
- Chemical digestion: Use enzymes to break down food.

Oral cavity (Mouth)

The first structure in the gastrointestinal system. It receives food.

● **Functions**

Mechanical digestion	Teeth are used to break down large food into smaller ones. Increasing the surface area of the macromolecules. Allowing the enzymes to act on larger areas. Not break down chemical bonds, just break down physical size.
Chemical digestion	Enzymes break down the bond. ● **Amylase (Ptyalin)** From the salivary gland Break down: Carbohydrates → Smaller maltase, dextrin Not efficient: Polysaccharides → Oligosaccharides ● **Lipase** Breaks down lipids.

- Bolus: Chewing form of a round mass food. Perfect for movement along the esophagus.
- Saliva: Water, proteolytic enzymes, antibacterial molecules from the salivary glands.
  Lubricating the food → reduces friction while moving along the esophagus

Pharynx

The passageway connects the nasal cavity + oral cavity → Larynx, trachea, esophagus
Allows the movement of air in/out of the lungs and movement of food bolus → Esophagus
Movement of food bolus → Esophagus

● **Esophageal sphincter**: Opens and allows the bolus to the esophagus.

● **Epiglottis**: Forms a protective barrier to block the food from entering the larynx.
Tongue, voluntary muscle forces the bolus into the larynx → respiration momentary stops

- Open: breathing (Air → Larynx)
- Close: digestion (Food, liquid → Esophagus) ↔ Failed: cough

Esophagus

Long and narrow passageway that connects the pharynx to the stomach.
It runs along the back of the windpipe, in front of the spinal cord.
It carries food and liquid from the pharynx to the stomach.

- Peristalsis: Wave-like contraction of smooth muscle
  Allows the food to move down the esophagus.

- Upper esophagus: Skeletal muscle (voluntary) that starts a movement of the bolus voluntarily.

- Rest of the esophagus: Smooth muscle (involuntary) that the bolus continues moving in the esophagus via involuntary movement.

- Cardiac sphincter: Bottom of the esophagus → allows the bolus moves into the stomach

Stomach

Flexible sac, which receives food from the esophagus.

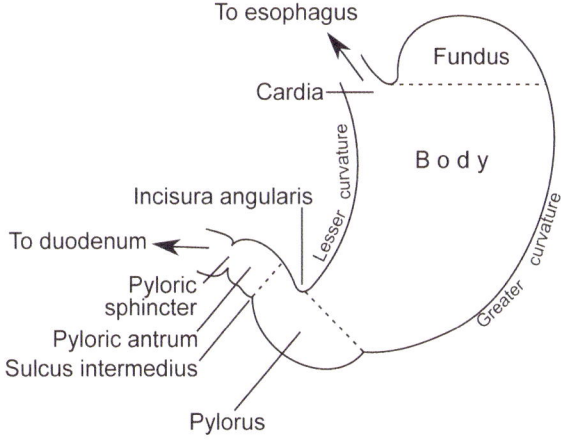

[15-2] Stomach

● Structures and functions

Chemical digestion	Pepsin (enzyme in gastric juice) breaks down proteins into smaller polypeptides. Chyme: Mix of gastric juice + food
Absorption	Lipid-soluble substances: Aspirin, Alcohol, Caffeine
Motility	Movement of the food
Secretion	Exocrine glands (gastric glands) on the wall secretes gastric juice to the stomach lumen. ● **G cells** Deep exocrine glands Acetylcholine stimulates G cells to release Gastrin. (peptide hormone) Gastrin - Stimulates parietal cells to make HCl. - Stimulates the chief cells to release Pepsinogen. ● **Parietal cells** Secrete HCl. (hydrochloric acid) HCl (hydrochloric acid) - Raises the stomach acidity: Pepsinogen → Pepsin - Denatures proteins. - Makes pepsin break down protein bonds. - Kills bacteria. - Secretes gastric intrinsic factor: Small intestine absorbs vitamin B12. ● **Chief cells** Deeper in the exocrine glands Release pepsinogen by gastrin hormone. Pepsin - HCl increases acidity → pH 2: Pepsinogen (zymogen) → converted into Pepsin (active enzyme) - Pepsin: Breaks down proteins into smaller polypeptides. ● **Mucous cells** Upper exocrine glands, stomach walls Secrete a sticky mucus. (glycoprotein, water, ions) Lubricate the lining of the stomach. Protect the lining of the stomach from degradation. (high acidity)

15 Digestive system

● **Stomach pathway**
G cells: Gastrin stimulates the parietal cells: HCl → increases acidity → at pH 2, Chief cells convert Pepsinogen to Pepsin: protein digestion ↔ Mucous cells: acidity protection

Small intestine

An organ in the gastrointestinal tract where most of the absorption of nutrients from food takes place. Majority of the digestion, almost all absorption occurs.

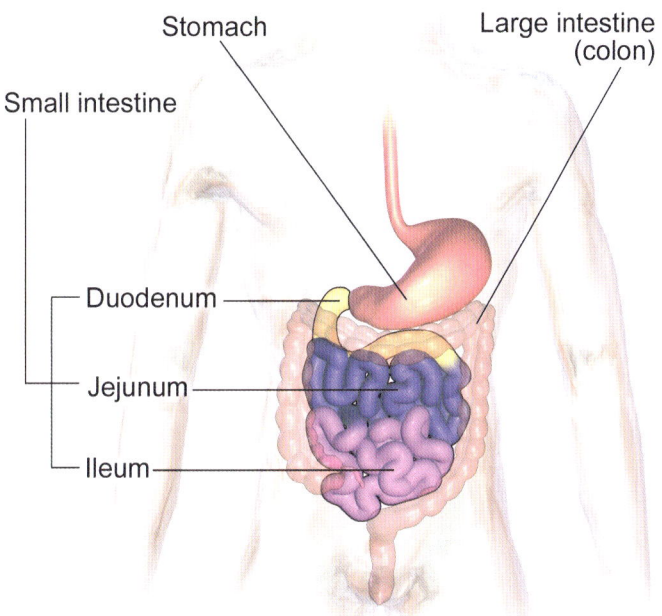

[15-3] Small intestine

- Duodenum: Most of the digestion occurs.
- Jejunum, Ileum: Most absorption
- Enterocytes: Intestinal cells
- Villi: Projections, consists of the small intestine walls.
- Microvilli: Hair-like projections that increase the surface area of the small intestine. Mucosal folds, intestinal villi, and microvilli increase the small intestine surface.

● Functions

Chemical digestion	**● With the Pancreatic enzymes** Pancreas makes Pancreatic enzymes → releases into the small intestine <u>Pancreatic amylase:</u> Breaks down carbohydrates. <u>Pancreatic peptidase:</u> Breaks down proteins. - Trypsin, Chymotrypsin, Carboxypeptidase <u>Pancreatic lipase:</u> Breaks down lipids. - Chylomicron: Fatty acids + Glycerol → Liver: Lipoprotein → cells **● With the Small intestine enzymes** Brush borders secret the small intestine digestive enzymes. Most digestion occurs in the duodenum. Enterocytes membrane + Membrane-bound proteins → proteolytic function <u>Disaccharidase</u> Breaks down disaccharides glycosidic bond. Location: Brush border (microvilli) - Maltase: Breaks down maltose - Sucrase: Breaks down sucrose - Lactase: Breaks down lactose <u>Peptidase, Dipeptidases</u> Proteolytic enzymes Break down dipeptide, peptide bonds. <u>Enterokinase</u> Converts Trypsinogen (zymogen) → Trypsin (active enzyme) Location: Villi
Mechanical digestion	**● With Bile salt** Liver makes bile salt and stores it in the gallbladder. <u>Bile salt</u> Liver → stored in the gallbladder → Small intestine Amphiphilic: Lipid emulsification - Lipid emulsification: Bile salt helps mechanically digest the lipid in the small intestine → increases the areas where lipase can act on

15   Digestive system

Absorption	Absorb monomers, vitamins, and electrolytes → Liver ● **Lipid transportation** Small intestine: Chylomicron (Fatty acids + Glycerol) → Liver: Lipoprotein → cells
Digestive hormones secretion	Secretin Peptide hormone by S-cell Stimulates the pancreas → release the pancreatic juice Cholecystokinin (CKK) Peptide hormone Stimulates the pancreas → releases the pancreatic juice Enterogastrone Slow down the movement of chyme along the small intestine. Proteolytic enzymes need time to break down macromolecules.

Pancreas

Helps digestion by making enzymes to break down sugars, fats, and peptides.
Controls blood sugar levels by secreting hormones.
Pancreatic juice → Pancreatic ducts → Small intestine

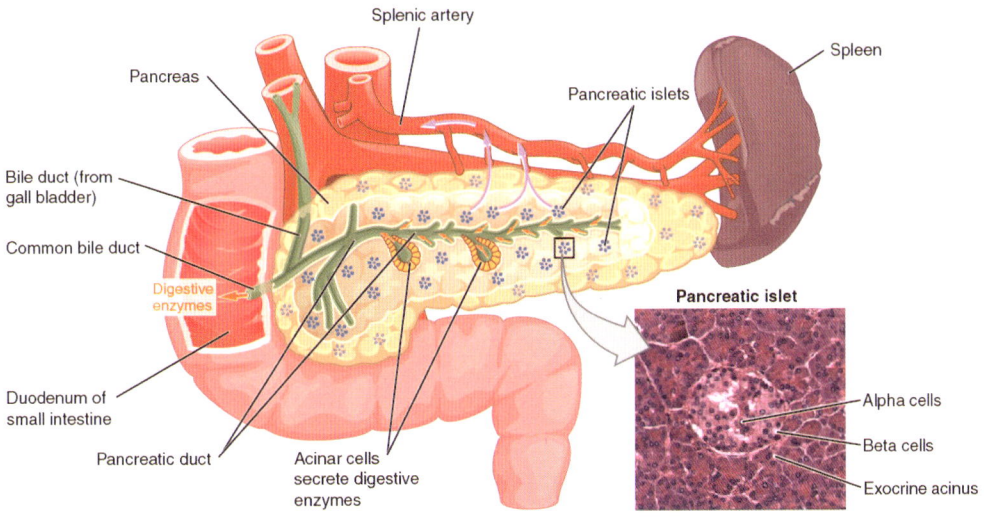

[15-4] Pancreas

- **Functions**

Endocrine	Pancreas secretes hormones. - Islets of Langerhans: Special cells inside the pancreas - Hormones: Insulin, Glucagon, Somatostatin, Pancreatic polypeptide

Exocrine	Pancrease secretes digestive enzymes.
	
	Pancreatic amylase
	Breaks down carbohydrates: Starch, Glycogen + α-linkage
	
	Pancreatic lipase
	Breaks down complex fat → Fatty acids
	
	Pancreatic peptidase
	Proteolytic enzymes
	Various peptidases: Each protease splits an only certain portion of a protein.
	
	- Trypsin: Breaks down peptide bonds.
	  Enterokinase makes Trypsinogen (zymogen) → Trypsin
	
	- Chymotrypsin: Breaks down peptides at aromatic amino acids.
	  Trypsin, Chymotrypsin activates Chymotrypsinogen (zymogen)
	  → Chymotrypsin
	
	- Carboxypeptidase: Hydrolyzes proteins with carboxyl-end.

Liver

Organ in the upper right abdomen

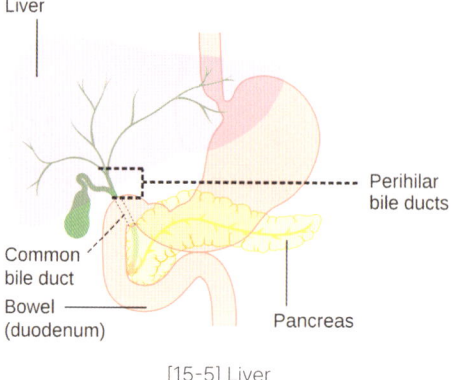

[15-5] Liver

• Functions

Macromolecule energy metabolism	Break down fats, synthesis and store macromolecules. All of the macromolecule, nutrients absorption
	
	● **Carbohydrates**
	Liver controls blood glucose levels.
	
	- Glucose level ↓: Liver cells release glycogen → break it down into glucose → send it into the blood plasma
	
	- Glucose level ↑: Liver cells absorb glucose → transform → Glycogen
	
	- Excessive glucose: Stored as glycogen
	  + Insulin: converted into Fatty acids, Glycerol → Triglycerides (fats)
	
	Glycogen is too big to move around the blood: Glucose → Blood → Liver → synthesized as glycogen form
	
	- Gluconeogenesis: Liver cells produce glucose from non-sugar constituents.
	
	● **Fats (Triglycerides)**
	Produce bile salts → emulsify fats (in the small intestine)
	Triglycerides: Store fats → broken down via beta-oxidation → ATP
	Cholesterol synthesis: Produce and clear cholesterol in the body.
	
	- Lipid transportation: Lipid cannot move around the blood vessel alone.
	- Small intestine: Chylomicron (Fatty acids + Glycerol) → Liver: Lipoprotein (Protein cover + Lipid) → move around the blood vessels
	
	● **Proteins**
	Most protein synthesis goes in the liver. (rough ER)
	Produce non-essential amino acids.
	Produce proteins: Albumin, Fibrinogen
	
	- Deamination: Liver deaminates excessive amino acids.
	   Removes amino group → Ammonia → Urea → excreted
	   Removes amino group → Glycolysis, Acetyl CoA → ATP
	   Removes amino group → stored into Fatty acids

Detoxification	Detoxify toxic substances: Drugs, Alcohol, Metabolic end-products Ex) Lactic acid, Ammonia, Pollutants Convert fat-soluble toxins to water-soluble → excreted as bile, urine, sweat

Blood management	Blood storage, Filtration, Red blood cell recycling - Blood storage: Liver cell blood vessel → expands to store extra blood - Kupffer cells (filtration): Phagocytic cells engulf and destroy bacterial cells. - Cell recycling: RBC dies → Macrophages phagocyte → Liver breaks down → recycle RBC, nutrients
Vitamins storage	Store vitamins, cofactors: Lipid-soluble vitamins (D, A, E, K), Iron
Hormone producer	Angiotensin 1, 2: Na^+ absorption Thrombopoietin: Glycoprotein hormone, produces platelets.
Bile salt production	Mechanical digestion Bile salts → stored in the gallbladder → released to the small intestine → Bile salts: emulsify fats → divide into small species → widen the surface areas → Small intestine can dissociate fat globules → better digestion, absorption fats - Bilirubin: Orange-yellow pigment - Anti-bacteria: Inhibits harmful bacteria

Large intestine

The organs follow the small intestine.
It has a large diameter and shorter length than the small intestine.
It absorbs water, salts, and nutrients from the material that has not been digested as food and eliminates leftover waste products.

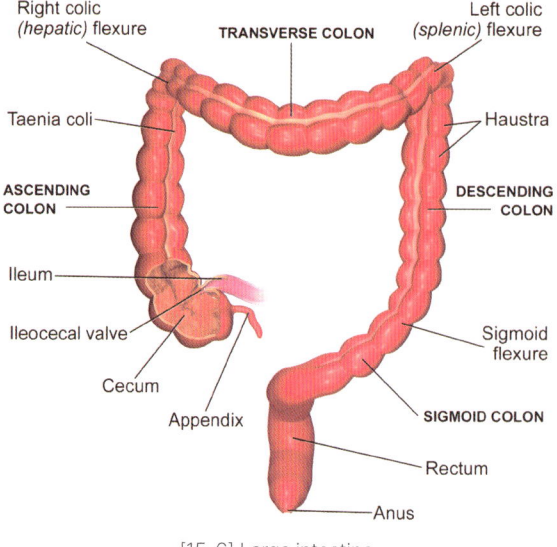

[15-6] Large intestine

15   Digestive system

• Structures and functions

Cecum	Small pouch which receives digestive chyme from the ileum. The appendix organ Connects the small intestine to the ascending colon. Push remaining chyme → rest of the large intestine Herbivores: Cecum contains specialized bacterial cells → breaks down cellulose
Colon	4 segments: Ascending, Transverse, Descending, Sigmoid (s-shaped) colons It absorbs water, ions, and vitamins which have not been absorbed from other sides of the body. It makes all the essential molecules and minerals to be absorbed entirely.

Rectum	Feces is stored before being excreted out.
	Rectum walls can expand to fit more feces.
	
	- Feces: Water, Dead bacterial cells, Fiber (indigestible cellulose),
	  Proteins (enzymes), Bile
	- Bacteria: Produce essential molecules. (Vitamin B12, Vitamin K)
	- Vitamin B12: DNA synthesis final component
	- Vitamin K: Synthesized by bacteria in the large intestine,
	  and act as a coagulation factor.

Anus	Opening where the feces is excreted. Internal sphincter muscle (involuntary movement) + External sphincter muscle (voluntary movement)

Nutrients digestion

Nutrients (proteins, carbohydrates, fats) are broken down into a simple unit.

Carbohydrates	● Breaking down pathway Monosaccharide → Glycolysis → ATP (4kcal/1g) - Excessive glucose: Stored as glycogen + Insulin: converted into Fatty acids, Glycerol → Triglycerides (fats)
Lipids	● Breaking down pathway Fats hydrolyzed → Fatty acids → Beta-oxidation (oxidized → split into 2C acetate) + CoA → Acetyl CoA → Citric acid cycle → ATP (9kcal/1g) Energy source, Cell membrane, Steroid hormones Bile salt: Fat emulsification Triglycerides (triacylglycerol): Body's neutral fats - Lipid transportation: Lipid cannot move around the blood vessels alone. (hydrophobic) - Small intestine: Chylomicron → Liver: Lipoprotein → Blood vessels - LDL (Low-Density Lipoprotein) Bad cholesterol High LDL level leads to a buildup of cholesterol in the arteries. Transport all fat molecules around the body in the extracellular water. - HDL (High-Density Lipoprotein) Good cholesterol Absorbs cholesterol and carries it back to the liver. The liver then flushes it from the body. High HDL cholesterol levels can lower the risk for heart disease and stroke.

Proteins	● Breaking down pathway
	Amino acid → Small intestine → Liver
	
	Essential building blocks of cells
	Enzymes, essential component: Receptors, Hemoglobin, Myosin
	
	- Deamination: Liver deaminates excessive amino acids.
	  Removes amino group → Ammonia → Urea → excreted
	  Removes amino group → Glycolysis, Acetyl CoA → ATP (4kcal/1g)
	  Removes amino group → stored into Fatty acids

- Acetyl CoA: Key intermediate molecule in the metabolism of all the nutrients.

15 Digestive system

• Nutrients digestion by pathways

	Carbohydrates	Proteins	Lipids
Mouth	**Amylase** Polysaccharides ↓ Disaccharides, Oligosaccharides		
Stomach	Acidic pH inactivates salivary amylase ↓	**Pepsin** Protein ↓ Short polypeptides	
Pancreas /Liver	**Pancreatic Amylase** Polysaccharides ↓ Maltose, Disaccharides ↓	**Pancreatic Peptidases** **Trypsin, Chymotrypsin** **Carboxypeptidase** Polypeptides ↓ Short polypeptides, Peptides ↓	**Bile salt** (Liver) Triglycerides ↓ Emulsified fat droplets ↓ **Pancreatic Lipase** Fatty acids + Glycerol
Small Intestine	**Disaccharidases** Maltase: Glucose + Glucose Sucrase: Glucose + Fructose Lactase: Glucose + Galactose	**Peptidase** **Dipeptidase** Amino acids	Digestion

Vitamins, Minerals

• Vitamins

Organic compounds, which are required in the diet in relatively small amounts.
Components of coenzymes
Deficiency, large overdoses of vitamins can be harmful.

Fat-soluble	Vitamin D, A, E, K Surplus: Not easily excreted and accumulated to harmful levels.
Water-soluble	Vitamin C, B Excreted in the urine.

- Vitamin A: Helps retina
- Vitamin K: Coagulation (with calcium)
- Vitamin B12: Final component of DNA synthesis
- Vitamin D deficiency: Loss of bone density, Rickets, Insomnia, Dizziness, Hair loss, Anxiety, Mood problem, Hypertension

• Minerals

Inorganic nutrients ingested in the form of salts dissolved in food and water.
Necessary components of body tissues and fluids.
Vital in maintaining the fluid balance of the body: Lost in sweat, urine and feces
Deficiency: Dehydration
  Ex) Na, Cl, K, Ca, P, Mg, Ma, S

- Antioxidant: Enzymes that destroy free radicals. (catalase, peroxidase)
  Ex) Phytochemicals

- Phytochemicals: Antioxidants, essential nutrients, and plant compounds promote health.
  Ex) Lycopene (red), Flavonoids (cocoa), Carotenoids (yellow, orange)

chapter 16

Reproduction

● Definition: Make zygotes through fertilization and give birth to offspring.

● Functions
- Produce sexual hormones.
- Genetic recombination
- Maintain and pass on genetic materials to offspring.
- Give birth to offspring.
- Produce, nourish and sustain gametes. (egg cells, sperm cells)

Asexual reproduction	A single parent gives birth to offspring that are genetically identical to the parent. 　Ex) Invertebrates, Sponges, Cnidarians, Rotifers, Flatworms, Annelid
Sexual reproduction	Two gametes (sperm and eggs) become a zygote (fertilized egg) through fertilization and give birth to offspring. (genetic variation)
Internal fertilization	The male generally delivers sperm cells directly into the female's body.
External fertilization	Gametes meet outside the body and simultaneously release eggs and sperms into the water. 　Ex) Aquatic animals
Hermaphroditism	A single individual produces eggs and sperms.

● **Clinical signal**
- Female human: Menstruation
- Other mammals: Estrus

Male reproduction

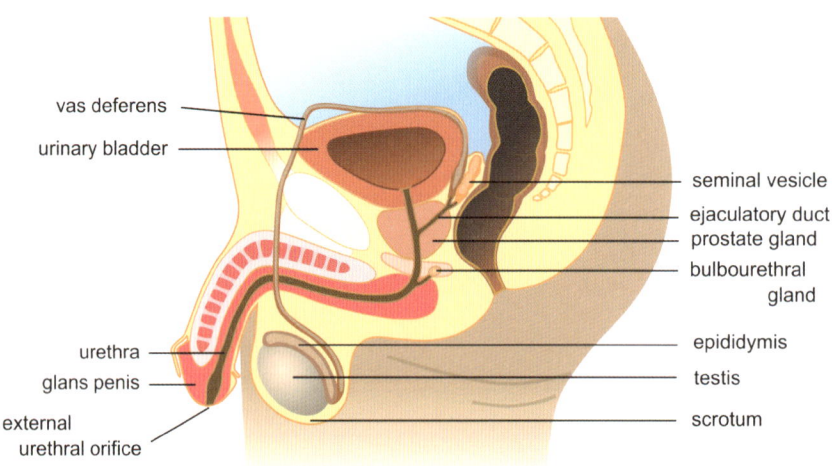

[16-1] Male reproductive system

Pathway: Testis (seminiferous tubules) → Epididymis → Vas deferens → Ejaculatory duct → Urethra

Testis	Starts making sperms.
Seminiferous tubules	Located in the testis. Produce immature sperm cells. (spermatogenesis) - Spermatogonium: Makes sperms through meiosis. - Leydig cells: Produce testosterone and make primary spermatocytes.
Epididymis	Store and mature sperm cells. - Sperm maturation: For about five weeks, sperms travel through the epididymis, completing their development.
Vas deferens	Transports sperm cells: Epididymis → Ejaculatory duct
Ejaculatory duct	
Urethra	Final canal which moves the sperms along and out of the body.

16 Reproduction

	Accessory glands Add nutrients and fluid to sperms and semen. - Semen: Grayish white bodily fluid, Sperm + Fructose + Enzymes It helps sperms survive in fertilization.
Seminal vesicle	Secretes nutrients (sugar, fructose, protein) needed by sperm cells.
Prostate	Secretes an alkaline fluid → helps neutralize the acidity inside the vaginal tract
Bulbourethral gland	Releases a fluid substance → helps neutralize the acidity of the vagina during the pre-ejaculatory phase

Spermatogenesis

The origin and development of the sperm cells within the male reproductive organs, the testes.

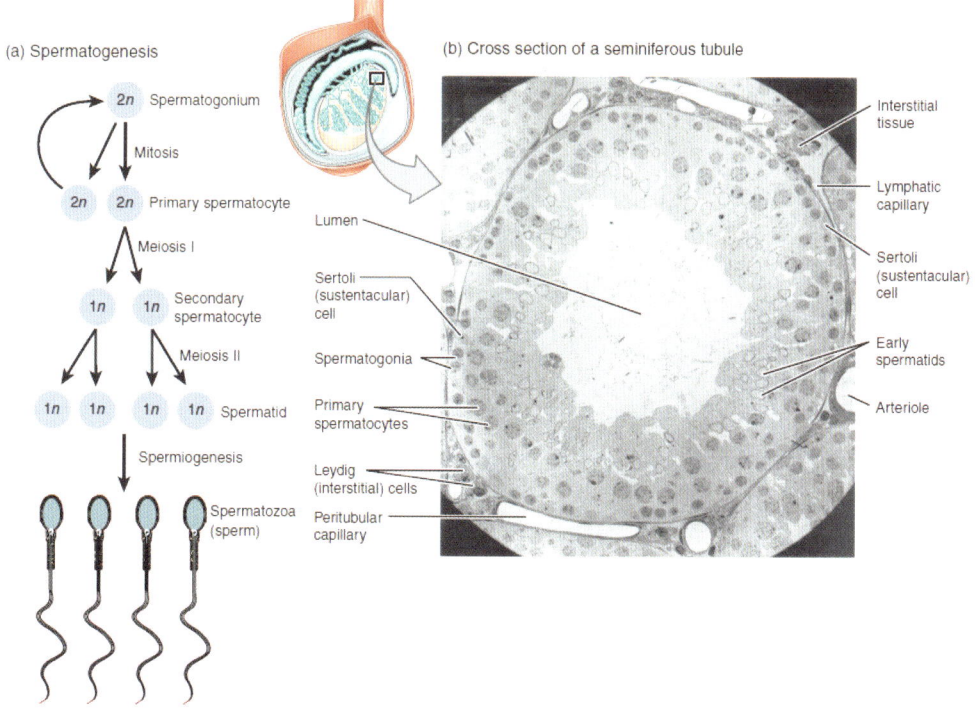

[16-2] Spermatogenesis

Spermatogonium	In the seminiferous tubules Diploid (2n) 46 chromosomes, precursor stem cells → give rise to sperm cells
Leydig cells	Produce testosterone. (steroid hormone) Stimulates spermatogonium → Primary spermatocytes (diploid, 2n)
Meiosis 1	Produces secondary spermatocytes (haploid, n x 2)
Meiosis 2	Secondary spermatocytes → 4 spermatids (haploid, n x 4) → Sperm cells

● **Sertoli cells**

Provide nutrients to growing sperm cells and help remove the unwanted cytoplasm.
Male reproduction: Continuous reproduction (until ages 70-80)
↔ Female reproduction has a limited period.

● **Sperm cells**

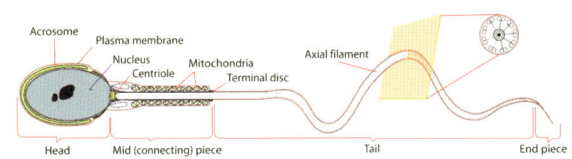

Head: nucleus (haploid)
- Acrosome: Enzymes help the sperm penetrate the egg coat

Middle: mitochondria
Tail: flagellum

[16-3] Sperm cell

● **Male reproductive system hormones**
- GnRH: Stimulates LH, FSH
- LH: Stimulates testosterone production
- FSH: Stimulates sperm production

Female reproduction

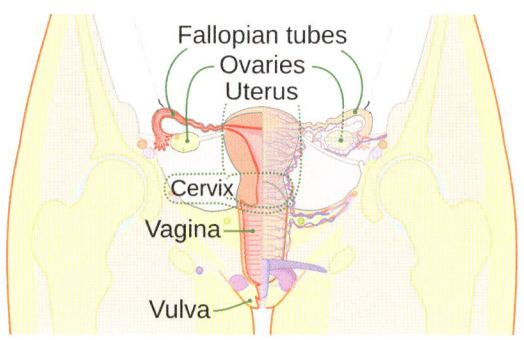

[16-4] Female reproductive system

Pathway: Ovary → Oviduct (fallopian tube) → Uterus/Endometrium → Cervix → External genitals

Ovary	Oogenesis Gametes production: Ova (ovum) Female sex hormone production: Estrogen, Progesterone Ovulation
Oviduct (Fallopian tube)	Moves the ovum along with the uterus. Fertilization: Egg cell + Sperm cell Lined with smooth muscles + cilia
Uterus	Pear-shaped organ Lined with thick, smooth muscle layers (myometrium) Contracts during childbirth.
Endometrium	Mucous layer Thickens in preparation for fertilization. Zygotes implantation: Onto the endometrium → grows + embryological development Cf. Uterine horn: Mammal females (not in human)
Cervix	Tiny opening, connects the uterus to the vagina. Closes the gate to block pathogens to provide protection, lower pH.
Vagina	Elastic, muscular tube Connects uterus to outside. Sperm enters here.

- **Female breast**

Estrogen and progesterone increase the breast size.
15 to 20 lobes of glandular tissue
Breastfeeding promotes recovery of the uterus.

- Breast milk: Immune cells (B-cells, T-cells, Neutrophils, Macrophages)
- Lactation: Production of milk for nourishing the young (hormone: prolactin)
- Prolactin: Secreted by the anterior pituitary, it stimulates milk production.
- Oxytocin: By the posterior pituitary, it stimulates the ejection of milk from the alveoli into the ducts and uterus contraction.

Oogenesis

Process in which female gametes are produced in the ovaries.
1st oocytes are produced during fetal development.

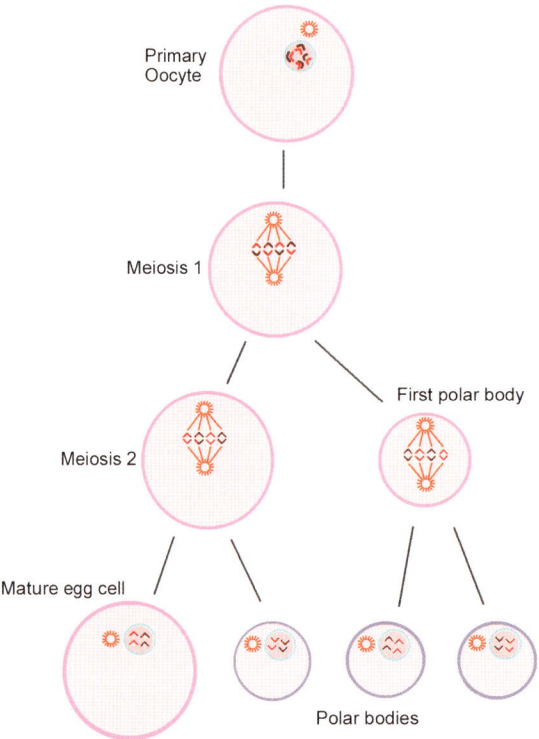

[16-5] Oogenesis

Oogonium Precursor of stem cells made during fetal development Oogonia → Primary oocytes	2n	**Meiosis**
Primary oocyte Puberty: Menstrual cycle starts Primary oocytes → Meiosis 1 → Secondary oocyte +1st polar body: Eliminates one-half of the diploid chromosome	2n	**Meiosis 1**
Secondary oocyte Secondary oocyte → remains frozen in Metaphase 2 ● **Fertilization** Sperm cell enters → Fertilization: Secondary oocyte finishes Meiosis 2 → Ovum (matured egg) ● **Menstruation** Frozen secondary oocyte → Menstruation	n	**Meiosis 2**
Ovum (matured egg) +2nd polar body: Eliminates one-half of the diploid chromosome	n	**Fertilization**

Ovarian follicles

Fluid-filled sacs, develop oocytes and mature other cells.
Regulate oogenesis process.
Produce sex steroid hormones. Ex) Estrogen

- Location: Ovaries
- Components: Oocyte + Theca cell + Granulosa cell

Every month: Primary follicle (+ primary oocyte)
→ developed into Secondary follicle (+ secondary oocyte)

Theca cell	Granulosa cell
Stimulated by LH (Luteinizing hormone)	Stimulated by FSH (Follicle-stimulating hormone)
Cholesterol → Androgen	Androgen → Estrogen

Follicle (Theca cell + Granulosa cell) development
Estrogen ↑↑ → LH levels peak → Ovulation

- LH, FSH: Steroid hormones
- Cholesterol: Converts androgen into estrogen

Menstrual cycle

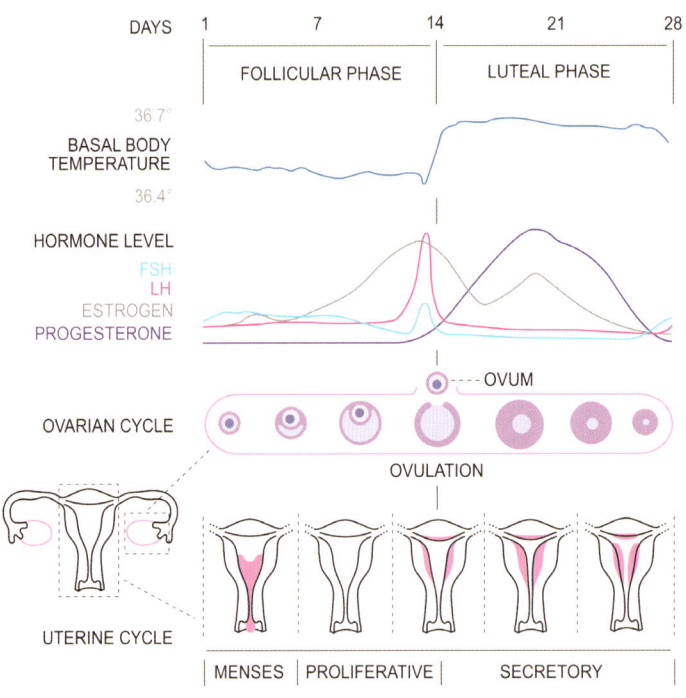

[16-6] Menstrual cycle

Ovulation (14 days) + Luteal phase (14 days)
Sequence of events that lasts about 28 days, prepares the woman for pregnancy.
Fertilization does not occur → 2nd oocytes in the endometrium → discharged (bleeding)

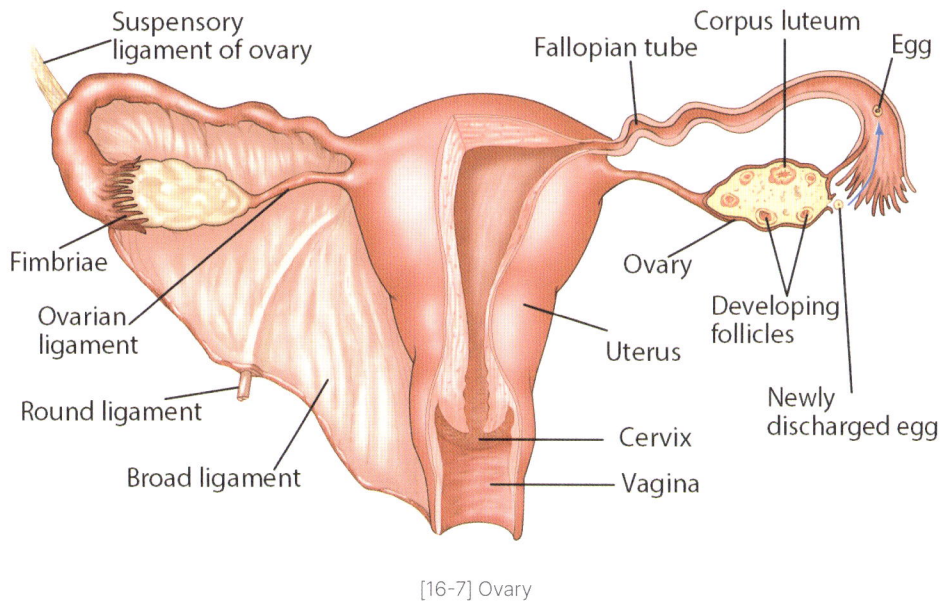

[16-7] Ovary

● **Pathway**

Menstruation → GnRH: stimulates LH, FSH → Follicles development
(theca cell, granulosa cell) → Estrogen ↑↑ → Negative feedback to GnRH
→ Follicles die → Dominant follicle survives → Positive GnRH feedback
→ LH, FSH levels peak → Ovulation → Corpus luteum: secretes Progesterone, Estrogen
→ Fertilization (pregnant) or Menstruation (not pregnant)

Hormone/Phase	Location	Process
Menstruation	Endometrium Uterus	Developing follicles
GnRH	Hypothalamus	Hypothalamus: secretes GnRH Stimulate the release FSH, LH Stimulate the immature follicle to mature Primary follicle → meiosis 1 → Secondary follicle produces Estrogen
FSH		Anterior pituitary: secretes LH, FSH, stimulates follicles development
LH	Anterior pituitary	- Theca cell by LH: Cholesterol → Androgen - Granulosa cell by FSH: Androgen → Estrogen Estrogen: GnRH negative feedback → Many follicles die, the dominant follicle survives Estrogen: GnRH positive feedback → LH, FSH levels up + levels peak → Ovulation (Endometrium thickening)
Ovulation (day 14)	Ovary	LH, FSH levels up + Levels peak → Ovulation Secondary oocyte goes out: Ovary → Oviduct (until fertilization) ↔ Other oocytes degenerate (apoptosis)
Luteal Phase (day 15-28) **preparing pregnant**	Ovary	Secondary follicle ruptured → Corpus luteum (in the ovary) Corpus luteum: secretes Progesterone, Estrogen Progesterone: GnRH negative feedback → FSH, LH ↓ ● **Fertilization** (pregnant) - Corpus luteum: Continues until the end of the pregnancy. - 2nd oocyte → Ovum (egg) → Embryo: In the endometrium, uterus ● **Menstruation** - Corpus luteum + 2nd oocyte: Slough off (endometrium)
Fertilization	Oviduct	Egg cell (Ovum) + Sperm cell → Zygote (embryo) in the oviduct Implantation: Endometrium
Menstruation	Endometrium Uterus	When the fertilization does not occur: - Corpus luteum: Starts to break down between 9-11 days after ovulation. - 2nd oocyte: Starts to break down in menstruation. LH ↓ Corpus luteum deteriorated, Progesterone ↓ Endometrium breaks down, sloughed off.

Menstruation hormones

• Cycle

Menstruation → Corpus luteum broken down → GnRH releasing: Positive feedback to LH, FSH → Follicles development → Estrogen levels up → LH, FSH levels up → LH peaks → Ovulation → Corpus luteum: produces Progesterone → Negative feedback to GnRH → Fertilization (or) Menstruation

GnRH	(Gonadotropin-releasing hormone) Synthesized in the hypothalamus. Stimulates the release of FSH and LH. Stimulates immature follicles to mature.
FSH	(Follicle-stimulating hormone) Stimulates granulosa cells.
LH	(Luteinizing hormone) Stimulates theca cells.

Estrogen	Thickens the layer of the uterus.
	Increases the size of the endometrium, preparing for zygote implantation indirect genomic signal.
	No signal transduction: Immediate transcription
	
	- Negative feedback: Inhibits GnRH
	   Many follicles die off → dominant follicle survives
	   Degenerates the corpus luteum.
	   The menstrual cycle restarts.
	
	- Positive feedback: Estrogen → GnRH, FSH, LH ↑
	   LH, FSH levels peak → Ovulation
	   Initiates the thickening of the endometrium.

Progesterone	Maintains the thickening of the endometrium. Pregnancy preparation Inhibits uterine contractions. - Negative feedback: Inhibits GnRH → FSH, LH ↓

Fertilization

A sperm cell fuses with the mature ovum (secondary oocyte → ovum) to produce the zygote.

● Functions
- Restores the diploid number of chromosomes: Ovum (n) + Sperm (n) → 2n
- Activates the egg + stimulates reactions → starts embryological development
- Location: Oviduct

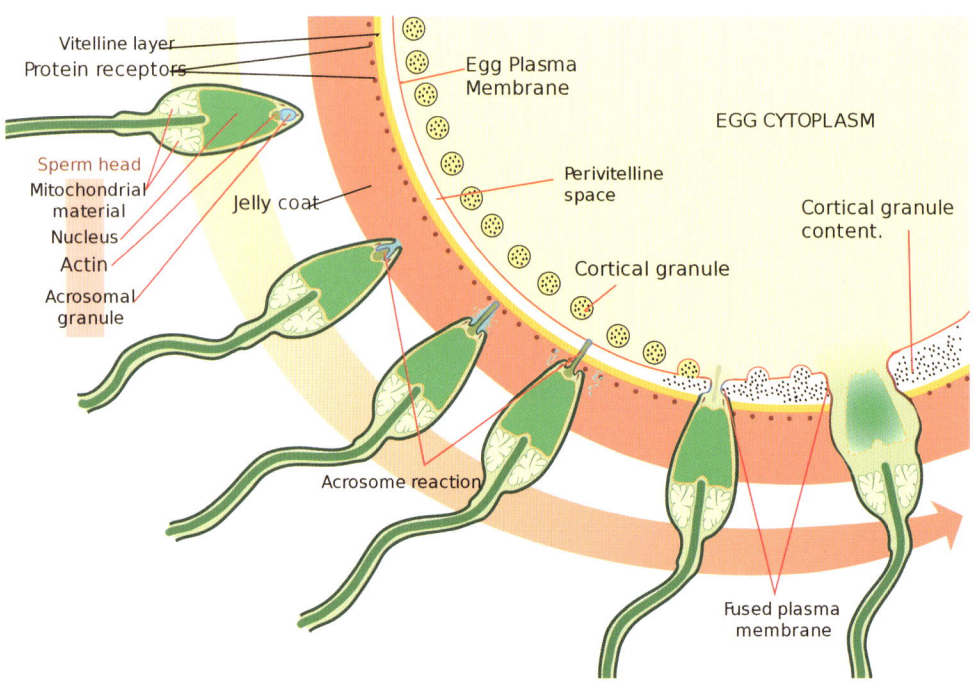

[16-8] Fertilization

1. Sperm cells approach the egg.

2. Sperm cells contract the Zona pellucida.
- Zona pellucida: Glycoprotein, Thick layer

3. Sperm cells release the acrosome. (digestive enzyme)

4. Acrosome drills a hole until the sperm reaches the egg's plasma membrane.

5. Membranes of the sperm + egg fuses → Cortical reaction starts

1) Membrane depolarization: Egg's membrane ion channels open → allows Na^+ → cells → depolarizes the cell + changes the membrane's polarity

2) Cortical reaction: Egg's membrane depolarization → Ca^{2+} movement → Cortical granules exocytosis → Cortical granules are released + changed the composition of the zona pellucida → prevents any other sperm fuse with the egg

6. Sperm nucleus enters the egg + 2 Nuclei fuses
→ restores the diploid number + initiates embryological development

chapter 17
Endocrine system

● Definition: The glands and organs that make hormones and release them directly into the blood.

● Functions: Regulates all biological processes in the body, such as metabolism to growth, emotions, mood, sexual function, and sleep.

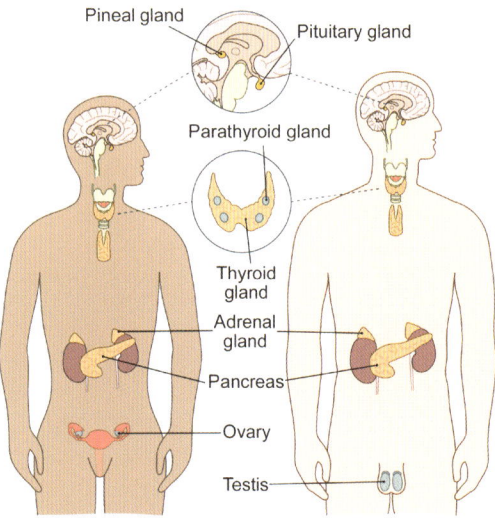

[17-1] Endocrine system

● Endocrine system
Produces and releases hormones → into the internal environment (blood, lymph)

● Exocrine system
Produces and releases the enzymes, mucus, and sebum through ducts and glands → into the external environment
   Ex) Sudoriferous glands: Release sweat directly to the skin via ducts.
   Ex) Oil glands: Secrete sebum.

● Chemicals
For multicellular organisms such as humans to function efficiently and effectively, many cells must be able to communicate with one another. This communication generally takes place through chemicals. These chemicals are released by cells and can either activate or inhibit the activity of other cells.
   Ex) Hormones, Neurotransmitters

Hormone	Neurotransmitter
Endocrine system releases chemicals	The nervous system releases chemicals
Released into the blood, lymph → travel long distances (throughout the body)	Released into neurons → travel very short distances (locally)
Not specific to any one cell → can affect many different types of cells Inhibit some cells + Activate other cells	Attach only to specific cells
Slow-acting response	Rapid-acting response
Long-term effect	Short-lived effect

Types of signaling

Contact-depending signaling	A type of cell-cell or cell-extracellular matrix signaling in multicellular organisms that requires close contact. Ex) Paracrine signaling, Endocrine signaling, Autocrine signaling, Gap junctions
Autocrine signaling	A cell releases a chemical that binds onto a receptor on that same cell → exhibits some types of response Ex) Immune system
Paracrine signaling	A cell releases a chemical → into the extracellular fluid → affects another cell nearby Ex) Prostaglandins
Endocrine signaling	A cell releases a hormone → enters the blood and lymph → travels a long distance to affect cells throughout the body
Neurotransmitter (synapse)	A neuron passes electrical signals to another through neurotransmitters. Transmit electrical signals between neurons or from neurons to muscles. Made in the neuron's cell body and then transported down the axon to the axon terminal.

Types of hormones

- Peptide hormones: Synthesized in the rough ER
- Steroid hormones: Synthesized in the smooth ER

- Phospholipid bilayer cell membrane: Phosphate (thin) + Lipids (thick)

- Peptide hormones (water-soluble, hydrophilic) cannot pass through the membrane
  → bind receptors and usd secondary messengers

- Steroid hormones (lipid-soluble, hydrophobic) can pass through the membrane.

Peptide hormone (water-soluble)	**Steroid hormone** (lipid-soluble)
Travel through blood vessels. (by itself)	Travel with carrier proteins.
Plasma membrane: Facilitated diffusion	Plasma membrane: Simple diffusion
Cannot move across the plasma membrane → binds to receptor proteins on the target cell's membrane → opens up channels, stimulates cellular change via secondary messenger system (cAMP) - Cannot bind directly to the target cell. - Directly transported in the blood. (hydrophilic)	Moves across the plasma membrane → directly binds to protein receptors in the target cell's cytosol → directly goes to the nucleus - Can bind directly to the target cell. - Cannot be directly transported in the blood. - Can transport in the blood with carrier proteins: Chylomicron, Lipoprotein

- Anterior pituitary: HGH, ACTH, TSH, Prolactin, Gonadotropin, MSH
- Posterior pituitary: ADH, Oxytocin
- Pancreatic: Insulin, Glucagon
- Adrenal medulla: Adrenaline, Norepinephrine
- Kidney: Erythropoietin
- Stomach: Gastrin
- Liver: Thrombopoietin, Angiotensin
- Heart: ANP
- Thyroid: Calcitonin
- Parathyroid: Parathyroid hormone
	- Kidney: Calcitriol
	- Thyroid: T3, T4
	- Thymus: Thymosin
	
	- Sex hormones
	   Testosterone: Testis
	   Estrogen: Ovaries
	   Progesterone: Corpus luteum
	   Androgen: Ovaries, Adrenal cortex
	
	- Corticosteroid
	   Adrenal cortex: Aldosterone, Cortisol

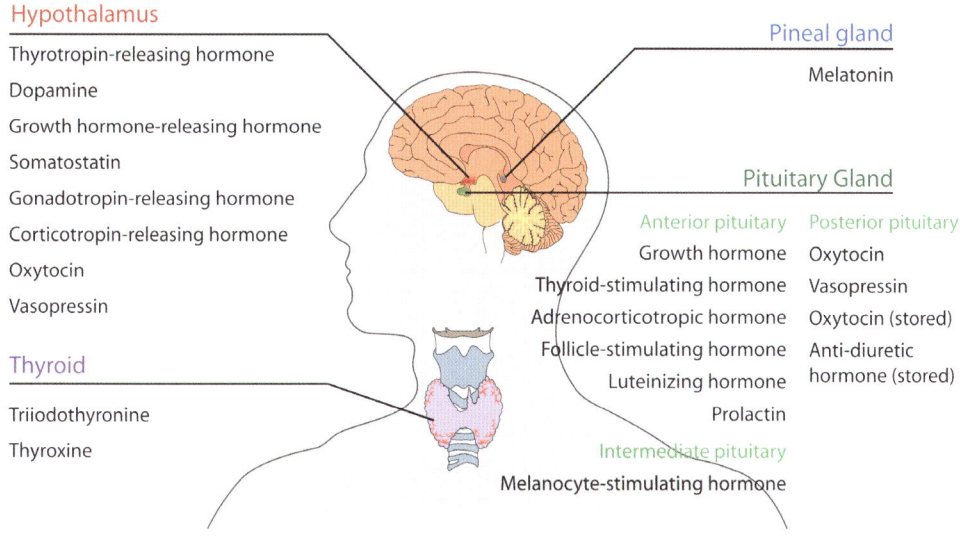

[17-2] Hypothalamus, Thyroid, Pineal gland, Pituitary gland

Hypothalamus

The highest regulatory organ
Region of the forebrain
A gland in the brain that controls hormone systems.
It releases hormones to the pituitary glands, send hormones out to different organs.
Controls pituitaries: Releasing hormones, Inhibiting hormones

● **Pathway**
Hypothalamus controls → Anterior/Posterior pituitaries release hormones
→ control target organs releasing hormones

● **Hypothalamus hormones**
- CnRH: Corticotrophin-releasing hormone
- GhRH: Growth hormone-releasing hormone
- GnRH: Gonadotrophin-releasing hormone
- TtRH: Thyrotrophin-releasing hormone
- Dopamine
- Somatostatin

Anterior pituitary

● Pathway
Blood→ Superior hypophyseal artery → Medium eminence → Hypothalamus secretes a hormone → Capillaries carry the hormone → Anterior pituitary releases the corresponding hormone

● Hypophyseal portal system
Entire network of arteries, capillaries, and veins
Between the hypothalamus to the anterior pituitary
→ through the hypophyseal portal system, the anterior pituitary produces hormones by itself (↔ Posterior pituitary cannot secrete directly)

● Anterior pituitary hormones
Peptide hormones
Synthesized in the rough ER, modified in Golgi complex.
Water-soluble: No carrier protein transport in the blood.
Binds onto protein receptors on the target cell's membrane.

Human Growth Hormone (HGH)	● Pathway Hypothalamus releases GhRH (Growth hormone-releasing hormone) → stimulates the release of HGH → Muscles, Bones ● Human growth hormone (HGH) Affects all the cells of the body. (anabolic) Non-growing cells: Stop using glucose → use fatty acids for energy Glucose supply ↑ + Cell growth (muscles, bones) Increases mitosis + Protein synthesis → cells can grow in size
Adrenocorticotropic Hormone (ACTH)	● Pathway Hypothalamus releases CTF (Corticotropin-releasing factor) → stimulates release ACTH → Adrenal cortex ● Adrenocorticotropic hormone (ACTH) Released during stress time. Adrenal cortex: Releases glucocorticoids (mineralocorticoid, cortisol via secondary messenger) Too much → Negative feedback: degrades the secreting system

Thyroid-Stimulating Hormone (TSH)	● Pathway Hypothalamus releases TRH (Thyroid-releasing hormone) → stimulates release TSH → Thyroid ● Thyroid-stimulating hormone (TSH) Thyroid increases the number of cells and cell sizes. Increases the thyroid T3 and T4 hormone production.
Prolactin	● Pathway PIF (Prolactin-inhibitory hormone): Inhibits releasing Prolactin PRLH (Prolactin-releasing hormone): Stimulates releasing Prolactin ● Prolactin Enable milk production in female.
Gonadotropin Hormone	● Pathway Hypothalamus releases GnRH (Gonadotropin-releasing hormone) → stimulates release FSH, LH → Ovary, Testis ● Luteinizing hormone (LH) - Female: Stimulates ovulation. - Male: Stimulates testosterone production. ● Follicle-stimulating hormone (FSH) - Female: Helps follicle formation. - Male: Helps sperm cell formation.
Melanocyte-stimulating Hormone (MSH)	● Pathway Hypothalamus → stimulates release MSH → Pigment cells in skin ● Melanocyte-stimulating hormone (MSH) Stimulates melanin production in vertebrates. Regulates appetite, energy, and body weight.

Posterior pituitary

Produces peptide hormones.
Cannot synthesize any hormone by itself.
Not an true endocrine glands
Water-soluble: No carrier protein transport in the blood.
Binds onto protein receptors on the target cell's membrane.

- **Pathway**

Hormones are synthesized in the hypothalamus and transported by neurons → Axon → Posterior pituitary (transport, storage)

- **Neurohypophysis**

Transport, store the hormones from the hypothalamus → Blood, Lymph

- **Posterior pituitary hormones**

Antidiuretic Hormone (ADH, Vasopressin)	● Pathway
	Made in Hypothalamus → packaged into vesicles → Axons → Posterior pituitary gland: stored in a secretory vesicle + released → Kidney increases the water reabsorption
	
	- When the body dehydrates,
	  Blood volume ↓ Blood pressure ↓
	  Salt concentration ↑ in the blood (osmotic pressure ↑)
	  Hypothalamus: 'Thirst center' is sensitive to the osmotic pressure → signals to the posterior pituitary → releases ADH (Antidiuretic hormone) → Kidney water reabsorption ↑ → hydration, Blood volume ↑ Blood pressure ↑
	
	● ADH (Antidiuretic hormone)
	Increases water absorption.
	Makes collecting ducts more permeable to water
	→ Water reabsorption: small urea
	Acts on aquaporin: Membrane protein. Makes a water channel in the collecting ducts.
	
	Cf. Diabetes insipidus: Not enough ADH is released → lots of urine

Oxytocin	● Pathway Made in Hypothalamus → Axon → Posterior pituitary gland → stored in a secretory vesicle (herring bodies) → released to the uterus, female breast ● Oxytocin Released during childbirth. Contraction of the smooth muscle of the uterus: Baby birth Stimulates the ejection of milk after childbirth.

Thyroid glands

Endocrine gland, on the front side of the trachea
Blood, lymph vessel supply

- T3, T4: Steroid hormones (lipid-soluble)
- Calcitonin: Peptide hormone (water-soluble)

● **Pathway**
Hypothalamus: TRH → Anterior pituitary gland TSH controls → stimulates release T3, T4

● **Thyroid hormones**

T3 (Triiodothyronine)
 T4 (Thyroxine)
	Steroid hormone: Lipid-soluble
	 T3: 3 Iodine, Triiodothyronine
	 T4: 4 Iodine, Tetraiodothyronine
	
	 ● Pathway
	 Pass through the membrane → Target cell's nucleus → affect the cell on a transcriptional level
	
	 ● T3, T4
	 Affect the basal metabolic rate: Increase or decrease the metabolic process rate.
	   Ex) T3, T4 ↑ → Cellular respiration ↑ Protein synthesis ↑
	   Heart concentration ↑
	
	 Important for growth and development of children
	 Iodine deficiency: Thyroid gland enlargement
	
	 ● **Hyperthyroidism**
	 Overstimulation of the thyroid → excessive levels of T3 and T4
	 Anxiousness, Increasing heart rate and respiratory rate, Weight loss
	
	 ● **Hypothyroidism**
	 Inability of the thyroid to produce a sufficient T3 and T4.
	 Lack of energy, Enthusiasm, Lower respiratory rate and heart rate
	
	 - Medicine: Hypothalamic TRH (thyrotropin-releasing hormone) production ↓

	● Negative feedback system Regulation of the thyroid hormone secretion depends on a negative feedback loop between the anterior pituitary and the thyroid glands. - Thyroid hormones ↑ : Thyroid-stimulating hormone (TSH) ↓ - Thyroid hormones ↓ : Thyroid-stimulating hormone (TSH) ↑
Calcitonin	Peptide hormone (water-soluble) Made in the thyroid parafollicular cells (c-cells) Decrease the blood Ca^{2+} concentration levels. Calcium concentration in the blood ↑ Calcitonin ↑ → Calcitonin: decrease the Ca^{2+} concentration levels Increase osteoblasts activity ↔ Decrease osteoclasts activity → More Ca^{2+} is stored in bone Make kidney excretes more Ca^{2+} Make intestine absorbs less Ca^{2+}

Parathyroid glands

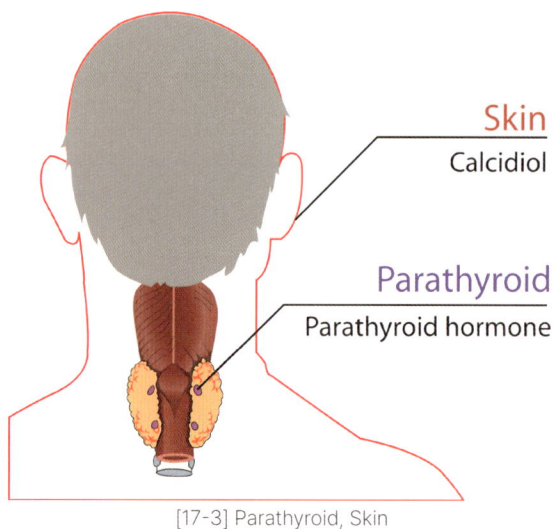

[17-3] Parathyroid, Skin

Produce peptide hormones.
Synthesized in the rough ER, modified in Golgi complex.
Water-soluble: No carrier protein transport in the blood.
Binds onto protein receptors on the target cell's membrane.
4 tiny glands
Round on the back of the thyroid gland.

● Pathway

Calcium in the blood ↓: PTH ↑ → increases the Ca^{2+} concentration levels

Decreases osteoblasts activity ↔ Increases osteoclasts activity
  → More Ca^{2+}, P^{3-} released in the blood

Make kidney absorbs more Ca^{2+}
Kidney produces an active form of Vitamin D → Intestine absorbs Ca^{2+} ↑

● Parathyroid hormones
Secreted in the parathyroid chief cells.
Regulating the concentration of calcium in the blood ↔ reverses the effects of Calcitonin
Increase blood Ca^{2+} concentration levels ↔ Calcitonin: blood calcium level ↓

- Calcium control: Thyroid (calcitonin) + Parathyroid (parathyroid hormone)

Skins

● Pathway
Synthesized by using UV radiation → to the Liver → transformed into Calcidiol
→ Kidney converts into
- Cholecalciferol: Vitamin D3 (Type of Vitamin D)
- Calcitriol: Regulates the calcium concentration.

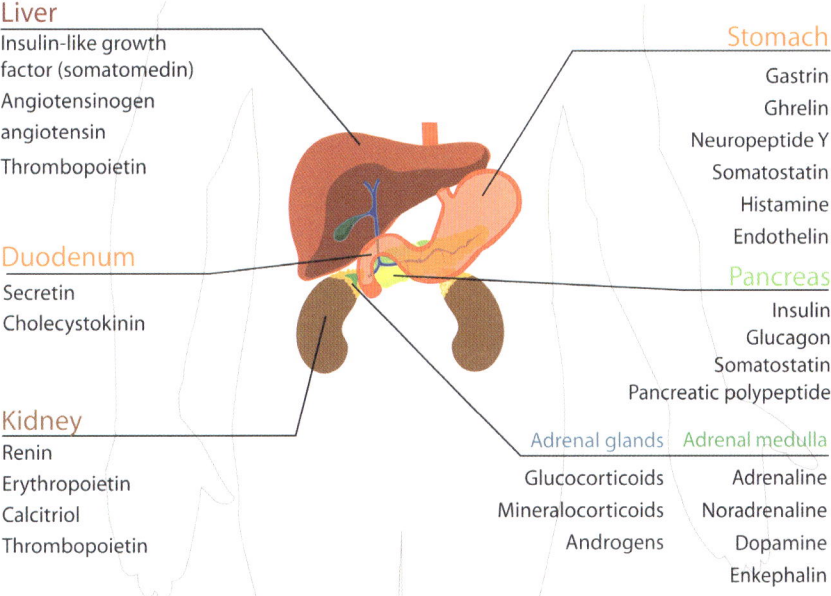

[17-4] Liver, Stomach, Duodenum, Kidney, Pancreas, Adrenal cortex, Adrenal medulla

Adrenal glands

- **Adrenal cortex**

Produces steroid hormones.

- Corticosteroid: Steroid hormone + Synthetic derivatives
  Stress, Immune, Inflammatory, Carbohydrate metabolism, Proteolysis metabolism
  Controls electrolytes in the blood.
  Ex) Aldosterone, Cortisol, Cortisone, Androgen

- **Adrenal medulla**

Produces peptide hormones.
Respond to physically and emotionally stressful situations.
  Ex) Adrenaline (Epinephrine), Norepinephrine

Connected to the sympathetic division: Neurotransmitters of the postganglionic neurons
- Neurotransmitters: Dopa, Dopamine, Epinephrine, Norepinephrine

- **Adrenal gland hormones**

	Adrenal cortex (outer region) Corticosteroid hormones: Mineralocorticoid, Glucocorticoid
Aldosterone	● Mineralocorticoids Maintain a good mineral balance in the blood. Increase kidney reabsorption of Na^+, Cl^- → back to the blood Increase blood sodium levels and blood pressure.
Cortisol (Cortisone)	● Glucocorticoids Control stress Receive stress → increase blood glucose level → repair tissues - Negative feedback: Degrades hormone-secreting system.
Androgen	Made in the adrenal cortex and gonads. - Male: Seminal vesicles and prostate development - Female: Converted into estrogen
	Adrenal medulla (inner region) Peptide hormones, respond to stressful situations and connect to sympathetic divisions
Epinephrine (Adrenaline) **Norepinephrine** (Noradrenaline)	Heart rate ↑ Heart contractile force ↑ Skeletal muscle's blood flow ↑ Liver's glycogen breaking down rate ↑ Dilate blood vessels leading to skeletal muscle ↑ Constrict blood vessels leading to higher blood pressure Constrict blood vessels leading to internal organs ↓ Digestive system peristalsis ↓

Pancreas

• Pancreas hormones (Islets of Langerhans)

Alpha cells	Increase the blood glucose concentration. ● Pathway Glucose concentration ↓ → synthesize and secretes Glucagon → Glucose concentration ↑ ● **Glucagon** Peptide hormone When glucose concentration ↓ Increase glucose concentration Water-soluble: Binds onto protein receptors of the target cell's membrane. - Glycogenolysis: Breaking down Glycogens → Glucose - Gluconeogenesis: Breaking down Proteins → Amino acids → Glucose, Acetyl CoA - Ketogenesis: Breaking down Triglycerides → Fatty acids → Acetyl CoA
Beta cells	Decrease the blood glucose concentration. ● Pathway Glucose concentration ↑ → synthesize and release Insulin → Glucose concentration ↓ ● **Insulin** Peptide hormone When glucose concentration ↑ Water-soluble: Binds onto protein receptor of the target cell's membrane. Insulin level is the highest when glucose uptake → gradually is decreased Make the membrane much more permeable to glucose and amino acids. - Cells convert: Glucose → Glycogen - Cells convert: Amino acid → Protein - Stimulates adipose tissue to convert: Fatty acids → Triglycerides
Delta cells	● **Somatostatin** Peptide hormone Inhibit the release of glucagon and insulin.
Gamma cells	● **Pancreatic polypeptide** Peptide hormone Regulate the pancreas activities: Pancreatic hormone excretion

Kidney hormones

Calcitriol	Steroid hormone Active form of vitamin D Circulates in the blood, regulates Ca, P Makes intestines absorb more Ca, P Makes bones absorb more Ca
Erythropoietin (Hematopoietic)	Peptide hormone Stimulates the red blood cell production
Thrombopoietin	Peptide hormone Promotes the platelet production
Antidiuretic Hormone (ADH, Vasopressin)	Production: Hypothalamus Function: Increase water reabsorption in the kidney. ● **Pathway** Body dehydration → salt concentration ↑ (osmotic pressure) → Hypothalamus: 'Thirst center' is sensitive to the osmotic pressure → signals to the posterior pituitary releases ADH → Kidney water reabsorption → hydration → Blood volume ↑ Blood pressure ↑ ● **ADH (Antidiuretic Hormone)** Increases water reabsorption Increases blood pressure Makes collecting ducts more permeable to water → Water reabsorption: less urea Acts on aquaporins: Membrane proteins Make a water channel in the collecting ducts. Cf. Diabetes insipidus: Not enough ADH is released → lots of urine releasing

Renin-Angiotensin-Aldosterone pathway

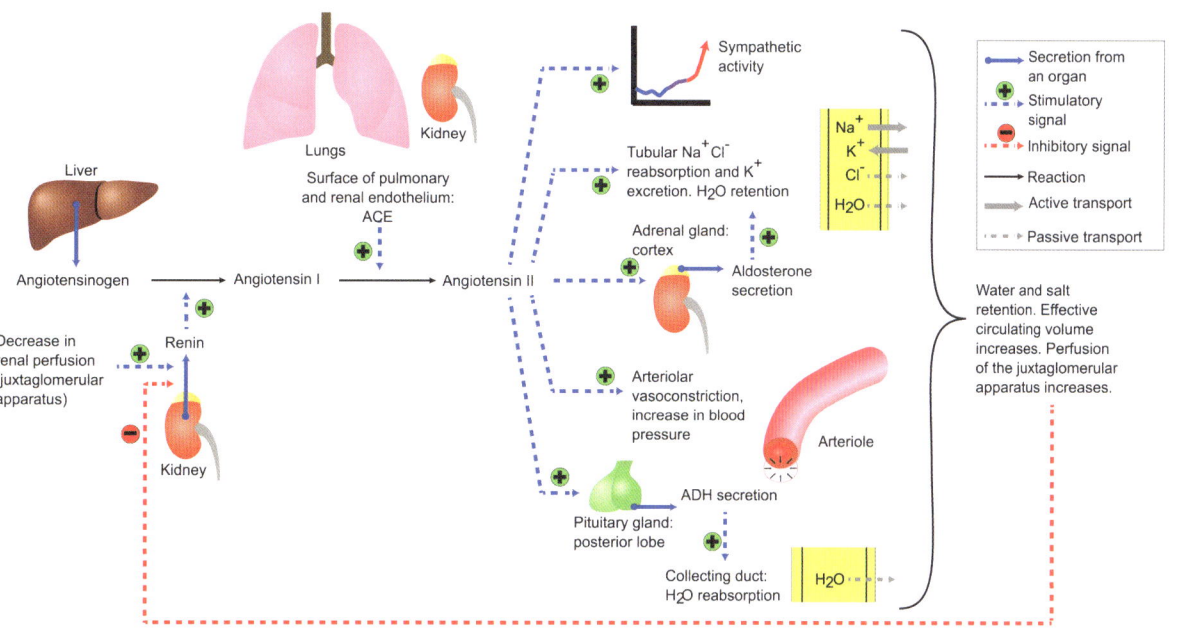

[17-5] Renin-Angiotensin-Aldosterone pathway

Production: Kidney, Liver, Adrenal cortex
Functions: Increase Na⁺ reabsorption and blood pressure in the kidney.

● Pathway
When blood pressure is low,
Juxtaglomerular apparatus: secretes 'Renin'
→ **Renin**: activates Angiotensinogen (Liver)
→ Renin + Angiotensinogen: **Angiotensin I**
→ ACE: converts Angiotensin I to **Angiotensin II**
→ Adrenal cortex secretes **Aldosterone**: Na⁺ reabsorption ↑ Blood pressure ↑

● Angiotensin II
Peptide hormone
Stimulates aldosterone secretion.

Blood pressure ↑ (by contracting blood vessels)
Stimulates releasing ADH ↑
Stimulates thirst.
Extracellular fluid volume ↑

- **Aldosterone**

Steroid hormone: Mineralocorticoid
Production and releasing: In the adrenal cortex
Increases Na^+ reabsorption, Blood pressure ↑

- Renin: Enzyme, produced and released in the kidney. (Juxtaglomerular apparatus)
- Angiotensin I, II: Peptide hormones, produced in the liver.
- Aldosterone: Steroid hormone, produced and released in the adrenal cortex.
- ACE (Angiotensin-converting enzyme): Produced by the endothelial cells in the walls of pulmonary capillaries.

Thymus

Two lobes
Hormone: Thymosin (peptide hormone)
Functions until puberty → slowly deteriorated → replaced by fat cells

● Immune system: Bone marrows produce the Thymocytes.

- Travel to the thymus → Thymosin is used to test the immunity of the thymocyte
    → Not pass the test: destroyed by the thymus
    → Pass the test: matured into T-cells → Lymph nodes

Other hormones

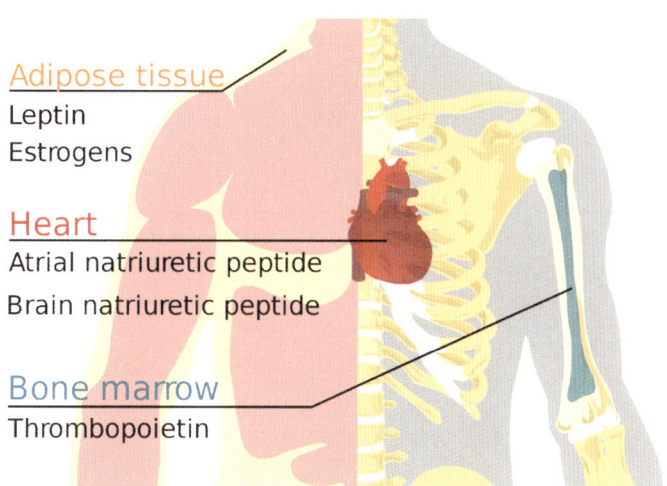

Adipose tissue
Leptin
Estrogens

Heart
Atrial natriuretic peptide
Brain natriuretic peptide

Bone marrow
Thrombopoietin

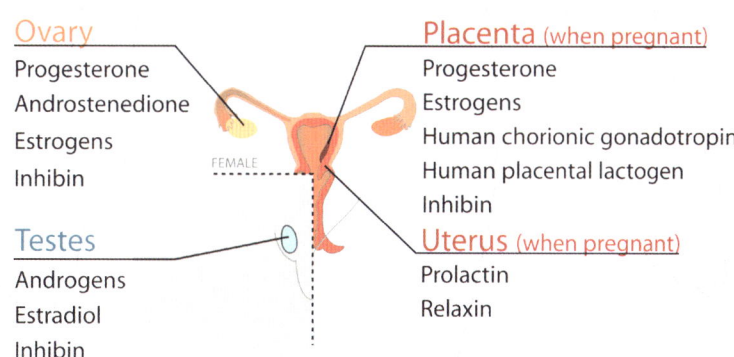

Ovary
Progesterone
Androstenedione
Estrogens
Inhibin

Testes
Androgens
Estradiol
Inhibin

Placenta (when pregnant)
Progesterone
Estrogens
Human chorionic gonadotropin
Human placental lactogen
Inhibin

Uterus (when pregnant)
Prolactin
Relaxin

[17-6] Adipose tissue, Heart, Bone marrow [17-7] Sex hormones

Atrial Natriuretic Peptide (ANP)	Production: Heart atrium Functions: Promotes urine output and Na⁺ excretion, Blood pressure ↓ ● **Pathway** When Na⁺ concentration ↑ Blood volume, pressure ↑ → Heart atria: releases ANP → Inhibits Na⁺ reabsorption, inhibits Aldosterone secretion → Large urine volume comes out: Blood volume ↓ Blood pressure ↓ ● **ANP** Dilates afferent arterioles. Inhibits Na⁺ reabsorption. (collecting ducts) Inhibits Renin secretion → inhibits Aldosterone secretion Large urine volume comes out ↑ Na⁺ excretion ↑ Decreases the blood volume and pressure.
Liver	● **Thrombopoietin** Peptide hormone Promotes platelet production.
Stomach	● **Gastrin** Peptide hormone Stimulates HCl (Gastric acid) and Pepsinogen.

chapter 18
Nervous system

● Definition
How different cells can communicate with one another rapidly and directly.
In vertebrates, a system of the body that includes the brain, spinal cord and nerves.
It senses organs and receives, interprets, and responds to stimuli from inside and outside the body.

● Functions
- Controls everything we do, including breathing, walking, thinking, and feeling.
- Helps all the parts of the body to communicate with each other.
- It also reacts to changes both outside and inside the body.

Neurons

Basic functional unit of the nervous system. (nerve cells)
Neurons depend almost entirely on glucose for energy generation.
Neurons cannot store much glucose in the cell, so they depend on glucose in the blood.
Glucose is brought into the neuron through a special facilitative transporter protein in the membrane.
Neuron cells do not depend on insulin to bring glucose into the cell.
Not in every living organism: Bacteria, prokaryotes, and plants do not have neurons.

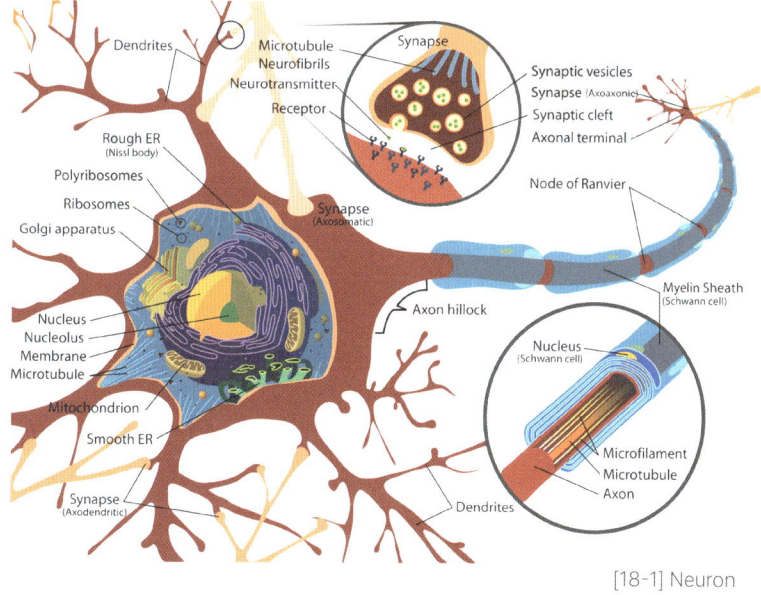

[18-1] Neuron

- Dendrites: Projection of the cell body that receives electrical signals from other neurons.
- Cell body: Region of the neuron that contains the nucleus and other organelles.
- Axon hillock: A special region that connects to the axon. Generates the action potential.
- Axon: A long extension of the nerve cell that carries the electrical signal away from the cell body to the axon terminal.
- Axon terminal: Projections at the end of the axon which transmit the signals to the postsynaptic cells.
- Projections: Bulb-shaped structure, release neurotransmitters. Stimulate the postsynaptic cells.
- Myelination: The acquisition of the highly specialized myelin membrane around axons.
- Myelin: Covers neuron fiber. It insulates action potential.
  Ex) PNS: made by Schwann cells, CNS: made by Oligodendrocytes.
- Oligodendrocytes: Glial cells in CNS. Produce myelin.
- Schwann cells: Glial cells in PNS which produce myelin. The membrane covers PNS axons helically.
- Node of Ranvier: Action potential saltatory conduction location
- Saltatory conduction: An electrical impulse skips from node to node down the full length of an axon, speeding the arrival of the impulse at the nerve terminal in comparison with the slower continuous progression of depolarization spreading down an un-myelinated axons.

● **Propagation of electrical signals**

Dendrites	Electrical signal is accepted by the dendrites. Dendrite → Membrane of the cell body → pass down the signal to the axon hillock
Axon hillock	When stimulation is high enough (exceeds the threshold value) → generates an action potential → causes the electric current to flow along the axon
Axon	The electric current flows along away from the cell body.
Synaptic bouton	The electrical signal reaches → stimulates it to release neurotransmitters → bind to the postsynaptic cells (effector cell) → change the postsynaptic cell membranes → initiate a signal

18 Nervous system

Glial cells (Neuroglia)

Found in the nervous system.
Improve the functionality of the activity of the neurons and support the neurons.

CNS: Central Nervous System

Astrocytes

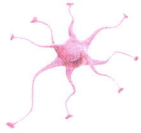

Containing extensions: Wrap around the neurons.
Provide physical support to neurons holding them in place.
Connect the neurons to the blood supply.
Help maintain the ions and nutrients concentration outside the neurons.

Oligodendrocytes

Cover the axon of the neurons with myelin.
Insulating material
Produce myelin in CNS.

Ependymal cells

Line the spinal cord to sections of the brain. (CNS)
Use cilia to move the cerebrospinal fluid.

Microglia

Protect the neurons of CNS.
Engulf debris and harmful things.

PNS: Peripheral Nervous System

Satellite cells

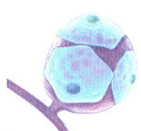

Cover the surface of the neurons in PNS.
Provide structural support.
Provide nutrients to the neurons.
Provide a protective, cushioning effect.

Schwann cells

Attach to sections of the axon.
Secrete the myelin covering.
Produce myelin in PNS.

[18-2] Astrocyte, [18-3] Oligodendrocyte, [18-4] Ependymal cell
[18-5] Microglia, [18-6] Satelite cell, [18-7] Schwann cell

Electrical signals transmission

Voltage across its membrane
Voltage = Stimuli (differences +/- charges) = Electrochemical
Determined by concentration gradients of ions across the membrane and membrane permeability to each ion.
Action potential speed is determined by axon diameter, internode distance, myelin sheath thickness, and temperature.
Signals between neurons are bidirectional.
Synapses can exist between a neuron and a non-neuron cell.
Action potential moment is one-directional.

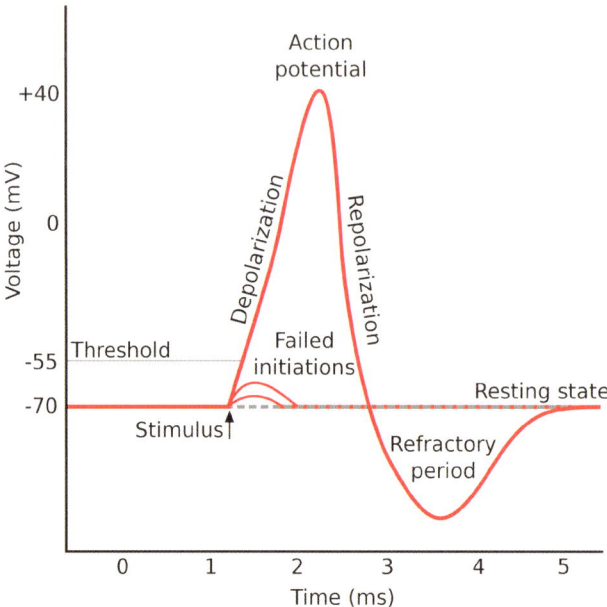

[18-8] Electrical signals transmission

18 Nervous system

Resting potential	Voltage (electrochemical gradient): -70mV
Hypopolarization	Initial increase of the membrane potential to the value of the threshold potential. Voltage: Resting potential < -70mV to -55mV < Threshold potential
Action potential (Threshold potential)	Opens voltage-gated Na⁺ channels: Many Na⁺ come inside. Inside of the cell becomes more electropositive. (+) Exceeds the threshold: -55mV
Depolarization	Too many Na⁺ come inside. Inside of the cell becomes too much electropositive. (+)
Overshoot	Extremely positive: +61mV
Repolarization	Voltage-gated Na⁺ channels closing → Na⁺ permeability decreases Voltage-gated K⁺ channels open → many K⁺ go out → decreasing the cell's electropositivity → electronegative (-)
Hyperpolarization	Membrane potential is more negative than the default membrane potential.
Resting potential	Voltage (electrochemical gradient): -70mV

Resting potential

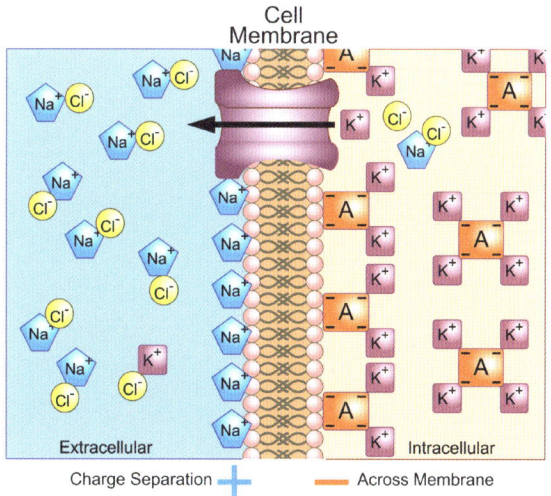
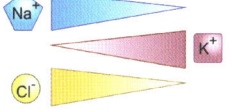

[18-9] Resting potential

Resting membrane potential: When there is no action potential, the membrane is resting.

• Sodium-Potassium pump
Membrane is selectively permeable to ions that cannot move freely.
- Outside: Na^+ ↑ ($3Na^+$)
- Inside: K^+ ↑ ($2K^+$)
  → Outside is more (+) charged
  → Makes voltage: Electrochemical gradient (net negative charges)

- Voltage: -70mV
  Electrochemical gradient difference between outside and inside.
  Inside membrane charge is 70mV less positive.

- Sodium-Potassium pump: Active transport
  → Requires energy because it transports against the gradient

• Resting potential flow
Electroneutrality: Both charges cancel the +/- charges, so the membrane is neutral.

1. Membrane is more permeable to K^+ > Na^+
→ Contains more protein channels for K^+
→ More K^+ leave the cell than Na^+ enter

2. K^+ leave the cell → Inside (+) ↓ Outside (+) ↑
→ Electric force brings K^+ back inside

- Equilibrium: Electric force pushing inside = Pushing outside
- Membrane proteins are closed.

Action potential

Axon hillock generates the action potential.
Spikes and impulses by temporary changes in membrane permeability for diffusible ions.

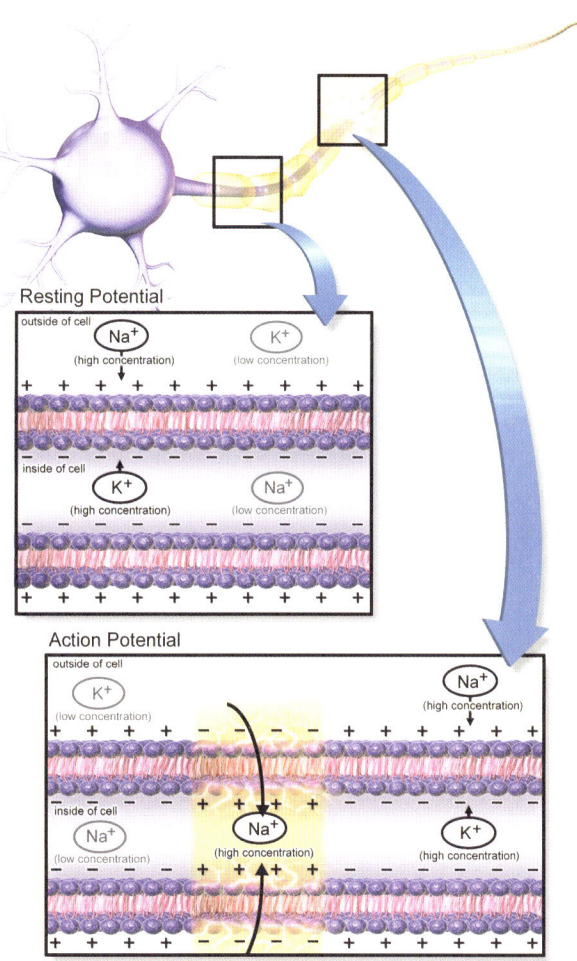

[18-10] Action potential

Initiation

Action potential is coming from the ex-neuron.
A neuron is waiting for the coming action potential to generate and pass the action potential.

When the action potential passes, it opens the 'Voltage-gated channels.'
- When rest: Membrane protein is closed (-70mV)
- When open: Voltage changes

When the action potential comes,

1. Na⁺ voltage-gated channels
→ Na⁺ voltage-gated channels open
→ Membrane is more permeable to Na⁺ > K⁺
→ Na⁺ moves down the electrochemical gradient
→ Na⁺ comes inside the membrane
→ Add more + charges inside
→ Membrane voltage gap decreases

2. Hypopolarization
Initial increase of the membrane potential to the value of the threshold potential.

- Voltage: Between -70mV to -55mV

3. Action potential generation
Voltage (electrochemical gradient) exceeds the threshold value (-55mV)
→ Action potential can be generated

- Voltage: 70mV

4. Depolarization
More Na⁺ come to the membrane inside
→ Depolarization: Membrane polarity ↓

5. Overshoot
Membrane inside voltage up to +61mV
→ Na⁺ voltage-gated channels shut down (inactivate)
→ Signals to K⁺ voltage-gated channels to activate
→ Gives action potential unidirectional

- Voltage: Up to +61mV

6. Repolarization
K⁺ voltage-gated channels open
→ Membrane will be more permeable to K⁺ > Na⁺
→ K⁺ moves down the electrochemical gradient
→ K⁺ go out of the cell

→ Outside is more positively charged
→ Some Na⁺ voltage-gated channels re-activate

- Voltage: Over - 55mV

7. Hyperpolarization
When the permeability (K⁺ > Na⁺) is too much, the voltage will drop below the resting voltage. (-70mV)
It ensures that action potential is unidirectional.

- Voltage: Lower than -70mV

● ATPase pump: Returns the neurons to the resting membrane potential.
→ Moves 3Na⁺ out of the cell
→ Moves 2K⁺ into the cell
→ Back to the resting potential

Before stimulus, neuron membrane: Inside (-) Outside (+)

After stimulus (action potential),

Propagation

1. Na⁺ channels open
→ Na⁺ rush inside
→ Reverse the polarity
→ Inside (+) Outside (-)
→ Inside (+)
→ Adjacent regions (+)
→ Stimulate Na⁺ channels to open in adjacent areas

2. Na⁺ channels closed
→ K⁺ channels open in the stimulus region
→ Na⁺ channels in the adjacent areas open
→ Depolarization: Gaining (+) charges, less negative between membranes
→ Consecutive regions all depolarized

● Absolute refractory stage: No type of stimulus can cause an action potential there.
→ Na⁺ channels are inactivated
→ Action potential moves along the axon membrane, away from the body

- Action potential is 'All-or-nothing.'
- If the stimulus increases, the wave's amplitude will remain the same, and the frequency of oscillation will increase.

● Resting potential, Action potential pathway
Resting potential: Voltage between membranes: -70mV → Ions movement → Voltage (electrochemical gradient) exceeds the threshold: -55mV → Action potential → Depolarization: Na⁺ channels open → Na⁺ come inside → Repolarization: K⁺ channels

open → K⁺ movement → Hyperpolarization → Resting membrane potential (-70 mV)

chapter 19
Central nervous system, Peripheral nervous system

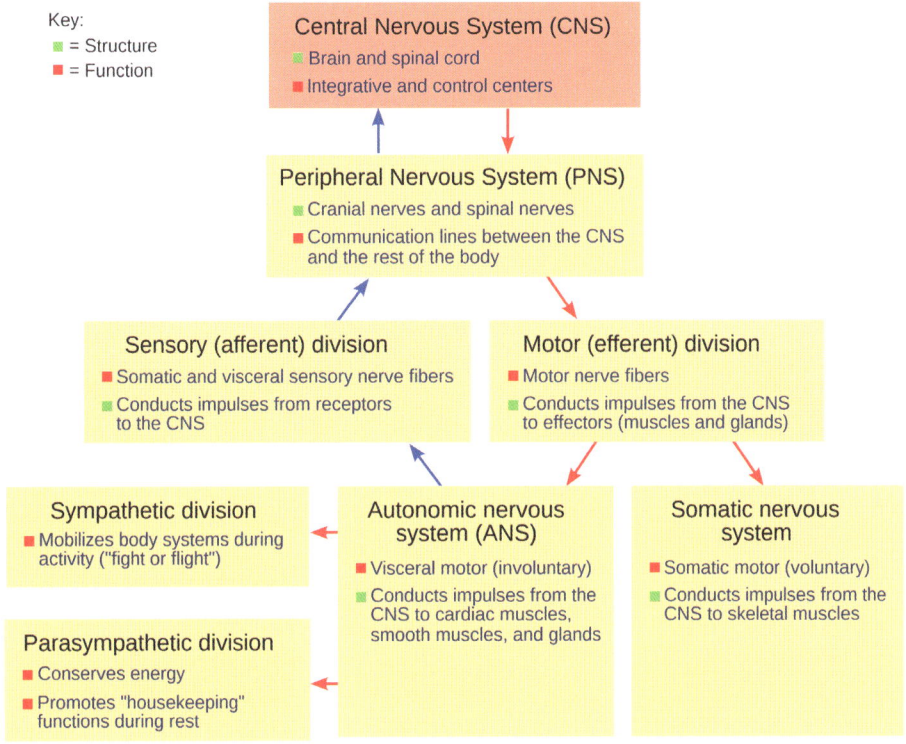

[19-1] Nervous system

Nervous system: Central nervous system (CNS), Peripheral nervous system (PNS)
Nervous system is found in almost all multicellular animals but vary significantly in complexity.
The only multicellular animals with no nervous system are sponges and microscopic blob-like organisms called placozoans and mesozoans.

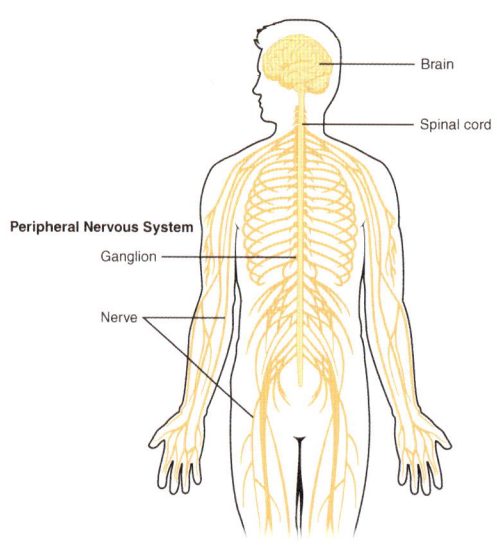

[19-2] CNS, PNS

Central nervous system (CNS)	Peripheral nervous system (PNS)
The central nervous system (CNS) includes the brain and the spinal cord.	The peripheral nervous system (PNS) includes all the nerves that branch out from the brain and the spinal cord and extend to other body parts, including muscles and organs.
● **Brain:** PNS, Spinal cord ⇆ Brain ● **Spinal cord:** PNS ⇆ Spinal cord ⇆ Brain	● **Somatic nervous system** - Voluntary movement - Motor neurons: CNS → Motor neurons - Sensory neurons: Sensory neurons → CNS ● **Autonomic nervous system** - Involuntary movement - Sympathetic neurons: boost up - Parasympathetic neurons: calm down
Axons: Slender projections	
Short nerve impulse	Long nerve fibers
Organize, analyze information from sensory organs.	Transmit sensory information → CNS Pass out motor impulses → Effector organs
Damage causes a global effect on the body.	Damage causes a local effect on the body.
It cannot regenerate nerve fibers.	It can regenerate nerve fibers.

- Ganglia: Groups of cell bodies, which are found in the peripheral nervous system.
- Preganglionic neurons: Cells that synapse between CNS and PNS ganglia.
- Postganglionic neurons: Cells that synapse between preganglionic neurons and effector organs.
- Interneurons: The majority of the neurons in the body. Connect other neurons.
  Ex) Sensory neurons, Motor neurons

Central nervous system

The central nervous system (CNS) includes the brain and the spinal cord.

● Functions
- Controls most functions of the body and mind.
- Itself can determine, make decisions, and order to PNS.
- Receives information from each other (Brain ⇆ Spinal cord) and secretes hormones.

Brain

Controls most bodily functions, including awareness, movements, sensations, thoughts, speech, and memory.

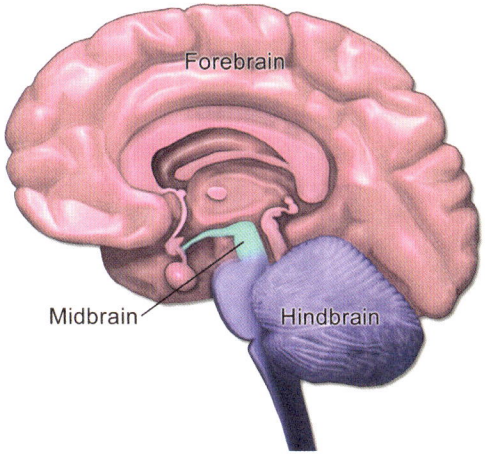

[19-3] Brain

Forebrain	● **Cerebrum** Consists of right and left cerebral hemispheres, connected by the corpus callosum. - Cerebral cortex: Outermost portion of the cerebrum. Memory and thought (the highest-level functions) - Functions: Somatic nervous system (voluntary actions) corresponding, Speech, Judgment, Thinking, Reasoning, Problem-solving, Emotions, Sensing (thalamus → cerebrum sensing cortex, olfactory epithelium → cerebrum olfactory cortex) ● **Hippocampus** Limbic system - Functions: Memory, Learning ● **Basal ganglia** A collection of neurons - Functions: Controlling voluntary motion ● **Thalamus** Limbic system - Functions: Relaying sensory and motor signals, Controlling consciousness, Sleeping, Waking up, Somatic nervous system control, Delivering sensory signals to the cerebrum ● **Hypothalamus** Limbic system - Functions: Regulating the endocrine system via the pituitary glands, Body temperature control, Receiving information from sensory neurons ● **Pituitary glands** Endocrine system Consist of the anterior pituitary and the posterior pituitary. - Functions: Hormone secretion, storage, and transportation
Midbrain	Midbrain = Mesencephalon The forward-most portion of the brainstem - Functions: Vision, Hearing, Motor control, Sleep, Wakefulness, Arousal (alertness), Temperature regulation

19 Central nervous system and Peripheral nervous system

Brain stem + Cerebellum

● Brainstem
Brainstem: Pons + Medulla
Life maintaining part

● Pons
From the forebrain → deliver signals → to the cerebellum

- Functions: Generating the respiratory rhythm, Postural control

Hindbrain

● Medulla (Medulla oblongata)
Transmit signals between the spinal cord and the brain.
Vital centers: Cardiac center, Respiratory center, Vomiting and vasomotor center

- Functions: Regulating the autonomic nervous systems (involuntary movement), Controlling the cardiovascular system, Swallowing, Vomiting, Respiration, Respiratory rate, Heart rate, Blood pressure, Digestion

● Cerebellum
Maintenance of balance and posture
Modify the signal of movement from the cerebrum: Alcohol affects this part
→ when drunken, challenging to control walking

● **Limbic system**

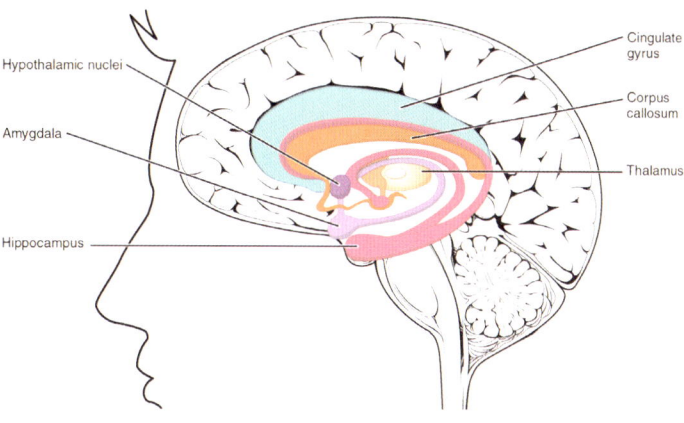

[19-4] Limbic system

A part of the brain involved in memory storage, emotions and retrieval.

Components
- Thalamus: Relays information to the cerebrum.

- Hypothalamus: Controls homeostasis with hormones.
- Hippocampus: Memory
- Amygdala: Emotion

Spinal cord

Connected to the brainstem and runs through the spinal canal.
Accepts and delivers signals back and forth between PNS and the brain.
Where sympathetic nervous system and parasympathetic preganglionic neurons are located.

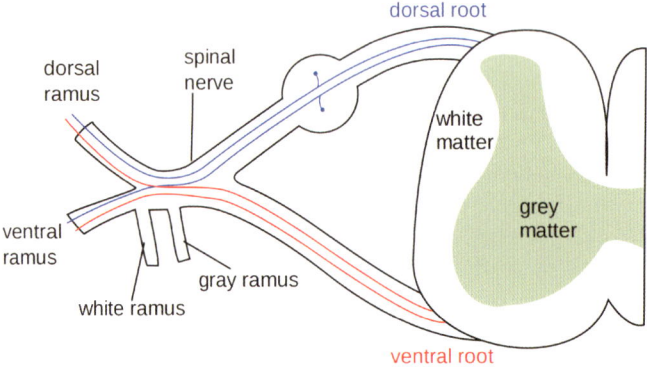

[19-5] Spinal cord

Afferent (in): Sensory neurons → (dorsal horn) Dorsal root + Ganglion → CNS
Efferent (out): CNS orders → (ventral horn) Ventral root → Motor neurons → Muscles

Central canal	Central hole, which contains cerebrospinal fluid.
White matter	Conduct, process, and send nerve signals up and down the spinal cord. Relay communication between different brain regions. - Composition: Myelinated axons, Glial cells, Nerve fibers
Gray matter	Butterfly shape Muscle control, Sensory perception (seeing, hearing), Memory, Emotions, Speech, Decision making, Self-control - Composition: Interneurons, Motor neurons, Unmyelinated axons, Dendrites, Ganglions - Axon terminal: Neuron synapse occurs.

- **Spinal reflex**

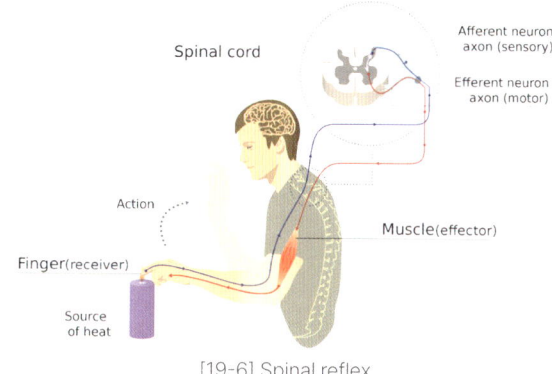

[19-6] Spinal reflex

Some reflex movements can occur via spinal cord pathways without the participation of the brain.

- Reflex arc: Neural pathway
  Sensory neurons → Spinal cord (no brain participation): fast reaction
- Stretch reflex: Contraction of a muscle in response to its passive stretching
- Flexor reflex: Contraction of limb flexor muscles

Peripheral nervous system

Nervous system except for CNS
Extend from CNS to other parts of the body.
Deliver signals to the organs, limbs, and skin.

Somatic nervous system	Autonomic nervous system
- Sensory neurons: (Afferent) Nerves sense → deliver → CNS	- Sympathetic nervous system: Excite the body to expand energy
- Motor neurons: (Efferent) CNS → decide → body motors	- Parasympathetic nervous system: Calm the body to conserve and maintain energy
Voluntary movement	Involuntary movement
Innervate skeletal muscles	Innervate smooth muscles, Cardiac muscles, Glands
Less complex signaling way	Complex signaling way
Transmit signals: One efferent neuron	Transmit signals: 2 Efferent neurons, Ganglia

Somatic nervous system

Voluntary nervous system
Voluntary movement control via skeletal muscles

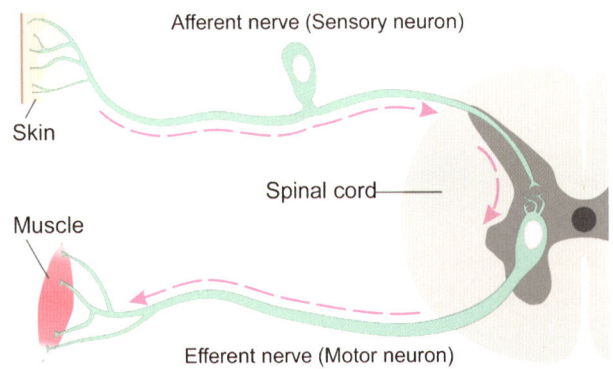

[19-7] Somatic nervous system

Motor neurons	Receive electrical signals from CNS and send to the target tissues, glands, organs, motor neuron dendrites, and cell body originate in the spinal cord. Carry the electrical signals via a single axon → Skeletal muscle Dendrites pick the signal → send through the axon + travel through PNS → axon terminal → ends at the effector (target) muscles → neuron uses the neurotransmitters (acetylcholine) → initiates muscle contraction - Efferent neurons: Exit the spinal cord ventral side. (front)
Sensory neurons	Sensory receptors pick up stimuli from the environment and transform them into an electrical signal by sensory neurons. Carry the signal via a single axon → Spinal cord → Brain - Afferent neurons: Enter the spinal cord dorsal side. (back) - Cell bodies: Located in the dorsal root ganglia.
Reflex arcs	Neural pathway Sensory neurons → Spinal cord (no brain participation, fast reaction) Quick, automatic response to stimuli: Cannot be controlled voluntarily. - Monosynaptic reflex arcs: Only contain one synapse. - Polysynaptic reflex arcs: Contain more than one synapse.

19 Central nervous system and Peripheral nervous system

Autonomic nervous system

Involuntary nervous system.
Involuntary movement control via cardiac muscles and smooth muscles.

Sympathetic nervous system	● 'fight-or-flight' response Arise the body to expand energy. - Increasing the blood flow to the cardiac muscles and skeletal muscles - Pupil dilation - Increasing the heart rate - Increasing the respiratory rate - Increasing sweat Decreasing the activity of the gastrointestinal system - Smooth muscle inhibition - Inhibiting peristalsis - Decreasing the digestive rate Signal pathway ● **Preganglionic neurons** Cell body: Spinal cord Axons extend out from the front side of the spine (ventral) → PNS Short distance: Axons travel a short distance before synapsing with the postganglionic neurons. - Neurotransmitters: Acetylcholine ● **Postganglionic neurons** Cell body: PNS, close to CNS Long distance: Long axons connect to the effector organs. - Neurotransmitters: Epinephrine (adrenaline), Norepinephrine (noradrenaline)

Parasympathetic nervous system	● **'Rest-and-digest' activities** Calm the body to rest and maintain energy. - Increasing the blood flow to digestive organs and excretory system - Decreasing the blood flow to skeletal muscles (adrenaline receptors organs) - Decreasing sweat, heart rate, and respiratory rate Signal pathway ● **Preganglionic neurons** Cell body: Spinal cord, Brain Long distance: Carry the electrical signal via a long axon → synapse - Neurotransmitters: Acetylcholine ● **Postganglionic neurons** Cell body: PNS, close to the target organs - Neurotransmitters: Acetylcholine

Synapse

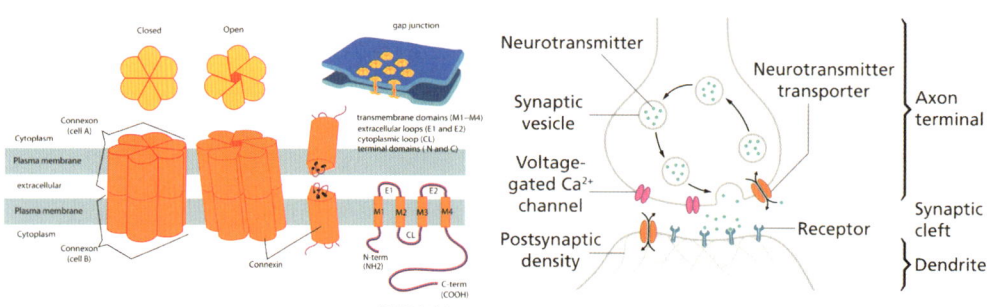

[19-8] Gap junction, [19-9] Neurotransmitter

19 Central nervous system and Peripheral nervous system

Electrical synapse (Gap junction)	Channels that physically connect adjacent cells. Mediate the rapid exchange of small molecules between neurons and muscles. It directly passes through a regulated gate between cells. - Location: CNS, Cardiac muscles, Smooth muscles - Targets: Small molecules, Ions, Inorganic salts, Sugars, Amino acids, Nucleotides, Vitamins
Chemical synapse (Neurotransmitter)	Neurons pass the electrical signals (action potential, receptor potential) to other neurons or skeletal muscles through neurotransmitters. - Location: PNS, Skeletal muscles - Target: Electrical signals (action potential, receptor potential) • **Neuromuscular junction** Synapse between a motor neuron and a muscle cell through neurotransmitters In skeletal muscles • **Neurotransmitter** Transmit electrical signals (action potential, receptor potential) between neurons or from neurons to skeletal muscles. Made in the neuron's cell body and transported down the axon to the axon terminal. Vesicle form is released at the presynaptic membrane. - Hydrophilic: Neurotransmitters cannot pass the membrane by themselves, so they bind onto receptor proteins on the postsynaptic cells. - Active transport: When a nerve impulse is produced, neurotransmitters leave the vesicles and open channels of the adjacent cell at the point of the synaptic contact. - Presynaptic neuron: Transmits the signal toward a synapse with neurotransmitters. - Postsynaptic neuron: Transmits the signal away from the synapse with neurotransmitters.

● **Neurotransmitters**

Somatic nervous system	Motor neuron	Acetylcholine
	Sensory neuron	Glutamate
Autonomic nervous system	**Sympathetic**-Preganglionic	Acetylcholine
	Sympathetic-Postganglionic	Adrenaline (epinephrine) Norepinephrine
	Parasympathetic-Preganglionic	Acetylcholine
	Parasympathetic-Postganglionic	Acetylcholine

Chapter 20: Sensory system

- Definition: A part of the nervous system responsible for processing sensory information.

- Functions
- Inform the central nervous system about stimuli impinging from the outside or within the body.
- Stimuli: Vision, Hearing, Touch, Taste, Smell, Balance

Sensory receptors

Detect information about changes in the external and internal environment.
Consist of specialized neuron endings and cells in close contact with neurons.
Each sensory receptor is especially sensitive to one particular energy.

Receptor potential	Action potential
Transmembrane potential difference produced by sensory neuron's sensory receptors responding to stimuli	A temporary shift (negative to positive) in the neuron's membrane potential is caused by ions suddenly flowing in and out of the neuron
Only facilitate signal transduction or stimulate inward current flow.	Trigger the release of neurotransmitters in neurons → transmit the electrical impulses throughout the body → without receptor participation, generation of action potential will not occur
If the stimuli are over the threshold → generate the action potential	Send information down an axon away from the cell body by changing the resting membrane potential to reach the threshold level.
In the sensory receptors	In the neurons
Signals can be transmitted over short distances	Signals can be transmitted over long distances
Graded	Not graded
Variable-strength signals	Large depolarizations
Depending on strength and duration of stimuli	Depending on the frequency and energy of the electrical impulses (when the threshold level is reached in the cell)
Distribution of +/- ions at two sides of cell membranes	Distribution of +/- ions at two sides of cell membranes

Can be occurred in depolarization, hyperpolarization	Only occurred in depolarization
May lose the strength during transmission	Do not lose the strength during the transmission
Do not obey 'All-or-nothing' rule	Obey 'All-or-nothing' rule

Sensory processing

● **Pathway**

Stimulus → Sensory reception (sensory receptors receive and absorb the stimulus) → Energy transduction (stimulus) → Receptor potential → Energy transmission → Action potential → transmitted to CNS → Brain perception (selection → organization → interpretation)

Sensory reception	Sensory receptors Receive stimuli from the external, internal environment. Absorb a small amount of energy from the stimuli.
Energy transduction	Stimuli → Opening ion channels in the sensory receptor's plasma membrane → Depolarization of the membrane → Sensory receptors transduce and convert the receptor potential It does not directly make action potential. Graded response: Magnitude change depends on the energy of the stimulus. When the receptor is a separate cell, receptor potential stimulates neurotransmitters. (delivers electrical signals through the synapse) - Unstimulated: Sensory receptors maintain the resting potential. - Stimulated: Ion channels open, depolarize the membrane and create a graded receptor potential. ● **Receptor potential** Electrical signals: Information of the nervous system Ion distribution change → Membrane's voltage change - Hyperpolarized: Charge difference ↑ - Depolarized: Charge different ↓

Signal transmission

Receptor potential → If the receptor potential exceeds a threshold (-55mV) → Sensory neurons generate the action potential → CNS

● **Action potential**
All action potentials are qualitatively the same.
The ability to differentiate stimuli depends on: Sensory receptors, Brain
A receptor responds to only 1 type of the stimulus.

Sensory receptor impulses differ in
- The total number of sensory neurons transmitting the signals.
- Specific neurons transmit action potentials + their targets
- A total number of action potentials by neurons.
- Frequency of the action potentials by given fibers.

Stimulus intensity
- Coded by the frequency of action potentials.
- Receptor potential is variable by the graded response.

- Strong stimulus: Greater depolarization of the receptor membrane
  → Sensory neuron produces action potentials with greater frequency

- Weak stimulus: Weaker depolarization of the receptor membrane
  → Sensory neuron produces action potentials with less frequency

Brain perception

Sensory neuron's action potential → Brain perception
(selection → organization → interpretation)

● Perception
Process by which the brain gathers and interprets information that it receives through the senses.
Influenced by the state of mind at the time it receives sensory information.

- Process: Selection → Organization → Interpretation of sensory information
- Brain converts the perception → Stimuli

● Interpretation
Types of sensation depend on which interneurons receive the message.
The brain interprets messages from a particular receptor.

Sensory adaptation, Integration

Sensory adaptation	The response properties of neurons, in turn, dynamically adjust to the prevailing properties of sensory stimulation. Animals distinguish between unimportant background stimuli that can be ignored and new, important stimuli that require attention. Sensory receptors respond at the stimulus rate changes. - During a sustained stimulus, the receptor sensitivity decreases, produces a smaller receptor potential → Low frequency of action potentials in sensory neurons - Changes occur at synapses in the receptor neural pathways. - Slowly adapt receptors: Adapt slowly and continue to trigger action potentials until the stimulus persists. Ex) Pain, Cold - Rapidly adapt receptors: Adapt rapidly and ignore persistent unpleasant, unimportant stimuli. Ex) Wearing tight jeans, Uncomfortable smells
Sensory integration	The process that it receives information through senses, organizes this information and uses it to participate in everyday activities. Begins in the receptor in CNS: Spinal cord, Brain

Types of receptors

• By location of stimuli

Exteroceptors	Receive stimuli from the outside environment. It enables an animal to know to explore the world, search for food, find a mate, recognize friends, and detect enemies.
Interoceptors	Sensory receptors within the body organs. Detect changes in pH, osmotic pressure, body temperature, and chemical composition of the blood.

• By generators

	Type of energy	Example
Photoreceptors	Light energy	Eyes
Auditory receptor	Sound energy	Ears
Mechanoreceptors	Mechanical energy Change shapes as a result of being pushed or pulled Touch, Pressure, Gravity, Stretching, Movement	● Tactile receptors: Touch, Pressure - Free nerve endings - Merkel cells - Meissner corpuscles - Ruffini endings - Pacinian corpuscles ● Proprioceptors: Movement, Position - Muscle spindles: Muscle contraction - Golgi tendon organs: Tendon stretch - Joint receptors: Ligament movement ● Auditory receptor: Sound waves - Vestibular apparatus: Gravity - Organ of Corti: Sound wave pressure ● Invertebrates - Statocytes: Gravity - Lateral line organs: Vibration in water
Nociceptors	Physical force Strong touch, Pressure, Heat, Temperature extremes, Damaging chemicals	Neuron endings in the skin and other tissues
Electroreceptors, Electromagnetic receptors	Electrical potential Magnetic field	Electrical currents: Fish, Amphibian Sensitive to the Earth's magnetic field
Chemoreceptors	Specific chemical compounds	Gustation: Taste buds Olfaction: Olfactory epithelium
Thermoreceptors	Heat, Cold	Temperature receptors Pit organs in pit vipers Nerve endings and receptors

Photoreceptors

Organ transforms the light energy into electrical signals and delivers it through the optic nerves to the brain's visual cortex.

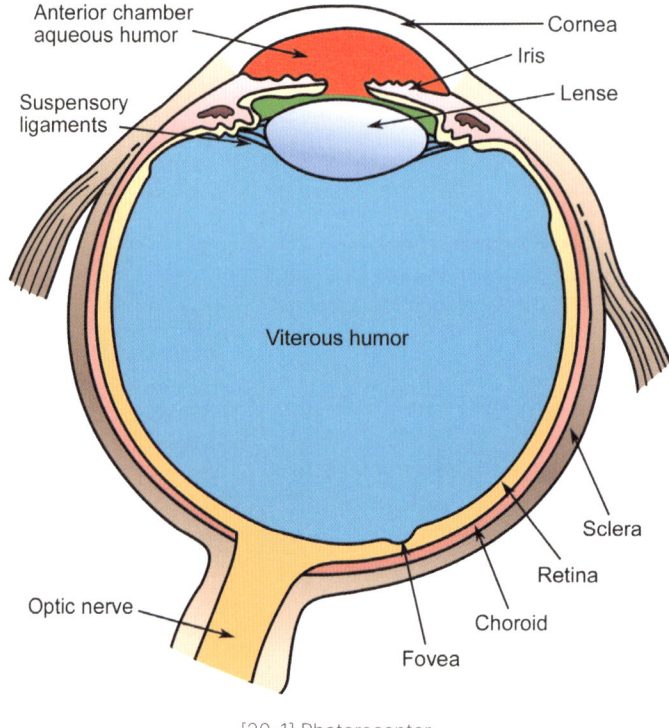

[20-1] Photoreceptor

• Visual pathway

Light → Cornea → Iris → Pupil → Lens → Vitreous humor → Retina → Optic nerves: carry signals → Brain visual cortex: turns the signals into images → Vision

Cornea	Clear, dome-shaped surface that covers the front of the eyes. Transparent layers Difference between the air and the cornea: Most of the bending of light occurs at the cornea. Not covered by the sclera.
Iris	Controls the amount of light passing through to the pupil. The colored part of the eyes Made of radial, circular muscles. Controlled by the autonomic nervous system.

Pupil	Opening of the eyes
	Allows light into the eyes.
	The amount of light is controlled by the iris.
	
	● **Sympathetic division**
	Innervates the radial smooth muscle
	- Dark conditions: Sympathetic system contracts the radial muscle
	  → dilates the pupil → allows more light in
	
	● **Parasympathetic division**
	Innervates the circular smooth muscle
	- Bright conditions: Parasympathetic system contracts the circular muscle
	  → decreases the size of the pupil → allows less light in

Lens	Clear structure inside the eyes Focus light rays onto the retina. Convex lens Used for fine-tuning. Shape and the lens focal length are controlled by the ciliary muscle. ● Ciliary body Secretes fluid. Controls the lens thickness.
Vitreous humor	Between the retina and the lens Water + Proteins, Salts, Electrolytes, Sugar, Collagens Colorless, transparent, gel-like material that fills the center of the eyes. Helps keep the eyes round in shape.

Retina	Light-sensitive nerve layer that lines the back of the eyes. Here the image is inverted. - Blindspot: Where the optic nerves are passing. - Collection of specialized cells: Rods, Cones - Rods, Cones: Contain pigments (phytochemicals, detect photons of light) ● **Rod** Pigment: Rhodopsin (protein) Detect all wavelengths of visible light. Cannot distinguish between different colors. (only light and shade) Detect faint light. ● **Cone** Pigment: Opsin (protein, synthesis Rhodopsin) Sensitive to some particular wavelength. Can distinguish between colors. ● **Fovea** Point of the retina where the image appears sharpest. Distinguish colors and objects. Higher concentration of cones than rods Photons of light hit the rods and cones → Causing a conformational change in membrane proteins → Production of electrical signals → travel → Optic nerve → Brain
Optic nerves	Carry signals
Visual cortex (Brain)	Turn the signals into images → Vision

● **Other structures**

Sclera	Majority of the outside of the eyes is covered by the sclera. White layers Composed of collagen + elastic fibers Protective layer
Choroid	Vascular portion Provides the eyes with various nutrients and oxygen.
Aqueous humor	Provides nutrients to the eyes. Drains out excess materials and waste. The anterior cavity of the eyes with fluid Predominately of water Maintains pressure in that region of the eyes.

Mechanoreceptors

Receptors detect mechanical stimuli such as touch, pressure, vibration, equilibrium, sound, and body balance.
Activated when they change shapes from the external mechanical stimuli.

● Functions
- Transduce mechanical energy, permitting animals to feel, hear, and maintain balance.
- Provide information about the shape, texture, weight, topographic relations of an object, and operation of internal organs. (food in the stomach, urine in the bladder)
- Enable organisms to maintain body positions with respect to gravity. (head up, feet down)
- External stimuli are usually in the form of touch, pressure, stretching, sound waves, and motion.
- When displaced from a normal position, animals quickly adjust their body to reassume the normal orientation.
- Continuously send information to CNS regarding the position and movements.
- Some extremely sensitive receptors: Alligator pressure receptors detect the movement in the surrounding water.

Proprioceptors	● Functions Help animals maintain postural relations. Continuously respond to tension and movement. The position of one part of the body. Locomotion, Skilled movement, Maintaining balance Animals can perceive positions of arms, legs, heads, and body parts. Preceptor impulses help coordinate the muscle contractions in a single movement. More numerous and active than other sensory receptors. - Receptor potentials: During stimuli existed. - Action potentials: Continuously generated. ● **Muscle spindles**: Detect muscle movement. ● **Golgi tendon organs** Respond to tension in contracting muscles. Respond to tension in the tendons. (attach to muscle bonds) ● **Joint receptors:** Detect movement in the ligaments.

Auditory receptors	● Functions Sensing mechanical waves in the air → transforming into electrical signals → Brain ● **Organ of Corti:** Detects sound wave pressure. ● **Vestibular apparatus:** Controls equilibrium. Senses the position of the body with respect to gravity. Detects rotational acceleration of the body. - 2 Chambers: Saccule, Utricle - 3 Semicircular canals
Tactile receptors	● Functions Free nerve endings in the skin Detect touch, pressure, vibration, pain when stimulated by contacting the body face. Sense the body's orientation in space with respect to gravity. Receptor potential develops. Raw action potentials develops. ● Pathway Compression → Displacement of the layers → Receptor potential falls to zero → stimulates the axon: Action potential (sensory adaptation) ● **Hair/Bristle** Tactile receptor's base Detect air, water vibration contact with other objects. Stimulated indirectly when the hair is bent or displaced. Receptors respond only when the hair is moving. Even though the hair is maintained in a displaced position, the receptor is not stimulated unless there is motion. ● **Merkel cells** Light tough Enable to distinguish softness, fuzziness, and hardness. Adapt slowly: Sense the object continuously to touch the skins. - Location: Form discs in deep epidermis → extend into the dermis ● **Messner corpuscles** Light touch, Vibration Encapsulated endings Adapt quickly - Location: Upper dermis ● **Ruffini endings** Heavy, continuous pressure, a stretch of the skin

	Fingers and hand information Adapt very slowly. - Location: Dermis ● **Pacinian corpuscles** Deep pressure that causes rapid movement of the tissues. Stimuli, Vibration Composition: Neuron endings + Connective tissue layers + Fluid - Location: Deep dermis
Hair cells	● Functions Detect movement. Help maintain position, equilibrium, and hearing. No action potentials - Surface: Kinocilium (long) + Stereocilia (shorter) - Fish: In lateral lines, detect water movement. ● **Kinocilium:** Long, 9+2 arrangement of microtubules ● **Stereocilia** Shorter Microvilli Actin filaments Mechanical stimulation: Voltage changes, Depolarization, Hyperpolarization, Neurotransmitters ● Pathway Water moves cupula, stereocilia to bend → change hair cell membrane potential → release neurotransmitters → Sensory neuron stimulated → Axon: action potential → CNS
Invertebrate	● **Statocyte** Gravity receptors Simplest organs of equilibrium Infolding sensory hair cells: Epidermis lined with receptor cells, with sensory hairs Invertebrates: Jellyfish, Crayfish ● **Statoliths** Allow certain invertebrates, plants to sense gravity and balance. Pulled downward by gravity, stimulate the sensory hair cells. ● **Lateral line organs** Inform the animal of obstacles in the way of moving objects. (prey, enemies) Long canal running the length of the body. Fishes and aquatic amphibians: Detect vibrations in the water.

Auditory receptors

Sensing mechanical waves in the air and transform them into electrical signals to the brain.

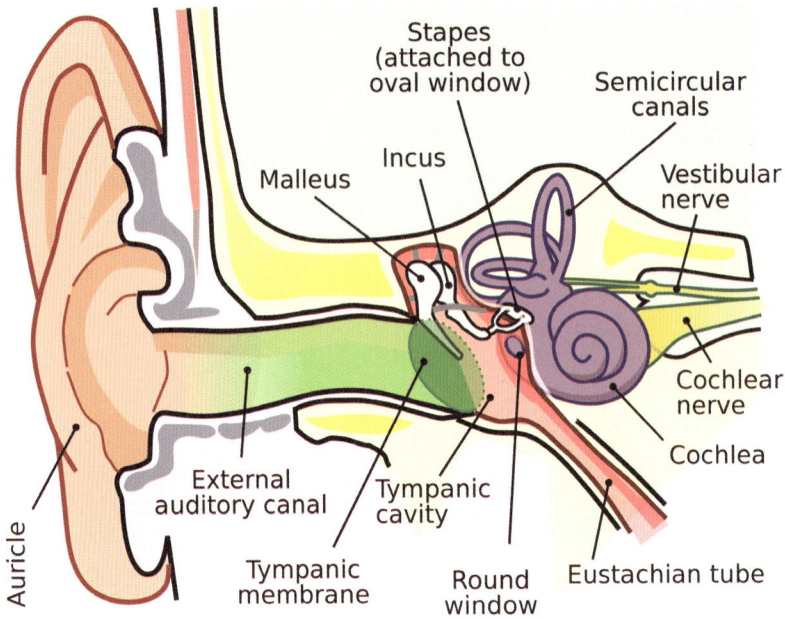

[20-2] Auditory receptor

● Sound pathway
Sound → Pinna: sound amplification → External auditory canal → Eardrum: sound amplification → Ossicles (malleus, incus, stapes): sound amplification, vibration → Oval window: vibration → Cochlea (perilymph → endolymph) → Organ of Corti: depolarization hair cells + generates action potential → Cochlear nerve → Brain

Outer ear	Ears can detect variations in air pressure. (mechanical waves) ● **Pinna** (Auricle) Captures much of the energy of the mechanical wave. Sound amplification Transmits through the external auditory canal. - Pathway: Mechanical wave → Pinna → **External auditory canal** → Middle ear

	● **Eardrum** (Tympanic membrane) At the ear canal, the mechanical wave hits → vibrates the eardrum Sound amplification Membrane is smaller than the pinna. Force the membrane feels because the mechanical waves are amplified. - Pathway: Force → transmitted → Ossicles

Middle ear	● **Ossicles**
	Sound amplification
	Lever system
	- 3 bones: Malleus (hammer), Incus (anvil), Stapes (stirrup)
	
	- Pathway
	  Force: Malleus → Incus → Stapes → increase the force
	  → vibration of the 3 bones → **Oval window** (inner ear)

Inner ear	→ **Oval window** → transmitted into the **Cochlear perilymph**
	→ Cochlea: Round window (perilymph, endolymph) to vibrate (vibration pressure) → **Endolymph** feels the vibration change
	→ **Basilar membrane's Organ of Corti:** Depolarizes hair cells
	→ generates the action potential → **Cochlear nerves** → Brain
	
	● **Cochlea**
	Transform the vibrations of the cochlear liquids and associated structures into a neural signal.
	Detect body angle and balance.
	
	- Organ of Corti: Mechanoreceptor, hair cells, sound waves
	  Hair cells depolarized → sends the action potential → Vestibular nerves
	
	- Perilymph
	  Inner ear air-fluid boundary
	  Many resistance to the mechanical waves.
	  To overcome this resistance, 3 levels of sound amplification are needed.
	
	- Endolymph
	  Fluid in semicircular canals
	  Fluid experiences a pressure change.
	  Organ of Corti: Generates the action potential → Vestibular nerves
	
	- Vestibular apparatus
	  Mechanoreceptor helps the body balance and equilibrium.
	  Allow detecting acceleration. (accelerometers)
	  2 chambers: Saccule, Utricle
	  3 Semicircular canals
	
	● 3 levels of sound amplification
	- Pinna
	- Eardrum
	- Ossicle bones: Malleus, Incus, Stapes
	
	● Mechanoreceptors
	- Organ of Corti
	- Vestibular apparatus

Chemoreceptors

Specialized cell groups responsible for acquiring information about the chemical environment and deliver the information to neurons.

Animals detect chemical substances in food, water and air, find mates and avoid predators.
The same species use chemoreception to communicate.
When the material is directly existing.
Activated by small amount.
Insects: By sensilla (sensillum), taste, smell, and sense.

Gustation (taste)	● Pathway: Gustation system → Thalamus → Cerebrum: gustatory cortex
	● Location: Taste buds, Taste receptors
	
	- Vertebrates: A sense of taste depends on materials dissolved in saliva.
	- Aquatic animals: By blur
	
	● **Taste buds**
	Oval epithelial capsule + Taste receptors
	Tiny elevations (papillae) on the tongue
	
	● **Taste receptors**
	Replaced every 10 days.
	Tips (microvilli): Extend into taste pores bathed in the saliva.
	G protein: Signal transduction process
	
	- Basic tastes
	  Sweet, Sour, Salty, Bitter, Umami
	  Flavor depends on the combination of smell, texture, and temperature.
	  Smell: Affects flavor for odors passing from the nasal chamber to the mouth.
	  (Nasal cavity blockage reduces the olfactory reception.)
	
	- PCT test: Some feel bitter, some feel non-taste.

Olfaction (smell)	● Pathway: Olfactory system → Cerebrum: olfactory cortex ● Location: Olfactory epithelium Most invertebrates main sensory system depends on this a lot. Adapt 50% after stimulation. Humans can detect camphor, musky, floral, peppermint, and ether. Gaseous substances → Olfactory receptors → Air More sensitive than gustation - Olfactory epithelium: Olfactory receptors respond to a small amount of substance.

Electroreceptors, Electromagnetic receptors

Electroreceptors	Sense differences in electrical potentials.
	Some predatory species of sharks, rays, and bony fishes detect electric fields in the water from prey's muscle activity.
	Some fishes have electric organs, specialized muscles, and nerve cells, emit electrical signals, and receive feedback signals.
	
	- Some species produce a weak electric current to help navigation.
	  Ex) Murky water (visibility is poor)
	
	- Recognizing a potential mate: Male and female have different frequencies of electric discharge.
	
	- Sharks, eels: Electric rays have electric organs in their heads
	  → deliver powerful shocks

Electromagnetic receptors	Sensitive to detect the Earth's magnetic field. Electromagnetic information integrated into the brain → helps animals orient themselves Use the information to orient themselves: Bony fishes, Insects, Amphibians, Reptiles, Birds, Migratory birds Ex) Sharks, rays, skates: Swim across one of the Earth's magnetic field lines, the receptor detects changes of the electric currents.

Nociceptors

Pain receptors
Free nerve endings of certain sensory neurons in almost every tissue.
Neuropeptides (substance P): Enhance and prolong the actions of glutamate.

- Thalamus: Pain perception begins.
- Limbic system: Emotional aspects of the pain are processed.

• Pain pathway

When stimulated, nociceptors transmit signals → Sensory neurons → releases Glutamate, Neuropeptides → Interneurons (spinal cord) → the opposite side of the Spinal cord → Thalamus → Parietal lobe + Other cortical regions (Limbic system: emotional aspects of the pain made) → Cerebrum → Aware the pain

Mechanical nociceptors	Respond to strong tactile stimuli. Ex) Cutting, Crushing, Pinching
Thermal nociceptors	Respond to temperature extremes.
Others	Respond to a variety of damaging stimuli. Ex) Certain chemicals

Thermoreceptors

Respond to heat and cold.

● Arthropods
Use for searching for an endothermic host: Mosquitos, ticks, and blood-sucking insects.

● Mammals
Endothermic
Free nerve endings + Specialized receptors: Skin and tongue detect temperature changes in the outside environment.
Pain receptors sense extreme temperatures threaten the body.

● Hypothalamus
Detects internal changes in temperature.
Receives and integrates information from receptors on the body surface
→ initiates homeostatic mechanisms → ensures a constant body temperature

Credits

© 2022 WIKIHOUSE, Inc. All rights reserved.

No part of this publication may be reproduced, distributed, or transmitted in any form or by any means, including photocopying, recording, or other electronic or mechanical methods, without the prior written permission of the publisher, except in the case of brief quotations embodied in reviews and certain other non-commercial uses permitted by copyright law.

Periodic table Adapted from Double sharp, based on File:Simple Periodic Table Chart-en.svg by User:Offnfopt at Wikimedia Foundation, Inc. © 2022 Printed by WIKIHOUSE, Inc., Seoul, South Korea.

Chapter 1

[1-1] Prokaryote Adapted from Mariana Ruiz Villarreal, LadyofHats at Wikimedia Foundation, Inc. © 2022 Printed by WIKIHOUSE, Inc., Seoul, South Korea **[1-2] Eukaryote** Adapted from Mariana Ruiz Villarreal, LadyofHats at Wikimedia Foundation, Inc. © 2022 Printed by WIKIHOUSE, Inc., Seoul, South Korea **[1-3] Eukaryote** Adapted from Mariana Ruiz Villarreal, LadyofHats at Wikimedia Foundation, Inc. © 2022 Printed by WIKIHOUSE, Inc., Seoul, South Korea **[1-4] Phospholipid bilayer cell membrane** Adapted from Mariana Ruiz Villarreal, LadyofHats at Wikimedia Foundation, Inc. © 2022 Printed by WIKIHOUSE, Inc., Seoul, South Korea **[1-5] Phospholipid** Adapted from Dhatfield at Wikimedia Foundation, Inc. © 2022 Printed by WIKIHOUSE, Inc., Seoul, South Korea **[1-6] Nucleus** Adapted from Mariana Ruiz Villarreal, LadyofHats at Wikimedia Foundation, Inc. © 2022 Printed by WIKIHOUSE, Inc., Seoul, South Korea **[1-7] Mitochondria** Adapted from Mariana Ruiz Villarreal, LadyofHats at Wikimedia Foundation, Inc. © 2022 Printed by WIKIHOUSE, Inc., Seoul, South Korea **[1-8] Cilia** Adapted from Mariana Ruiz Villarreal, LadyofHats at Wikimedia Foundation, Inc. © 2022 Printed by WIKIHOUSE, Inc., Seoul, South Korea **[1-9] Flagella** Adapted from Mariana Ruiz Villarreal, LadyofHats at Wikimedia Foundation, Inc. © 2022 Printed by WIKIHOUSE, Inc., Seoul, South Korea **[1-10] Centrosome** Adapted from Kelvin Song at Wikimedia Foundation, Inc. © 2022 Printed by WIKIHOUSE, Inc., Seoul, South Korea **[1-11] Simple diffusion** Adapted from Mariana Ruiz Villarreal, LadyofHats at Wikimedia Foundation, Inc. © 2022 Printed by WIKIHOUSE, Inc., Seoul, South Korea **[1-12] Facilitated diffusion** Adapted from Mariana Ruiz Villarreal, LadyofHats at Wikimedia Foundation, Inc. © 2022 Printed by WIKIHOUSE, Inc., Seoul, South Korea **[1-13] Active transport 1** Adapted from Mariana Ruiz Villarreal, LadyofHats at Wikimedia Foundation, Inc. © 2022 Printed by WIKIHOUSE, Inc., Seoul, South Korea **[1-14] Active transport 2** Adapted from Mariana Ruiz Villarreal, LadyofHats at Wikimedia Foundation, Inc. © 2022 Printed by WIKIHOUSE, Inc., Seoul, South Korea **[1-15] Osmosis** Adapted from Mariana Ruiz Villarreal, LadyofHats at Wikimedia Foundation, Inc. © 2022 Printed by WIKIHOUSE, Inc.,

Seoul, South Korea **[1-16] Exocytosis** Adapted from Mariana Ruiz Villarreal, LadyofHats at Wikimedia Foundation, Inc. © 2022 Printed by WIKIHOUSE, Inc., Seoul, South Korea **[1-17] Endocytosis** Adapted from Mariana Ruiz Villarreal, LadyofHats at Wikimedia Foundation, Inc. © 2022 Printed by WIKIHOUSE, Inc., Seoul, South Korea **[1-18] Bacteria** Adapted from Mariana Ruiz Villarreal, LadyofHats at Wikimedia Foundation, Inc. © 2022 Printed by WIKIHOUSE, Inc., Seoul, South Korea **[1-19] Virus** Adapted from Vector Stock © 2022 Printed by WIKIHOUSE, Inc., Seoul, South Korea **[1-20] Virus** Adapted from Vector Stock © 2022 Printed by WIKIHOUSE, Inc., Seoul, South Korea **[1-21] Animal cell** Adapted from Mariana Ruiz Villarreal, LadyofHats at Wikimedia Foundation, Inc. © 2022 Printed by WIKIHOUSE, Inc., Seoul, South Korea **[1-22] Plant cell** Adapted from Mariana Ruiz Villarreal, LadyofHats at Wikimedia Foundation, Inc. © 2022 Printed by WIKIHOUSE, Inc., Seoul, South Korea **[1-23] Energy pyramid** Adapted from Swiggity.Swag.YOLO.Bro at Wikimedia Foundation, Inc. © 2022 Printed by WIKIHOUSE, Inc., Seoul, South Korea.

Chapter 3

[3-1] Fatty acid Adapted from Mariana Ruiz Villarreal, LadyofHats at Wikimedia Foundation, Inc. © 2022 Printed by WIKIHOUSE, Inc., Seoul, South Korea **[3-2] Saturated fatty acid** Adapted from Calvero at Wikimedia Foundation, Inc. © 2022 Printed by WIKIHOUSE, Inc., Seoul, South Korea **[3-4] Triglyceride** Adapted from Erica Soyoon Bae © 2022 Printed by WIKIHOUSE, Inc., Seoul, South Korea **[3-5] Steroid** Adapted from NEUROtiker at Wikimedia Foundation, Inc. © 2022 Printed by WIKIHOUSE, Inc., Seoul, South Korea **[3-6] Carbohydrate** Adapted from ClockworkSoul at English Wikipedia © 2022 Printed by WIKIHOUSE, Inc., Seoul, South Korea **[3-7] α Anomer** Adapted from Wikimedia Foundation, Inc. © 2022 Printed by WIKIHOUSE, Inc., Seoul, South Korea **[3-8] β Anomer** Adapted from Wikimedia Foundation, Inc. © 2022 Printed by WIKIHOUSE, Inc., Seoul, South Korea **[3-9] Protein** Adapted from Chemistry-grad-student at Wikimedia Foundation, Inc. © 2022 Printed by WIKIHOUSE, Inc., Seoul, South Korea **[3-10] Amino acid** Adapted from Smokefoot at Wikimedia Foundation, Inc. © 2022 Printed by WIKIHOUSE, Inc., Seoul, South Korea **[3-11] 4 Types of protein structure** Adapted from Mariana Ruiz Villarreal, LadyofHats at Wikimedia Foundation, Inc. © 2022 Printed by WIKIHOUSE, Inc., Seoul, South Korea **[3-12] Nucleic acid** Adapted from Sponk at Wikimedia Foundation, Inc. © 2022 Printed by WIKIHOUSE, Inc., Seoul, South Korea **[3-13] DNA, RNA** Adapted from Sponk at Wikimedia Foundation, Inc. © 2022 Printed by WIKIHOUSE, Inc., Seoul, South Korea.

Chapter 4

[4-1] DNA replication Adapted from Mariana Ruiz Villarreal, LadyofHats at Wikimedia Foundation, Inc. © 2022 Printed by WIKIHOUSE, Inc., Seoul, South Korea **[4-2] Transcription** Adapted from Sulai by National Human Genome Research Institute © 2022 Printed by WIKIHOUSE, Inc., Seoul, South Korea **[4-3] Splicing exons** Adapted from Mariana Ruiz Villarreal, LadyofHats at Wikimedia Foundation, Inc. © 2022 Printed by WIKIHOUSE, Inc., Seoul,

South Korea **[4-4] Translation** Adapted from Mariana Ruiz Villarreal, LadyofHats at Wikimedia Foundation, Inc. © 2022 Printed by WIKIHOUSE, Inc., Seoul, South Korea.

Chapter 5

[5-1] Chromosome Adapted from Traducció d'Imartin6 a partir d'un treball de Phrood~commonswiki at Wikimedia Foundation, Inc. © 2022 Printed by WIKIHOUSE, Inc., Seoul, South Korea **[5-2] Cell cycle** Adapted from Richard Wheeler, Zephyris at Wikimedia Foundation, Inc. © 2022 Printed by WIKIHOUSE, Inc., Seoul, South Korea **[5-3] G1 phase** Adapted from Mariana Ruiz Villarreal, LadyofHats at Wikimedia Foundation, Inc. © 2022 Printed by WIKIHOUSE, Inc., Seoul, South Korea **[5-4] S phase** Adapted from Mariana Ruiz Villarreal, LadyofHats at Wikimedia Foundation, Inc. © 2022 Printed by WIKIHOUSE, Inc., Seoul, South Korea **[5-5] G2 phase** Adapted from Mariana Ruiz Villarreal, LadyofHats at Wikimedia Foundation, Inc. © 2022 Printed by WIKIHOUSE, Inc., Seoul, South Korea **[5-6] Mitosis** Adapted from Mariana Ruiz Villarreal, LadyofHats at Wikimedia Foundation, Inc. © 2022 Printed by WIKIHOUSE, Inc., Seoul, South Korea **[5-7] Interphase** Adapted from Mariana Ruiz Villarreal, LadyofHats at Wikimedia Foundation, Inc. © 2022 Printed by WIKIHOUSE, Inc., Seoul, South Korea **[5-8] Prophase** Adapted from Mariana Ruiz Villarreal, LadyofHats at Wikimedia Foundation, Inc. © 2022 Printed by WIKIHOUSE, Inc., Seoul, South Korea **[5-9] Metaphase** Adapted from Mariana Ruiz Villarreal, LadyofHats at Wikimedia Foundation, Inc. © 2022 Reprinted and electronically reproduced by WIKIHOUSE, Inc., Seoul, South Korea **[5-10] Anaphase** Adapted from Mariana Ruiz Villarreal, LadyofHats at Wikimedia Foundation, Inc. © 2022 Reprinted and electronically reproduced by WIKIHOUSE, Inc., Seoul, South Korea **[5-11] Telophase** Adapted from Mariana Ruiz Villarreal, LadyofHats at Wikimedia Foundation, Inc. © 2022 Reprinted and electronically reproduced by WIKIHOUSE, Inc., Seoul, South Korea **[5-12] Cytokinesis** Adapted from Mariana Ruiz Villarreal, LadyofHats at Wikimedia Foundation, Inc. © 2022 Reprinted and electronically reproduced by WIKIHOUSE, Inc., Seoul, South Korea **[5-13] Meiosis** Adapted from Ali Zifan, Oganesson007 at Wikimedia Foundation, Inc. © 2022 Reprinted and electronically reproduced by WIKIHOUSE, Inc., Seoul, South Korea **[5-14.1] Prophase 1** Adapted from Ali Zifan, Oganesson007 at Wikimedia Foundation, Inc. © 2022 Reprinted and electronically reproduced by WIKIHOUSE, Inc., Seoul, South Korea **[5-14.2] Synapsis** Adapted from Miguel Gutierrez at Wikimedia Foundation, Inc. © 2022 Reprinted and electronically reproduced by WIKIHOUSE, Inc., Seoul, South Korea **[5-15] Metaphase 1** Adapted from Ali Zifan, Oganesson007 at Wikimedia Foundation, Inc. © 2022 Reprinted and electronically reproduced by WIKIHOUSE, Inc., Seoul, South Korea **[5-16] Anaphase 1** Adapted from Ali Zifan, Oganesson007 at Wikimedia Foundation, Inc. © 2022 Reprinted and electronically reproduced by WIKIHOUSE, Inc., Seoul, South Korea **[5-17] Telophase 1** and Cytokinesis 1 Adapted from Ali Zifan, Oganesson007 at Wikimedia Foundation, Inc. © 2022 Reprinted and electronically reproduced by WIKIHOUSE, Inc., Seoul, South Korea **[5-18] Prophase 2** Adapted from Ali Zifan, Oganesson007 at Wikimedia Foundation, Inc. © 2022 Reprinted and electronically reproduced by WIKIHOUSE, Inc., Seoul, South Korea **[5-19] Metaphase 2** Adapted from Ali Zifan, Oganesson007 at Wikimedia Foundation, Inc. © 2022 Reprinted and electronically reproduced by WIKIHOUSE, Inc., Seoul, South Korea **[5-20] Anaphase 2** Adapted from Ali Zifan, Oganesson007 at Wikimedia Foundation, Inc. © 2022 Reprinted and electronically reproduced by WIKIHOUSE, Inc., Seoul, South Korea **[5-21] Telophase 2** and Cytokinesis 2 Adapted from Ali Zifan, Oganesson007 at Wikimedia Foundation, Inc. © 2022 Reprinted and electronically reproduced by WIKIHOUSE, Inc., Seoul, South Korea **[5-22] Homologous chromosomes and sister chromatids** Adapted from Emw at Wikimedia Foundation, Inc. © 2022 Printed by WIKIHOUSE, Inc., Seoul, South Korea **[5-23] Chromosomes nondisjunction** Adapted from Tweety207 at Wikimedia Foundation, Inc. © 2022 Printed by WIKIHOUSE, Inc., Seoul, South Korea.

Chapter 6

[6-1] Allele Adapted from 2010-2022 Freepik Company S.L. © 2022 Printed by WIKIHOUSE, Inc., Seoul, South Korea **[6-2] Human chromosome** Adapted from National Human Genome Research Institute © 2022 Printed by WIKIHOUSE, Inc., Seoul, South Korea **[6-3] Mendel's law** Adapted from Mariana Ruiz Villarreal, LadyofHats at Wikimedia Foundation, Inc. © 2022 Printed by WIKIHOUSE, Inc., Seoul, South Korea **[6-4] Incomplete dominance** Adapted from Spencerbaron at Wikimedia Foundation, Inc. © 2022 Printed by WIKIHOUSE, Inc., Seoul, South Korea **[6-5] Codominance** Adapted from YassineMrabet at Wikimedia Foundation, Inc. © 2022 Printed by WIKIHOUSE, Inc., Seoul, South Korea **[6-6] Epistasis** Adapted from Thomas Shafee at Wikimedia Foundation, Inc. © 2022 Printed by WIKIHOUSE, Inc., Seoul, South Korea **[6-7] Pleiotropy** Adapted from Alphillips6 at Wikimedia Foundation, Inc. © 2022 Printed by WIKIHOUSE, Inc., Seoul, South Korea **[6-8] Norm of reaction** Adapted from Karin Langner-Bahmann © 2022 Printed by WIKIHOUSE, Inc., Seoul, South Korea **[6-9] Punnett square** Adapted from Pbrks at Wikimedia Foundation, Inc. © 2022 Printed by WIKIHOUSE, Inc., Seoul, South Korea **[6-10] Dihybrid cross** Adapted from Wikimedia Foundation, Inc. © 2022 Printed by WIKIHOUSE, Inc., Seoul, South Korea **[6-11] Linked genes** Adapted from Aweir03 at Wikimedia Foundation, Inc. © 2022 Printed by WIKIHOUSE, Inc., Seoul, South Korea **[6-12] Sex chromosomes** Adapted from YassineMrabet at Wikimedia Foundation, Inc. © 2022 Printed by WIKIHOUSE, Inc., Seoul, South Korea **[6-13] Lac operon** Adapted from Wikimedia Foundation, Inc. © 2022 Printed by WIKIHOUSE, Inc., Seoul, South Korea **[6-14] Pedigree** Adapted from Madibc68 at Wikimedia Foundation, Inc. © 2022 Printed by WIKIHOUSE, Inc., Seoul, South Korea.

Chapter 7

[7-1] Cellular respiration Adapted from Darekk2 at Wikimedia Foundation, Inc. © 2022 Printed by WIKIHOUSE, Inc., Seoul, South Korea **[7-2] ATP** Adapted from Wesalius at Wikimedia Foundation, Inc. © 2022 Printed by WIKIHOUSE, Inc., Seoul, South Korea **[7-3] Glycolysis** Adapted from Sylvie Loh at Wikimedia Foundation, Inc. © 2022 Printed by WIKIHOUSE, Inc., Seoul, South Korea **[7-4] Acetyl CoA formation** Adapted from Innerstream at Wikimedia Foundation, Inc. © 2022 Printed by WIKIHOUSE, Inc., Seoul, South Korea **[7-5] Citric acid

cycle Adapted from Narayanese, WikiUserPedia, YassineMrabet, TotoBaggins at Wikimedia Foundation, Inc. © 2022 Printed by WIKIHOUSE, Inc., Seoul, South Korea **[7-6] Electron transport chain** Adapted from Originally by Fvasconcellos at Wikimedia Foundation, Inc., modified by Erica Soyoon Bae. © 2022 Printed by WIKIHOUSE, Inc., Seoul, South Korea **[7-7] Alcohol fermentation** Adapted from Erica Soyoon Bae (2022) © 2022 Printed by WIKIHOUSE, Inc., Seoul, South Korea **[7-8] Lactic acid fermentation** Adapted from Erica Soyoon Bae (2022) © 2022 Printed by WIKIHOUSE, Inc., Seoul, South Korea **[7-9] Chloroplast** Adapted from Kelvin Song, Kelvin13 at Wikimedia Foundation, Inc. © 2022 Printed by WIKIHOUSE, Inc., Seoul, South Korea **[7-10] Enzyme** Adapted from Mariana Ruiz Villarreal, LadyofHats at Wikimedia Foundation, Inc. © 2022 Printed by WIKIHOUSE, Inc., Seoul, South Korea **[7-11] Activation energy graph** Adapted from Mariana Ruiz Villarreal, LadyofHats at Wikimedia Foundation, Inc. © 2022 Printed by WIKIHOUSE, Inc., Seoul, South Korea **[7-12] Inhibitions** Adapted from Boghog at Wikimedia Foundation, Inc. © 2022 Printed by WIKIHOUSE, Inc., Seoul, South Korea.

Chapter 8

[8-1] Simple squamous epithelial tissue Adapted from Mikael Häggström at Wikimedia Foundation, Inc. © 2022 Printed by WIKIHOUSE, Inc., Seoul, South Korea **[8-2] Stratified squamous epithelial tissue** Adapted from Berkshire Community College Bioscience Image Library © 2022 Printed by WIKIHOUSE, Inc., Seoul, South Korea **[8-3] Simple cuboidal epithelial tissue** Adapted from Berkshire Community College Bioscience Image Library © 2022 Printed by WIKIHOUSE, Inc., Seoul, South Korea **[8-4] Stratified cuboidal epithelial tissue** Adapted from Wbensmith at Wikimedia Foundation, Inc. © 2022 Printed by WIKIHOUSE, Inc., Seoul, South Korea **[8-5] Simple columnar epithelial tissue** Adapted from Berkshire Community College Bioscience Image Library © 2022 Printed by WIKIHOUSE, Inc., Seoul, South Korea **[8-6] Stratified cuboidal epithelial tissue** Adapted from Echinaceapallida at Wikimedia Foundation, Inc. © 2022 Printed by WIKIHOUSE, Inc., Seoul, South Korea **[8-7] Pseudostratified epithelial tissue** Adapted from Berkshire Community College Bioscience Image Library © 2022 Printed by WIKIHOUSE, Inc., Seoul, South Korea **[8-8] Dense connective tissue** Adapted from J Jana at Wikimedia Foundation, Inc. © 2022 Printed by WIKIHOUSE, Inc., Seoul, South Korea **[8-9] Elastic connective tissue** Adapted from Berkshire Community College Bioscience Image Library © 2022 Printed by WIKIHOUSE, Inc., Seoul, South Korea **[8-10] Loose connective tissue** Adapted from Berkshire Community College Bioscience Image Library © 2022 Printed by WIKIHOUSE, Inc., Seoul, South Korea **[8-11] Reticular connective tissue** Adapted from Berkshire Community College Bioscience Image Library © 2022 Printed by WIKIHOUSE, Inc., Seoul, South Korea **[8-12] Adipose connective tissue** Adapted from Berkshire Community College Bioscience Image Library © 2022 Printed by WIKIHOUSE, Inc., Seoul, South Korea **[8-13] Cartilage** Adapted from Berkshire Community College Bioscience Image Library © 2022 Printed by WIKIHOUSE, Inc., Seoul, South Korea **[8-14] Bone** Adapted from Berkshire Community College Bioscience Image Library © 2022 Printed by WIKIHOUSE, Inc., Seoul, South Korea **[8-15] Blood** Adapted from Berkshire Community College Bioscience Image Library © 2022 Printed by WIKIHOUSE, Inc., Seoul, South Korea **[8-16] Lymph** Adapted from Wikimedia Foundation, Inc. © 2022 Printed by WIKIHOUSE, Inc., Seoul, South Korea **[8-17] Skeletal muscle tissue** Adapted from Berkshire Community College Bioscience Image Library © 2022 Printed by WIKIHOUSE, Inc., Seoul, South Korea **[8-18] Cardiac muscle tissue** Adapted from Berkshire Community College Bioscience Image Library © 2022 Printed by WIKIHOUSE, Inc., Seoul, South Korea **[8-19] Smooth muscle tissue** Adapted from Berkshire Community College Bioscience Image Library © 2022 Printed by WIKIHOUSE, Inc., Seoul, South Korea **[8-20] Neuron** Adapted from Mariana Ruiz Villarreal, LadyofHats at Wikimedia Foundation, Inc. © 2022 Printed by WIKIHOUSE, Inc., Seoul, South Korea.

Chapter 9

[9-1] Skin Adapted from Madhero88 and M.Komorniczak at Wikimedia Foundation, Inc. © 2022 Printed by WIKIHOUSE, Inc., Seoul, South Korea **[9-2] Skeletal system** Adapted from Mariana Ruiz Villarreal, LadyofHats at Wikimedia Foundation, Inc. © 2022 Printed by WIKIHOUSE, Inc., Seoul, South Korea **[9-3] Bone** Adapted from OpenStax College from Wikimedia Foundation, Inc. © 2022 Printed by WIKIHOUSE, Inc., Seoul, South Korea **[9-4] Osteoclast** Adapted from Laboratoires Servier, France © 2022 Printed by WIKIHOUSE, Inc., Seoul, South Korea **[9-5] Osteoblast** Adapted from Laboratoires Servier, France © 2022 Printed by WIKIHOUSE, Inc., Seoul, South Korea **[9-6] Joint** Adapted from Madhero88 at Wikimedia Foundation, Inc. © 2022 Printed by WIKIHOUSE, Inc., Seoul, South Korea.

Chapter 10

[10-1] Muscle filaments Adapted from Wikimedia Foundation, Inc. © 2022 Printed by WIKIHOUSE, Inc., Seoul, South Korea **[10-2] Sarcomere and muscle contraction** Adapted from Richfield, David (2014). "Medical gallery of David Richfield". WikiJournal of Medicine 1 (2). DOI:10.15347/wjm/2014.009. ISSN 2002-4436. © 2022 Printed by WIKIHOUSE, Inc., Seoul, South Korea **[10-3] Muscle fiber** Adapted from OpenStax College from Wikimedia Foundation, Inc. © 2022 Printed by WIKIHOUSE, Inc., Seoul, South Korea **[10-4] Muscle contraction 1** Adapted from OpenStax College from Wikimedia Foundation, Inc. © 2022 Printed by WIKIHOUSE, Inc., Seoul, South Korea **[10-5] Muscle contraction 2** Adapted from OpenStax College from Wikimedia Foundation, Inc. © 2022 Printed by WIKIHOUSE, Inc., Seoul, South Korea **[10-6] Skeletal muscle** Adapted from Berkshire Community College Bioscience Image Library © 2022 Printed by WIKIHOUSE, Inc., Seoul, South Korea **[10-7] Cardiac muscle** Adapted from Berkshire Community College Bioscience Image Library © 2022 Printed by WIKIHOUSE, Inc., Seoul, South Korea **[10-8] Smooth muscle** Adapted from Berkshire Community College Bioscience Image Library © 2022 Printed by WIKIHOUSE, Inc., Seoul, South Korea.

Chapter 11

[11-1] Respiratory system Adapted from Mariana Ruiz Villarreal, LadyofHats at Wikimedia Foundation, Inc. © 2022 Printed by WIKIHOUSE, Inc., Seoul, South Korea **[11-2] Inhalation

Adapted from Mariana Ruiz Villarreal, LadyofHats at Wikimedia Foundation, Inc. © 2022 Printed by WIKIHOUSE, Inc., Seoul, South Korea **[11-3] Exhalation** Adapted from Mariana Ruiz Villarreal, LadyofHats at Wikimedia Foundation, Inc. © 2022 Printed by WIKIHOUSE, Inc., Seoul, South Korea **[11-4] Alveoli** Adapted from Mariana Ruiz Villarreal, LadyofHats at Wikimedia Foundation, Inc. © 2022 Printed by WIKIHOUSE, Inc., Seoul, South Korea **[11-5] Gas exchange** Adapted from Original: Cruithne9 Vector: Pixelsquid at Wikimedia Foundation, Inc. © 2022 Printed by WIKIHOUSE, Inc., Seoul, South Korea **[11-6] Oxygen transport graph** Adapted from Ratznium at Wikimedia Foundation, Inc. © 2022 Printed by WIKIHOUSE, Inc., Seoul, South Korea **[11-7] Carbon dioxide transport graph** Adapted from OpenStax College from Wikimedia Foundation, Inc. © 2022 Printed by WIKIHOUSE, Inc., Seoul, South Korea.

Chapter 12

[12-1] Excretory system Adapted from Jordi March i Nogué at Wikimedia Foundation, Inc. © 2022 Printed by WIKIHOUSE, Inc., Seoul, South Korea **[12-2] Kidney** Adapted from Blausen.com staff (2014). "Medical gallery of Blausen Medical 2014". WikiJournal of Medicine 1 (2). DOI:10.15347/wjm/2014.010. ISSN 2002-4436. © 2022 Printed by WIKIHOUSE, Inc., Seoul, South Korea **[12-3] Nephron** Adapted from OpenStax College from Wikimedia Foundation, Inc. © 2022 Printed by WIKIHOUSE, Inc., Seoul, South Korea.

Chapter 13

[13-1] Circulatory system Adapted from Mariana Ruiz Villarreal, LadyofHats at Wikimedia Foundation, Inc. © 2022 Printed by WIKIHOUSE, Inc., Seoul, South Korea **[13-2] Blood vessels** Adapted from Kelvin Song, Kelvin13 at Wikimedia Foundation, Inc. © 2022 Printed by WIKIHOUSE, Inc., Seoul, South Korea **[13-3] Blood circulations** Adapted from OpenStax College from Wikimedia Foundation, Inc. © 2022 Printed by WIKIHOUSE, Inc., Seoul, South Korea **[13-4] Alveoli** Adapted from Mariana Ruiz Villarreal, LadyofHats at Wikimedia Foundation, Inc. © 2022 Printed by WIKIHOUSE, Inc., Seoul, South Korea **[13-5] Gas exchange** Adapted from Original: Cruithne9 Vector: Pixelsquid at Wikimedia Foundation, Inc. © 2022 Printed by WIKIHOUSE, Inc., Seoul, South Korea **[13-6] Heart** Adapted from Wapcaplet at Wikimedia Foundation, Inc. © 2022 Printed by WIKIHOUSE, Inc., Seoul, South Korea **[13-7] Heart layers** Adapted from OpenStax College from Wikimedia Foundation, Inc. © 2022 Printed by WIKIHOUSE, Inc., Seoul, South Korea **[13-8] Cardiac cycle** Adapted from OpenStax College from Wikimedia Foundation, Inc. © 2022 Printed by WIKIHOUSE, Inc., Seoul, South Korea **[13-9] Platelet** Adapted from Tleonardi at Wikimedia Foundation, Inc. © 2022 Printed by WIKIHOUSE, Inc., Seoul, South Korea.

Chapter 14

[14-1] B-cell Adapted from Fred the Oyster at Wikimedia Foundation, Inc. © 2022 Printed by WIKIHOUSE, Inc., Seoul, South Korea **[14-2] Antibody** Adapted from Fvasconcellos at

Wikimedia Foundation, Inc. © 2022 Printed by WIKIHOUSE, Inc., Seoul, South Korea **[14-3] Antibody chains** Adapted from Fred the Oyster at Wikimedia Foundation, Inc. © 2022 Printed by WIKIHOUSE, Inc., Seoul, South Korea **[14-4] Primary immune system** Adapted from Sciencia58 an the makers of the single images Domdomegg, Fæ, Petr94, Manu5 at Wikimedia Foundation, Inc. © 2022 Printed by WIKIHOUSE, Inc., Seoul, South Korea **[14-5] T-cell** Adapted from Rehua at Wikimedia Foundation, Inc. © 2022 Printed by WIKIHOUSE, Inc., Seoul, South Korea **[14-6] Major histocompatibility complex** Adapted from BQmUB2011048 at Wikimedia Foundation, Inc. © 2022 Printed by WIKIHOUSE, Inc., Seoul, South Korea.

Chapter 15

[15-1] Gastrointestinal tract Adapted from Mariana Ruiz Villarreal, LadyofHats at Wikimedia Foundation, Inc. © 2022 Printed by WIKIHOUSE, Inc., Seoul, South Korea **[15-2] Stomach** Adapted from Henry Vandyke Carter (1831–1897) at Wikimedia Foundation, Inc. © 2022 Printed by WIKIHOUSE, Inc., Seoul, South Korea **[15-3] Small intestine** Adapted from Blausen.com staff (2014). "Medical gallery of Blausen Medical 2014". WikiJournal of Medicine 1 (2). DOI:10.15347/wjm/2014.010. ISSN 2002-4436. © 2022 Printed by WIKIHOUSE, Inc., Seoul, South Korea **[15-4] Pancreas** Adapted from OpenStax College from Wikimedia Foundation, Inc. © 2022 Printed by WIKIHOUSE, Inc., Seoul, South Korea **[15-5] Liver** Adapted from Cancer Research UK © 2022 Printed by WIKIHOUSE, Inc., Seoul, South Korea **[15-6] Large intestine** Adapted from Blausen.com staff (2014). "Medical gallery of Blausen Medical 2014". WikiJournal of Medicine 1 (2). DOI:10.15347/wjm/2014.010. ISSN 2002-4436. © 2022 Printed by WIKIHOUSE, Inc., Seoul, South Korea.

Chapter 16

[16-1] Male reproductive system Adapted from Wumingbai at Wikimedia Foundation, Inc. © 2022 Printed by WIKIHOUSE, Inc., Seoul, South Korea **[16-2] Spermatogenesis** Adapted from OpenStax College from Wikimedia Foundation, Inc. © 2022 Printed by WIKIHOUSE, Inc., Seoul, South Korea **[16-3] Sperm cell** Adapted from Mariana Ruiz Villarreal, LadyofHats at Wikimedia Foundation, Inc. © 2022 Printed by WIKIHOUSE, Inc., Seoul, South Korea **[16-4] Female reproductive system** Adapted from CDC, Mysid at Wikimedia Foundation, Inc. © 2022 Printed by WIKIHOUSE, Inc., Seoul, South Korea **[16-5] Oogenesis** Adapted from Sciencia58 at Wikimedia Foundation, Inc. © 2022 Printed by WIKIHOUSE, Inc., Seoul, South Korea **[16-6] Menstrual cycle** Adapted from Isometrik at Wikimedia Foundation, Inc. © 2022 Printed by WIKIHOUSE, Inc., Seoul, South Korea **[16-7] Ovary** Adapted from https://zealthy.in/en at Wikimedia Foundation, Inc. © 2022 Printed by WIKIHOUSE, Inc., Seoul, South Korea **[16-8] Fertilization** Adapted from Mariana Ruiz Villarreal, LadyofHats at Wikimedia Foundation, Inc. © 2022 Printed by WIKIHOUSE, Inc., Seoul, South Korea.

Chapter 17

[17-1] Endocrine system Adapted from OpenStax & Tomáš Kebert & umimeto.org © 2022 Printed by WIKIHOUSE, Inc., Seoul, South Korea **[17-2] Hypothalamus, Thyroid, Pineal gland, Pituitary gland** Adapted from Mariana Ruiz Villarreal, LadyofHats at Wikimedia Foundation, Inc. © 2022 Printed by WIKIHOUSE, Inc., Seoul, South Korea **[17-3] Parathyroid, Skin** Adapted from Mariana Ruiz Villarreal, LadyofHats at Wikimedia Foundation, Inc. © 2022 Printed by WIKIHOUSE, Inc., Seoul, South Korea **[17-4] Liver, Stomach, Duodenum, Kidney, Pancreas, Adrenal cortex, Adrenal medulla** Adapted from Mariana Ruiz Villarreal, LadyofHats at Wikimedia Foundation, Inc. © 2022 Printed by WIKIHOUSE, Inc., Seoul, South Korea **[17-5] Renin-Angiotensin-Aldosterone pathway** Adapted from Soupvector at Wikimedia Foundation, Inc. © 2022 Printed by WIKIHOUSE, Inc., Seoul, South Korea **[17-6] Adipose tissue, Heart, Bone marrow** Adapted from Mariana Ruiz Villarreal, LadyofHats at Wikimedia Foundation, Inc. © 2022 Printed by WIKIHOUSE, Inc., Seoul, South Korea **[17-7] Sex hormones** Adapted from Mariana Ruiz Villarreal, LadyofHats at Wikimedia Foundation, Inc. © 2022 Printed by WIKIHOUSE, Inc., Seoul, South Korea.

Chapter 18

[18-1] Neuron Adapted from Mariana Ruiz Villarreal, LadyofHats at Wikimedia Foundation, Inc. © 2022 Printed by WIKIHOUSE, Inc., Seoul, South Korea **[18-2] Astrocyte** Adapted from Blausen.com staff (2014). "Medical gallery of Blausen Medical 2014". WikiJournal of Medicine 1 (2). DOI:10.15347/wjm/2014.010. ISSN 2002-4436. © 2022 Printed by WIKIHOUSE, Inc., Seoul, South Korea **[18-3] Oligodendrocyte** Adapted from Blausen.com staff (2014). "Medical gallery of Blausen Medical 2014". WikiJournal of Medicine 1 (2). DOI:10.15347/wjm/2014.010. ISSN 2002-4436. © 2022 Printed by WIKIHOUSE, Inc., Seoul, South Korea **[18-4] Ependymal cell** Adapted from Blausen.com staff (2014). "Medical gallery of Blausen Medical 2014". WikiJournal of Medicine 1 (2). DOI:10.15347/wjm/2014.010. ISSN 2002-4436. © 2022 Printed by WIKIHOUSE, Inc., Seoul, South Korea **[18-5] Microglia** Adapted from Blausen.com staff (2014). "Medical gallery of Blausen Medical 2014". WikiJournal of Medicine 1 (2). DOI:10.15347/wjm/2014.010. ISSN 2002-4436. © 2022 Printed by WIKIHOUSE, Inc., Seoul, South Korea **[18-6] Satelite cell** Adapted from Blausen.com staff (2014). "Medical gallery of Blausen Medical 2014". WikiJournal of Medicine 1 (2). DOI:10.15347/wjm/2014.010. ISSN 2002-4436. © 2022 Printed by WIKIHOUSE, Inc., Seoul, South Korea **[18-7] Schwann cell** Adapted from Blausen.com staff (2014). "Medical gallery of Blausen Medical 2014". WikiJournal of Medicine 1 (2). DOI:10.15347/wjm/2014.010. ISSN 2002-4436. © 2022 Printed by WIKIHOUSE, Inc., Seoul, South Korea **[18-8] Electrical signals transmission** Adapted from Original by en:User:Chris 73, updated by en:User:Diberri, converted to SVG by tiZom © 2022 Printed by WIKIHOUSE, Inc., Seoul, South Korea **[18-9] Resting potential** Adapted from Д.Ильин: vectorization at Wikimedia Foundation, Inc. © 2022 Printed by WIKIHOUSE, Inc., Seoul, South Korea **[18-10] Action potential** Adapted from Blausen.com staff (2014). "Medical gallery of Blausen Medical 2014". WikiJournal of Medicine 1 (2). DOI:10.15347/wjm/2014.010. ISSN 2002-4436. © 2022

Printed by WIKIHOUSE, Inc., Seoul, South Korea **[18-11] Synapse** Adapted from Thomas Splettstoesser (www.scistyle.com) from Wikimedia Foundation, Inc. © 2022 Printed by WIKIHOUSE, Inc., Seoul, South Korea.

Chapter 19

[19-1] Nervous system Adapted from Fuzzform at Wikimedia Foundation, Inc. © 2022 Printed by WIKIHOUSE, Inc., Seoul, South Korea **[19-2] CNS and PNS** Adapted from OpenStax College from Wikimedia Foundation, Inc. © 2022 Printed by WIKIHOUSE, Inc., Seoul, South Korea **[19-3] Brain** Adapted from BruceBlaus at Wikimedia Foundation, Inc. © 2022 Printed by WIKIHOUSE, Inc., Seoul, South Korea **[19-4] Limbic system** Adapted from OpenStax College from Wikimedia Foundation, Inc. © 2022 Printed by WIKIHOUSE, Inc., Seoul, South Korea **[19-5] Spinal Cord** Adapted from Mysid (original by Tristanb) at Wikimedia Foundation, Inc. © 2022 Printed by WIKIHOUSE, Inc., Seoul, South Korea **[19-6] Spinal reflex** Adapted from MartaAguayo at Wikimedia Foundation, Inc. © 2022 Printed by WIKIHOUSE, Inc., Seoul, South Korea **[19-7] Somatic nervous system** Adapted from Helixitta at Wikimedia Foundation, Inc. © 2022 Printed by WIKIHOUSE, Inc., Seoul, South Korea **[19-8] Gap junction** Adapted from Mariana Ruiz Villarreal, LadyofHats at Wikimedia Foundation, Inc. © 2022 Printed by WIKIHOUSE, Inc., Seoul, South Korea **[19-9] Neurotransmitter** Adapted from Thomas Splettstoesser (www.scistyle.com) from Wikimedia Foundation, Inc. © 2022 Printed by WIKIHOUSE, Inc., Seoul, South Korea.

Chapter 20

[20-1] Photoreceptor Adapted from Original: Holly Fischer, Vector: Pixelsquid at Wikimedia Foundation, Inc. © 2022 Printed by WIKIHOUSE, Inc., Seoul, South Korea **[20-2] Auditory receptor** Adapted from Lars Chittka Axel Brockmann at Wikimedia Foundation, Inc. © 2022 Printed by WIKIHOUSE, Inc., Seoul, South Korea.